SERMONS

ON THE

PUBLIC MEANS OF GRACE,

ON THE

Fasts and Festivals of the Church,

SCRIPTURE CHARACTERS, AND VARIOUS PRACTICAL SUBJECTS.

BY THE LATE

RIGHT REV. THEODORE DEHON, D. D.,

RECTOR OF ST. MICHAEL'S CHURCH, CHARLESTON, AND BISHOP OF THE PROTESTANT EPISCOPAL CHURCH IN THE DIOCESE OF SOUTH CAROLINA.

Second American Edition,

WITH ADDITIONAL SERMONS NEVER BEFORE PUBLISHED.

IN TWO VOLUMES....VOL. I.

NEW YORK:
PUBLISHED BY THOMAS N. STANFORD,
637 BROADWAY.
1856.

Billin and Brother, *Printers and Stereotypers*, 20 *North William Street.*

TO

THE PROTESTANT EPISCOPAL CHURCH,

OF THE

UNITED STATES OF AMERICA,

This Edition

OF

THE DISCOURSES OF THE RT. REV. THEODORE DEHON, D. D.,

IS RESPECTFULLY DEDICATED

BY THE PUBLISHER.

PREFACE.

In presenting a second American edition of the Sermons of the late Bishop Dehon, first published in 1821, together with several discourses not contained in the first edition, the publisher feels assured that he is making a contribution to the sacred literature of the country, which will be appreciated not only by those to whom it is dedicated, as an exemplification of the practical faith and doctrines of their church, but by Christians of all denominations, as a devout and beautiful commentary on the teachings and characters of the Holy Scriptures.

It is due to the lamented author to state, that these Sermons were not written with any view to publication, but only for parochial use, and never had the benefit of his revision; yet, notwithstanding the disadvantages of a publication under such circumstances, they have proved to be most popular and useful both here and in England.

The first American edition has long since been entirely exhausted; and of three editions printed in England not a copy remains unsold. And the learned gentleman who had charge of the publication in England writes, that "each edition was of a thousand copies, and that he knew of no instance of such a sale for any English sermons;" and a leading bookseller in London adds, "that his sale of the work proved it to be equally esteemed by all parties in the Church, and scarcely less by dissenters."

The perfect piety and faith which pervade the Sermons of this gifted divine; his high conceptions of the relations and responsibilities of man to his Maker; the deep and touching pathos with which he portrays the beauty of holiness; the tender solicitude with which he comforts the afflicted, and pours consolation into the broken and contrite heart; and the natural and graceful eloquence by which he seeks to persuade all men to become Christians, cannot fail to impress and elevate the thoughtful reader, to whatever sect he may belong.

These discourses are indeed models of practical pulpit sermons, glowing with the spirit of the Scriptures, and instinct with a living sense of God's presence, and are worthy to be disseminated everywhere, "from sea to sea, and from the rivers to the ends of the earth," for they will lead to "fountains of living waters," and to "the tree whose leaves are for the healing of the nations."

The publisher has selected from a memoir written by the late Rev. Dr. Gadsden, of Charleston, the following particulars of the life and death of Bishop Dehon:

"He was born in Boston, in December, 1776. At the public school where he received his early education he was for seven years at the head of his class. He entered Harvard University in 1791, and was graduated in 1795, with the highest honors of his class. He immediately commenced his studies for the ministry, for which from early childhood he had evinced a strong inclination, and was ordained in 1797, and elected rector of Trinity Church, Newport, R. I., where he remained till 1810, devotedly attached to his people, when, his health failing, he was advised by his physicians to try a residence in a milder climate. An invitation to the rectorship of St. Michael's Church, Charleston, S. C., was shortly afterwards tendered to him, which he accepted, having previously declined two invitations from a church in that city, in consequence of his disinclination to leave his church in Newport.

"In 1812 he was elected bishop of the diocese of South Carolina, and was consecrated to that holy office, by the venerable Bishop White, at Philadelphia.

"He continued thereafter to perform his duties both as rector and bishop, with eminent zeal, discretion, and success, until he fell a victim to the yellow fever, in Charleston, on the 6th of August, 1817.

"He met death in conscious serenity, trusting with undoubting faith in the promises of the Redeemer he had served through life. His body was buried, by the request of the vestry, beneath the chancel of the church, at the altar where he had so often ministered.

"This circumstance was thus eloquently alluded to in an oration delivered by the late Hon. William Crafts, before the Phi Beta Kappa Society of Harvard University, in 1817.

"'The sun shines not upon his grave, nor is it wet with the morning or the evening dew; but innocence kneels upon it, purity bathes it with tears, and the recollections of the sleeping saint mingle with the praises of the living God.'

"Bishop Dehon was loved and revered wherever he was known; and those who saw his daily conversation and life, and knew what manner of man he was, erected in St. Michael's Church, in Charleston, a monument to his memory, which bears this inscription:

SACRED TO THE MEMORY

OF

The Right Rev. Theodore Dehon, D. D.,

LATE RECTOR OF THIS CHURCH, AND BISHOP OF THE DIOCESE,

WHO CEASED TO BE MORTAL ON THE 6TH DAY OF AUGUST, 1817, IN THE 41ST YEAR OF HIS LIFE, AND THE 20TH OF HIS MINISTRY.

GENIUS, LEARNING AND ELOQUENCE,
ADDED LUSTRE TO A
CHARACTER
FORMED BY CHRISTIAN
PRINCIPLES, AND A CONSTANT
STUDY OF THE CHRISTIAN'S MODEL. MEEK:
HE WAS SWIFT TO HEAR, SLOW TO SPEAK, SLOW TO
WRATH; HUMBLE: HE ESTEEMED OTHERS BETTER THAN HIM-
SELF; MERCIFUL: HE SOUGHT OUT THE POOR AND THE AFFLICTED;
DEVOTED TO GOD: HE COUNTED HIS LIFE NOT DEAR TO HIMSELF,
SO THAT HE MIGHT FINISH HIS COURSE WITH JOY, AND THE
MINISTRY, WHICH HE HAD RECEIVED OF THE LORD JESUS,
TO TESTIFY THE GOSPEL OF THE GRACE OF GOD;
ZEAL FORTIFIED BY DISCRETION, AND FIRMNESS
BY MODERATION, SANCTITY UNITED WITH
URBANITY, AND GOODNESS WITH
CHEERFULNESS, RENDERED HIM
THE DELIGHT OF HIS
FRIENDS; THE ADMI-
RATION OF HIS
COUNTRY;
THE GLORY
AND HOPE
OF THE CHURCH; HIS DEATH WAS CON-
SIDERED A PUBLIC CALAMITY. THE
PIOUS LAMENTED HIM AS A
PRIMITIVE BISHOP, THE
CLERGY AS A FATHER,
AND YOUTH AND
AGE LINGERED
AT HIS GRAVE. HE WAS
BURIED UNDER THE CHURCH BY
DIRECTION OF THE VESTRY, WHO ALSO
CAUSED THIS MONUMENT TO BE ERECTED IN
TESTIMONY OF THEIR AFFECTION, AND HIS MERIT.

QUIS DESIDERIO SIT PUDOR, AUT MODUS TAM CHARI CAPITIS!

CONTENTS OF VOL. I.

SERMONS I, II.

ON THE SCRIPTURES.

2 Timothy, iii. 16, 17.

SERMON III.

ON RELIGIOUS ORDINANCES.

1 Samuel, ix. 13.

SERMON IV.

ON BAPTISM.

Acts, ii. 16.

SERMON V.

ON BAPTISM.

St. Mark, x. 14.

SERMON VI.

ON BAPTISM.

Acts, viii. 36, 37.

SERMON VII.

ON BAPTISM.

St. Matthew, xxviii. 19, 20.

SERMON VIII.

ON BAPTISM.

St. Luke, ii. 22.

SERMON IX.

ON THE LORD'S SUPPER.

1 CORINTHIANS, xi. 23–27.

SERMON X.

ON THE LORD'S SUPPER.

1 CORINTHIANS, xi. 28.

SERMON XI.

ON THE LORD'S SUPPER.

ST. LUKE, xiv. 18.

SERMONS XII., XIII., XIV.

ON THE SABBATH.

EXODUS, xx. 8.

SERMON XV.

ON THE SANCTUARY.

LEVITICUS, xxvi. 2.

SERMON XVI.

ON THE SANCTUARY.

PSALM, cxxxii. 7,

SERMON XVII.

ON THE LITURGY.

PSALM, xlv. 13.

SERMON XVIII.

ON PSALMODY.

2 CHRONICLES, v. 13, 14.

SERMON XIX.

ON PUBLIC INSTRUCTION.

ROMANS, x. 14, 15.

SERMON XX.

ON ADVENT.

ST. MATTHEW, xxi. 5.

SERMON XXI.

ON ADVENT.

ST. MATTHEW, xi. 3.

SERMON XXII.

ON CHRISTMAS-DAY.

JOHN, iii. 16.

SERMON XXIII.

ON CHRISTMAS-DAY.

NEHEMIAH, viii. 10.

SERMON XXIV.

ON CHRISTMAS DAY.

ISAIAH, xliv. 23.

SERMON XXV.

ON THE CIRCUMCISION.

LUKE, ii. 21.

SERMON XXVI.

ON NEW-YEAR'S DAY.

EPHESIANS, v. 16.

SERMON XXVII.

ON NEW-YEAR'S DAY.

ST. LUKE, xii. 7, 8.

SERMON XXVIII.

ON THE EPIPHANY.

ISAIAH, lx. 3.

SERMON XXIX.

ON THE EPIPHANY.

MATTHEW, ii. 9, 10, 11.

SERMON XXX.

ON THE EPIPHANY.

ST. JOHN, viii. 12.

SERMON XXXI.

ON THE TEMPTATION.

MATTHEW, iv. 1.

SERMONS XXXII., XXXIII.

ON THE TEMPTATION.

MATTHEW, iv. 2.

SERMON XXXIV.

ON THE TEMPTATION.

MATTHEW, iv. 5–11.

SERMON XXXV.

ON THE TEMPTATION.

MATTHEW, iv. 8–12.

SERMON XXXVI.

ON REPENTANCE.

1 JOHN, i. 8, 9.

SERMON XXXVII.

ON THE PASSION.

ECCLESIASTES, iii. 4.

SERMON XXXVIII.

ON THE PASSION.

MATTHEW, xxvi. 18.

SERMON XXXIX.

ON GOOD FRIDAY.

JOHN, i. 29.

SERMON XL.

ON GOOD FRIDAY.

LUKE, xxiii. 48.

SERMON XLI.

ON GOOD FRIDAY.

ISAIAH, liii. 5.

SERMON XLII.

ON EASTER-DAY.

LUKE, xxiv. 5, 6.

SERMON XLIII.

ON EASTER-DAY.

PSALM cxviii. 24.

SERMON XLIV.

THE GOSPEL TO BE GLORIED IN.

ROMANS, i. 16.

SERMON XLV.

THE DANGER OF NEGLECTING THE GOSPEL.

HEBREWS, ii. 3.

SERMON XLVI.

GLORYING NOT IN THE THINGS OF THIS LIFE, BUT IN THE LORD.

2 TIMOTHY, iii. 4.

SERMON XLVII.

GLORYING NOT IN THE THINGS OF THIS LIFE, BUT IN THE LORD.

JEREMIAH, ix. 23, 24.

SERMON XLVIII.

HOPE.

SERMON XLIX.

STABILITY IN RELIGION.

SERMON L.

THE TRUTH MAKING THE FAITHFUL FREE.

SERMON I.

ON THE SCRIPTURES.

2 Timothy, iii. 16, 17.

"All Scripture is given by inspiration of God; and is profitable for doctrine, for reproof, for correction, for instruction in righteousness; that the man of God may be perfect, thoroughly furnished unto all good works."

IN this chapter, which has just been read to you from the desk, St. Paul, after warning Timothy of the errors and vices which should prevail in the last days, is anxious for the preservation of him, in the faith first delivered to the saints. "Continue thou in the things which thou hast learned and hast been assured of, knowing of whom thou hast learned them." He reminds him, "that from a child he had known the holy Scriptures;" which, rightly understood, and faithfully applied, could not fail to become to him a source of wisdom and salvation. This led him to give that interesting account of the sacred writings, which I have selected for your present consideration—"All Scripture is given by inspiration of God; and is profitable for doctrine, for reproof, for correction, for instruction in righteousness; that the man of God may be perfect, thoroughly furnished unto all good works."

The words call our attention to three things; the inspiration, the completeness, and the end or use of the sacred writings. Topics, these, which we should ponder with seriousness, with humility, and with sanctified affections. They have a strong bearing upon our faith, and may have a happy influence upon our practice.

I shall first speak to you of the inspiration of the sacred writings—"All Scripture is given by inspiration of God." The high and Holy One who inhabiteth eternity, commiserating the ignorance, and anxious for the salvation of the wayward children of men, hath graciously condescended to give them instructions, by which they may attain to knowledge, to virtue, and to eternal life. These instructions are contained in the Bible, which is emphatically styled the word of God. The contents of this holy volume, are not the offspring of reason, applying itself to the discovery of truth and duty. "The world by wisdom knew not God." They are not the devices of politic men, aiming to provide means for controlling and regulating mankind. A house divided against itself would not stand. But they are the dictates of the spirit of the Almighty. They are the advices and lessons of our heavenly Father to his children, tabernacling in the flesh. The sacred penmen wrote them under his guidance and direction. So far as their natural faculties could be useful to them in their work, these faculties we may presume were used. But his eye was constantly upon them. Wherever their judgment might have erred, he restrained them. Wherever the subjects were above the reach of their reason, he enlightened them. Wherever their recollection failed, or their knowledge was deficient, the Holy Ghost called all things to their remembrance, and guided them into all truth. They wrote what they have written, by the incitement, and under the superintendence, and with the assistance, whenever it was needed, of the Spirit of God. So that in the sacred volume, there is nothing but what is true, and worthy of all men to be thankfully received, and devoutly considered. It is, as it has been emphatically styled, the word of truth.

Of this high character of the Scriptures, there are testimonials many, various, and very weighty; and I presume you will attentively listen to some of the reasons for believing in the inspiration of the sacred writings.

In the first place, human ability has been inadequate to the production of any thing which would justify us in attributing to it the production of the Scriptures. In their account of the creation; of the origin of man; of his sinfulness and miseries, and of his future destiny; in their view of God, his nature, character, and government; in their revelation of the way, in which God has provided for us pardon and deliverance, and by which we may acceptably approach and serve him; in the prophecies they contain of events, developed and to be developed, in all portions of time, even to the end of the world; in the purity, spirituality, and universal applicability of their moral instructions; in their exact and perfect adaptation to the condition and necessities of human nature, and their wonderful operation, when attentively perused, upon the heart and life; and, I might add, in the transcendent sublimity of conception and expression, which is to be found in many parts of them, there is a height of wisdom and a degree of glory, to which no work of uninspired man has ever yet attained. If reason, in some of her most successful efforts, has disclosed some truths of great worth and divine import, the best of her productions are, nevertheless, but as the image in Nebuchadnezzer's dream. Though the head be of gold, the feet are of iron and clay. And the volume of inspiration, like the typical stone cut out of the mountain without hands, has overturned them, and broken them in pieces, and made them as the chaff of the summer threshing floors, and the most precious of their fragments is rendered by it of little value or utility. Now human reason, it may safely be supposed, has, in the course of the ages since the creation, been excited by as powerful motives as can ever excite it, and has acted under as great advantages as, in this present state, it can ever act under, without the special assistance of the Almighty. If, then, it have never arrived at such views of the divine nature and character; if it have never attained to such knowledge of the means of salvation and eternal life; if it have never discovered such a perfect system of righteousness and holiness, as the Scriptures reveal; nay, if its best works do but betray its weakness, and its sincerest confessions acknowledge the necessity of such a revelation, as the Scriptures contain, what can be more unreasonable, than to attribute to it a work, whose contents would oblige us to suppose, not only that it had once surpassed itself and overleaped the limits of its former exertions, but also, that it had a foresight of the purposes of God, and a familiar acquaintance with the counsels of his mind. To me it appears, that there would hardly be more absurdity in supposing, that frail man, with the little taper, wherewith in the shades of the evening he enlightens his own dark dwelling, had kindled the fire of that glorious body, which God hath set in the heavens, to enlighten and rule the day. All the productions of human ability with which we are acquainted, bear marks, that, like their authors, they are of the earth, earthy; but the contents of the holy Scriptures do manifest of themselves, that they are given by inspiration of God.

Again. God having graciously resolved to recover the human race from the state into which they had fallen, and to this end having spoken, in times long past, to the Fathers by the Prophets, and in the latter days to the world, by his Son, it is reasonable to suppose, that, for the benefit of the generations to come for ever, he would cause a record to be made of the communications of his will. In all his revelations, the whole human race are interested, and there would be great danger of their receiving them impaired and corrupted, and without sufficient evidence of their authenticity, if they received them only by oral tradition. We may presume that he would cause his instructions which concerned the world, as they were gradually completed, to be written in a table and noted in a book. But in this record there are some things, such as prophecies of events yet in the womb of time, explanations of the mystery of redemption hidden from ages and generations in the bosom of God, long and important discourses of our blessed Saviour, and of others, his servants, which the writers cannot be conceived capable of recording, without the immediate suggestions and aid of the Holy Spirit. And when we reflect upon the vast importance of the whole, that to it men were to recur and appeal, as the only rule of faith and life, it would be a just expectation that the scribes, whom God vouchsafed to employ, would be constantly under his own inspection and guidance, in every part of their work. Accordingly, we find, that Moses and the Prophets were full of the Holy Ghost, and have recorded their instructions as the word of God; we find the Apostle of the Jews testifying that, "the prophecy came not in old time by the will of man, but holy men of God spake as they were moved by the Holy Ghost;" and we find, also, our blessed Lord, and the first preachers of his gospel, referring to the books of the Old Testament as of infallible truth, and divine authority. With regard to the New Testament, Christ promised to his Apostles, to send them power from on high, to qualify them for their office of establishing his Church, and promulgating his religion. This power they received by the miraculous descent of the Holy Ghost upon them, to be to them, by his presence, instead of their master, after his ascension to glory. By his inspiration they wrote, as well as spake. In the consciousness of it, they deliver to the Church their several records, as the instructions of the Lord. And the favoured disciple, who closes the sacred code, leaves us impressed with an awful sense of our obligation, to reverence it as the hallowed Scripture of God, by uttering at its close, the very solemn declaration, that "if any man shall add unto, or take away from the words of the prophecy of this book, God shall take away his part out of the book of life."

Further: The connection and agreement of the several parts of the sacred volume, intimates strongly its divine inspiration. That so many writers, in so many and distant ages, many of them without any knowledge of each other, should have written divers books, every one connected with the rest, and all tending, with wonderful combination, to introduce, unfold, and establish one grand, supernatural system of religious truth, would, were it admitted as true, be a wonder, hardly surpassed by the Atheist's formation of a world, by the fortuitous concurrence of atoms. Though many hands be discernible in the sacred volume, there is evidently but one mind. It is the work of that being, who, by the gradual production of six successive days, completed the beautiful fabric and furniture of nature, and who, by adding revelation to revelation according to the counsel of his will, has raised in the moral world, this stupendous monument of his wisdom and mercy. We see one spirit pervading the whole. It is the design of one master, accomplished by many servants. Every book is perfect as a part; and all together form, if I may be allowed the figure, one temple of truth and salvation, into which the mind, that enters with sanctified affections, feels sensible of the presence of the deity.

Once more: Tradition has accompanied the holy volume in all ages and places of its being, testifying its claim to be considered as the word of God. The Jews, to whom were committed the most ancient oracles, esteemed and reverenced them as dictated by Jehovah. So great was their regard for their authenticity, that in every transcript they counted the letters, and compared the number with the original, that no part might be lost of the sacred word. In the earlier ages of the Christian Church, the canon of Scripture was adjusted with great care, and the acknowledged inspiration of any book was its title to admission into the sacred code. This tradition of the inspiration of Scripture, undoubtedly had its origin in the holy writers themselves; men who were pre-eminent for all the qualities which should entitle them to credibility, and to whose veracity, in most cases, there were given supernatural attestations; God working with them, and endowing them with miraculous powers, and confirming their word with signs following. From them, it has descended to us, strengthened with the consent of many generations. It is a consent in which is heard the voice of the primitive Fathers, who lived nearest to the Apostles' times, and whose evidence is amply given, that the holy writings were dictated by the Spirit of God. It is a consent in which is heard, in subsequent ages, the voice of Constantine and Alfred, of Newton and of Locke, of sages and philosophers without number, of piety and learning, in their most exalted characters, and loftiest attainments. It is a consent, in which is heard the voice of the universal Church in all ages, raising the sacred volume above all human improvements, exalting it to be the unerring standard of what men are to believe and do, and thus imparting to it, the only real seal of infallibility, the seal of the inspiration of God. This holy reverence, with which time and truth have clothed the Scriptures, what hand shall dare to tear away? As of the common consent of all nations in acknowledging the existence of a Supreme Being, so, also, of the common consent of the Christian world, in acknowledging the inspiration of the sacred writings, it may be well observed, that he who shall deny it, must have a most vain and perilous conceit of his own wisdom, and be ready to impute both ignorance and folly, to the wisest and most virtuous part of his race.

I would further observe, that the providential care of God over the holy Scriptures, may well lead us to believe that they are his offspring. When we consider the age of these writings, some of them being the most ancient in the world; when we reflect to how many perils they have been formerly exposed, by the captivities of the Jews, the persecutions of Christians, and the enmity of the world to the true faith; when we call to mind, into how many languages they have been translated, and how many copies of them have in later ages been multiplied; that they should every where have been preserved, and preserved the same, without any essential loss or variation, indicates that there is something in them, not in any other writings, which recommends them to the special protection of the Providence of God. The flood of time, which sweeps away every thing, has swept away most other writings of equal antiquity. But this holy volume, like the ark of Noah, upborne and protected by the invisible hand of the Almighty, has surmounted the waves, unchanged and entire; the shelter of the faithful, and the safe deposit of man's last hopes. If, indeed, the Scriptures have the Most High for their author, and are the only sources of knowledge and salvation to the children of men, it were natural to believe that they should never be lost, but that he would specially provide for their preservation and safety. And from his actual care, and wonderful Providence over them, it is reasonable to infer that, they are in reality the oracles of truth, to the inhabitants of this lower world, given by inspiration of God.

I add, finally, that the inspiration of the sacred volume is to be believed, because there are difficulties attending any other supposition, which no sober mind can remove or surmount. To what a dilemma are we reduced, if we receive not the Scriptures as the word of God! We must not only suppose, that reason has in one instance, surpassed her powers, overleaped the limits of her excursions, and penetrated into the very cabinet and bosom of the Almighty; we must not only suppose, that a number of men, unacquainted with each other, have acted together in all ages of time, in framing prophecies, and connecting them with events, and introducing one consistent, admirable, and wonderful scheme of religion; but we must also believe that, the most perfect and virtuous characters with which we are acquainted, have, without any view to present or future benefit, with one consent been deceivers of mankind; we must believe, that the holy and unaspiring Jesus, has confirmed their fraud and promoted the delusion; we must believe, that by investing the Prophets and Apostles with miraculous and prophetic powers, the Almighty himself has connived at, and befriended iniquity; and we must believe, what of all things it is most difficult to believe, that the kind and gracious Father of our race, who hath formed us to know and to serve him, and to find happiness under the shadow of his wings, has left us without any certain knowledge of himself; destitute of any instruction or advice from him; exposed, continually, to uncertainty and error, to doubt and despair. For, let it be remembered, if the Scriptures are rejected, there is no other letter of love, no other paternal counsel and direction, from our heavenly Father, to be found in our world. If the sacred volume is not his word, there is no certain evidence, that between the Creator and the creature, in this part of his dominion, there has been any communication of his will. A very gloomy consideration!

Whoever soberly weighs it, and adds to it the other difficulties we have enumerated, and duly appreciates the evidences on the contrary part, which have been adduced, he cannot but be persuaded, that the holy writings are inspired by God; and, like the faithful witness in heaven, shall stand fast for ever and ever, a light to lighten the Gentiles, and to be eventually the glory of his people Israel.

You see, then, my brethren, the character of the sacred volume, that it is the sacred record of that chain of communications which from time to time the Almighty has made, to the inhabitants of this lower world; a record made, by such scribes as he has pleased to choose, under his own inspection, and the guidance of his spirit; and, consequently, containing nothing but what is true and important, and worthy of all men to be most thankfully received.

The next head of discourse is the completeness of the sacred writings, whereby I mean, their sufficiency and perfection as a rule of faith and conduct; their adequateness to our necessities in this present state.

This, in the first place, we may clearly deduce from what has already been established. Being given by inspiration of God, the Scriptures must be perfect for the purpose whereunto he sends them; and if they are finished, so that no further addition to them is to be expected, they must be perfect in all generations for ever, for the use of the children of men. The Old Testament was to them, to whom it was given, a complete rule of conduct; and had they given heed to it in simplicity and sincerity, it was able to have made them wise unto salvation. It had respect, however, to fuller dispensations to come. God, in his great mercy, having provided some better things for us, the devout mind under the Mosaic economy was filled by faith, with the certain expectation of more glorious revelations. But now, that God hath sent into the world his chief and dearest messenger, his beloved Son, and hath disclosed by him the whole scheme of redemption, to which all preceding dispensations had reference, and in which they are all explained, there is no reason to expect from him any further general communications. The revelation of his will is finished. And the same reasons which would lead us to hope, that he would give any revelation to our race, would lead us also to believe, that such revelation, if he vouchsafed to bestow it, would, when finished, be fully adequate to our necessities in this present state. For what man is there among you, who if he were counselling his son, would leave him ignorant of any thing which he wished him to understand or perform? How much less, then, shall your Heavenly Father, having condescended to instruct his children by his word, leave them uninformed of any thing which they are to believe or do. If the Scriptures are given by inspiration of God, as we have abundantly proved, and if, as we have remarked, there is no reason to expect any further addition to them, it would imply a strange idea of the divine wisdom and goodness, not to be persuaded that they are a sufficient and perfect rule, both of faith and conduct. The Most High, surely, does nothing imperfectly, and the word which he hath provided for the government of our lives, is unquestionably adapted in every respect to our nature and necessities.

And this, if we now, in the second place, advert to the sacred writings, will be found to be really the case. Upon every subject of a religious or moral nature, concerning which mankind have been inquisitive, we may here find ample information. And concerning the conduct which is proper in every situation in which mankind may be placed, we may here find explicit instruction. No man who recurs to these holy oracles with a docile mind and a sincere spirit, will find them silent upon any serious subject, about which his thoughts can be reasonably exercised.

It appears from the natural inquiries and desires of our own souls, and from what we discover to have been the desires and inquiries of thoughtful men among the heathens, in all ages, that to the religious and moral necessities of human nature, nothing can be adequate, but knowledge of the being and character of God, assurance of a way in which he may be propitiated and the pardon of sins obtained, instruction in what is right and virtuous with respect to God, our fellow-beings, and ourselves, and certain information of eternal life. These points comprehend all the subjects about which the thoughts of considerate men may be anxious; and upon each of them the instructions of Scripture are abundantly sufficient, for the fixing of our principles and the regulation of our lives.

Fundamental to all true virtue and durable happiness, are clear and right views of the divine nature and government. For what thinking mind can be happy, what course of life can be satisfactory, without some knowledge of God? The light which the Scriptures diffuse upon this point is clear and sufficient for all the purposes of life. The Supreme Being here assures us that He Is, that he is One, that he is Eternal, that he is infinitely Wise, infinitely Good, infinitely Powerful, and infinitely Holy, that he is omnipresent, and that he is unchangeable. Concerning his providence we are informed that it never sleeps, and that it is extended every where, over the minutest works of his hands. Concerning his government we are taught that it is a moral government; that it embraces in its care all the affairs of all worlds, and that it is conducting all things with an unerring hand, to the production of the greatest possible good of the universe. We are assured that we are his creatures, that he takes a perpetual interest in us, that we may approach him in devotion, and that he notices our services and iniquities. To assist our conceptions of him, he hath given us in his word a portrait of his Son, who is the brightness of his glory and express image of his person, and we are hereby enabled, without having our understandings dazzled or our hearts dismayed, to behold the light of the knowledge of the glory of God, in the face of Jesus Christ. These are such instructions concerning the Supreme Being our Creator, as can no where else be found; and I know not that there is any further information we can desire, which might not be shown to be unsuited to our condition, or beyond the capacity of our nature in its present state. At any rate, I am sure that these instructions are sufficient for all the purposes of duty and happiness, and that every man who recurs to the Scriptures may have his mind satisfied with regard to the existence and character of the Being whom no man can see, and who dwelleth in that light unto which it is not wonderful that no mortal can approach.

All men are conscious of sinfulness; and we every where behold mankind endeavouring to appease and propitiate their deities with such anxiety, and with so many devices, as plainly indicate that assurance of the mercy and pardon of God is another thing essential to the happiness of our nature. And, indeed, when we look into our own bosoms, and review our own lives, what can be more desirable to us than the knowledge of a way in which all our unrighteousness may be forgiven, and our sin covered, and the great and holy God reconciled to us, and made the patron and protector of our happiness. This assurance has been universally the object of man's most anxious concern. He has tasked himself with penances and pains, he has offered in sacrifice thousands of rams; he has poured out in libations ten thousands of rivers of oil; we may see him sacrificing his first-born; offering in the fear and anxiety of his soul the fruit of his body, the offspring of his love; and all this, from a consciousness of his sinfulness, and an earnest desire to attain to an assurance of the remission of his sins and the favour of his maker. But this assurance he finds not till he is brought to the foot of the cross. He returns from his sacrifice and libation, and is still filled with uncertainty. It is in the word of God only that his fears are composed, and the peaceful confidence for which he seeks is found. Here he is not only assured of the placability and mercy of the Deity, but also that God, foreseeing the fall and degeneracy of man, hath actually provided the means of expiating his sins and securing his salvation. Here he beholds the Almighty managing, in all ages of time, a stupendous apparatus of promise, prophecy, and type, whereby is introduced and explained, promulgated and confirmed, this scheme of his mercy for the redemption of man. Here the Everlasting Father declares his love for the world, and his pity for the erring children of men; and his desire that all men should come to repentance, and be pardoned and saved through the intervention of his beloved Son, whom he sets forth, offered upon the cross, a full, perfect, and sufficient sacrifice for their transgressions. From the benefit of this sacrifice none are excluded. In its blood, sins of the deepest stain may be washed away. By its efficacy it hath restored to man the good will of God, and opened his arms to every returning offender. In the Scriptures, then, man finds that mediator between him and his Maker that he needs; and the worthy and acceptable sacrifice which he himself is unable to procure. That token for good for which his soul longeth, is here attained, in the enlivening declaration, "that if any man sin we have an advocate with the Father, Jesus Christ the righteous, who is also the propitiation for our sins." How adapted to man's necessities is the knowledge of this salvation! How sufficient these overtures of mercy for his peace! He looks to the Son of God lifted up upon the cross for his redemption, as the Israelites looked to the brazen serpent in the wilderness; and when he looks with faith and repentance, becomes presently conscious of the cessation of his pains, and the healing of his wounds.

There is in every human being some sense of his moral nature and of his accountability. This, together with the inquisitiveness and native tendency of reason, urges him to investigations concerning duty and virtue, concerning right and wrong. Every man who indulges himself in sober reflection, will find it among the first of his inquiries, "What is good, and what does the Lord my God require of me?" These are inquiries upon which the heathen sages appear to have employed the most utmost exertions of their minds; and without a solution of them there can be but little satisfaction or merit in the conduct of life. And here the Scriptures are the perfect and only source of indubitable instruction. I say perfect source, because they contain principles and rules which are applicable to every case that can occur. I say only source, because the law of nature written in the heart, is defaced and weakened by corruption, and the fruits of the researches of human reason are partial in their extent, and of little efficacy. It is to the sacred volume we must look for complete instruction in the principles and obligations of righteousness. Do we inquire what is right and virtuous conduct with respect to the Deity? They teach us to have faith in his word and to obey his requirements; to carry ourselves towards him with love and reverence, with gratitude and humility, with confidence and filial fear; to worship him in simplicity and sincerity, with our bodies and our souls, in spirit and in truth. Do we inquire what is right and virtuous conduct with respect to our fellow-beings? They teach us to render to all their due; to be patient, and kind, and courteous towards all men; to forgive and bless our enemies; to be grateful to our friends; to hurt no person either by injuring his right, or neglecting to promote his benefit; and, in one word, to do to others as we would wish, if they were in our situation and we in theirs, that they should do to us. Do we inquire what is right and virtuous with respect to ourselves? They instruct us to keep our hearts with all diligence, as the sources of the issues of life; to cleanse ourselves from all filthiness of flesh and spirit; to be industrious and temperate, meek and gentle, honest and peaceable, and, in short, to keep ourselves pure habitations of God, through the spirit. There is, indeed, not a vice to which human nature is liable, that the word of God does not describe and denounce. There is not a virtue of which human nature is capable, that the word of God doth not illustrate and commend. So complete is it as a rule of life, that it may be questioned, whether any situation can be supposed, in which a man can be placed, in which it would not furnish him with principles for determining what ought to be his conduct. And its instructions are not complicate, but plain and explicit, adapted to every capacity. They are not arbitrary, but grounded upon the eternal distinction of things, and commend themselves to reason as soon as they are understood. They are not grievous in the practice of them, for they are made easy to the obedient heart, by the spirit which ever accompanies them, and are productive of internal satisfaction and peace. They cannot mislead us, nor need any addition to their authority or certainty, for they came from God. Let a man govern his life by them, and he may have full assurance that he will not fail to attain to the highest perfection of his nature, and to answer the true end of his existence.

But, though man be informed of the being and character of God; though he have hope of the pardon of his sins; though he have instruction in the way of righteousness, he yet must find himself mortal. Reflection tells him that he must die. Existence is dear to him; dissolution is terrible; and it is essential to his happiness and virtue, both under the loss of his friends, and under the consciousness of his own mortality, that he should have some certain information of a future being. He wishes eagerly for assurance of eternal life. But where shall this assurance be found? Shall he ask it of the dead? They, none of them return to disclose their fate. Shall he ask it of the living? They, none of them have passed the grave to make any discovery. Shall he ask it of nature? Shall he ask it of reason? Alas! conscious, since the fall, of their unworthiness, and forgetful of the power of God, they give, at best, but a dubious reply. Of this part of wisdom it may well be declared, "the depth saith, it is not in me; and the sea saith, it is not in me; it cannot be gotten for gold, neither shall silver be weighed for the price thereof." It can be given us only by that Being, who holds the keys of hell and of death. And nothing can more commend his Scriptures unto us, than the consideration that in them we have the words of eternal life. God, upon whom our immortality or annihilation must depend, here teaches us that he hath ransomed us from death, to which we became subject by transgression. He here gives us his immutable word, that we shall pass through the gate of the grave to another, and, if we are faithful and obedient, to a better existence. The declaration of this joyful doctrine he hath ratified and confirmed by raising up his Son Jesus from the dead, and making him to sit in our nature in heavenly places, even at his own right hand, in his celestial kingdom. So that life and immortality are brought to light in the sacred volume; and we have, perhaps, the fullest evidence of it which is compatible with the trial of our faith, and the continuance of the partition, with which, in his wisdom, he hath separated this world from the next.

Who now, that considers the clearness of the light which the Scriptures give upon these several subjects, under one or other of which may be comprehended every moral topic about which human nature is anxious and inquisitive, does not perceive their perfect adaptation to the necessities of man, and their adequateness to his wants as a rule of faith and conduct?

But it may be objected, if the Scriptures are thus complete, whence is it that so many to whom they are sent are neither brought by them to right faith nor right practice? And this brings me to observe, thirdly, in illustration of the completeness of the sacred volume, that if any who have access to it are deficient in knowledge or virtue, the cause of the deficiency is altogether in themselves. The law of the Lord is perfect; and his spirit is ready to render his word efficacious to every attentive and humble mind. But we must approach it with docility; we must remove from our bosoms whatever is unfriendly to its influence; we must adhere to its precepts, and continue in the way which it points out to us, if we would have any experience of its sufficiency for the necessities of our nature. It is owing to men's lusts and passions, to the pride of their minds, to the perverseness of their hearts, to the carnality and viciousness of their lives, that they do not all perceive the excellence and perfection of the Word of God, and find it a savour of life unto life to their souls. "If our gospel be hid," says an Apostle, "it is hid to them that are lost; in whom the God of this world hath blinded the minds of them who believe not." But what disparagement is it to the orb of day, if any shut their eyes, or retire into the caves of the earth, and complain of darkness? Or what does it detract from the clearness and utility of its beams, if any, whose sight is jaundiced and diseased, see the objects on which they rest, in confused and false colours? In like manner, it diminishes not the excellence and sufficiency of the word of God, that men who refuse to open the eyes of their understanding, or who suffer their spiritual discernment to be weakened and vitiated by vice and folly, live in the full brightness of its beams, without any rectitude in their principles, or correctness in their lives. In the parable of the sower, our Lord hath taught us, that the seed of the word to be fruitful, must fall upon good and honest hearts. It may fall upon careless and volatile minds, which are open to every idea that passes; but in them it will be like seed by the way-side, the fowls of the air will devour it up. It may fall upon hearts stupid and insensible, and hardened through the deceitfulness of sin; but in them it will be like seed upon a rock; as soon as it springs up it withers. It may fall upon souls overrun with the cares, and pleasures, and passions of the world; but in them it will be like seed among thorns, the rank and noxious weeds will overtop and choke it. In order to be fruitful, it must fall upon hearts prepared with humility, and ready to retain and nourish it, being cleared of the passions and affections which would obstruct its growth. Let a man study the Scriptures with an inclination to be benefited by them; let him bring to them such reverence and attention as he would carry into the presence of their Author; let him conform his life to their requirements, and supplicate the Spirit to descend as the dew of heaven upon his soul; and then let him say what doctrine there is essential to his faith or virtue which they do not illustrate; what vices or errors there are in his heart which they do not reprove; what sorrow of a temporal or a spiritual nature there is which they do not console, and what peaceful or ennobling virtue there is which they do not promote? Such a man, and such an one only, is qualified to judge of the merits of the sacred writings; for "the natural man receiveth not the things of the spirit of God; neither can he know them, because they are spiritually discerned."

The grand principle upon which the divine spirit acts, is that laid down to us by our blessed Lord; if any man will do his will, he shall know of the doctrine whether it be of God or men. The inestimable treasure which he hath given us in the volume of his word, contains, indeed, the medicine which will heal our sickness, and the food whereby our souls may live. But, in order to the efficacy of the one and the other, the directions he hath prescribed must be obeyed. If any man depart from these prescriptions, or counteract them with contrary indulgences, the holy word, instead of being a savour of life unto life, may be a savour of death unto death to him. And hence the solemn admonition of St. Paul, that we "be not conformed to this world, but be transformed by the renewing of our minds, if we would prove what is that good, and acceptable, and perfect will of God."

You see, then, my brethren, the completeness of the sacred volume; that it is now finished, and is perfect as a rule of faith and life, adapted in all respects to the wants of our nature in this present state. When thy word goeth forth it giveth light unto the simple. It is "profitable for doctrine, for reproof, for correction, for instruction in righteousness." "The wayfaring man, though a fool, shall not err therein."

SERMON II.

ON THE SCRIPTURES.

2 TIMOTHY, iii. 16, 17.

"All Scripture is given by inspiration of God; and is profitable for doctrine, for reproof, for correction, for instruction in righteousness; that the man of God may be perfect, thoroughly furnished unto all good works."

IN a former discourse from these words, I called your attention, in the first place, to the Inspiration of the Scriptures; and secondly, to their completeness.

You are now, therefore, prepared to consider, in the third place, what is the end for which God hath condescended, by inspired writings, to furnish us with this perfect rule of faith and conduct. We find ourselves in possession of a volume wonderfully adapted to the necessities of our nature, and given by inspiration of God. It becomes us to inquire what is the object for which it is given?

And let me, in the first place, observe, what is very necessary to our right estimation of this gift, that it is for no purpose of benefit to the Almighty, that the volume of his word is given to our world. Neither our faith nor our obedience can profit the Most High. It is, indeed, a declaration of his character and glory; but we should ever remember that his character and glory are declared, not for any exaltation of himself, but for communication of happiness to the beings he has created. Were mankind wholly ignorant of his word; were they all extinct upon the earth; yea, were the globe itself which he hath given them for an habitation, removed from amongst his works, there could be no diminution of his happiness or glory. He still would exist, the perfect God. It is not with any view to his own interest that he hath given us the holy Scriptures.

I must also premise that, whether any other beings than ourselves are interested in them, and whether their contents will be of utility to us in the other world, are questions which need not be discussed, as essential to the inquiry we are about to consider. It is enough, in order to raise our estimation of them, to be assured, that into the mysteries revealed to us the angels desire to look, and that by the dispensations to the Church, is made known to higher orders of beings the manifold wisdom of God. From the nature of things we may also be certain, that those general principles of duty and virtue, which have not respect to mutable stations and relations, are the principles by which the conduct of perfect beings is regulated in all parts of the universe, and by which our own conduct will be regulated, if we are among the ransomed, when our present condition shall have passed away, and we shall have entered upon the scenes of the eternal world. And this, by the by, is a high motive to induce us to reverence these principles, and to form by them the habits of our hearts and lives.

But what I am now principally concerned to consider, is the end or uses of the sacred volume to us men, to whom it is given in the present world. And this is nothing less than our recovery from the state of ignorance, sinfulness, and misery into which we are fallen, and our exaltation to the hope of eternal life. God having, by the sacrifice of his beloved Son, ransomed the world from destruction, hath also, with paternal care and unspeakable mercy, made us acquainted by his word with this redemption, and with the way in which we may attain to all its blessed fruits and benefits. Our salvation, and the faith, repentance and obedience which lead to it, are the burthens of the sacred volume. The law was a schoolmaster to bring them to whom it was given unto Christ; and the gospel was written that we might believe in him, and "that believing we might have life through his name." God hath given his word for no other purpose than the recovery of our apostate race. The sacred writings are the means he hath appointed to inform us of that capacity for everlasting salvation into which we are brought by the redemption that is in Christ Jesus, and also to train us up in that faith and holiness which are necessary, both as conditions and qualifications for the enjoyment of his heavenly kingdom. The doctrines which these writings contain we must embrace; to the reproofs which they administer we must harken; the reformation which they require we must promote; the instructions in righteousness which they give we must follow, if we would rise from the awful state of sin and ignorance in which we find ourselves, and attain to any tolerable degree of faith and holiness in this life, and to the hope of immortality and bliss in the world to come. They are given by inspiration of God, for this end, that we may not doubt their certainty. They are made complete for this great and most gracious purpose, that we may be perfect in all the wisdom and knowledge and armour which is necessary to salvation; and "thoroughly furnished unto all good works."

That I may more distinctly set before you the gracious design of the Almighty in giving us the volume of his word, allow me more particularly to observe, that it is the efficacious means of all those changes and graces by which the Christian character is formed and perfected. We are told, you know, that we must be born again in order to the knowledge and enjoyment of the kingdom of God. It is through the instrumentality of the Scriptures that this regeneration is accomplished. They are the seed of his new birth. God's spirit always accompanying them as his institution, they are effectual in the heart of every one who reads them with the dispositions they require, to enlighten his mind and reform his heart, to bring him "out of darkness into God's marvellous light," and to turn him from "the power of Satan unto God." "In Christ Jesus," says St. Paul to the Corinthians, "I have begotten you through the gospel." "Of his own will," says St. James, "begat he us by the word of truth, that we should be a kind of first fruits of his creatures." We are "born again," says St. Peter, "not of corruptible seed, but of incorruptible by the word of God, which liveth and abideth forever." Our regeneration, like all our blessings, is solely and entirely from God; but it is wrought and perfected through the instrumentality of his word.

Again. It is necessary that we should be sanctified and made holy in heart and life, before we can enter into the kingdom of heaven. And the holy Scriptures are the means by which the spirit of God accomplishes this important part of our salvation. They teach us what is virtuous, and praiseworthy, and required of us; they set before us all the motives and encouragements which can influence us to forsake our sins, and they are mighty through the Spirit which always accompanies them in the humble heart, to break down the strongholds of vice, and to lead us into all the paths of righteousness and holiness. "Sanctify them," says our Lord in his prayer for his disciples, "sanctify them through thy truth; thy word is truth." "I commend you," says the Apostle to the elders from Ephesus, "I commend you to God, and to the word of his grace, which is able to build you up, and to give you an inheritance among all them that are sanctified." Our sanctification is the work of the Holy Ghost, but it is wrought by means of that word of truth which he himself hath inspired for this very purpose.

Further. It is required of us to grow in grace; and we have need to be constantly nourished in all goodness, if we would not relapse into our evil state, but advance to perfection in knowledge and virtue. The sacred writings are the granary from which this daily sustenance of our souls is to be obtained. They reveal the truths, they contain the virtues, they give efficacy to the ordinances by which we are nourished unto eternal life. They furnish milk for the infant Christian, and meat for those of maturer years. It is by constant and deep attention to their sublime doctrines, that our spiritual strength is increased; it is by frequently impressing our hearts with their divine instructions, that we must counteract the tendency of our spirits to evil, and advance to greater and greater maturity in all virtue and godliness. "The words that I speak unto you," says our blessed Lord, "they are spirit, and they are life." "Desire the sincere milk of the word," says St. Peter, to the youthful converts, "that you may grow thereby." And of the experienced Timothy, his spiritual father speaks, as "nourished up in the words of faith and of good doctrine, whereunto he had attained." For the sustenance of our spiritual as of our animal life, we are dependent wholly upon the invisible power of the Most High; but this power is exerted in and through the means which he hath provided and blessed for the purpose, namely, the revelations, and persuasions, and promises, and ordinances which are contained in his holy word.

Finally, it is necessary to our comfort, and to the full accomplishment of our deliverance from the miseries of our natural state, that we should have joy and peace in believing. And the reservoir of all spiritual joy is the word of God. We must read its comfortable doctrines to be relieved from the anxieties and sorrows of this sinful life. Its assurances of pardon and favour through the blood of Jesus, cheer and compose the conscience. The examples of the worthies it has immortalized, illustrate to us the efficacy of faith, the safety of the righteous, and the fidelity of God. Its precious promises, and the glorious prospects which it opens, rejoice the heart, and enable the human pilgrim to pass on his way, wet, perhaps, with many a shower, and afflicted with the apprehension of many a danger, but happy in the hope that his sins will be forgiven, and that his pilgrimage will terminate in a rest from his cares, and an enjoyment of immortal felicity. The burthen of God's word is styled by a prophet and angel, glad tidings of joy to all people. And "whatsoever things were written aforetime," we are told by an Apostle, "were written for our learning, that we, through patience and comfort of the Scriptures, might have hope." The source, the well-spring of all joy is in God, and from him alone it must be derived to us; but it hath pleased him to communicate it to us through the channel of his word; which is therefore called, "the gospel of our salvation," and "the word of life."

It appears, then, from the views we have taken, that the end and use of the sacred volume, is to recover us from the awful and unhappy state into which our nature is fallen, to wisdom and righteousness, and the blessed hope of everlasting life. It is given to bring us to Christ; to establish our faith, and order our goings; that we may be comforted with the knowledge and fitted for the enjoyment of immortality. By the instrumentality of the doctrines it reveals, God would rescue our understandings from the ignorance and blindness with which they are encompassed. By means of the reproofs, corrections, and instruction in righteousness, which it furnishes, he would bring us from the servitude of sin to the love and practice of virtue. And by the overtures of mercy which it contains, and the acts of faith and devotion which it dictates, he would draw us to himself, and enable us, with peaceful hope, to pass through this probationary state; looking for a final redemption and glorious immortality beyond the grave. So that the end of that faith in and obedience to his word, unto which we are called, is nothing less than the salvation of our souls.

I am aware, that there are some persons to whom I may seem to have attributed too much efficacy to the sacred writings. Actuated by the occasional experience of devout fervour, and by the ardor of undisciplined imagination, they cherish in themselves, and encourage in others, the expectation of extraordinary internal illuminations, and supernatural assistances. Into this error, they are led, by certain expressions of Scripture, which they have not properly considered. We are said to be "born of God." And this is, indeed, true. But it is, as you have seen, through the instrumentality of his word. We are said to be "born of the Spirit;" but the Spirit is also God, and acts by the same means, the word of truth which he hath dictated. We are said to be "born of water;" and this is indeed true; for baptism is the laver of our regeneration. But it is efficacious by the authority of the Scriptures. We are cleansed with the washing of water by the word. The word of God, is, indeed, the only seed which his ministers can sow. From this seed, when it falls into good and honest hearts, will spring, through his blessing, that faith, and hope, and charity, which are the principles, and characteristics, of the new and divine life. Nothing can we teach, or inculcate, but what we derive from the Scriptures. Nowhere but to the sacred writings can we send you, for that knowledge which must remove your ignorance; for that light which may make the paths of duty, and virtue, plain before you, or for that assurance of salvation, and eternal life, which may fill you with hope and peace. Indeed, when the Almighty, with the most gracious condescension, hath spoken his will, in times past, by the Prophets, and, in these latter days, by his Son; when with great care he caused a record of his communication to be made under the guidance and inspiration of his Spirit; when this volume of his word is perfect as a rule of faith and conduct, and adequate to all the necessities of our nature, it is not reasonable to suppose, that all this has been done in vain, and that we are to find the knowledge, and means of salvation, in supernatural interpretations. We are not to look out of the word for that which the word is given to furnish. The Spirit of God is indispensably necessary, to open our understandings to receive the Scriptures, and to assist the infirmities of our nature, in complying with their requirements. But it operates by making no new revelation; it furnishes no new light; it acts in, and by, the word, which it accompanies, and blesses, in the heart of every sincere inquirer.

It is true; that there have been some instances, of men's being brought to the knowledge of salvation, without the intervention of the word. The penitent thief has been suddenly sealed upon the cross, unto redemption. And a Paul, has been converted to the faith, by immediate revelation from heaven. But so, also, in the natural world, the shadow has gone back upon the dial, and the sun has stood still at noon day. But these were miraculous events for extraordinary purposes; and can only teach us, that though we are bound by God's laws, he, himself, is not. *Generally* speaking, the course of nature, we may clearly perceive, is according to uniform laws. And from the analogy which pervades the ways of the Most High; from his essential love of order; and from express intimations of his word, we may also conclude, that his moral government is ordinarily conducted by uniform and stated principles. Having given us his inspired word, to be to us a source of wisdom, and salvation, every way adapted to our nature, and adequate to our necessities, we are not to wander from it in search of other illuminations, nor to expect any illuminations without it. To this full and glorious light which he hath given us, we must recur, that we may see ourselves, and our condition; that by it, we may discern the paths of duty, and salvation; that in it, we may behold the glory, and loving-kindness of God; that through the beams of its promises, we may be cheered and strengthened; and that, conducting ourselves in the ways which it reveals, we may please our Creator, and attain to the enjoyment of him, in his heavenly kingdom.

This appears to me, to be the doctrine of the Scriptures concerning the end, or uses, of the sacred volume. It is answerable to our nature, as reasonable beings, and moral agents. And in confirmation of it, I shall adduce to your notice a plain, but very instructive passage, from one of those admirable homilies, which were composed with pious care, in the morning of the reformation, and then set forth to be read in the Churches: "The Scripture of God is the heavenly meat of our souls. The hearing and keeping of it maketh us blessed, sanctifieth us, and maketh us holy. It is a light to our feet. It is a sure, steadfast, and everlasting instrument of salvation. It giveth wisdom to the humble, and lowly hearts. It comforteth, maketh glad, cheereth, and cherisheth our conscience. It hath in it everlasting comfort. The words of Holy Scripture be called, words of everlasting life; for they be God's instrument, ordained for the same purpose. They have power to turn, through God's promise; and they be effectual, through God's assistance; and being received in a faithful heart, they have ever a heavenly spiritual working in them. They are lively, quick, and mighty in operation; and sharper than any two-edged sword; and enter through, even to the dividing asunder of the soul and the spirit, of the joints and the marrow. Christ calleth him a wise builder, that buildeth upon his word; upon his sure and substantial foundation. By this word of God we shall be judged; for the word that I speak, saith Christ, is it that shall judge in the last day. He that keepeth this word, is promised the love and favour of God, and that he shall be the dwelling-place, or temple, of the blessed Trinity."

I have now pursued this important subject, according to the plan proposed, at the opening of these discourses; and have set before you, the inspiration, the completeness, and the end, or uses, of the sacred writings. You have seen, from numerous and irrefragable evidences, that the Scriptures are the sacred record of a chain of communications made by the Almighty, from time to time, to the inhabitants of this lower world; a record, written, by such scribes as he was pleased to choose, under his own inspection, and the guidance and assistance of his Spirit; and, consequently, containing nothing but what is true, and important, and worthy of all men to be thankfully received. You have seen, that these Scriptures are now finished, and are perfect, as a rule of faith and conduct, furnishing light, and instruction, upon all the points about which the human mind is anxious and inquisitive; and adequate, in all respects, to the necessities of our nature, in this present state. And you have seen, that the great and gracious end, for which God hath vouchsafed to furnish us, by inspired writings, with this perfect rule of faith, and conduct, is nothing less than our recovery from the state of ignorance, sinfulness, and misery, into which we are fallen; and our exaltation to the hope of eternal life. And more particularly, that through its instrumentality, we are regenerated, and sanctified, and nourished in all goodness, and filled with joy and peace, in believing; being brought by it to the knowledge, and incited to the pursuit of holiness and immortality, and conducted by it, if we follow its directions, to the favour of God, and the salvation of our souls. From these truths, which we have so amply discussed, there are several inferences, of a very serious nature, ard great practical importance, to which I must now ask your attentive consideration.

And, in the first place, from the views we have taken of the sacred volume, we may perceive its claim to our highest estimation. Imagine yourselves living in that age and state of the world, in which human nature is found unenlightened by revelation. Fancy yourselves, for a moment, encompassed with the darkness of heathenism, the paths of virtue and safety obscured; your Maker hidden from your view; your origin, your duty, your destination, unknown; the way to the tomb, your inevitable course haunted with spectres of doubt and dismay; your spirits turning on every side for light and direction; but finding on every side darkness and uncertainty. In the midst of this gloom, suppose the heavens opened, and there descended to you a messenger, bringing to you a book which informed you of your origin and destiny; which revealed to you the true God, and assured you of his love and favour; which made the path of every virtuous excellence plain before you; and disclosed to you a title, an eternal title to immortality. With what transports of delight would you receive the messenger! I see you, in imagination, falling prostrate at his feet. The book which he gives you, you would press to your lips; you would hold it to your bosom; you would drop on it the tears of excessive joy. As the messenger returned to the skies, you would follow him with benedictions till he vanished from your view; and the precious volume you would carry to your habitation with care and unspeakable exultance. Your wife and your children would be called to behold the gift. Your neighbours and friends would be shown the treasure. And were the wealth of the world offered you in exchange for it, you would again clasp it in your hands, and declare it above all price. But, my brethren, take away the Scriptures, and what is your condition but the condition of unenlightened nature? Consider their inspiration of God and their important contents, and what is their value less than if they were brought to you immediately from the skies? And yet, how imperfectly are they appreciated? Who hath sufficiently regarded them? Of the worth of the sacred volume, no estimation would be too high. For the kindness and condescension of the Almighty in giving it to us, no measure of gratitude would be excessive. But because we have always been in the enjoyment of it, and its light and comfort are familiar to our minds, we behold it as we behold the sun in the heavens, unmindful of the majesty and benignity of its author, and almost unconscious of the importance of its beams. Surely, if the views we have taken of the subject are remembered, this insensibility to the value of the best blessing of life, will be reproved by your consciences, and carefully corrected. When you think of the inspiration of the Scriptures, of their completeness, and of their end and uses, unless you are ungrateful to your Maker and unjust to yourselves, you will be, like the Psalmist, as glad of God's word as one that findeth great spoils.

But if we value the Scriptures, we shall also study them. And an obligation to do so is the second thing I would urge upon your notice, as peculiarly enforced by the account which has been given of the sacred volume. It is a deplorable fact, and too plain to be disguised, that the Scriptures are little read and imperfectly understood. If we look into the natural world, we see every object guided and governed by the laws of its Maker. Could we look upon the hosts of spiritual beings who compose the court of the King of Heaven, we should behold them, with eager and constant attention, "harkening unto the voice of his word." But man, whom he hath condescended to furnish with an inspired gospel for the guidance of his life, possesses the treasure with heedless indifference, and rests satisfied with a partial knowledge of its contents. In how many families does the sacred volume repose undisturbed upon the desk, from Sabbath to Sabbath? And are there not many individuals who never are induced, even by the solemnity and disengagedness of this holy day, to recur to its important pages?

Surely, its origin, and the design of the Almighty in bestowing it upon us, are forgotten, or it would not thus be neglected. What being, who should visit us from another sphere, would suppose that these neglected Scriptures are given us by inspiration of God? Who that should observe our indifference to them, would believe that in them we have the words of eternal life? If habit had not bound us with a fatal spell; if we were not in a state, a dangerous state, of spiritual insensibility, we should not have in our houses such an oracle of truth and salvation, without recurring to it for instruction every morning, and for consolation and benediction every night.

The consequences of not reading the holy Scriptures are of a more serious nature, and greater in extent than you may suppose. It is to this, I apprehend, that we are to attribute, in a great measure, the total ignorance of religion in some, and the decay of it in others. It is in this that we are to look for the cause of the instability of Christians. Here we may find the reason why error prevails. Here we may discover the source of fanaticism and of superstition. To this it is owing that the best seem unconscious of the degree of holiness to which they are called; and that all rest easy under imperfections of knowledge and deficiencies of virtue, which a thorough acquaintance with the Scriptures would both reprove and correct. Such were the consequences when, in unhappy days, a spiritual tyranny locked up the sacred writings from the people in an unknown tongue. And the effects will not be greatly different, if, when these writings are easily accessible to you, in your own language, you keep yourselves ignorant of them. Education may give you a respect for them; you may think of them with a kind of abstract reverence. But unless you study them; unless you enlighten your understandings with their doctrines, and impress your hearts with their spirit, they can be to you no more than the Koran of Muhammed, or the dialogues of Plato. You will neither be well informed concerning your salvation, nor acquainted with the extent of your privileges or duties. "Ye do err," said our Lord to the Sadducees, "not knowing the

Scriptures." And it is assigned as the cause both of the faith and of the high commendation of the Bereans, that they searched the Scriptures with a ready mind.

Were it calling you to an unnecessary, an unprofitable task; were it merely to engage you in dubious speculations; were it only to fit you to be able disputants upon theological subjects; far, very far would it be from me to press upon you the importance of frequently and attentively perusing the holy volume. Unhappy they, who gather water from this sacred spring, only to sport with it in the fields of contention. But the Scriptures are the rule of faith and life. They are provided with infinite condescension by the care of God. His purpose in giving them to us is the salvation of our souls. In them, if any where, we must seek the knowledge of "the truth as it is in Jesus." By them, if by any means, we must be "thoroughly furnished unto all good works." But how shall their end be accomplished in you if they be not known? In what shall they be useful to you if they be not read and applied? Will you trust to the portions of them which your spiritual pastors feebly bring to your notice? This would devolve more upon them than they can discharge, and expose you to imperfection in knowledge and holiness. Will you trust to your prayers; and while you neglect his word, expect that he will enlighten and save you? This would be like beseeching him to sustain you in life, while you refused to use the bread which he hath provided for your sustenance. Having given us his word, perfect instructions in wisdom and holiness, in the way and in the means of salvation, he requires that, as reasonable beings, we employ our faculties in apprehending these instructions, and applying them to the government of our lives. It is incumbent, therefore, upon every man to study the sacred writings. If he value the knowledge of God; if he desire to have the paths of duty and virtue marked out to him; if he would understand the mystery of redemption, and the terms upon which his Maker's favour is obtained; if he would be consoled with the hope of immortality, and advance from strength to strength in knowledge and virtue, he will study them assiduously and thoroughly; he will have his meditation in them day and night. When these fountains of divine truth are set open unto us, to neglect to recur to them is to affront the Spirit who presides over them, and to merit perpetual subjection to darkness and delusion. It is saying to the Almighty in practice what we should shudder to avow in words, that we desire not the knowledge of his ways.

Again. In the course of our observations upon the holy Scriptures, we have shown that God hath a merciful purpose in conferring them on us; even to recover us from our ignorance, sinfulness, and misery, and exalt us to the hope of everlasting life. It behoves us, therefore, to inquire how far his desire and gracious intention hath been accomplished in us? And this inquiry you will most safely answer, not by adverting to your occasional feelings and transient fervours, but by looking to your principles and your lives. Are you brought to a clear knowledge of the only true God, and of Jesus Christ whom he hath sent? Have you embraced God's offer, and do you confide in his promise of mercy in and through his beloved Son? Do you possess and cherish an enlightened reverence and a filial love for your Creator, Redeemer, and Benefactor? Have you renounced the hidden things of darkness, and the malevolent passions, the sinful appetites, the criminal pursuits, and the polluting indulgences wherewith your God and Redeemer is grieved and displeased? Are those traits of excellence which are distinctly exemplified in the lives of the Scripture worthies, and which are all combined and perfected in the example of our blessed Lord, are they imitated by you in the several conditions and relations in which the Most High hath placed you? Is your faith such as hath wrought by love and purified the heart, so that in your affections, and temper, and conduct, as well as in the relations and hopes to which you have been begotten through the gospel, you are new creatures? These are important inquiries. And you owe it to God, who hath vouchsafed to give you a perfect rule of life; you owe it to yourselves, who have been ennobled and strengthened by such an inestimable gift, to see if these fruits of his word have been produced in you.

There is nothing, perhaps, which men so seldom ask themselves as, whether the end of God's instructions is accomplished in them? And yet there is nothing against which his indignation hath been more strikingly expressed, than against the frustration of the use of his word by the heedlessness or perverseness of those to whom it is given. Look at his peculiar people, to whom were once exclusively committed the oracles of truth. They became proud in the imaginations of their heart. They knew not the Scriptures. They despised the simplicity of truth, and made the word of God of none effect. And behold, they are scattered under the whole heavens; their temple is demolished; their oracles are to them obscured; and not till their minds are humbled, and they are ready to embrace the Messiah, whom their neglect of the Scriptures led them to reject, will they be gathered again to the favour of God. Look at those regions of the eastern world, which, in the morning of Christianity, were blessed with the first light of the gospel. Unhappy countries! The people became lukewarm and careless; they held the truth in unrighteousness; its end was not answered in them; they loved the dominion of error and sin; and behold, they are left, as they were threatened, to the delusions of darkness; for the light of God's word hath been taken away. The absurdities of the mosque have been substituted for the worship of the Christian temple; and ignorance and imposture now revel on the spots which were once hallowed by the presence of truth. These are dreadful tokens of the Almighty's indignation, when his word is unproductive of its proper effects.

It may be, that to such temporal vengeance we may never be exposed. Willingly would I persuade myself, that there never will be wanting among us, such fruits of faith and knowledge, of piety and virtue, as will induce the Father of all mercies, to continue to our country the light of his glorious word. But, as individuals, we are fast hastening to the grave; and, after death, is the judgment! The most distinguishing privilege, the principal talent, for which we shall then be called to account, is the possession we have had of the Scriptures of truth. These are capable of exalting us to sublime attainments of divine wisdom and holiness; and having furnished us with these, great are the improvements which our Maker may require at our hands. And if at his tribunal, in the day of retribution, we shall be found, notwithstanding our advantages, to have remained unchanged, and unrenewed, the very heathens will rise up in judgment and condemn us; and we can only expect to be driven from the presence of God, as unprofitable servants, who have disregarded his instructions, and despised his reproofs.

On this solemn account, I cannot forbear adding, in the fourth place, what is powerfully enforced by our subject, the importance of bringing to the oracles of truth, whenever we recur to them, becoming dispositions, and conduct. You have seen, that the Scriptures are completely adequate to the necessities of your nature, in the present state. They teach you fully, what you are to believe, and what you are to do; and the Holy Spirit is ever present with them, to render them efficacious in the humble heart, to all the purposes of everlasting salvation. So that you can never plead, either ignorance, or inability, in extenuation of your errors, or vices. That you may not, therefore, through any default of your own, come short of the kingdom of God, let me exhort you, to use the sacred volume in that way, which experience, and its own directions, commend to your observance. Having seen the evidences of its inspiration, recur to it, always, as the word of God. Carry to it inquiring, and docile minds. Read it with a humble desire to be made wiser, and better by it. Since nothing can be efficacious without the power of the Almighty, bow to him your knees, and supplicate his blessing upon your use of it. Make a fair experiment of its principles. Whatever it denounces, as opposed to its efficacy, avoid. Whatever it recommends, as promotive of your good, pursue. Endeavour, if possible, to make it the standard, by which you would regulate all your thoughts, and actions. Such confidence, obedience, and good will, as you would repose in the physician for whom you had sent, to relieve you of bodily disease or pain, repose also in the word, which the great spiritual physician hath provided, for the restoration of your souls. In this way, avail yourselves of the Scriptures of truth; and you will find by an experience, more satisfactory than many testimonies, that the ways it recommends to you, are ways of pleasantness, and the paths into which it hath brought you, are the paths of peace.

Lastly. The character of the sacred writings, and your privilege in possessing them, impose on you an obligation to extend the knowledge of them, as far as you are able, and, especially, to make them the source from which you furnish your children, with the principles and rules of life. "These words which I command thee," says the Almighty, "shall be in thine heart; and thou shalt teach them diligently unto thy children; and shalt talk of them when thou sittest in thine house, and when thou walkest by the way, and when thou liest down, and when thou risest up." Pliant is the infant mind. Free from pride and prejudice, and the perversion of vice, it readily receives the instructions of the Bible, as the word of God. If a reverence for it be impressed, and a knowledge of its contents communicated, in early life, they will, in all probability, be carried through every stage of existence. It was the happiness of the distinguished young Bishop, to whom the text was addressed, that from a child he had known the holy Scriptures: And the preeminent Apostle who addressed it to him, was brought up piously, at the feet of Gamaliel, in all the knowledge of the law.

I know not, indeed, what there is, to which you should be so anxious to conduct your children, as to the fountains of divine wisdom and virtue, in the holy Scripture. You are careful to accomplish their bodies. You are solicitous to have them initiated in human sciences. You spare no pains to give them the graces and the knowledge, which are esteemed in the world. And we do not desire, to denounce any innocent and rational attainments, which may soften the asperities of social intercourse, and give intelligence and usefulness to life. But the sphere of all these attainments is transient. The best temporal accomplishments are of short and uncertain utility. Your children are heirs of immortality. They are rapidly hastening to leave this state, and enter an eternal world. It is the highest wisdom, it is the tenderest affection, to imbue them with the principles, and furnish them with the graces, which will be esteemed and used, in the societies of heaven, when earthly accomplishments will have been left upon earth, and human knowledge will have vanished away. Train up the young, then, in the principles and spirit of the word of God. In so doing, you will be just to the Most High, who hath put you in trust with the sacred oracles; you will give to your children instructions and hopes, for which they may bless you at the bar of God; and you will be instrumental in conveying to posterity, those sacred records, which he, who considers their inspiration, their completeness, and their use, will esteem the most important blessing, that posterity can receive.

I have now, my brethren, finished my remarks upon this all important subject. Persuaded that if ever you are made wise and good, it must be through the instrumentality of the Scriptures: Believing that an acquaintance with them is the best preservative from irreligion, on the one hand, and fanaticism on the other; and fearful, that from the neglect of them proceed ignorance, indifference, and vice, I have assayed to set the subject before you, in a great extent, and under various aspects. It is highly probable, that many parts of it have been tedious, and that in all parts, I have fallen far short of the clearness, sublimity, and ardor, which such a topic should have inspired. But such as my remarks have been, I know, that God is able to bless them, and to render them productive in you, of an increased attachment to his holy word. To his blessing I commend them; and shall close all, with two passages from the sacred volume, which are peculiarly pertinent and impressive. The one is from the mouth of the ablest Minister of the Old Testament; and the other, from the blessed Author of the New:

"Set your hearts," says Moses, "unto all the words which I testify among you this day, which ye shall command your children to observe to do, all the words of this law; for it is not a vain thing for you; because it is your life."—"If ye continue in my word," says our Lord, "then are ye my disciples indeed; and ye shall know the truth, and the truth shall make you free."

SERMON III.

ON RELIGIOUS ORDINANCES.

1 Samuel, ix. 13.

For the people will not eat until he come, because he doth bless the sacrifice; and afterwards they eat that be bidden.

THERE is a striking resemblance between the outlines of the Mosaic, and of the Christian Church. Each arose upon a divine basis. Each had its form of initiation and symbolic rites. Each had its three orders of Ministers in the sanctuary. And each boasts of a divine Being at its head. As in the one, so in the other, the covenant is in the hands of a Mediator, and its principles and laws are deposited in a sacred code. In both, to explain the covenant, to bless the children of it, and to speak from the appeased Deity the remission of their sins, appertained to the Priesthood; and this honor no man could take to himself, but it was received in a way of divine appointment. There is, indeed, in the Christian Church, a higher degree of spirituality than is found under any other dispensation. Here, the shadows of the law find their substance. Here, the types of antiquity meet their fulfilment. Here, the daily sacrifice and oblation cease, absorbed in their significance in that great sacrifice, of which, to the eye of faith, they all were figures. But in the constitution of his Church, our blessed Lord did not overlook the ancient pattern of heavenly things, nor forget the nature of Man. Under the protection and blessing of the divine Spirit, the Church in her militant state, is now, as formerly, to be known and preserved, to be propagated and improved, by the word, the sacraments, and the ministry. It will not, therefore, be an uninteresting employment, nor foreign to the business for which we are here convened, to contemplate, my brethren, the propriety and utility of religious rites; the consequent necessity (of an authorized order) of men to administer them; and the obligations which are hence devolved upon both ministers and people.

The first point to which I would call your attention, is the fitness and utility of Religious Ordinances. When any number of men become associated into one body, with peculiar principles, purposes, and advantages, there seems a propriety in their having some characteristic badges. It is necessary, in the induction of new members, that there be some form; how else shall the person introduced know his title, or those who were already of the community, be assured of their acquisition, and his claim? It is necessary that there should be some external properties, or rites, common to every one; how else can he always manifest his relation to the rest, and discover their relation to him; and the whole body, however various and scattered its parts, be kept distinct, pursue uniformly its purposes, and attract the notice of the world? Will it be said, that by the name of a community all its members may be known? But it is certainly expedient, that this name should be given, or taken, with some ceremony, in some established way; for otherwise, it might be assumed and resigned at will; and it would be difficult to know to whom it regularly belonged. Will it be said, that their sentiments and purposes are sufficient to distinguish any body of men? But the sentiments of every man are not always avowed; and the views of different members of the same community, are frequently various. My knowing that I have the same opinions which distinguish any society, may convince me that I am related to them, so far as similarity of principles can connect us; but they cannot know it till I declare my feelings; and when each knows the other, we cannot be associated without some mutual act; nor our relation be perceived by mankind, without some public demonstration of it. There is, in truth, no such obvious, simple, and universal means of preserving communities distinct, and manifesting their members to the world and to each other, as characteristic rites and peculiar badges. Nature prompts to the use of them; for the savage of the woods has the song and the ceremonies of his ancestors, and by the gashings and daubings with which he disfigures his form, denotes his tribe. Reason and policy have discovered their utility; for the armies of the ambitious have their uniforms and their standards; and almost every nation has its mode of naturalizing subjects, its oaths of allegiance, and its arms. Indeed, so fit and necessary are they, that few communities continue long without them, or survive the loss of them; and they who denounce all rites as useless, are obliged ro recur to peculiarity of dress, of phrase, or of gesture, when they would be known to each other, and distinguished from the world.

Hitherto our observations have been of a general nature, applicable to any community. What, then, shall we say of the propriety and importance of rites, and ordinances, in the service of religion? If we had nothing more to add, the reasons which have already been adduced, will equally prove the necessity of some proper forms in religious, as in other, institutions. But if we consider the nature of man, and the design of religion, we shall find them requisite on other accounts. Composed of body and spirit, man is obligated to honor his Maker with both. The bended knee befits his homage, as well as the humbled soul. A worship suitable to his nature cannot be wholly spiritual in his present state, for then would many of his faculties be unemployed, which should bring praise to their Author, and that part of him which is specially adapted to his probationary residence, would be useless in his noblest, and most important work. There is, too, an aid derived by the mind from the co-operation of the body in religious services. Easily, and strongly impressed by present objects, having his understanding, his imagination, and his affections closely connected with his senses, man's devotion is warmed, and his spirits relieved, by symbolic representations of the truths he should feel, and sensible indications of the worship he would render. Accordingly, in almost all theories of religion which have been devised, some hallowed rites have found a place. The heathen had his feasts, his purgations, and his sacrifices. To the Jews, God appointed a system of ceremonies, to connect them together, and shadow forth the sublime subjects of faith to their understandings. And our adorable Redeemer, instituted for his followers a baptism, which should represent their "death unto sin, and new birth unto righteousness;" and a supper, in which they should commemorate the foundation of all their hopes and joys, his offering himself in the body once for all.

But further: Religious ordinances are of unspeakable advantage, in uniting members of the same body, and attaching them affectionately to each other. They form a kind of visible chain connecting men together; the first and last links of which, are connected with God. They open, as it were, a common resort for the same benefit, in which men perceive, affectingly, their mutual relation, and from the coincidence of their hopes, their interests and pursuits, acquire a regard for each other's welfare. Whenever we perceive in another, sentiments and feelings congenial with our own, we invariably feel a fondness for him. If we discover in him the same profession, name, country, or expectations with ours, the bond of attachment is strengthened. Community of interest begets confidence; and while we are pursuing the same objects, under consciousness of the same infirmities, but with reliance upon the same hopes, we are filled, involuntarily, with affection for each other. Analogous, is the effect of sacred rites, in which, one discovers in another, the same holy badge which he himself wears; and all perceive in the unity of their object and care, a bond of fellowship which is pleasant and impressive. This is strikingly illustrated in the natural tendency, and no doubt was strong in the Redeemer's view, at the gracious institution of the Lord's Supper. How can the feelings of brotherly kindness and charity, be more strongly excited, then when Christians are gathered around the same table, to recognize their relation to the same head; to feed upon memorials of the same deliverance from a common destruction; and, to receive, at the same hands, the pledges of a joint inheritance of everlasting life? Here, if Satan have not possession of the soul, strife will retire, and animosity be appeased. Here, if any where, revenge will abhor its purpose, and mankind will learn to have the same care one for another. For who, as he joins in the holy ordinance, can be insensible to the Apostle's beautiful appeal; "The cup of blessing which we bless, is it not the communion of the blood of Christ? The bread which we break, is it not the communion of the body of Christ? For we being many are one bread, and one body; for we are all partakers of that one bread."

On the accounts which have been mentioned, we see the fitness and utility of external rites and ordinances in religion. It is true that they may be ill chosen or ill used, and thus be made instruments of superstition and folly. But it would lead to the greatest impoverishment of our nature, if we should infer from the abuses of things their absolute inutility. We may remark, too, in passing, that the ordinances of the gospel are unexceptionable in their number and nature; being few, simple, pure, and significant. By one baptism we are made members of Christ, children of God, and inheritors of the kingdom of heaven; and by one eucharistic feast we commemorate the sacrifice of the death of Christ, and the inestimable benefits which we receive thereby. If these pure and sublime ordinances have at any time been perverted to injurious purposes, we can only bewail the more the propensity of our nature to error. The melancholy fact would evince the necessity of restraining men by established rites, to a uniform worship and simple truths, instead of leaving them to the unlimited wandering of their own imaginations.

Having seen, then, the importance of religious ordinances, let us haste to consider the necessity of a distinct and authorized order of men for the administration of them. A few words will set this point in a clear and convincing light. The very idea of a rite or sacrament supposes some one to administer it. Now, there is no other alternative than that every man administer to himself and others, or that particular men be set apart, authorized and obligated to wait continually upon this very thing. And who, after a moment's reflection, perceives not which of the two is most eligible? Who sees not which must be most conducive to convenience, to regularity, to solemnity, and to the ends for which ordinances are instituted? What confusion would the indiscriminate exercise of sacred functions occasion! How would the solemnity of ordinances disappear if they were in every man's hand, like his common occupation, without uniformity or distinction! What debate and discord might arise if every man's will was his criterion for hallowing and applying sacraments and rites, and no one apprehended an appointed order, to which he was accountable, and the community could appeal.

Independent of the difficulty of preserving ordinances the same, and without urging the improbability that they would, in this way, be preserved at all, it must be evident to every considerate mind, that the committing of them to the administration of a qualified order of men must magnify their importance, add to their solemnity, be most likely to accomplish their design, and best preserve them from degeneracy and abuse. Would you know the common sentiment of mankind upon the subject? Look through the Pagan world, and observe every where a priest where you find an altar; a sacred office where you find a god. Would you know the divine counsel in this particular? Behold the Deity in the dispensation to his chosen people, selecting a particular tribe for his service, and confining to them the right and the duty of ministering in holy things. Above all, it should satisfy our minds upon this topic, that our Saviour did ordain selected men, authorizing them to send others as he sent them to preach his Gospel, to administer his ordinances, and to guide and govern his visible Church. "Go," said he, when about to leave our earth, to the Apostles, whom for this purpose he had chosen, "Go ye, therefore, and teach all nations, baptizing them in the name of the Father, and of the Son, and of the Holy Ghost, teaching them to observe all things whatsoever I have commanded you, and lo, I am with you alway, even unto the end of the world."

There arises, from the nature of the Christian ordinances, a peculiar necessity for an authorized ministry. These sacraments are of high and holy import. Like the ark of the covenant, they are not to be carried by unhallowed hands. They are seals of an engagement between God and men. They are compacts between the Almighty Father and his repentant children, in which he pledges himself, upon condition of their faith and obedience, to give them the pardon of their sins, the blessing of his Spirit, and the enjoyment of eternal life. And who can sign the covenant of such mercies unto men but they who act in God's behalf, but they who act by God's authority? Not, oh, not, that in those to whom this ministry is committed, there is any elation above the ordinary qualities of their fellow-beings. Every priest appointed to this service must be taken from among men; and, consequently, be subject to like passions with the rest of their race. It is, indeed, infinite condescension in the great God, to employ, in the accomplishment of his mighty and gracious purposes, beings frail as we are; but, perhaps, we may say it is also wisdom. For hereby is secured to him, to whom alone it belongs, all the honour, all the praise, all the glory, of the efficacy of the ministrations. "We have this treasure," says St. Paul, speaking of the great Christian behests entrusted to the ministry, "we have this treasure in earthen vessels, that the excellency of the power may be of God, and not of us." It is presumable from the nature of the thing, that there would be found in the world an established priesthood, unto whom this ministry of reconciliation would be committed for the edification of the Church. And blessed be our adorable Head, such a priesthood there has been among his redeemed from the first ministry of his Apostles unto the present day! Nor can we doubt his will, that after the way of his appointment, it should be perpetuated in the world until his coming again. When, under that strong image of endearment, by which the Holy Spirit reveals to us the love and unity of Christ with his Church, she addresses him as her spouse, "Tell me, O thou whom my soul loveth, where thou feedest; where thou makest thy flock to rest at noon?" What is his reply? "If thou know not, O thou fairest among women, go thy way forth by the footsteps of the flock, and feed thy kids beside the shepherds' tents."

There results from the nature of man, from the requirements of a state of society, and from the very scope of the Redeemer's purposes, a reasonable expectation that there should be appointed shepherds, around whose tents, pitched in the second Eden, which himself hath planted, the kids should feed, and all his followers, to the end of time, moving in the same paths, by the footsteps of their predecessors, be gathered together to the same shades, and fountains, and pastures, to enjoy the same guidance and protection, and partake of the same sustenance and delights.

Here we are brought to notice the obligations which the truths we have been considering, devolve upon ministers and people. The first and most obvious inference is, that it is incumbent upon us all to respect and observe the institutions of the gospel. It is the duty of every person to keep the laws, to respect the rites, and to promote the interests of every useful community to which he belongs. This common obligation upon members of any institution, is binding upon the Christian. As a follower of Christ, he owes it to his Lord, and to the reputation and interest of his Church, devoutly to observe the ordinances which, for the edification of his people, he hath seen fit to appoint. Not that a mere outward and formal observance of the sacraments of Christianity will accomplish in us the purposes of the mission of the Son of God. But in these sacraments are deposited the mercy, the gifts, the refreshments, the renewals, the hopes, which we need; of all which, they who resort to them with the requisite qualifications, cannot fail to participate. On this account it was that attendance upon them constituted so large a part of the religious business of the primitive Christians, and that they spake of them in such lofty terms, as the laver of regeneration, the seed of immortality, the earnests of a resurrection. Far different was the estimate of these ordinances in their days from that which seems to prevail in ours. They were then the Christian Bethesdas, by which the penitent and believing waited, that when the angel moved the waters, they might wash in them from sin and uncleanness, and be restored to hope, and soundness, and vigour. And should we go about to ascertain why the gospel is not now productive in so great a degree as in the Apostolic times, of its proper peace, and joy, and holiness, we should probably find among the chief causes, the uninformed manner in which some go to its sacraments, and the entire disregard with which the many neglect them. For besides the general reasons to observe them, there are, to every individual, peculiar motives for this obedience. The sacraments of Christianity are ordained, not only to be of general use, but also for his individual benefit. He himself is washed in its Baptism from the defilement of sin, and in its Supper he himself is nourished with the bread of immortality, which came down from heaven. These ordinances are to every man the channels of divine mercy, the resort where the Church findeth her Lord. Here, he leadeth her by the still waters. Here, he causeth her to lie down in green pastures. Here, he maketh his flock to rest at noon. Enjoined by divine authority, we may not question their necessity; crowned with the divine promise, we cannot doubt their efficacy; but we do owe it to ourselves as well as to the Redeemer who appointed them, and the Christian community to which we belong, to endeavour to walk after the footsteps of his ancient servants, "in all his commandments and ordinances blameless."

But the truths we have been considering, press upon our observation the holiness, and importance, and duties of the ministry. They are the keepers of the fountain which is set open for mankind to wash in from sin and uncleanness, and they are the dispensers of the word by which we are instructed in righteousness and begotten again to the blessed hope of everlasting life. If there be any ground upon which, more than all others, the distinct and solemn character which we have been considering, of the priesthood, rests, it is perhaps this. The internal influences of grace; they are with the Holy Spirit. The written word, it is nigh unto every man, even in his mouth, and in his heart and in his hand. But the signs and seals of grace and truth, they are confided to the faithfulness and discretion of the "Stewards of the mysteries of God." With the care of these ordinances are necessarily connected the care of the principles of faith; the care of the duties of life; the care of men's souls, even of their salvation. It was, most probably, with respect to these, that our Lord said, when he breathed upon his first ministers, "Whose soever sins ye remit, they are remitted; and whose soever sins ye retain, they are retained." "Whatsover ye shall bind on earth shall be bound in heaven; and whatsoever ye shall loose on earth shall be loosed in heaven." Having such high and momentous functions entrusted to them, great care should be used, as far as human agency is concerned, to commit the office only to such men as will pitch their tents where the tents of the first shepherds stood, willingly and faithfully to feed Christ's sheep and feed his lambs. For if the tents of the Shepherd are moveable, the grounds which they choose variable, how shall they go their way forth by the footsteps of the flock? and if they retire into their tents, and disregard what is done around them, and strengthen not the diseased, neither heal that which is sick, neither bind up that which is broken, neither bring again that which is driven away, neither seek that which is lost, but suffer them to wander through all the mountains, and to be scattered upon every hill, to what purpose do they occupy the tents; how shall the flock be benefited and the kids fed, and the owner of the flock receive his increase? Entrusted with the word and ordinances, whereby men are born again and nourished unto eternal life, they should endeavour to imitate the Chief Shepherd, of whom prophecy when she contemplated him, said in her finest tone, "He shall gather the lambs with his arm, and carry them in his bosom, and shall gently lead those that are with young." Ambassadors from the living God to a sinful and ignorant world, it is their duty, in simplicity and dignified sincerity, without listening to the speculations, or yielding to the innovations of restless men, to "set forth his true and lively word, and rightly and duly to administer his holy sacraments." Impressed with the importance of the end for which ordinances were instituted and a priesthood ordained, for which God gave his Son, and Jesus died, the recovering of man from sin and destruction to wisdom, virtue, and immortality, they should assiduously seek and faithfully use all those attainments of knowledge, powers of mind, influence of character, acquaintance with revelation, and assistances of the Spirit, which will qualify them to establish men truly in the faith, to instruct them clearly in righteousness, and to persuade them irresistibly to come into the paths which will lead them to heaven. Set, moreover, to watch and bear together the ark of God's most precious mercies towards the human race, community of office should in them especially produce affection and brotherly love. How shall their hearts be at variance when their hands carry for men, in behalf of God, the same treasure of reconciliation? Like the Cherubim around the mercy-seat in the ancient temple, their faces should be always towards each other, and their wings should meet. Hereby all men should not only know them to be Christ's disciples, but admire them also as the ministers of the Lord, if they have love one for another. Above all, they should preserve the purity as well as the authority which belong to tho mantle he has left them. Be ye clean who bear the vessels of the Lord. If, under the Jewish economy, much more under the Christian dispensation, there should be written upon the foreheads of the priesthood and upon all their sacred vestments, "Holiness unto the Lord."

But, finally, we must remark, that there arises from what has been said, an obligation upon the people to abide by, and cooperate with those, who are regularly appointed to minister in holy things. In vain will God have instituted ordinances in the Church, in vain will he have established in it Pastors and Teachers, if the body of Christians neglect or profane these sacred institutions, or with Gallio's temper, "care for none of these things." It is theirs, to go their way by the footsteps of the flock, not forming for themselves new and various paths, but abiding with zealous attachment, by the appointments of God, contentedly following, in faith and practice, the examples of the saints who have gone before and entered into their rest. It is theirs to bring their lambs to the fold of the Redeemer, and to come with their kids, and to accustom them to feed beside the Shepherds' tents. It is theirs to make such provision for those to whom Christ has committed the care of the Church, as will preserve them from temporal cares and perplexities, and enable them to give themselves wholly to this very thing. It is theirs, by their attendance on sacred institutions, to encourage the labours; by their prayers to aid the exertions, and with their charity to cover the imperfections, of those who are set as Shepherds of the flock. In a word, they should be of one heart and one mind, and though they discountenance the promiscuous exercise of those functions, which reason, Scripture, and the practice of primitive Christians teach us should be confined to a distinct and authorized order of men, they should, nevertheless, be active in the cause of the Redeemer, by "letting their light so shine before men, that they may see their good works and glorify their Father who is in heaven." Happy state! If Ministers and people thus, in their distinct spheres, co-operated with each other! Happy state! if men thus hearkened to the solemn admonition, stand in the way, and see and ask for the old paths where is the good way, and walk therein! Verily, we might then expect once more to realize that perfect condition of the visible Church, of which, as it existed in the days of apostolic purity, the pencil of inspiration hath left us the picture. They who "gladly received the word were baptised," and with one heart and one soul, "they continued steadfastly in the Apostles' doctrine and fellowship, and in breaking of bread, and in prayers."

Thus I have set before you the fitness and utility of established rites and ordinances in religion; the consequent necessity of a distinct and authorized order of men, for the administration of them; and some of the obligations which these truths devolve upon Minister and people. What remains, but that we, my brethren, Clergy and laity of the Episcopal Church, should give to these considerations a practical effect. With our high privileges correspondent duties are connected. It has pleased God to grant us our Christian vocation in a Church whose rites and ordinances are of primitive origin, and the authority of whose ministry has never been questioned. Amongst a people taking their position upon such elevated ground, and surrounded by so many advantages, it might justly be expected, that Christianity would be seen in the full glory of its nature and happiest influence of its power. Has this been the case? Are we conspicuously a wise and pious, a devout and charitable people? During the rest which the Churches in this land have been permitted to enjoy, have they been found walking in the fear of the lord, and in the comfort of the Holy Ghost, and are they multiplied?

As parts of the Christian community, there is upon us a solemn and weighty responsibility. We have in our hands, treasures of unspeakable importance to our country and posterity. I know not that there is promised to any people, a continuance of the gospel among them, any longer than its authority is reverenced, and its institutions observed. Look at the regions which were first visited by the beams of the sun of righteousness. What do we behold? Alas! the Turkish mosque now occupies the place of the Christian temple, and deluded Mussulmen now mumble their absurdities, where once the Ministers of the Redeemer preached the glad tidings of peace! What has been the cause of this melancholy change? In some places the Christians were lukewarm; in others they were dissolute. In some Churches the Ministers of the gospel were negligent, or depraved; in others, its doctrines were corrupted, and its ordinances polluted. And should we fall into a similar degeneracy, should we corrupt the faith, debase the ministry, neglect the ordinances, and trample upon the principles of our holy religion, what assurance have we, that the golden candlesticks will not be taken away and our country, in time, instead of rejoicing in the light they once benignly shed, be left like unhappy Asia, to the darkness, vices, and horrors, of spiritual night. It is a solemn consideration! On our conduct may depend the religious advantages of our posterity. We may be instrumental by our zeal and fidelity, in preserving to our country, even for successive generations, the precious blessings of the gospel, or by our coldness, corruptions, and depravity, may provoke the Almighty to take them away. My hearers, be induced by a regard for the souls of others, as well as by concern for your own, to cherish for the Church, and its institutions, a holy affection and respect. To render us faithful in our several spheres, let us remember, that it is but a little while we shall have it in our power to be thus useful in the cause of truth. Fast roll the hours which are bearing us to the tomb. On rapid, though noiseless feet, the day is approaching, when opportunity of promoting the interests of our Redeemer will have passed away. Let us "work the work of him that sent us, while it is day." Let us shelter the fountains by which the Shepherds have pitched their tents. Let us seek the peace and prosperity of his Church, and by our individual and joint exertions endeavour, that the whole "building fitly framed together, and compact by that which every joint supplieth," may grow up into a durable and extensive temple unto the Lord. Then will the Holy Spirit dwell amongst us. Then will the Son of Man walk in the midst of us. And when the militancy of the Church is accomplished, we shall be taken to the triumphant company, which shall eternally surround the throne of heaven, clothed with white robes, and having palms in their hands. Thither, O adorable Redeemer, vouchsafe to bring us! There, when thou comest unto judgment, make all thy saints partakers of thy glory. But especially, O Christ, enable us, thy Ministering servants, to say to thee in that day, without any abatement of our joy, Behold, here am I, and the people whom thou hast given me!

SERMON IV.

ON BAPTISM.

ACTS, ii. 16.

"And now why tarriest thou? arise and be baptised, and wash away thy sins, calling on the name of the Lord."

HAVING, in a former discourse, set before you the necessity and utility of Ordinances in religion, I come now to treat of the first Christian sacrament, Baptism. In approaching this ordinance, I am struck, brethren, by one thing; that under a form so simple, as almost to want hold upon attention, are contained the sublimest truths, and most important interests. There is little in it that meets the eye; little that excites curiosity, engages investigation, or produces astonishment; and yet Baptism is the most solemn and momentous transaction respecting individuals, that takes place upon our globe. In this there is an analogy with the other works of God; whose peculiar character it is, to produce the most important effects by the fewest causes, the sublimest results by the simplest operations.

Simple, however, as is this ordinance in its form, and great as is its significance, there is no subject upon which more indefinite opinions prevail, or more erroneous ones have been propagated. There are many who consider it as nothing more than a decent formality of the Christian world. Others view it as of so tremendous and exclusive a nature, that a large part of our race, and that the most innocent part, are incapable of receiving it. Others seem to think it the mysterious charm which does all for their salvation which needs to be done, leaving them to advance towards heaven on the wings of inconsideration, through the polluted paths of vice and folly. And of those upon whom the ordinance hath been bestowed, the number, it is to be feared, is comparatively small who preserve an adequate sense of the magnitude of the benefits it conveys to them, or of the sacredness of the obligations it devolves upon them.

On these accounts, you perceive, that it is neither an uninteresting nor unprofitable subject to which your attention is invited. Christians, surely, should understand the first rite of Christianity. And it is to Christians I speak. To others, indeed, who reject the Gospel, disquisitions upon its sacraments will not have much interest, and can be of little utility. In endeavouring to explain to you this ordinance of our religion, I purpose to adopt the simplest arrangement, and to use the most unadorned illustrations. You will not here look for flowers of rhetoric, nor for flights of eloquence, but, as becomes the subject, for truth in its plainest form. This, then, is the method: We will consider why mankind should be baptised; when they should be baptised; how they should be baptised; by whom they should be baptised; and where they should be baptised. Under these inquiries may be comprehended all which it is important for you to know, concerning this leading ordinance of the Gospel.

We are first to consider, why mankind should be baptised. And the reasons to be adduced shall be drawn from the authority of the Institutor, and the benefits to be derived from the institution; the one involving its nature, the other its obligation.

All positive institutions rest upon the authority of him by whom they are ordained. The highest authority in the Christian world is that of Christ. It is not left optional with us, whether we will do what he has commanded, or not, if we would enjoy his favour. Now, baptism is the ordinance which he hath appointed for the purposes to which he hath consecrated it. "Go ye," said he to his eleven disciples, and in them to their successors unto the end of the world, "go ye, and teach," or disciple "all nations, baptising them in the name of the Father, and of the Son, and of the Holy Ghost." Do you ask, whether he meant to have this rite considered as of *essential* importance, where the other graces and virtues of Christianity are not wanting? Hear him declaring to the stewards of his mysteries, "He that believeth and is baptised shall be saved." Hear them proclaiming to the anxious multitude inquiring what they should do, "Repent and be baptised every one of you, in the name of Jesus Christ, for the remission of sins, and ye shall receive the gift of the Holy Ghost." Do you ask whether the ordinance may not be dispensed with, where it may be had, but is to be considered as generally necessary to salvation? Hear him saying to the wavering Nicodemus, "Except a man be born of water and the Spirit, he cannot enter into the kingdom of God." If, then, there be any respect for the authority of God, nay, if we may not claim his mercies in any other way than that in which he chooses to bestow them, this ordinance is of the highest and most solemn obligation, in every case, where there are proper subjects of it. If children are among the proper subjects of it, as we shall, by and by, show that they are, what Christian parent can safely neglect to procure it for his offspring? And what adult, who believes the Scriptures, and desires to partake of the salvation that is in Christ, can allow himself to remain unbaptised? That it is the will of the Being who is our God and guide, our Redeemer and Sanctifier, from whom, alone, we can receive pardon of our sins and eternal life, is sufficient reason why this ordinance should be observed, even if we knew not its utility, and there were no other considerations to entitle it to our devout regard.

But we shall better understand this ordinance, its use and importance will be seen in a strong light, if we proceed from the authority of the Institutor, to the benefits to be derived from the institution. And what are these? It does nothing less than seal to us, visibly, the conveyance to us on the part of God, of all the infinite treasures of the gospel; its precious salvation, its enlivening promises, its glorious privileges, its blessed hopes.

Mankind are by nature born in sin and the children of wrath. Under the holy law of God they cannot live. But it hath pleased their compassionate Creator, in consideration of his own tender mercy, and of the mediation for them by his beloved Son, to place them under a new and lenient covenant of grace, in which are provided a covering for their sins, sanctification for their spirits, and redemption from death to everlasting life. This covenant is most mercifully adapted to their situation since the fall. Without it their condition had been hopeless; in the sight of the Almighty no flesh living could have been justified. With a condescension as great as the mercy, God was pleased when he communicated this covenant to his faithful servant Abraham, to adapt the dispensation of it to the nature of man. He stipulated with his creature, and for his better assurance added signs to his word. He gave him circumcision to be to him a sensible and significant seal of the righteousness which is by faith; a visible and sure token, pledge, and remembrancer, of the mercies and promises to which he had adopted him. When the ever-blessed Negotiator of this new covenant, in the fullness of time appeared in the flesh, that he might conform all things to the tender character of the dispensation by him, he substituted instead of that painful rite, the easier and not less significant ordinance of baptism. And this is now to us what circumcision was to God's ancient people, a token and means of our birth to new life; a seal of the pardoning mercy and covenanted favour of God, and a pledge of salvation unto eternal life, if we forfeit not, by a neglect of the condition of the covenant, our title to the inheritance. Whoever, therefore, would have an interest in that covenant of grace assured to him, under which alone mankind can hope for forgiveness and immortality, it is needful he should be baptized in the name of the Lord Jesus.

That you may the better apprehend the greatness of the benefits which baptism confers upon us, by bringing us under the covenant of grace, let us descend to a more particular consideration of some of the leading ones; adducing, as we pass, the evidences from Scripture of their certainty; and from the articles and liturgy of our Church, that they are embraced in our belief. In the choice and order of them we will be guided by the Church, than whom, upon this subject, we can have no better human instructor. She teacheth us that, in baptism we are made "members of Christ, children of God, and inheritors of the kingdom of heaven."

We are by baptism made members of Christ; that is, united to him; made parts of the body of which he is the head, and so long as we continue living members of the same, partaking of his life, of his care, and of his glory. For, saith the Apostle, the Church is his body; and "baptism," as it is expressed with much precision in the twenty-seventh Article, "is not only a sign of profession, and mark of difference, whereby Christian men are discerned from others that be not christened, but it is also a sign of regeneration, or new birth, whereby, as by an instrument, they that receive baptism rightly are grafted into the Church."

In this union with the Church, we become entitled to its instruction and prayers, to a participation of that light with which God hath illumined it; to access to the fountains of living water which are set open to the members of it; to the bread of life which is provided for the sustenance at its holy table, and to the aids of the spirit which proceedeth from the Father and the Son. For from the head all the body hath nourishment ministered, and being knit together by joints and bands, increaseth with the increase of God. It is on account of the inestimable value of this union with Christ, that we are instructed, whenever baptism is conferred upon any one, "with one accord" to give thanks to Almighty God, "that it hath pleased him to regenerate" such person, "and graft him into the body of Christ's Church."

Again. By baptism we are made, in a peculiar manner, children of God. Man was by nature the offspring of the Almighty. But by the fall, he lost his resemblance to his Maker, and forfeited all claim to his favour. Yet God, in the greatness of his mercy and pity, hath devised a way of adopting him again to himself, and restoring unto him his forfeited possessions. By the precious blood of his Son he is freed from the guilt, and by the purifying influences of his Spirit, is cleansed from the dominion of sin; and in baptism receives, as it were, in symbol, this inestimable grace, being washed in its waters from the stain of the original transgression and all past offences, and blessed with the gift of the Holy Ghost. "Arise," said Ananias to the converted Paul, "be baptized and wash away thy sins, calling upon the name of the Lord." "Repent," said St. Peter, "and be baptized for the remission of sins, and ye shall receive the gift of the Holy Ghost." "Because ye are Sons," saith the great Apostle of the Gentiles, "God hath sent forth the Spirit of his Son into your hearts, crying Abba, Father." Pardoning their sins, and renewing them by the Holy Ghost, the Almighty, in this ordinance, formally receives them anew into his family, and conveys to them visibly, as by a deed authenticated with his seal, a provisional title to all the privileges and expectation which he hath revealed, as belonging to the children of adoption. By baptism, says the Article of the Church upon the subject, the promises of the forgiveness of sin, and of our adoption to be the sons of God, by the Holy Ghost, are visibly signed and sealed.

"I suppose," says the profoundly learned and eminently pious Mede, "that in the baptism of our Saviour the mystery of all our baptisms was visibly acted, and that God says to every one truly baptised, as he said to him, (in a proportionable sense,) thou art my son in whom I am well pleased."

But this leads me to observe, further, that in this ordinance we are made inheritors of the kingdom of heaven. It is the title and pledge, to those who truly receive it, of immortality and eternal life. God, as it were, puts into our hand the charter of our interests in a better world, sealed with his sacramental seal, that we may be assured of the immutability of his counsel, and have strong consolation, who have fled for refuge to the hope set before us in the gospel. Thus, according to the Scripture, we are made not only children, but also "heirs; heirs of God, and joint heirs with Jesus Christ." Being "buried with him in baptism," and therein also risen with him, we are "begotten by the resurrection unto a lively hope, to an inheritance incorruptible and undefiled, and that fadeth not away, reserved in heaven for us."

In short, in the gracious covenant, that is in Christ Jesus, are provided for mankind, the pardon of their sins, the promise of God's spirit and eternal life. In the ordinance which he hath most graciously appointed for the purpose, God meets us with this covenant, he puts it into our hands and says, be faithful to the conditions therein contained, and I add my oath to my word, that the mercies thereof shall never fail.

There are two objections to what has been said, which may arise in your minds; but which, it is incumbent upon you, if you would not be spoiled through philosophy and vain deceit, instantly to repel. The first reproaches the simplicity of the ordinance. Can it be, it may be asked, can it be, that on the simple ceremony of washing with water, so great and important interests depend? Ah, my hearers, dare not to question the sufficiency of the means which the Almighty hath chosen for the accomplishment of any of his purposes. Reverence, humbly, the institutions of God; and allow not yourselves to be drawn to doubt, that he will render them effectual to the ends for which he hath ordained them. The objection proceeds from not considering, that where the word and power of God are engaged, the result does not depend upon human perception of the efficacy of the means. Cannot he whose healing power rendered the waters of Jordan effectual, by the word of his servant, to recover the Syrian from his leprosy, accompany the waters of baptism by the power of his grace, and render them effectual, to cleanse his redeemed from the guilt and consequences of sin? Cannot he, who, at the baptism of his beloved Son, caused the Spirit to descend like a dove and rest upon him, in every administration of baptism cause the same Spirit, in as significant character, though not in visible form, to descend upon the souls of those whom he is receiving to the adoption of sons? What, though no cloud overshadow them, and no voice be heard from the cloud, cannot he, who has as easy access to the spirits as to the bodies of men, in a still majesty move upon the chaos of their affections, and, in due time, restore order and harmony and beauty to their nature? To those who make the objection, we would give the reasonable reply of his servants to the cavilling Naaman; "If the prophet had bid thee do some great thing, wouldest thou not have done it? how much rather, then, when he saith unto thee, Wash and be clean."

But there is another objection of a more melancholy aspect. It reproaches the consequences of this ordinance. How is it possible, it may be asked, if baptism is thus efficacious, that so many who have received it are destitute of all faith, and live in trespasses and sins? We are obliged to concede the truth of the afflicting fact; but this with some qualifications. There are persons, and blessed be God, the number of them is not small, in whom the seeds which were sown in the infancy of their new life, after having been choked for years by weeds, which have had their growth and withered, do spring up and produce their proper fruits, holiness and everlasting life. This is, doubtless, many times the result of the mercies which were sealed to them in baptism; for though man may depart from his stipulations, the gifts and calling of God are without repentance. It must, however, be confessed, that there are many who have tasted of the heavenly gift, and been made partakers of the Holy Ghost, that seem to fall away; and go on still in iniquity, and die, as well as live, without God or holiness. But this only teaches us, that there is nothing irresistible in the moral operations of God; that the covenant of his grace and mercy, in Christ Jesus, is conditional; and that in the performance of the conditions, we are left perfectly free. Will it be said, that on such persons remains the burthen of the original guilt of their nature? No. From this, in their baptism, they were entirely delivered; they perish by their own transgressions. Will it be said, that to them the Holy Spirit was not given? No. It hath moved many times in the heart of every one of them. It hath often called to them, and in a tone of anxious concern, "This is the way, walk ye in it, when they have turned to the right hand, and when they have turned to the left." But its movements they have stifled; to its voice they have been "like the deaf adder that stoppeth her ears;" they have resisted, and grieved it, and turned it away. Will it be said, then, that for them there was proffered no glorious inheritance? No. Heaven was within their reach. And it is this, which, in the day of retribution, will aggravate their condemnation, and vindicate the justice of their Judge, that when a title to the joys and honours of God's kingdom was put into their hands, they preferred the dominion and pleasures of sin. The objection does not affect the doctrine which has been delivered concerning this important ordinance. It teaches us, rather, when God hath, in baptism, lifted us from the mire, and set our feet upon a rock, and ordered our goings; to take heed lest we fall. Whatever in the covenant which is signed and sealed by this rite, our merciful Creator hath vouchsafed to promise, "he, for his part, will most surely keep and perform." But if, when he hath set open the prison in which we were captive, and broken the fetters with which we were bound, and bidden us go forth to the joys of freedom, and the light of day, any prefer to remain in their prison, or go forth to such life as must bring them thither again, does it set at naught the acts of the Almighty, if, persisting in their perverseness, they die in the pit after their bread has failed. The case of such was foreseen by the Spirit of God; and it is by a humbling figure that he hath illustrated their state. It is unto them, according to the true proverb, "The dog is turned to his own vomit again, and the sow that was washed, to her wallowing in the mire."

The next inquiry in the order of treating this subject, is, when mankind should be baptised? in which is embraced the question concerning infant baptism, But I have already greatly trespassed upon your patience, and must defer this inquiry to another opportunity. Meanwhile, my Christian hearers, who in your infancy or adult state have been admitted to baptism, consider, soberly, how unspeakable are the blessings, how momentous the interests, how solemn the duties, which were involved in that transaction.

Under the Captain of our salvation we have been delivered from the bondage of sin. In the waters of baptism we have passed through the sea. This probationary life is the wilderness before us. The grave is as the river between us and our inheritance. Heaven is the Canaan of our rest and felicity. While we sojourn in the wilderness we shall encounter difficulties, be surrounded with temptations, and many times be in danger of having our faith fail. If we are entangled in these dangers, and by these trials are overcome, we shall not enter into his rest. But, have faith in your God; resist the temptations to murmur, or to doubt; avoid the sins, which on every side beset you; bear up patiently under your privations and sorrows, follow steadfastly the steps of your leader, and joy unspeakable awaits you in the world to come.

SERMON V.

ON BAPTISM.

St. Mark, x. 14.

"Suffer the little children to come unto me, and forbid them not."

IN a former discourse we have considered, why mankind should be baptised; and have adduced the reasons of it from the authority of the Institutor, God in Christ, and from the benefits received in the institution. Under this latter head, we have shown, that it doth nothing less than seal to us, visibly, on the part of God, conveyance of all the infinite treasures of his gospel; its precious redemption; its merciful conditions; its enlivening promises; its glorious privileges; its blessed hopes; particularly that in it "we are made members of Christ, children of God, and inheritors of the kingdom of heaven." And let me here add, before I proceed further, that this high view of the importance of baptism is authorized; this account of its interesting nature confirmed, by the language of the first Christian writers, who style it, with impressive eloquence, the sacrament of absolution; the regeneration of the soul; the robe of light; the communication of the passion and resurrection of Christ; the garment of immortality; the seal of God.

If such be the importance of this ordinance, it becomes an interesting inquiry, when mankind should be baptised? which was the second thing proposed in the order of treating this subject. And what Christian parent, that looks upon his children, and considers their exposures in this life, and their liability to be snatched away by death, is not ready to meet me with his little ones, at the threshold of the inquiry, and say, may I not obtain for these, this blessed initiation into the school of Christ; this remission of sin, and protection of the Holy Spirit; this adoption by new birth, into the family and favour of God; this title and pledge of eternal life? Yes, Christian parents, this is not only your privilege, but your duty. The Church teaches you not to doubt, that our heavenly Father favourably alloweth the charitable work of bringing infants to his holy baptism; and instructs her ministers, in every parish, to "admonish the people, that they defer not the baptism of their children longer, than the first or second Sunday next after their birth, or other holy day falling between, unless upon a great and reasonable cause."

In answer, then, to the inquiry, when mankind should be baptised? we say, in the first place, as soon after they are born as it can conveniently be done. But there are those, who, for some cause or other, have not been so happy as to receive baptism in their infancy. To their case we shall, in the second place, give a separate consideration.

Obvious upon the first reflection it is, that benefits, so unspeakably momentous as those conferred in baptism, have been shown to be, should be secured to every human person, as soon as it can with propriety be done. Now, if there be nothing in the nature of the thing; nor in the instructions of Christ; nor in what we know of the practice of the Apostles and primitive Christians, to exclude infants from this ordinance, but on the contrary, many reasons, and strong evidences, that from the beginning they were admitted to a participation of it, and moreover, difficulties which are awful and insuperable, attend any other supposition, who will not perceive, that it is the right and duty, the privilege and obligation of every Christian, to claim early for his offspring, the benefits of this sacrament. These several points I hope, my hearers, through the assistance of God, to establish to your satisfaction.

We are first to inquire, if there be any reason arising from the nature of the thing to exclude children from this important ordinance. Now it is to be remembered, that in baptism, the subject of it is altogether a recipient of favours. He does nothing in the act to merit the gifts he receives. There are, indeed, qualities requisite to bring him into a condition for the application of these favours; but this requisition supposes him in a state in which these qualities are needed and attainable. If his state be such as not to admit of their existence, they cannot be necessary; and it would be unreasonable to suppose that God, in such cases, requires them; or will withhold those benefits of the ordinance, which are absolute and applicable, on account of the absence of qualities, for which, in fact, there was no place. God hath graciously given to mankind in the gospel, a charter of redemption and eternal life. He hath, too, given them baptism, to be, as it were, his visible seal of that charter, a means of enabling them to realize its grace, "and a pledge to assure them thereof." Repentance and faith are, indeed, required of adult persons, before they are received to baptism; and with great fitness; for it could neither honour God, nor benefit themselves, to be baptised into that which they believed to be false, or to seek remission of sins which they were willing to retain. But this requirement supposes, in the very making of it, that they of whom it is made have occasion and power to repent, and opportunity and capacity to believe. And I cannot see how, without instructions to that effect, it can be inferred from such requirements of such persons, that others, who are incapable of the qualities required, are cut off, on that account, from the mercies of the covenant, as far as they are capable of them, or from the benefits of its use. Repentance was a condition of the baptism which John preached. Our blessed Lord knew no sin, and therefore could exercise no repentance. Yet for the sake of other advantages appertaining to the act, Jesus was baptised of John in Jordan. Now, of active faith infants are incapable. And unless we suppose that they may, at this initiation into the school of Christ, have faith, as it were, in the seed, which if it be not suffered to perish, will spring up, in due time, and produce fruit, I do not know how they can have any faith. Having, moreover, committed no actual sin, they are not capable of repentance. The stain of the original transgression is their misfortune, not their crime. And surely, the innocence which they bring to the waters of baptism, cannot render them less acceptable to God, than the most penitent sinner, for actual transgressions, is rendered by his repentance. They are, therefore, to be baptised for those advantages of baptism which they need, and of which they are susceptible. And do they not need to be relieved from the doom of the original trangression, to be adopted anew into the family of God, and to have the renewing influences of his Holy Spirit? That repentance, faith, and obedience, which afterwards become necessary, and by which the Christian life is not only begun, but continued and perfected, may, as will presently appear, be stipulated for them, in their unknowing and helpless state, by those whom God has made the guardians of their interests.

Shall I be told, that under the gospel dispensation, repentance and faith are qualifications without which there can be enjoyed no spiritual blessing? Look back to the conduct of the Redeemer. In the days of his flesh, "they brought young children unto Christ, that he should touch them. And he took them up in his arms, laid his hands upon them, and blessed them." What but spiritual blessings could our poor and despised Lord have then bestowed? And if by the imposition of his hands they could receive spiritual blessing, why not by the application to them of those waters of baptism, by his ministers, which he hath ordained as the means of conveying his grace, and the "pledge to assure us thereof?"

Shall I be told that baptism is, as we have stated, the seal of a covenant; and that children are incapable of entering into a covenant? I ask, whether it is not the right, nay, I go further and say, the duty, of every parent to make, in behalf of his yet unconscious child, such temporal contracts as will be for its advantage? How much rather, then, such coutracts as will be for its spiritual and eternal benefit; especially if the good contracted for, and the conditions stipulated, be such as it would have been not only his interest but his duty to have pursued, whether any covenant binding him thereto had been made for him or not. But the objection that children are incapable of entering into covenant, is overturned by sacred fact and the authority of God. "Ye stand this day," said Moses to the people of Israel, in the plains of Moab, "ye stand this day, all of you before the Lord your God; your little ones and your wives, to enter into covenant with the Lord thy God, and into his oath which the Lord thy God maketh with thee this day, that he may establish thee to-day for a people unto himself." And above all this, was not circumcision the seal of a covenant? Was it not the seal of a covenant which involved spiritual blessings and religious obligations? Was it not a covenant, the same in substance with that in which we rejoice, having Christ for its Mediator, and for its end, the acceptance of the righteousness which is by faith? Yet, were not children subjects of the seal of this covenant? Was it not the command of God to the parent to give to his infant offspring this seal, and his solemn declaration that the man child who had not received it should be cut off from his people?

What reasons, then, arise, from the nature of the thing, to exclude infants from the baptism of the gospel? Surely, it is a consistent and most excellent charity; surely, it is not only the right, but the duty of those whom Providence has made the guardians of the welfare of any infant, to think and act for him in those important concerns in which he is unable to think or act for himself; and especially to obtain for him the unspeakable benefits of the Christian baptism, by promising those things in his name, which, unless they disbelieve the Christian religion, they must know such infant, when he comes to age, would, whether they had stipulated for him or not, be bound to perform.

I have dwelt thus long on the difficulties arising from the nature of the thing, because these are most frequently urged. You have seen that they are without foundation. Is there, then, secondly, any reason arising out of the instructions of Christ upon the subject, to exclude infants from his holy baptism? Let us advert to the commission which, when about to return to the Father, he left with his Apostles. "Go ye and make disciples in all nations, baptizing them in the name of the Father, and of the Son, and of the Holy Ghost." Children are a part, and no small part of every nation. They are a part, for the welfare of which, God, in the transactions concerning Nineveh, hath declared himself to be tenderly careful. They are a part of which Jesus always manifested himself to be a fond and zealous friend. Unless, then, there were any customs or circumstances prevailing at the time, to have led them to the opinion, what was there in the instructions given to his Apostles, to induce them to suppose that children might not be received as pupils to be taught of him, and have in this ordinance the seal and means of grace. Were there, then, any such customs or circumstances? On the contrary, there were prevalent ideas and usages which sufficiently explain why our Lord gave no express instructions upon the point; and must have left his Apostles without such instructions to infer, that to infants as well as adults, this sign of the covenant was to be given. It was matter of notoriety to them that circumcision, of which this rite took place, was conferred generally upon its subjects in childhood. And, moreover, baptism was not to the Apostles a new ceremony. The Jews, from the first sanctification of their ancestors by water, had used it. And to whom were they in the habit of applying it? Not only to every adult proselyte, but to all his children; and, as would appear from their best writers, to their own infant offspring. Certain, however, it is, that they received no convert to their religion without washing him with water; that they baptized, at the same time, all his offspring; and that they considered them after this application of this ordinance as new born, and the ordinance as the instrument of their regeneration. This explains our Lord's surprise, that Nicodemus, a master in Israel, understood him not when he said, in allusion to his holy baptism, a person "must be born again before he can enter the kingdom of God." This was probably the reason which induced our blessed Lord, who seems to have avoided doing any unnecessary violence to the customs of his nation, to adopt the washing with water to be the token of initiation into his Church. It is this alone which can satisfactorily explain to us why he did not deem it necessary to give any express instructions upon this important question. Yea, this is sufficient to induce us to believe, that as no exceptions were made in the command to baptize, the Apostles would naturally, I had almost said unavoidably, be led to apply the ordinance to all such as they had been accustomed to consider subjects of circumcision and of baptism.

This we shall find to have been actually the case, if we proceed to consider, thirdly, what we know of the Apostles' practice. There is no mention upon record of the reception or rejection of children, as such, in the administration of this ordinance by the first Apostles of our Lord. To him who knows that there was in their nation an established usage, this silence will afford a presumptive evidence that they introduced no innovation. The silence of their enemies affords a similar presumption. When we consider the tenacity with which men cleave to their religious rites when they are invaded, and especially the horror and indignation with which they would meet an attempt to deprive their offspring of religious blessings to which they had been accustomed, it is a strong ground for presuming that the first Christians did not cut off children from such benefits as they were used to receive, that the adversaries of the gospel, who were sufficiently eager to disparage it in the estimation of the populace, did never charge it with what would have been a very popular objection, the diminishing of the privileges and blessings which had before been enjoyed by their children.

But though we have no positive record; as, indeed, if the thing were done by no new command, but in conformity with a prevalent usage, we should expect none; yet have we strong intimations, and these, such as upon the supposition are most naturally given, that the Apostles received children into the Church by this ordinance of their Lord. St. Peter exhorted the multitude to be baptized, because the promise was to them and to their children; and if the children were heirs of the promise, is it probable he refused them the seal; especially, when he knew, that the ancient sign of it was given to the little ones, and had heard his Lord say, "that of such was the kingdom of heaven?" All the members of a family, also, in more instances than one, received this ordinance, on the conversion of a parent, by the Apostles' hands. Of the pious woman of Thyatira, it is recorded, that when the preaching of Paul brought her to the knowledge of the truth, she was baptized, and her household. And the astonished jailor, who was converted at midnight, by a miracle, "was straightway baptized," we are told, "he and all his." Under this head, it is to be added, that St. Paul, in his epistle to the Corinthians, tells them, as an advantage of a believing parent's abiding with an unbelieving one, "that thereby their children became holy;" that is, according to the meaning of the phrase in the sacred dialect, and particularly in the writings of the same Apostle, were devoted to God, which could only be done by baptism. And, accordingly, the most pious commentators of the first ages, and the most learned ones of modern times, in interpreting this singular passage, consider it as a declaration that, by the right and influence of the pious parent, the children were baptized.

Still, it may be, you ask for more certain demonstration of the Apostolic practice. It is to be obtained; for we have full and unequivocal testimonies how they conducted, who succeeded the Apostles, and from them derived their instructions. If it would not be considered as an affected display of learning, unbecoming this holy place, I might adduce to you Justin Martyr, who lived only forty years after the age of the Apostles, testifying, that in his time there were many persons living, of sixty and seventy years old, who were regenerated and made disciples of Christ, in their infancy. I might adduce a work of the same age with this writer, in which it is stated, that children are allowed to enjoy the good things that come by baptism, by the faith of them that bring them to the ordinance. I might adduce to you, Ireneus, who lived among those that had seen the Apostles, and received his instruction under Polycarp, the venerable disciple of St. John, saying, that the Redeemer makes infants holy, and saves infants and little ones, and children and youths, and elder persons, all who, through him, are born anew, or baptized unto God. I might adduce, not long after him, the learned Tertullian, representing the children of a Christian as sanctified by the discipline of the institution, whereby it is manifest, from the context, he intended baptism. I might adduce to you, from the next age, the renowned Origen, of Tyre, whose father and grandfather were Christians, and who demands, as concerning a thing which had always been established, why, if they are not encumbered with original sin, infants are baptized? Nay, and declares, that the Church had received from the Apostles a tradition, to give baptism to little ones; for they, says he, to whom the divine mysteries were committed, knew that there is, in all persons, the natural pollution of sin, which must be removed by water and the Spirit. Not far after him, I might adduce to you the zealous Cyprian, relating, that in his time a question was started, not whether baptism might be administered to infants, but whether it should not be deferred till the eighth day. This most credible witness would testify to you, that he sat in a convention of sixty-six bishops, who were unanimously of opinion, that from baptism, and the grace of God, who is benignant to all, none ought by us to be prohibited, and as this is to be observed with respect to all, so, especially, is it to be observed and retained with respect to infants, and those who are just born, who, by their tears with which they begin the world, might in reason obtain more from our help, and the divine mercy. In the fourth century, I might adduce Gregory Nazianzen, replying, in an oration upon the subject, to the question, whether children, who can neither know the loss, nor be sensible of the grace of this ordinance, should be baptized, that it is better for them to be sanctified when they have no sense of it, than that they should die unsealed. I might go on to adduce to you witnesses, increasing with the years, till I brought you to the active and elaborate Augustin, who, after declaring that the baptism of infants rests upon the authority of the universal Church, delivered by the Lord, and by the Apostles, says, "Let no man whisper to us other doctrines. This the Church hath always had; this it hath received upon the faith of the predecessors; this it keeps perseveringly to the end."

Such, my brethren, are the grounds upon which we maintain the doctrine of the Church, that baptism is to be administered as soon after birth as it can conveniently be done. They are grounds which she can never leave. Upon any other, she is surrounded with difficulties, awful and insuperable. Take from her the right of admitting your children to the benefits of baptism, and she must believe that the tender and liberal dispensation of her Lord is less indulgent to them than the rigorous dispensation of the law. She must believe that the sweet innocence of the new-born babe is less acceptable to God than the penitence of a hoary offender. She must believe, that while they who are mature, are required to become as little children, before they can enter the kingdom of God, little children are excluded from being initiated into that kingdom because they are such. Yea, she must stand by the graves of the infant offspring of her members, and have no covenanted assurance of their salvation and immortality. For if they are cut off from admission into the Church militant on earth, what certainty can she have of their admission into the Church triumphant in heaven. She shrinks from the difficulties; and rejoices that grounds are so clear, so strong, and so extensive, upon which she can perpetuate her Master's tender words, "Suffer the little children to come unto me, and forbid them not."

SERMON VI.

ON BAPTISM.

Acts, viii. 36, 37.

"See, here is water, what doth hinder me to be baptized?" And Philip said, "If thou believest with all thine heart, thou mayest."

HAVING, in a previous discourse, shown, at large, why mankind should be baptized, deducing from the authority of the Institutor, and the benefits of the institution, its solemn obligations and unspeakable importance, we, the last Lord's day, entered upon the second inquiry proposed, at the opening of these discourses, in the order of treating this subject, viz: when they should be baptized? At the threshold of this inquiry, I could not forbear fancying myself met by the Christian parent, bringing with him his beloved children, and under the consciousness of their exposures in life, and liability to death, demanding of me eagerly, may I not obtain for these this initiation into the school of Christ; this remission of sin, and protection of the Holy Spirit; this adoption by a new birth into the family and favour of God? Having shown, that there is nothing in the nature of the thing; nor in the instructions of Christ; nor in what we know of the practice of the Apostles and primitive Christians, to exclude infants from this ordinance, but that, on the contrary, there are many reasons, and strong evidences for believing, that from the beginning they were admitted to a participation of it, and, moreover, that there are difficulties which are awful and insuperable attending any other supposition, we arrived at the conclusion, than which there is no doctrine of the

Church established upon a broader basis, that it is not only the right, but also the duty, of every Christian parent, to obtain early for his offspring, the benefits of this sacrament. After a very full investigation of the question, it appeared most clearly evident, in the first place, in answer to the inquiry when mankind should be baptized? that this ordinance should be administered where sureties for the child can be found, as soon after birth as it can, conveniently, be done. As there are many persons, who, for some cause or other, have not been so happy as to receive baptism in their infancy, it was proposed to give to their case, in the second place, a separate consideration. An attention, as brief as it well may be, to the inquiry with respect to them, now asks your indulgence; and this, with some inferences, from the interesting truths, to which the inquiry will have conducted us, shall close our observations upon the second part of the general division of the subject.

At the first promulgation of the gospel, a large part of those, to whom the Apostles and Evangelists administered baptism were, necessarily, adults. From among the Jews and Gentiles, they came to the Church as doves to the windows; and in admitting them, the ministers of the Church governed themselves by those requirements which arose out of the nature of the thing, or were suggested to them, in the instructions of their Lord.

It is evident, the case of infants is very different from that of adults. The latter bring with them to the waters of baptism, actual sins which are their crime, as well as the inherent corruption of their nature, which is their misfortune; and from the former, God gives no remission but upon repentance. They bring, also, matured understandings, capable of hearing, and weighing, and embracing the gospel, and God requires that they to whom it is preached should believe if they would be saved by it. They, moreover, are capable of making for themselves any stipulations which are necessary; and God, in great wisdom and mercy, has annexed to the covenant of his grace, conditions, on the part of the subjects of it to be fulfilled, to which it is meet and right that they who are of age to do it, should, when they are receiving the seal of the covenant, in their proper person, manifest their assent. It was, probably, with such persons in his view, that St. Peter said, "Baptism doth now save us, not the putting away the filth of the flesh, but the answer of a good conscience towards God."

It would seem, then, upon a very little reflection, that until they possess and are able to profess, "repentance towards God and faith in the Lord Jesus," persons of mature age should not receive Christian baptism. For, as we have already intimated, it can neither honour the Deity nor benefit themselves, to be baptized into a faith which they believe to be false, or to seek remission of sins which they are willing to retain. Accordingly, if we advert to the proceedings of the Apostles and primitive Christians, we shall find that these qualifications were required before admission to baptism, of all those in whom they could exist. When the multitude, upon the powerful preaching of St. Peter, were pricked at the heart, and demanded of him and the rest of the Apostles, "Men and brethren, what shall we do?" he replied and said, "Repent and be baptized every one of you in the name of Jesus Christ, for the remission of sins, and ye shall receive the gift of the Holy Ghost." And when the devout treasurer of the queen of Ethiopia, to whom Philip had showed, from the wonderful prophecies of Isaiah, that Jesus is the Son of God, said to the Messenger of the Most High, "See, here is water, what doth hinder me to be baptized?" The holy Deacon answered, "If thou believest with all thine heart, thou mayest." Indeed, the necessity of these qualities seems implied in the commission to baptize, first given to the Apostles; for it is difficult to conceive how any person can be made a disciple of Christ who neither believes his authority as a teacher, nor desires his instructions and grace. On this necessity, arising from the nature of the thing and the words of the commission, were founded those solemn renunciations and promises which the Church hath required to be made at every administration of baptism, from the earliest age to the present day. To renounce the Devil and every evil work; to believe the doctrines revealed by Christ, and to be obedient to the will of God, are conditions upon which the mercies of the gospel are to be inherited, and without specifying them and requiring a promise to observe them, from every adult candidate for baptism, I know not that the zeal of the conveyance of those mercies, was, even in the earlier ages of Christianity, permitted to be given. These renunciations and promises are retained by our Church in the baptismal office; and she hath expressed her sense of the necessity of the substance of them, when to the question "What is required of persons to be baptized?" she replies in her Catechism, "Repentance, whereby they forsake sin; and faith, whereby they steadfastly believe the promises of God made to them in that sacrament."

But though without repentance and faith, there is no baptism for those who are capable of repenting and believing, yet where these qualifications are possessed, the ordinance should not be delayed. As soon as the heart is turned from sin unto God, and unto Jesus Christ whom he hath sent, and the mind is sufficiently instructed in the great doctrines of his gospel to know what it embraces, the person should hasten to this holy fount, that in its waters he may "die from sin and rise again unto righteousness," prepared for the holy and exalted duties, and invested with all the glorious privileges and immortal hopes, unto which, by this new birth, the children of adoption are begotten. It is not necessary, I conceive, that he should tarry till the Christian life is perfected in him. It is sufficient that he is prepared and ready to begin it. There are many truths to be learned, and many excellencies to be acquired in the teaching which follows the ordinance, yea, even unto the end of the Christian's career. In the Apostolic Church the interval was not long between conversion and baptism. "Why tarriest thou?" said Ananias to the newly converted Paul: "Arise, and be baptized, and wash away thy sins, calling on the name of the Lord." The pious treasurer of Candace, who came from far to Jerusalem to worship, and as he returned read in his chariot the word of God, had but just become acquainted with the wonderful character, and sufferings, and mediation of the Redeemer, when he desired to be sealed as one of his, and going down with Philip into the water, received in baptism the token and pledge of the mercies that are in Christ Jesus. And though in subsequent ages, a discipline was assigned to candidates for the ordinance, this was rather a matter of prudence than necessity; as appears from the considerations, that the term of preparation was of various duration in different places; and that the ordinance was immediately administered upon a profession of faith and penitence, whenever the circumstances of the case required it. When Arintheus, a Roman consul, was on his sick bed converted to Christianity by his pious wife, he was immediately baptized, and the sentiment is established among the earlier Christian writers, that unto those who are brought to the first principles of the truth, baptism, if they are in danger of death, should be immediately given, in hopes of the resurrection. It is at the entrance of the Christian life, when the soul has turned to its Creator, and is willing to be led by his Son to righteousness and peace, that God, if I may so speak, meets us with this animating and efficacious ordinance. And in this, he is seen the true Father of the returning prodigal. While yet he is a great way off, in his rags and poverty, the Father goes to meet him. He brings him to his house, the Church. He commands his servants, the ministers of his Church, to bring forth the best robe, the robe of his Son's righteousness, and, by baptism, to put it on his recovered child; at the same time they put, as it were, a ring, the signet of favour, the token of affection, upon his hand, and shoes upon his feet, when they have washed them, that he may walk pleasantly in the paths of holiness. In the holy eucharist the banquet of reconciliation and gladness is prepared for him; and the members of the family, whether militant on earth, or triumphant in heaven, partake of the Father's joy, that a child, who was dead, is alive again, that one who was lost, is found.

We have now considered the question of infant baptism, and have shown, that children are not excluded from this important ordinance, but that it should be administered as soon after birth as it can conveniently be done. We have also considered the case of those, who, from any cause whatever, have not been so happy as to receive baptism in their infancy; and have shown, that they should obtain for themselves this ordinance, as soon as their hearts are turned from sin unto God, and they find themselves desirous to embrace the truths and partake of the mercies which are revealed in Christ Jesus. These two inductions are sufficient to satisfy the second inquiry upon this important subject, viz: when mankind should be baptized?

And, in looking back upon them, some inferences press themselves upon my view, without a notice of which I cannot dismiss this head of discourse.

In the first place—parents! how great is your felicity in having for your offspring the benefits of this sacred ordinance. How consoling, as that babe slumbers by your side, to know that from the guilt of the nature in which it was born, it hath been washed in a fountain set open by God. How blissful as its little mind begins to expand, to reflect, that it shall endure and expand forever, having a charter of immortality sealed with the seal of God, and being destined, if it forfeit not its inheritance, to flourish among nobler beings in regions of eternal day. How happy, when thinking of the temptations and sorrows to which it must be exposed in this evil world, to be able to plead for it with the Father the promise of his protecting Spirit; and to say, I have caused it to be entered in the school of the Redeemer, where, if I keep it there, and it be diligent, it shall find wisdom, and safety, and consolation. What a fund of joy, then, with respect to the present condition of his offspring, is this simple ordinance to the truly Christian parent.

But there is lifted up to me a countenance overspread with gloom. It seems to say, I had a child. I brought it to be washed in the waters of baptism. It was just beginning to learn its duty and to lisp its love. But death came. He tore from my arms my struggling babe. I shall see my child no more!—Afflicted mother! learn a new motive to rejoice in God your Saviour. Your child, in its baptism, had been washed from sin, and adopted of God; and sooner shall heaven and earth pass away, than its little spirit shall fail. Its lot is happy. It has escaped the hazards of a probationary life, in which, though it had been washed, it might have become again defiled; perhaps, defiled beyond reclaiming, and thus have forfeited its heavenly inheritance. A seraph now, it is the care of angels. Amidst the spirits of the just, it "follows the Lamb, whithersoever he goeth." Be patient. Be holy. Be innocent and humble, like your child. And you shall one day find it in a situation—oh! how shall I express its bliss? It will greet you with smiles; reposing on the bosom of its God.

Again. How tender is the care, how condescending the mercy of our heavenly Father, that, though by committing many actual sins we have most grievously offended him, he hath, for our encouragement, provided a visible seal, a sensible pledge, of his pardon and favour, if we will turn unto him and live. Penitent offender in this laver of regeneration, "though your sins have been as scarlet, they shall be made white as snow; though they have been red like crimson, they shall be as wool." Hast thou been washed therein? Remember thy obligations. How shalt thou claim the love of the Almighty, if, having renounced the pollutions that are in the world, and promised to believe, and do, what he hath commanded thee, thou again givest thyself up to work iniquity, and departest from the living God? Art thou yet unwashed with baptism? Come to the waters. Repent, and be baptized for the remission of sins. Dost thou fear that thou art destitute of that faith and repentance which must be brought to the ordinance? Ah! remember that without the qualities which are necessary to fit thee for the Church upon earth, thou canst have no admission into the kingdom of heaven.

Once more. It is plain, from what has been said, that infants are admitted to baptism on the faith of those who bring them, and the stipulations which are made for their Christian education. How solemn, then, the responsibility which rests upon their parents and sponsors. The Church, indeed, is in some degree their guardian. And she does for them what she can. When she offers in her litany the tender petition for young children she has them in her thoughts. She has provided her catechism for their instruction, and commanded very solemnly her ministers to feed those lambs. In all the ministrations of the sanctuary, she furnishes means for their growth in grace, and in the knowledge of their Lord and Saviour Jesus Christ. But, for the better securing of their Christian education, she hath from the beginning required sponsors at their baptism to pledge themselves for the same. And to their arms she returns them as soon as they have been washed, to be their peculiar charge, till in confirmation they take upon themselves the promises and vows which, when they were helpless and unconscious, the charity of their friends made in their behalf.*

* The duties of Sponsors are explained in the Sermons on *Confirmation.* As these were not delivered as a part of the series on the Ordinances and Rites of the Church, they were given by the late Bishop DEHON to the *Protestant Episcopal Society for the Advancement of Christianity in South Carolina,* and were published in 1818. They may be had of *E. Thayer,* the Society's Bookseller, No. 25 Broad-street, Charleston.

SERMON VII.

ON BAPTISM.

St. Matthew, xxviii. 19, 20.

"Go ye, therefore, and teach all nations, baptizing them in the name of the Father, and of the Son, and of the Holy Ghost, teaching them to observe all things whatsoever I have commanded you, and lo, I am with you alway, even unto the end of the world."

SOME of you, my brethren, may remember, that in order to embrace all the interesting and important views of baptism, it was proposed when we first turned our attention to this subject, to consider why mankind should be baptized, when they should be baptized, how they should be baptized, by whom they should be baptized, and where they should be baptized? To the first and second of these heads we have given a very full consideration; a consideration necessarily rendered long by the greatness of the consequences involved in the inquiries, and the investigations which were necessary to clear and satisfy them. We come now, in the third place, to consider how baptism should be administered? And upon this head of discourse, I need not in this audience be very diffuse, but shall content myself with stating only such particulars as will explain and vindicate our mode, and furnish us with an answer to give to every man who asketh a reason of the practice of the Church to which we belong.

We observe, first, that baptism is always to be administered with water. There is represented in the ordinance the purifying and sanctifying of the whole man, by the pardoning mercy of God and the gracious influences of his Holy Spirit. Of this change, the action of water upon the body affords a most significant representation. This cleansing and refreshing element has, indeed, been used in all religions, to express in figure the state of purity in which man, when he would have the love and favour of his Maker, must endeavour to be found. Ablution with water was a part of the Pagan's worship, and the Jew had his holy washings appointed by the Most High. With great propriety, therefore, and condescension to our nature, did the blessed Institutor of the Christian baptism consecrate this element to be the emblem of his blood and spirit to his Church; these by their purifying, sanctifying, and invigorating influence doing that to the spirit which water by its cleansing and refreshing power does to the bodies of men. And as we can admit of no baptism as valid if administered with any *other* substance, neither can we conceive of any true and sufficient baptism without *this*. If the visions of men have led any to rely upon internal baptisms by the word or spirit, to the neglect of the external rite, we have no such doctrine in the Church of Christ. His declaration is, that a man must be born of water as well as of the spirit, if he would enter the kingdom of God. And when the devout Cornelius and his friend had been filled with faith and the Holy Ghost, the Apostle demands, "Can any man forbid water, that these should not be baptized, who have received the Holy Ghost as well as we?"

But though water is indispensably necessary in every Christian baptism, so much so that no man, be his other religious attainments what they may, can, without it, be said in the way of his appointment, to have put on Christ, yet the mode of applying the element, whether by immersion or affusion, seems not essential to the validity or efficacy of the sacrament. Had it been, the Scriptures would not have been silent upon the subject. They leave us unable to gather either from express instructions or from the import of the terms used, or from analogous cases, or from recorded facts, that it is of essential consequence or was of universal practice, to apply the waters of baptism in either manner, to the exclusion of the other. It is highly probable that under different circumstances each was used. And, indeed, if no command upon the subject was given by our Lord, it would appear reasonable, upon reflection, that the certainty and efficacy of the ordinance does not depend upon the quantity of water which is used, but that it is sufficient that there be preserved in the mode that emblematical representation of the inward and spiritual grace, for which the outward visible sign is chiefly instituted. The mode of affusion is generally practised in our Church; and the grace which is represented by the rite is frequently expressed in Scripture with manifest allusion to the cleansing, sanctifying, and blessing of beings and things under the law, by such phrases as pouring water upon the subjects of it; sprinkling them with pure water, and shedding upon them that which they receive. In climates, indeed, in which total immersion in water would not be safe nor pleasant, or would not be so consistent with decency and order as another mode, or in which the cleansing power of water is daily applied to a part only of the body, it is evident that the significance of the symbol is preserved with as great force and with greater propriety, by the use of affusion or sprinkling in baptism, rather than of immersion.

But it may be asked, does not the term by which this ordinance is named, intimate the necessity of immersion? I answer no. The passages are numerous in the sacred volume, in which partial washings and applications of water, or blood, by sprinkling, are expressed in the original language by the word from which we derive the term baptism. Thus, when St. Paul, in his epistle to the Hebrews, speaking of the ceremonial law, says, it "stood only in meats, and drinks, and divers washings," the word rendered in our translation, washings, signifies, in the original, and is elsewhere translated, baptisms. What were these baptisms? Unquestionably, those legal purifications and sanctifications, which were most of them, as the Apostle himself witnesses, made by sprinkling. Thus, also, when the Pharisee with whom our blessed Lord condescended to dine, is said to have marvelled that he had not washed before dinner, the word, rendered in our Bible, washed, in the original signifies baptized. But this customary baptism of the Jews, which Jesus had on this occasion omitted, was a partial application of water to the body, as you may learn by express declaration of holy writ, and by the account and use of the water pots, which stood, after the manner of purifying of the Jews, in that house, in Cana of Galilee, where the marriage was celebrated, which was honoured with the presence and first miracle of our Lord. Other passages are numerous which might be adduced, to show you, that baptism often signifies, in the sacred volume, a partial as well as total washing, and sometimes, by fair inference, a sprinkling of the subject of it.

But it may further be inquired, did not the Apostles administer this ordinance by immersion? I answer, we know not that they uniformly did; we believe that they never did to the exclusion of the other mode. When the jailor and his family were baptized, at midnight, by St. Paul, in the chambers of the prison, who can doubt that it was with affusion of water? And when that great Apostle himself was, after his conversion, baptized by Ananias, in Damascus, it would appear, from the face of the narrative, that in the house in which the minister found him, he stood up and received baptism. There is nothing in the account of the baptism of Cornelius, or of the treasurer of Candace, or of the three thousand who were baptized in the after part of the day of Pentecost, which assures us the ceremony of immersion was used in their respective cases. And though, in subsequent times, this mode of administering the ordinance appears to have become general, it was never exclusively so, nor considered as necessary to the perfection of the sacrament. For in every age and country, the sick and the feeble received baptism by affusion; which, if any particular mode had been derived from the Apostles, as essential to the validity of the ordinance, they could not have done; and from which, we may at least infer, that upon this, as upon other matters upon which he had given no express instructions, Christ left it with his Apostles, and their successors in the Church, to exercise their discretion as circumstances should require.

But it has been objected, and to the disquietude of many who were educated in correct principles, was not Jesus himself baptized by immersion, and should we not follow his example? I know not whence it is learned, that John the Baptist used this mode. We are told that he came baptizing *with* water, not *in* water; and it is difficult to conceive, unless he dwelt continually in the river, how he could have immersed the great multitudes who went forth to his baptism. With regard to our blessed Lord, as he had no sin unto which, in baptism, he could die, and needed no new birth unto righteousness, it is with great reason supposed his baptism was preparatory to his entrance upon the offices of his ministry, and that in submitting himself to it, he had respect unto that law of God, which required that every Levite should be set apart to his office by washing with water before he entered upon the sacred functions of the Priesthood. This was, most probably, the righteousness that our blessed Lord, at this eventful period, when he was about to enter upon the great works of his Priesthood, was anxious to fulfil. Do you ask how that washing of the Levites, in order to their consecration to their office, was performed? Not by immersion. No. "Thus shalt thou do unto them, to cleanse them," said the Almighty to Moses; "sprinkle water of purifying upon them." After this manner, therefore, if this law was in the view of Christ, it is reasonable to believe he was baptized. His holy feet stood probably in Jordan; and the venerable Baptist standing there with him, sprinkled its waters upon his sacred form; and as he came up from the river, the voice of God was heard from heaven, proclaiming his character, and accepting his ministry. Is it said that the sacred writers speak of a going into, and coming up out of the waters? It does not necessarily follow therefrom that those of whom they speak had undergone a submersion; for the same thing is said of him who gave, as well as of him who received baptism. And if it did, the original phrases which are thus rendered in our Bible, might, with equal correctness, have been translated by *going to*, and *coming up from* the waters, and, in fact, are so translated in many places of the New Testament. If, however, it were indubitable that John administered baptism only by immersion to his disciples and to our Lord, we could not infer from this the necessity of the same mode, under the Christian dispensation, in every climate, and in all circumstances. For this would suppose a close analogy between cases differing essentially in those very points by which, we contend, the question concerning the mode of baptism has, by the Church been generally decided.

Upon the whole, then, it appears that the manner of applying the water of baptism is not essential to the efficacy of the sacrament, provided it be always so applied as to express the spiritual sanctification, of which it is the symbol and pledge. If we consider, moreover, that the benefits which this ordinance represents and conveys are more frequently expressed in the types and language of Scripture, by sprinkling, than in any other way, we shall have ample reason to be satisfied with the mode used by the Church in which we have received this holy ordinance.

But though the manner of applying the element be not essential, nor established in the gospel, the words which accompany the application are. It would seem, my brethren, that our Lord foresaw to what assaults and exposures the peculiar and fundamental doctrine of his religion would be exposed; and endeavoured to secure it by introducing it into the very seal of the covenant which, at their initiation into his Church, his disciples should receive. "Go ye, therefore, and teach all nations, baptizing them in the name of the Father, and of the Son, and of the Holy Ghost." The faith of the Trinity is fundamental to Christianity. Take his divinity from the Son, and you destroy the value and efficacy of his blood. Take his being from the Holy Ghost, and you bereave yourselves of the Comforter, whose abode in the bosoms of the faithful, is the best, the only safeguard of their virtue and peace. To establish this faith, therefore, and perpetuate the recollection and reverence of it, Christ commanded his baptism to be administered in the name of the Trinity, and wherever this is omitted, the baptism which he instituted is not given. The use of this "form of sound words" is of inestimable importance. It is as a rampart round the Christian faith, which the power of its adversaries cannot penetrate, nor their subtlety undermine. For who that shall recollect under what authority and in what name he was baptized, shall be able to believe that Jesus, if a creature, exalted himself in this ordinance to a participation of equal honour with the Father, or commanded his followers to be baptized in the name of a Spirit which hath no personal existence!

SERMON VIII.

ON BAPTISM.

St. Luke, ii. 22.

They brought him to Jerusalem, to present him to the Lord.

AFTER some intermission, my Christian friends, we resume the subject of baptism; and come now to treat of the least of the inquiries, proposed at the commencement of the discourses, upon this ordinance, viz: where it should be administered? The question is interesting, and I am aware of the difficulties to be encountered in treating of it. Should I seem to be the advocate of a new practice, I must beg you to suspend your judgment as, I doubt not, I shall evidence to you that the practice advocated is the ancient usage, and most conformable to the nature, and promotive of the utility, of this holy institution. I purpose to show you, that baptism should be administered publicly, in the Church; and this, by reasons drawn from the authority of the Church, from the nature of the sacrament, and from the great and peculiar advantages attending the public administration of it.

There is no express command given in the gospel, concerning the place in which baptism should be administered. It is, therefore, left to wisdom to ascertain and fix upon the places, which are most suitable and advantageous; but not to the wisdom of every individual; for the opinions of men are so various, that in this way there could exist no order nor uniformity; but to the wisdom of the Church, with which there cannot but have been left discretionary powers, to be applied to the ordering of all matters not regulated by positive instructions, and whose authority, therefore, in such cases must be observed, if we would keep the "unity of the Spirit in the bond of peace." In proportion as you release men from the obligation to be bound by the rules of the society to which they belong, you loosen the bands of that society; you destroy the preservatives of its unity, its identity, its perpetuity, its health, perhaps of its very existence.

The primitive Christians had no churches. Watched not persecuted by their adversaries, they met, sequestered from notice, in those places where they could do it with the greatest safety. An upper room in the mansion of some Christian family, the convenient apartment of some pious believer, was the sanctuary in which the first disciples of our Lord assembled, for the purposes of communion and social worship. They, therefore, had no temples to which the subjects of baptism could be brought; but in the waters of some neighbouring spring, or river, or in water brought to the place where they were assembled, or wherever it was most convenient, they administered the holy rite. But even then the solemnity was public. The renunciations were made in the presence of a congregation. It was done, generally, before the faithful, that they might witness the deed.

When Christianity, under the protection and blessing of Almighty God, became established, and churches were erected for the use of Christians, these churches were furnished with baptisteries, or fonts, to which the candidates for baptism were brought, that with due solemnity, in his holy temples, they might be presented unto the Lord. In some cities in which there were many churches, the ordinance was administered only in the mother church; chiefly, to cherish the better the important doctrine, that they who are baptized are born again, and become heirs of all the instructions, hopes, and privileges of the Church, whom, to express the tenderness and indissolubleness of his union with her, the Redeemer had condescended to represent, as espoused to himself. In subsequent times, wherever we find Christian temples, we find fonts, for the public administration of baptism; and the Church to which we belong, while with great tenderness for the welfare of little infants, she permits this holy sacrament to be administered in private, whenever they are dangerously sick, with equal care for the sacredness of the office, and the most solemn and useful performance of it, requires her ministers, as you may read in the rubric at the head of the office for the "ministration of private baptism," that they warn the people, "that without great cause and necessity they procure not their children to be baptized at home in their houses." This, her order, is grounded not only in the ancient usage, but, also, as we shall presently show, in the nature of the thing, and with a regard to special advantages to be derived from the observance of it. And here, let me be allowed in passing, to state, that for the preservation in its integrity of her holy and beautiful system, and the more certain accomplishment of the spiritual benefits which this system is designed to promote, there is required of her ministers, before they are clothed with holy orders, a very solemn vow, that to the laws of her worship, as well as to the doctrines of her creed, they will religiously conform themselves. This, to your consciences, will excuse your clergy, if, at any time they find themselves obliged to ask of you, the gratification of having your children brought to the church, when you wish to have them baptized.

This you will the more readily do, if we now proceed to consider, in the second place, that this method of administering baptism publicly in the church is suited to the nature and end of the ordinance. Baptism is a public rite. It is, as you have heard in a former discourse, the initiation of the subjects of it into the school of the Redeemer, and the sealing to them, on the part of God, of an interest in that redemption and those precious promises of which every believer is a partaker. And shall this transaction, the most solemn, the most momentous in its import which takes place upon our globe, be done in secret?

Shall it be performed lightly, in some private chamber; or gayly, in some festive hall? Should not an initiation so interesting take place in the presence of the congregation, who are parties in this business, receiving hereby an accession to their number, and a new occasion for their praise and prayers? Should not the sealing, visibly, to a child of man of the mercies of the Almighty, take place in the temple set apart to his service, the places which he hath chosen to set his name there? Where but to his house should the children be brought who are to be dedicated unto him? Where but in the places in which the followers of the Redeemer are assembled, should *their* names be named who are to be enlisted under his banners, and embodied with those who are to "fight the good fight of faith?" Consider, I pray you, what is done for your children in baptism; that therein "they are made members of Christ, children of God, and inheritors of the kingdom of heaven;" and then say, if this thing should not be done publicly, both for the glory of God and the information of the Church; and with all the circumstances of place and manner which can give sanctity to the deed.

But it is objected, what interest can the congregation take in the baptism of a child of whom they know nothing? Ah, my hearers! at every rescue of one of our race from the dominion of evil, and translation of him into the kingdom of the Redeemer, "there is joy in the presence of the angels of God!" And do you, partakers of his nature, ask, What interest have I in this? At every administration of baptism, the Redeemer, in his high state of glory, sees of the travail of his soul, and is satisfied. And do you, professed followers of him, ask, What interest have I in this? Oh, Christian! a celebrated Roman could say, "I myself am a man, and think nothing foreign to me which concerns the welfare of man." And do you ask, when by the ordinance and seal of the Almighty, an infant of your species is taken from under the dominion of sin and death to the glorious liberty and exalted expectations of the children of God, do you then ask, What interest have I in this? Ah!

were we sufficiently alive to the mercies of God, the honour of the Redeemer, and the salvation of our fellow-beings, there could not be to us a scene more interesting than the new birth even of the humblest offspring of Adam, to the life and relations, and privileges and hopes, unto which we are begotten in baptism by Christ Jesus. Evident it is, that the pious compilers of our Liturgy supposed that all the faithful are deeply interested in every administration of this ordinance. For to whom is the earnest address at the commencement of the office made? Who are called upon to supplicate the Almighty in behalf of the present child? To whom are the appropriate gospel, and the affecting exhortation which follows it addressed? To whom is it declared, that we receive the "child into the congregation of Christ's flock?" And who are called upon to give "thanks unto Almighty God," for the mercies we have witnessed? The congregation. Whereby is intimated to us the absurdity of performing this service in private; and that every Christian is concerned in the matter when a new member is grafted into the body of the Church, and a new heir born to the kingdom of heaven. Nay, when it is said to the sponsors, "Ye have brought this child here to be baptized," who sees not that it is supposed to be in the church? And the reason why the ordinance is required to be administered immediately after reading the second lesson is, that then the greatest number of the faithful are usually present, to witness the interesting work, and unite in the devotions with which it is solemnized.

This brings me to notice, in the third place, some special advantages attending thereon, which recommend the public administration of baptism. And, in the first place, sponsors may hereby be more deeply impressed with the sacred obligations of their holy and important office. Here, where the eye of God is felt more immediately upon them, in his house, at his holy altar, they pledge themselves to see to the religious education of those whom, with a charity which is doubtless highly acceptable to the Most High, they are careful to bring to his holy baptism. Is not our nature such, that under circumstances like these, they will more soberly undertake the duties of their office, and be more solemnly impressed with the importance of faithfully discharging them?

Again. Who can estimate the benefits which may be derived to the child from this public consecration of him to religion and virtue? It cannot be considered by the serious as a mere superstition, to view it as a felicity, that an infant should be first blessed in the sanctuary. Samuel, whose piety and integrity we all may well emulate, was carried to the temple in his childhood, and devoted to God. Jesus himself, who, as he increased in stature, increased also "in favour with God and man," was brought in his infancy to Jerusalem by his pious parents to be presented in the temple unto the Lord. And it is at the places of his worship that the Almighty has been pleased specially to promise his blessing. Nor, further, can it be believed, that in the lips of a pious parent it would always be an inefficacious appeal to his rising offspring, "My child, in your infancy you were carried to the altar of God, and there, with prayers and tears, devoted to a virtuous life." Least of all can it be doubted, when all is performed with sincerity, that blessing should result to the infant who is offered to God in his house from the combined prayers of all his faithful people. An advantage this, of which it is difficult to conceive how any thoughtful person can be willing his child should be deprived, unless he contemn the institutions of religion, and disbelieves the efficacy of all prayer. For surely, if ever, it is on this occasion we may hope the voice of sincere supplication will be heard. When asking only spiritual blessings, when asking them for the helpless babe, who, as yet, has done no sin, when asking them with one accord, for Jesus' sake, we have the strongest encouragement to believe that the prayers of the faithful will reach unto the throne, and that nothing but the perverseness of the creature will turn away the blessings which they implore?

I add, once more, that from the administration of this ordinance in the Church, benefit may accrue to the whole congregation. Upon each one of us who has been baptized, there rest, unless to the perdition of our souls we have abjured them, "a solemn vow, promise, and profession." On our observance and fulfilment of these depend the pardon of our sins, our participation of the influences of the Holy Spirit, and our enjoyment of eternal life. By the attrition of the business, the pleasures, and the vices of the world, our remembrance of the import of this profession, and solemnity of this vow, is perpetually exposed to be worn away. We need to have it often renewed; and among the best means of renewing it may be reckoned the public administration of baptism, in which we see that acted for others which was once acted for us; and the mercies of the covenant, and the conditions of inheriting them, are brought to our view explicitly, solemnly, and in all their importance.

Finally, the influence and reputation of religion are involved, more than at first thought might be supposed, in the public and solemn administration of this ordinance. The respect of the mass of mankind for the doctrines and precepts of religion, will very much depend upon their respect for its institutions. Their respect for its institutions will, perhaps, not less depend upon the manner in which they are performed, than upon the reasons on which they are grounded. On this account it is of unspeakable importance, that the sacraments of Christianity should be generally administered in a holy place, and when it is practicable, on a holy day, and always in a holy manner. Nor is it easy to conceive a sufficient reason why one of them should, with suitable awe, be celebrated in the sanctuary, and the equal reverence which is due to the other, be exposed to hazard by stripping it of the solemnities of time, and place, and manner, with which it is wise it should be protected, and meet it should be adorned.

You see, then, how many and how weighty are the reasons for the administration of baptism publicly in the church. Suffer then the little children to come unto the Redeemer, where he is present with the congregation of his saints. Christian parent, when you consider the contagion and sorrows of the world, into which you have brought your offspring, where would you that they should make their first appearance but in the temple of God? Pious woman, who art grateful to the Almighty for thy preservation in the peril of childbirth, and art filled with joy that a man child is born into the world, what offering of gratitude so significant and acceptable canst thou send to his house, as thy new born babe to be dedicated to his name? Holy mother; wouldst thou not choose that that should be done for thy little one, which, in the days of his infancy, was done for thy Lord? Behold, then, his parents, with religious fidelity, taking him to the temple "to do for him after the custom of the law." See the child Jesus, in the morning of his being, presented at the altar for redemption and a blessing; and with thy little ones do thou likewise. And God grant, "that whosoever is here dedicated" to him "by our office and ministry, may also be endued with heavenly virtues, and everlastingly rewarded" through his mercy, "who doth live and govern all things, world without end."

SERMON IX.

ON THE LORD'S SUPPER.

1 CORINTHIANS, xi. 23—27.

"For I have received of the Lord that which also I delivered unto you, that the Lord Jesus, the same night in which he was betrayed, took bread; and when he had given thanks, he brake it, and said, Take, eat; this is my body which is broken for you; this do in remembrance of me. After the same manner, also, he took the cup, when he had supped, saying, This cup is the New Testament in my blood; this do ye, as oft as ye drink it, in remembrance of me; for as often as ye eat this bread and drink this cup, ye do show the Lord's death till he come."

HAVING set before you, my brethren, in several discourses, the nature and necessity, the subjects, the uses, and the laws of the first Christian sacrament, we come now to consider the second, the Lord's Supper. In approaching the consideration of this holy mystery, I am filled with anxiety that it should be rightly understood by you. If baptism is the great mean whereby we are born to a new life, new relations, and new hopes, the Lord's Supper is the great mean whereby that life is sustained, those relations are recognized, and those hopes enlivened and assured. Yet of the benefits of this sacrament, how large a part of the Christian community have no participation. God, of his mercy, has been pleased, in compassion to the infirmities of our nature, to provide for us sensible pledges of his pardon and favour; visible tokens of the near relations to him, and exalted hopes unto which he has begotten us by the covenant in Christ Jesus, that we may be encouraged and enabled to maintain a lively faith in his mercy, and reminded and strengthened to discharge the obligations, which, under that covenant, do necessarily rest upon us. But having either no thoughts upon the subject, or erroneous ones, the greater part of Christians turn their backs upon his altar, neglecting their peculiar inheritance, the best gift of their holy religion. What wonder then that the privileges of Christianity are imperfectly appreciated; and its virtues so frequently absent from bosoms in which they might flourish; yea, and in bosoms in which they have a partial growth but are so seldom matured!

On these accounts, I crave your indulgence, if I shall seem to treat with unnecessary fullness of this important ordinance. In the discourses upon it which will ensue, there are three things which I shall endeavour, through the divine assistance, to accomplish.

To set before you, in the first place, the considerations which should induce us to partake of this sacrament:

Secondly, to point out to you the qualifications with which we should receive it:

And, thirdly, to ascertain and obviate the principal causes which induce so many to neglect it.

We are first to attend to the considerations which should induce us to partake of this sacrament. These must be inferred from the history of its institution. Of this, there is an account given by the three first Evangelists, in their several gospels, and also by St. Paul, in his first epistle to the Corinthians, according to a special revelation of it which he received from the Lord Jesus. St. John, who wrote his gospel long after the others, and wrote to supply what was then wanting, rather than to repeat what was already written, omits this as a thing perfectly understood by the Church. Among the several accounts of this institution, there is scarcely any variation. I have taken for our guide that account of the institution of the Lord's Supper which is given by St. Paul; it being, perhaps, the fullest and most impressive which we have in the sacred records. You will recollect that this great Apostle received the knowledge of the gospel, not of man, but by the revelation of Jesus Christ; and when you consider, that he conferred not with flesh and blood, concerning the truths he should deliver, you will be struck with the harmony between him and the holy Evangelists in their several accounts of this institution, and may perceive the care of its Author, that its history should be indubitably recorded, and its importance unequivocally made known. The words of the Apostle I have read; and in the discourse which may ensue upon them, you will not look for flowers of rhetoric, nor displays of argumentation; you will not find affected conceits, nor mysterious allusions. No eloquence can adorn a rite so simple. No language can add sublimity to an ordinance so holy. My chief concern will be to conduct you, with great plainness, through the several parts of the Apostle's record, persuaded that you will find in it all that you have need to understand of the nature and obligation of this holy mystery.

The first thing which presents itself to our attention is the Person instituting this sacrament—the Lord Jesus. It is of the highest and most sacred authority. Its origin is not of men. Our obligation to observe it is not derived from the Church. It is appointed by that Being whom we are bound to love as our Saviour; whom it is our duty to reverence as "Lord of all" things; whom we have confessed as our Master and Instructor, and have pledged ourselves in our baptismal covenant, to serve and obey. It is a positive institution of that Christ, in a conformity to whose instructions, safety and happiness, improvement and final approbation will always be found. Nothing that he has ordained as generally necessary in his Church, can be consistently dispensed with by his followers, or deemed by any man optional or useless.

The injunction to the Apostles. to do what he had done, to take bread, and the cup, and bless them, and distribute them, as a memorial of his death and passion, necessarily implied that there should be recipients. And who, in the reason and nature of the thing, should receive his body and blood but the members of his Church, for whom they were given? Who should unite in this commemoration before God, of the sacrifice of the death of Christ, but all those who hope to obtain by it remission of sins? Who should eat, at the table of the Lord, of this feast upon the sacrifice, but all they who have need of pledges of God's favour and goodness towards them? Such was the way in which the matter was understood by the first Christians, who cannot be supposed to have been ignorant of the design of the ordinance, or intention of their Lord. On the first day of the week, in all their assemblies, the celebration of this Supper was the great act of their public worship. And every person who, by baptism, had been grafted into the body of the Church, and had not forfeited his privileges by notorious iniquities, was considered not only as having a right, but as being under an indispensable obligation to join in this holy Eucharist.

The second thing which you will notice, is the time in which Jesus appointed us this ordinance; "the same night in which he was betrayed." What! blessed Lord, couldst thou have required of thy followers in that night, which they will not all be anxious to observe and do! We are so constituted, that we are much influenced in our opinions and conduct by the circumstances of things. When this influence is promotive of good feelings, and friendly to virtue, it is commendable to indulge and cherish it. The circumstance of the time of the institution of the Lord's Supper, is carefully recorded, and renders it peculiarly interesting. In that night, "the heathen raged and the people were imagining a vain thing; the kings of the earth" stood up, "and the rulers were taking counsel together against the LORD, and against his anointed." In that night, the powers of hell were in array against the Redeemer, aiming at the subversion of his purpose, and the oppression of his spirit. In that night, he experienced the first wound in the house of his friends; the first treachery of one whom he had chosen; and beheld, in anticipation, the subsequent faithless desertion of all his followers. In that night, the soul of our Master was "exceeding sorrowful, even unto death," and the hour was near, when he would exclaim, under the power of darkness, "My God! my

God! why hast thou forsaken me!" In that night, he perceived his ministry drawing near to a close; he knew that the agonies of the cross were at hand. But under all the emotions which possessed his bosom, he is chiefly anxious for the welfare of his Church. In that same night, he collected his disciples, and appointed the thing which he would have us do in remembrance of him. Sacred are the requirements of the departing soul. Precious are the last bequests of parents and friends. This holy rite, what is it but the dying injunction of our Lord! This blessed sacrament, what is it but the parting legacy of Christ to his Church, to be to them a comfort and nourishment when he should be gone!

A third thing for our consideration, is the elements which are used in the Supper; "The Lord Jesus the same night in which he was betrayed, took bread;" and "after the same manner, also, he took the cup, when he had supped." Unquestionably, the Redeemer might have exalted, by his appointment, any creature which he chose, to be, to his Church, a memorial of his body and blood. But there are some obvious and affecting reasons for the selection of bread and wine, of which I would not have you ignorant. These were pure elements, which his followers would be able to procure in every age, and the Church, by the consecration of these to the purpose, would partake of the same symbols in every place. There were, too, before the Saviour, at the time, the loaf and the cup, which, among the Jews, the master of the feast at the close of the supper, distributed among the guests, in token of peace and good will; and with instructive felicity, were these converted into the elements of that sacrament, in which we receive from our Lord the assurance of his favour and love. "Wine," also, hath God provided to "make glad the heart of man," and bread hath he ordained to be the staff of our subsistence; and most significantly do they represent that refreshment of the soul and nourishment unto eternal life, which those find in the body and blood of Christ, who spiritually receive them in this sacred Supper. The faithful, moreover, in the use of these symbols, are impressively taught their joint communion in the mercies of Christ, and their union with each other in him. For though there be many grains, reaped, perhaps, from divers fields, yet is there in the same loaf but one bread; and though there are many grapes, gathered, perhaps, from several vineyards, yet is there in the same cup, but one wine. "The cup of blessing which we bless, is it not the communion of the blood of Christ? The bread which we break, is it not the communion of the body of Christ? For we being many are one bread, and one body; for we are all partakers of that one bread." Though, therefore, our blessed Lord might have set apart any of his gifts and creatures to this exalted use, and all things might well have vied with each other for this holy appropriation, yet, in the appointment of bread and wine, he hath consulted the convenience, and promoted the unity, of his Church; he hath furnished us with an ancient and significant pledge of peace and good will; he hath set before us, in a lively image, our eternal sustenance in, and by, him; and he hath taught us our common interest in his graces, and our near relation in him to each other. I might add, a further significance in the breaking of bread, and pouring out of the wine; but this will come more properly under another point to be noticed by you, viz: the act of the Lord in consecrating these elements.

In themselves, they were nothing more than means of corporeal strength and refreshment. Not till he had blessed, did he break the bread, and deliver the cup. Not till he had broken the bread, and taken the cup, and by his word and benediction hallowed them to this purpose, were they in any sense his body and blood. It was his consecration and offering of them, as symbolical of his sacrifice of himself, which gave them their sacred significance, and converted them into means of spiritual sustenance. And of bread and wine consecrated and offered to God, by the same authority, after the same manner, must we partake, when we would receive this sacrament; for, otherwise, we cannot be said to eat of *that* bread, and drink of *that* cup. This authority, therefore, Christ left with his Apostles and their successors forever, with power to commit it to others, as he had committed it to them. And to them, and such as they shall authorize, does it exclusively appertain in behalf of their Master, to bless the cup, and to break the bread. No man, not lawfully set apart to the office, and deriving his authority from the head of the Church, through the channels which he hath appointed to convey it, may administer these elements to himself or others, any more than Uzziah might acceptably offer incense, or Korah and his company be their own priests. In the act, indeed, of breaking the bread, is shadowed forth, as the text suggests, the breaking of his body who is the sustenance of the faithful, and in the pouring out of the wine is represented the shedding of his blood, as the libation which propitiates the Father, and washes away the sins of the world. And this commemorative representation, is it the memorial of a sacrifice without a priest? To whom is the care of it, with such advantage of order and significance, committed, as to those who have received from him the ministry of reconciliation, and are his organs and representatives to the Church? Not that there is in them any singular virtue. Alas, they are frail as their fellow men! The efficacy of their functions is not in them, but in the office and authority with which Christ has seen fit to invest them. The Lord is in all things a lover of order. The Church, according to the pattern of it in the heavens, is a system of holy and beautiful order. All the institutions of the Saviour are comformable to the same order. When he would miraculously feed the multitude, the people sit down, and the Apostles distribute to them the loaves and the fishes. When he would dispense the knowledge of the truth to Cornelius and to Paul, though present in person with the one, and by an angel with the other, he refers them both to members of the ministry, to which he had committed the preaching of his word, and government of his Church. He hath ordained a perpetual priesthood, to attend continually on this very thing. They are, in an especial manner, the depositaries on earth of the powers which are necessary to give validity to his sacraments; and now he hath ascended up on high, it is through their act of consecration in his behalf, that bread and wine are, by his word and spirit, made to the faithful, in the Supper, the symbols of his body and pledge of his love.

But it is time to pass to a consideration of the intent and use of his holy institution; "This do in remembrance of me; for as often as ye eat this bread, and drink this cup, ye do show the Lord's death till he come;" that is, to preserve a lively recollection of me, and of my sacrifice for the sins of the world, ye shall observe this ordinance for ever. As often as ye shall eat bread, and drink wine, like these, made by consecration in my name symbols of my body and blood, ye do show forth my death in an acceptable and effectual manner. Ye do show it forth to the Father, as the ground of your plea for pardon, grace, and immortality. Ye do show it forth to me, as gratefully impressed upon your hearts, and as an inducement to me to forgive and preserve my Church, having redeemed it with my blood. Ye do show it forth to the world, as the subject of your faith, whereof you are not ashamed; as the only ground of your reliance for pardon and immortality, to which they also should betake themselves, and through which, alone, they, and any of the human race have everlasting life. Ye do show it forth to each other, as a source and occasion of common joy, of mutual consolation and encouragement, of tender amity, and reciprocal good services. And ye do show it forth to your own souls, as the purchase of your redemption, as the sure foundation of hope and peace; as the sacrifice whereby your sins are taken away, and you are restored to the love and favour of God. "Do this," then, all of you, "in remembrance of me." Let it be the great act of Christian worship in all generations. In this simple, easy, and significant sacrament, commemorate often my love and my death, and the relations and hopes to which I have begotten you; and the benefits which I have purchased for you with my blood, you will thus acceptably celebrate and sensibly enjoy. This appears to be the full purport of the words which our blessed Lord is said to have used, at the institution of this sacred ordinance. It is obvious in them, that the intent and meaning of this holy rite is a commemoration of the sacrifice of the death of Christ; in which we avouch ourselves to be his disciples, believing in, and relying upon, the redemption and mercies that are in him; desiring, especially, to be fed with that bread of life which came down from heaven; to eat the flesh and drink the blood of the Son of Man, that we may have eternal life abiding in us. Whatever blessings the ordinance is calculated to represent or convey, we may be sure will be annexed to the faithful observance of it; for no institution of the Almighty, unless it be through our own fault, can ever fail of its proper effects.

You are prepared now to consider, lastly, by whom this sacrament is to be received. It was to the twelve alone, at its first celebration, that it was administered. But it was evidently designed to be a perpetual ordinance in the Church. By it, the Lord's death was to be shown until he comes. All, therefore, who stand related to Christ, as the disciples did; all who are sensible of their salvation by his death, and after the way of his appointment, have been grafted into his Church; all to whom Jesus has been manifested as Lord and Christ, are bound to fulfil this, his requirement. Every adult Christian in the primitive Church, who had not been set aside for his unworthiness, partook often of the Supper. And the command of the Lord is, drink ye all of it. The considerations which rendered it a significant, becoming and useful ordinance to the Apostles will render it so to every believer. For who that looks for salvation by the blood of Christ, is not concerned in the grateful commemoration of his death! Accordingly, the invitation of the Church is given "to all such as shall be religiously and devoutly disposed." And if, indeed, there can be among Christians one duty which may be raised above another, when all rest upon the same authority of their Lord, it is this, of observing, with proper affections, the rite he hath ordained, for the perpetual commemoration of his death. None of his followers is beyond the application of the request, "Do this in remembrance of me."

You see, then, my brethren, in the views we have taken, how interesting and obligatory, how holy and significant, how proper and useful this sacrament of the Supper is. Much it were to be wished that every Christian was in the habit of constantly observing it with suitable dispositions and affections. I cannot forbear to express my regret, that in this, and indeed in other Christian communities, so few males are found at the Supper of the Lord. Except here and there a beloved disciple, the holy women, as at the beginning, are alone by the cross, and first at the sepulchre. Surely, these things ought not so to be. You have seen by whom this ordinance was instituted—the Lord Jesus. You have adverted to the solemn time of its institution; "the night in which he was betrayed." You have observed with what attention to our convenience, instruction, and comfort he chose the elements, bread and wine. You have heard with how much care he hath appointed a ministry in his Church, and made them the depositaries of his authority; that of elements, hallowed by virtue of the same power which hallowed the first sacramental bread and wine, you also may partake. You have seen the intent and meaning of this holy institution; that it is a grateful commemoration of the death of Christ, made at his request, in remembrance of him, and for our own spiritual improvement. And you have been informed that it was designed for the benefit of the whole Church, and is among the most important of those duties which are obligatory upon all Christians. In these considerations, how great are the inducements, how powerful are the reasons, which should bring all the followers of the Lamb to his holy table! Will it be said by them that they are conscious of much sinfulness? "It is a faithful saying, and worthy of all men to be received, that Christ Jesus came into the world to save sinners." And for the benefit of sinners, who "with a true and penitent heart and lively faith," turn unto him, was this ordinance specially instituted. Will it be urged, that by reason of their want of repentance and faith they are unworthy? But, if they are not in a state to receive the Redeemer in his vailed presence at his holy table, how shall they approach him in the unvailed display of his glory when he cometh to judgment? That faith and repentance which they need, it is the most important concern of their lives immediately to acquire. Will it be said that they see many go to the Supper of the Lord who seem not, in any respect, to be benefited by it? Alas! it is an afflicting, a humbling consideration. But let it be remembered, that the deficiencies of others can never pollute the ordinance unto us. It is generally supposed that Judas, the basest and most ignoble of the human race, was present at the first celebration of the Supper, and we may draw from it this most important lesson, that duties which others prostitute or perform insincerely, we are not, on that account, to neglect. Will it be pleaded, that they are deterred by the fear that they may not subsequently live up to their obligations? Commendable, in some degree, is this humility. But they should consider, that under the same obligations they are already brought in their baptismal covenant, that the same faith is professed by them in their creed, and a consciousness of the same duties is implied in their prayers and praises. Besides, we should ever remember, that when our exertions are faithful, God's grace is sufficient for us, and that when we are weak, then he is strong.

Let me not be supposed to diminish the sacredness and most holy solemnity of this institution, or to encourage an unmeaning and presumptuous attendance at the altar of the Lord. No. If any of you be a blasphemer of God, a hinderer or slanderer of his word, an adulterer, or be in malice, or envy, or any other grievous crime, repent ye of your sins, or else come not to that holy table. But it is my desire to persuade you, if you have the Christian dispositions and principles, to avail yourselves of the comfort and encouragement of this ordinance; and if you have them not, to induce you to acquire them, by a sense of your separation from him on earth, and a dread of a consequent separation from him in his heavenly kingdom.

To you, my Christian friends, who expect at the approaching

festival,* to join in the celebration of this holy sacrament, I would say, in the language of the Apostle, "Examine yourselves." When you come to the altar of God, come with hands that are clean and hearts that are pure; come in the garments of humility and with the spirit of love. Come with a penitence which your Maker will accept as sincere, and a faith which he will approve as holy and immovable. And may that Spirit, for which the disciples were waiting on the day of Pentecost, with one accord, in one place, descend also upon you; to enlighten your understandings, to purify your affections, and to strengthen you unto "all such good works as God hath prepared for you to walk in;" that thus you may be fitted when you shall have passed through the gate of death, to celebrate the love and praises of your Redeemer in that temple above, in which angels and archangels, and all the company of heaven, in perfect felicity and uninterrupted joy, unitedly worship God and the Lamb.

* Easter Sunday.

SERMON X.

ON THE LORD'S SUPPER.

1 CORINTHIANS, xi. 28.

"Let a man examine himself; and so let him eat of that bread and drink of that cup."

WHEN we entered, in a former discourse, upon the subject of the Lord's Supper, it was proposed to set before you, in the first place, the considerations which should induce us to partake of this sacrament; secondly, to point out to you the qualifications with which we should receive it; and thirdly, to examine, and if possible remove, the principal causes which induce so many Christians to neglect it. To the first of these heads we then confined our attention; and found in the authority and character of the Being by whom the ordinance was instituted, in the peculiar time of its institution, in the reasons which induced him to choose for the elements of it bread and wine, in his care for the better assurance of the faithful, to leave in his Church a ministry instructed and qualified to perpetuate it and give it validity, in the intent, and meaning, and uses of the holy institution, and in the merciful and comprehensive design of applying it to the benefit of the whole Church; a body of motives to induce every believer in the Redeemer to partake of this sacrament, as strong, numerous, and affecting, if not more so, than those by which any other Christian duty is enforced. No man, therefore, who looks for the mercies of the Lord Jesus unto eternal life, may innocently, and without great detriment to his spiritual interests, neglect to do this, which he hath commanded for our benefit to be done, in remembrance of him. But, though every Christian is obligated, both in interest and duty, to join in the celebration of the Lord's Supper, it is of unspeakable importance that he do it rightly; "for as the benefit is great, if with a true penitent heart and lively faith, we receive this holy sacrament, so is the danger great if we receive the same unworthily." It is a holy mystery. It was styled anciently a tremendous mystery. It is represented in Scripture as a most efficacious mystery. And the reason why it fails to produce its proper effects upon the hearts and lives of any who partake of it, must be found in the ignorance or inconsideration, or wickedness with which it is received. You will, therefore, indulge me with your serious attention, while I proceed to the second thing proposed, in treating of this subject, namely, to point out to you what are the qualifications with which we should receive the Lord's Supper.

It may be well to observe, in the first place, that it is necessary, before a person receives this holy sacrament, that he should have been baptized. The Lord's Supper was instituted by the Redeemer exclusively for the nourishment and comfort of his Church. No man, therefore, can with any propriety partake of it who is not a member of his Church. Baptism is the mean, and the only mean which he hath appointed of grafting men into his mystical body; and when once they have been baptized, they are incorporated into his Church, and have a title, which, if they do not forfeit it by violating the conditions of their baptismal covenant, will be eternal; to all the instructions, assistances, and blessings, which, for his Church, he hath purchased with his blood. Among these, the benefits of the Lord's Supper are, upon earth, among the greatest. And it may be generally observed, that the Christian life which by our baptismal obligation we are bound to lead, is the best preparation for receiving rightly the holy communion. For in the detail which it will be useful to give of sundry qualifications, which we ought to carry whenever we go thither to the table of the Lord, you will perceive, and I could wish the thing might be observed and remembered, that it comprises those graces and virtues which Christians are obligated to possess, whether they partake of the sacrament of the Supper or not.

Thus, that we may descend to particulars, repentance is a qualification without which, we cannot consistently, nor with any advantage, go to the Lord's table. And this for many reasons. Do we not go thither to obtain the tokens and seals of our forgiveness? But can we hope, can we ask to be pardoned for the sins at the remembrance of which we feel no sorrow, and with the dominion of which over us we have no desire to part? Do we not go thither to commemorate the suffering and death of the Son of God, for the expiation of our sins? And can we do this sincerely and worthily without being penetrated with compunction, for the transgressions which required to be expiated at such a price; which put our merciful Redeemer to his unparalleled grief? Do we not go thither to recognize and be recognized, in our exalted relations to the family of God, and to participate of the glorious privileges which belong to the children whom he hath adopted? But can we think of these high and holy relations, can we plead our claim to those privileges without being sorrowful for the omissions of our duty and violations of our baptismal vows, into which, through the infirmity of our nature, or through the perverseness of our wills, we, at any time, have fallen? The Church, in framing the office for the holy communion, presumes that her children come to it truly and earnestly repenting of their sins. And what dangerous inconsideration, what solemn mockery is it to profess to bewail before God "our manifold sins and wickedness, which from time to time we have committed, by thought, word and deed, against his divine majesty," if our souls with heedless levity forget their trespasses; or, having them in remembrance, are not humbled on account of them, and turned suppliantly to God. "Let a man examine himself." Let him compare his life with the rule of God's commandments. Alas! he will find in himself many iniquities; "For there is no man that doeth good and sinneth not." But let him have a painful sense of them; let him be heartily sorry for them; let him earnestly resolve to relinquish them; "and so let him eat of that bread and drink of that cup;" that the Almighty may behold in him the humble and contrite spirit, without which there is no promise of remission. "For unto the ungodly God saith, Why takest thou my covenant in thy mouth; whereas thou hatest to be reformed and hast cast my words behind thee?" But to him who sincerely laments, and resolves to forsake his sins, the Redeemer doth vouchsafe to give, sacramentally, in this ordinance, his body and blood, to be the pledges and earnest of forgiveness.

This leads me to add, in the third place, that if we would receive this sacrament with propriety and benefit, we must bring to it a lively faith in Jesus Christ. The necessity of this qualification arises out of the nature of the thing. For with an infidel, a doubting or an indifferent mind, to pretend to show forth before God in solemn memorials, the death of his Son, would be a horrible impiety and base hypocrisy. Consider, my hearers, the necessity and character of this faith. It is not enough that we be free from unbelief. We must have a living and active faith in the Redeemer, in all his important offices; a faith that eagerly seizes hold upon him as mighty to save; a belief that God hath appointed him to be unto us "a Prince and a Saviour," "in whom we have redemption through his blood;" a confidence, especially, in the efficacy of the spiritual food and sustenance which he hath provided for us in this holy sacrament; that therein he is, as it were, evidently set forth, crucified among us; and we receive the assurances and comforts which arise from feasting upon the sacrifice, which the Almighty hath accepted, "are made partakers of his most blessed body and blood." It is by this faith alone, that we offer unto God in the eucharist, an acceptable sacrifice. It is by this faith only, that we discern in the holy Supper, the Lord's body. Without this faith our souls can no more be benefited by the body and blood of Christ, than without the use of the proper corporeal organs, our bodies can be, by bread and wine. The mere eating of the latter in the sanctuary, even if it be accompanied with prayer and some devout aspirations, can have but little significance or efficacy. Without respect to the offices of Christ and confidence in the divine mercy, through the merits of his death and passion, it will be little more than an unmeaning and useless ceremony. It is using it merely as a religious ceremony, that deprives many of the recipients of it of its sanctifying influences. "Let a man examine himself," then, "whether he be in the faith." Let him know and embrace the Lord Jesus, as "the author of eternal salvation to all them that obey him." Let him look to the cross as the instrument of his redemption, and to the Lamb expiring upon it, as the propitiation for his sins. Let him see in the sacramental bread, the body of his Redeemer broken for the offences of man, and in the sacramental wine, the blood of the Redeemer shed for his salvation. Let him be able, as he takes these elements, to say, Through him whom these represent I am pardoned and accepted; "and so let him eat of that bread and drink of that cup;" that thus he may join in this supper with that faith, without which it is impossible to please God. For whosoever cometh unto him in this ordinance, and would be benefited thereby, "must believe that he is" in it, "and that he is the rewarder of all those who diligently seek him" therein.

It is unavoidable to remark here, in the fourth place, that we should bring to the celebration of the Lord's Supper, hearts overflowing with gratitude to him, for his wonderful love. This sacrament is the commemoration of the most stupendous act of benevolence, and to us, the most beneficial act, which in this part of the universe is known; the death of the Son of God upon the cross, for the redemption of our sinful race. "Let a man examine himself," whether he hath appreciated justly, and with sufficient thankfulness, this death of his Lord? Let him impress upon his bosom the glory and happiness which his Redeemer left; the humiliation and misery which he endured; the awful destruction from which he ransomed, and the delightful expectations to which he hath raised the human race. Let him by pondering "the height and depth, and length and breadth," of his merciful purposes, fan into a holy flame, that love which the knowledge of his passion can hardly fail to kindle; "and so let him eat of that bread and drink of that cup," that with such affectionate gratitude as he would feel in fulfilling the wishes of a dying benefactor, he may "do this," which Jesus hath commanded, "in remembrance of him."

Once more. We should be filled with charity when we go to the Lord's Supper. The feast of the eucharist is a feast of love. One design in ordaining it was, to render it to Christians a bond of love. The deeds which it celebrates are deeds of unparalleled love. In the night in which he instituted it, Jesus said to his disciples, "A new commandment I give unto you, that ye love one another; as I have loved you, that ye also love one another." And who can contemplate his patient and infinite love, and not be warmed with the glow of his benevolence! Who can look upon the family for which he was contented to die, and feel ill will towards any of them! Who can stand by his cross, and behold him pouring out his soul unto death, a ransom for many, and not be excited to acts of beneficence and pity! Who can see his patience and forbearance, amidst the indignities of his passion, and hear him, while he offers himself upon the cross a sacrifice for his enemies, uttering a prayer for their pardon, and an apology for the wrongs they had done him; and not have his resentments towards those who have injured him stilled and subdued, and his heart softened to reconciliation and forgiveness! The character of Christ is so entirely benevolent; the events which we celebrate at his Supper, are of a character so consentaneous with the spirit and acts of charity, that he who carries to it any other temper than that of peace and good will, exhibits in himself a monstrous contrast to the qualities which he is professing to admire, and can hardly expect, that the spirit of the Redeemer will love and abide with him. "Let a man," then, "examine himself," whether the same mind be in him which was in Christ Jesus. Let him supplicate Charity to come from her seat by the throne of God, and shed abroad her heavenly influences upon his heart. Let her fill him with a sincere desire and lively regard, for the welfare of his fellow men; let her remove from his bosom all envy, hatred, and malice, and introduce in their stead, peace with all men and good will; let her excite him to generous alms-deeds, for the poor and needy; let her invest him with a part of the golden chain which binds one fellow being to another, and all to God; "and so let him eat of that bread and drink of that cup."

Now, these qualifications form the habit of every sincere Christian's life. They are carried by him into the scenes of his business and walks of his pleasure; they are found with him when he sitteth in the house, and when he walketh by the way; they constitute his character in the days which are given to the world, and in the Lord's day. To him, therefore, no opportunity to show forth his Lord's death need be lost. Like the ancient Christians, he should seize every occasion to eat of the bread which came down from heaven, and sprinkle himself with the blood which cleanseth him from sin.

But you may ask, is it not proper that we should especially prepare ourselves, when we would join in the celebration of this sacred ordinance? I answer, when we are sure that we are to approach the holy table, self-examination, prayer, and whatever may purify and elevate our affections, is both decent and useful. It is to be reckoned amongst the beneficial effects of receiving this sacrament frequently, and at stated times, that the preparatory recollections and devotions, to which it will naturally lead us, are most happily adapted to prevent the inconstancy of our minds to religious principles, and to check the wanderings of our feet from the paths of virtue. And St. Paul, in the text, seems to recommend and require a sober consideration and proving of ourselves, when we are about to join in this great act of Christian worship. But yet the habitual is far preferable to the occasional preparation. The sincere Christian can never be unwelcome at the table of his Lord. For is he not always ready to confess, and desirous to forsake his sins? Does he not always rest upon the merits of the Redeemer, and find gratitude warming his bosom at every remembrance of his love? It is not always his wish, however feeble his power, to be conformed to the will of his Maker, and is not benevolence towards his fellow beings the reigning principle at all times, by which he would regulate his feelings and conduct towards them? Is he not always a subject of his Redeemer's intercession, even when Satan may be desiring to sift him as wheat? Is he not constantly an object of his Redeemer's regard, even when, like Nathaniel, he is seen under the fig-tree, unconscious of the eye that observes him? Let not, then, the true follower of the Lamb, unnecessarily deny himself the refreshment of the holy Supper. If there be not upon his conscience some extraordinary impediment, let him be by the table of his Lord, whenever he beholds it spread. But let not this diminish the awe with which that table is guarded.

SERMON XI.

ON THE LORD'S SUPPER.

St. Luke, xiv. 18.

"They all with one consent began to make excuse."

IN discoursing upon the sacrament of the Lord's Supper, we have already attended to the considerations which should induce us to partake of it, and the qualifications with which it should be received. The former, we have seen, are very numerous and weighty, and the latter, attainable by all Christians, and such as they should possess, whether they partake of this sacrament or not. Whence, then, is it, that by so many Christians this ordinance is neglected? Whence is it, that before so many of his followers, the table of the Lord is spread in vain? This is the inquiry which we come now to consider; and with our remarks upon which we shall close our discourses upon the sacraments of Christianity.

The causes which prevent men from observing this ordinance of our religion are various. We shall speak only of those which are the most obvious, and in speaking of these, shall claim your indulgence for that plainness of speech which, in the discussion of such topics, is both necessary and useful.

It may be presumed, that a leading cause of the neglect of this ordinance, is a thoughtlessness of its nature and obligatoriness. There are many persons who have never seriously considered it as the great and proper act of Christian worship; as an ordinance which, by their baptismal vows, they are solemnly pledged to observe and keep; as a sacrament instituted for the whole body of the Church, of which no member of the same can neglect to partake without great detriment to his spiritual life. They have never said to themselves, This ordinance was appointed not for a few, but for all the followers of Christ. They have never asked themselves, How shall I live if I keep not up a communion with the source of life? What shall I reply, when he who shall judge the world shall say to me, Wherefore hast thou neglected to perform the services which I commanded to be done "in remembrance of me?" And yet, this inconsideration, though it may explain, can never excuse the neglect of this sacred duty. Can we innocently be thoughtless of the obligation of an ordinance, about which, for our benefit, the Redeemer of the world employed his care when the agonies of crucifixion were pressing towards him? This very thoughtlessness is surely a great crime when God and his ordinances solicit attention. It is the requirement of reason, as well as the precept of inspiration, "Be ye not unwise, but understanding what the will of the Lord is."

Again. The pressure of the business and cares of this world, is urged by many as a reason why they neglect to receive this sacrament. The avocations of life are so numerous and indispensable; their time is so taken up, and their minds so occupied with them, that they are not able to give that attention to this duty which it deserves, and they hope the Almighty will pardon their omissions. Now, does not this plea evidently imply that the requirements of the world are to be satisfied before the requirements of God; that the affairs of this life are more important than the things which belong to our eternal peace! But what is there in the cares and toils, or in the pursuits and pleasures of this transitory state to entitle them to this pre-eminence? What claim have they to monopolize our time and absorb our attention? Are they most properly our business here? No. We are destined for an immortal existence in another world, and are placed here to be trained up for it. Are they sources of greater and more substantial happiness? No.

Tell us, ye busy men, ye votaries of wealth, ye slaves of fashion, are the happiness and pleasure ye pursue either sure or satisfactory? Are they most noble in their nature and worthy of our first regard? No. They, in general, affect the inferior part and properties of man, and are perishable as the bodies they concern. Are they, in their influence or their advocates, furnished with pretensions of a more alluring character? No. The scenes of the one are time, of the other eternity; the advocate of the former is man; of the latter, God. So that if there be any incompatibility between the business of religion and the business of life, the former has the first claim to our attention; to use the latter in apology for neglecting the former, exposes us to the charge both of imprudence and impiety.

But it is apprehended, that there is nothing incompatible between the requirements of the gospel and an attention to all our lawful secular concerns. Is a man unable "to do justly, to love mercy, and to walk humbly with his God," because he has much business? Is a man unable to be industrious, to control his passions, to have trust and resignation towards his Maker, because he has many avocations? Is a man unable to rejoice in the knowledge of a Redeemer, whose blood may cleanse him from his sins, and whose intercessions may propitiate the Almighty in his behalf, because he has many cares? And concerning the appropriate duties of public and private worship, is there any man who, by a methodical arrangement of his matters, may not find time for these? Man is by nature social, and his situation in this world renders it necessary and proper that he should be occupied with many temporal concerns. Christianity is a religion adapted to him in that nature and condition in which it finds him. It is a religion for men of business as well as for men of leisure. It is a religion for the world as well as for the closet. Its ordinances are not something to which he who embraces it must betake himself, and abandon every thing else. They are rather provided to protect him in his necessary pursuits, and to encourage him in sustaining his temporal cares. And he who is just and benevolent in all his temporal transactions, who from a principle of obedience is faithful in discharging the duties of the relations into which his connection with the world has brought him, does thereby honour his Creator, as well as when he brings to him his prayers and praises. Is thy business criminal? Thou mayest well abstain from the altar of God. He who is engaged in the pursuit of a forbidden object, or pursues in a forbidden manner an object which is lawful, is in a state of awful liability to divine vengeance, whether he goes to the sacrament or not. But are your occupations, Christians, lawful? In your business, are you true and just, meek, compassionate, and beneficent? Throughout the paths into which your avocations lead you, are your steps regulated by the laws of God? Let not the multiplicity of your concerns, nor the greatness of your cares, keep you from the ordinances of the Church. Come rather the more willingly to the green pastures which in the holy eucharist are set open to you, that from the hurry and turmoils of the world you may there, at intervals, rest and be refreshed. Come the more gladly to the still waters by which the Redeemer, in this sacrament, would lead you, that you may be cooled from the heat with which intensity of earthly business may oppress you, that you may be cleansed often from the defilements which the best men may contract in the midst of this miserable world; yea, that you may be invigorated to pursue your temporal concerns in future with the firm step of undeviating integrity, amidst the numerous temptations by which you are surrounded, and the infirmities of nature which you carry within you.

Further. A sense of sinfulness deters many from approaching the table of the Lord. They are so oppressed with the consciousness of having transgressed many commands and omitted many duties, that they dare not go to so holy an ordinance. Such persons surely have not rightly pondered that "faithful saying," which St. Paul says, is "worthy of all men to be received, that Christ Jesus came into the world to save sinners." For sinners he became incarnate. For sinners he died. And for the benefit of sinners he instituted this holy sacrament.

Not for the whole who need no physician; not for the righteous, who need no repentance; but for the penitent offenders, over whom "there is joy in the presence of the angels of God," was this table of his compassion spread. Indeed, if none but sinless beings should go to that Supper from the family of man, no guest could be invited. If we would wait till we have put off all our imperfections, we must wait till we have put off our flesh. We do not go thither "trusting in our own righteousness;" and they go most worthily who feel that they "are unworthy to gather up the crumbs under the Lord's table." It is not the sinner who is excluded therefrom, but the obdurate and impenitent sinner. "If with true penitent hearts and lively faith, we receive that holy sacrament," "though our sins be as scarlet, they shall be as wool, though they be red like crimson, they shall be as snow." But, perhaps, you say, I have not this faith and repentance. Ah! is it so? Stay yet awhile from that holy table. Nevertheless, be not easy in your absence from it. Think not, because you abstain from this ordinance you shall be safer in your sins. Preposterous were the supposition, and in the highest degree dangerous and impious, that the neglect of one duty can diminish our accountability for other deficiencies. The truth is, without repentance and faith no man is in a state of safety. It is not the only consequence of the want of these that we cannot go acceptably to the Lord's Supper. Without them there can be no peace in life, no hope in death, no entrance into heaven.

There are many persons who have a lively sense of the holiness of this ordinance, and wish to join in the celebration of it, who are deterred by a fear that they shall not be able afterwards to live up to their obligations. Estimable in the sight of God is this diffidence of their own strength. When it is accompanied by an earnest desire to perform the duties for which they fear their insufficiency, it is one of the essential requisites to a worthy participation of this sacrament. But it may be carried too far. It may lead us to think our merciful Lord a hard man, and with wicked timidity, to wrap the talent with which he hath entrusted us, in a napkin. Let it be remembered that this ordinance devolves upon us no duties which, with the aid of that grace which it promises us, we are not able to perform. Under the same obligations we are already brought by our baptismal covenant; the same faith is professed by us in our creed, and a consciousness of the same duties, and a promise to perform them, is unquestionably implied in our prayers and our praises. Him who desires sincerely to please his God, this ordinance is calculated to encourage and strengthen, to protect and bless in the fulfilment of his obligations. And, diffident Christian, dost thou tremble, lest, going to his table, thou shouldst incur obligations which thy infirmities may not permit thee to discharge? Remember the power and faithfulness of thy Maker. What is the consolation which accompanies the elements of this Supper? "My grace is sufficient for thee." What are the truths which these holy symbols seal to thy soul? "He is merciful to them that fear him"—"He will ever be mindful of his covenant"—"His strength is made perfect in weakness."

Another cause which prevents men from receiving this sacrament, is the existence of anger and animosity in their bosoms; the consciousness of ill will between them and some of their fellow beings. Without charity we cannot, indeed, go safely to the table of the Lord. And without charity we cannot safely live in the world. We may not sit down quietly when this important Christian grace has departed from our bosoms, and trust that no ill consequences will result from her absence because we do not go to the Lord's table. She is the grace, without which man can have no continued unction from on high; no spiritual life and hope; no progress in the holiness; no joy and peace in lifting his eye to another world. If she be absent from his heart he will not receive the visitations of the Holy Spirit; for into a malicious soul he will not enter. If she be absent, he can know nothing of the pleasures of the new life; "for he that hateth his brother abideth in death." If she be absent, his praises and adorations to his Maker are unacceptable; for he that "loveth not his brother whom he hath seen, how can he love God whom he hath not seen." If she be absent, he shall in vain expect the pardon of his sins; for "if ye forgive not men their trespasses, neither shall your heavenly Father forgive you." If she be absent, he shall be destitute in the eternal world of the chief grace, which shall then be of utility; for faith will there be swallowed up in vision; and hope will be lost in the final decision. Charity only shall remain to guide the thoughts and regulate the conduct, and bless the joy of the redeemed; and by the lovely character which she will shed over them, causing the Almighty Father to smile complacently upon his offspring, and all heaven shall be glad as he smiles. Not a moment, then, should we allow ourselves to be destitute of this grace; much less, when we should together be gathered around the table of our Lord. What saith the Scripture? "If thou bring thy gift to the altar, and there rememberest that thy brother hath aught against thee, leave there thy gift before the altar, and go thy way; first be reconciled to thy brother; and then come and offer thy gift." Observe, you are not permitted to come to the altar of God with the knowledge of enmity between yourselves and your brethren; nor yet are you permitted to stay away. Reconciliation is enjoined. "Be reconciled to thy brother, and come and offer thy gift." But it may be you have conquered the enmity in your own bosom, but your adversary is implacable. In this case, what conduct ought the Christian to pursue? If, with our utmost endeavours, we have sought peace with all men, but have failed on account of the implacability of others, we are not, while we have only emotions of benevolence in our bosom, to debar ourselves from the comfort and privilege of discharging our duty to God. With them is the sin. To the table of the Lord we should go, that we may learn to perfect and perpetuate our forgiveness, and there, with godly sincerity, should pray for our enemies, that God would "give them repentance and a better mind."

It is urged by some who neglect this ordinance, that they see many go the Lord's table, who seem not, in any respect, to be benefited by it. Their dispositions are not more heavenly, nor their lives more virtuous than others. There is some foundation for this remark. It is an afflicting, a humbling consideration; and should teach the disciples of the Lord, who mind to come to the communion of his body and blood, to exercise a holy and vigilant circumspection, that others may not be deterred by their deficiencies from glorifying their "Father who is in heaven." But, at the same time, all men should be careful how they judge their fellow-beings. Perhaps the communicant laments with secret sorrow, at the foot of that table, the imperfections by which thou art offended. It may be, the strength shall one day be there obtained, by which those imperfections shall be vanquished.

There are many persons deterred from receiving this sacrament by a particular passage of Scripture, which is frequently misunderstood. I mean that striking observation by St. Paul, that "he who eateth and drinketh unworthily, eateth and drinketh damnation to himself, not discerning the Lord's body." There are two causes from which the misapplication of this passage proceeds; from affixing a meaning to the word damnation, which, in the original, it does not bear; and from indefinite or erroneous ideas of the unworthiness which the Apostle condemns. By damnation, is not here meant, as by many is supposed, everlasting destruction, but immediate disapprobation, the displeasure of the Most High; which displeasure is manifested, as the Apostle states, by visiting the unworthy recipients with divers temporal judgments; and this too, in order to their final salvation; if haply, being chastened of the Lord, they may not be condemned with the world. And, accordingly, the same word which is here rendered damnation, is rendered in one of the following verses of the same chapter, by condemnation. Moreover, we should have definite ideas what it is to eat and drink unworthily. The Corinthians, whom the Apostle here addresses, had fallen into an irreverent, and, in some cases, profane manner of celebrating the Lord's Supper. They brought their own bread and wine; they blended this sacred mystery with their common feast; the rich waited not for the poor; the poor were jealous of the rich; there was division in their bosoms, and confusion in their conduct. In the elements before them, the Lord's body was not discerned. Against this irreverence, the Apostle, with great propriety, pointed his sharpest reprehension. But his solemn sentence will not light upon those, who, with the qualifications which have been stated, are careful to receive this sacrament. Let a man, with a willing mind, go to the Lord's Supper, carrying to it repentance, faith, and charity, a thankful remembrance of the Redeemer's love, and a steadfast resolution to walk in newness of life; and he will be owned, by the master of the feast, as a welcome guest, and share in the peculiar benediction which blesses that Supper.

Finally. There is an objection which deters a large number of those, who have, by baptism, been grafted into the body of Christ's Church from discharging this most incumbent Christian duty; I mean, that they are too young. There is not, I conceive, an objection which would be more painful to our blessed Redeemer. The young are most endangered by the temptations and troubles of this evil world. They have most need of the ægis which he hath provided for the redeemed, in the sacraments of his Church. He himself dwelt not in the flesh to the period at which man arrives at the meridian of life; to teach us, perhaps, in our earliest years, with our earliest faculties, to do the will of him who sent us. In early piety, his Father had many times manifested his special delight, and he himself evidenced on earth, a partiality for the devotion of the youthful heart. The wise Solomon, the distinguished David, the good Josiah; and Samuel, who, at the close of his life, could challenge an impeachment of his integrity, all knew the Almighty in their youth; and of the disciples of our blessed Lord, he obtained most of his love who had seen the fewest years. Yes, happy John! "the disciple whom Jesus loved;" thou didst follow him in juvenile years; and it is among the recollections which now gladden thy spirit, that thou didst early devote thyself to the peaceful pursuits of his kingdom, that thou leanedst, in thy youth, on his bosom, at the first celebration of the holy Supper. My young friends, follow his example. Let not your youth deter you from manifesting your gratitude to the Being to whom you owe all the years of your existence. You most need in this dangerous world the protection of his wing. By an observance of his ordinances, place yourselves under it, and you shall not fail of his care who hath said: "I love them that love me, and they who seek me early shall find me."

Thus, my respected hearers, I have endeavoured to remove the obstacles which prevent so large a part of the Christian community from discharging what, in the right and ancient view of it, is the highest and most distinguishing Christian duty. Forgive me, that I have dwelt so long upon this subject. The late eminently pious and truly reverend Bishop of London considered the signs of the times as affording him a special reason for calling upon the Christians of his diocese, to return to the ancient practice of offering their devotions in the temple, humbly upon their knees. How much rather, then, may we call upon you, by the motives which have been suggested, by the judgments of the Almighty which are abroad in the world, and by the disparity in attainments of holiness between the Church in the primitive, and our own days, to gather yourselves together around that altar where your devotions may be offered most acceptably, and the best pledges of benediction are to be found. What Christian is now hearing me, who, if the trumpet which shall give notice of the second advent of our Lord should burst upon his ears, would not gladly be found at his holy table, with humility and gratitude commemorating his love? But oh! if he shall not find us there, let none of the obstacles which have been considered, prevent us from being of the number, concerning whom he shall say, in the day of judgment, presenting them unto the Ancient of Days, These are they who on earth were faithful. They have eaten of my bread "in remembrance of me," and have drank of the cup which I mingled. Father, I will that they forever be with me where I am, that they may behold my glory, and drink of the wine of which I desire to drink with them in thy eternal kingdom.

SERMON XII.

ON THE SABBATH.

EXODUS, xx. 8.

"Remember the Sabbath day, to keep it holy."

THAT God is to be worshipped, is a sentiment of nature, a dictate of reason, and a declaration of the written law. This point being established, there follows a necessity that there should be established times for discharging the duties of devotion. As regularity in transacting business of any kind is ultimately beneficial, so, in this particular, unless there be stated periods for paying our devotions to the Most High, inattention will produce indifference, indifference will form a habit of forgetfulness or neglect; and thus, in the noblest employment of a rational being, the mind would but seldom and accidentally engage. When we further consider, that there are favours which we unitedly need, and consequently, for which we ought unitedly to petition; that there are sins which we join in committing, and, consequently, ought to join in imploring remission of the same; that there are blessings which we enjoy in common, and, consequently, for which we ought to return a common tribute of praise; in a word, when we consider, that, social in everything else, man ought to be social in the worship of his God, we cannot but be convinced of the necessity that some definite part of time should be appropriated to the service of religion. Now, were it left for men to determine among themselves, how great, and what particular part of time should be thus consecrated, it would be rare indeed, if, differing in sentiment upon almost every other subject, they should be united upon this. The supposition is inadmissible. We can conjecture ten thousand circumstances which would inevitably operate against this unanimity. But, blessed be God, in this respect he has not left mankind a prey to uncertainty and discord. He himself has determined what portion of their existence his intelligent creatures shall dedicate to him. "Remember," says he, when promulgating his sacred laws, "remember the Sabbath day, to keep it holy." Permit me, beloved, to bespeak your attention, while I endeavour to state to you, in the first place, the nature of this day, and the reasons for remembering it; and, secondly, the suitable and reasonable methods of keeping it holy.

We learn from the history of the creation, that Deity employed himself six days in forming the heavens and the earth, and all the host of them. It could not have been necessary, that he should be occupied for this, or any other particular space of time, in effecting the purposes of his will. He, whose simple fiat could call light into existence, could, with equal ease, have said, "Let creation be," and instantly the universe would have appeared. But for some certainly wise and good end, perhaps, for our instruction, he chose to employ himself six days in creating our world. "The seventh day," says the sacred historian, "God blessed and sanctified, because that in it he had rested from all his work which God had created." Not that he was fatigued by the exertions which he had made, or exhausted by the greatness of the work which he had accomplished. Far otherwise. The Lord, the Creator of the ends of the earth, "fainteth not, neither is weary." When it is said, that God rested on the seventh day, the expression means, that he then ceased from that particular employment in which he had been engaged. And when he sanctified this day, he determined that every periodical return of it should be duly observed by his intelligent creatures, for commemorating the nativity of creation, when "the morning stars sang together, and the sons of God shouted for joy;" and for impressing upon their minds a remembrance, that he, to whom they dedicate the day, was the Author, and is the Preserver and Governor of the universe; of whom, and through whom, and to whom, are all things. Such was the origin of the Sabbath day; and there is a probability, that the observance of it commenced and continued, from the time when the reason first existed for which it was blessed and sanctified. It is true, that we have no account of the actual observance of the day, before the time of Moses. Many have inferred from this, that the notice of the day is to be dated from the solemn appointment of it by Moses. But if the Sabbath had been kept from the creation, as a matter of course, it is a circumstance which we should not expect to find mentioned in a history so concise, when the author himself must have viewed the thing as common as the resting at night, after the labours of the day. Now, we have no account from which we can possibly infer the neglect of the day; and it is observable, that the first observance of it, noticed by the historian, was previous to the promulgation of the law from Sinai. When the children of Israel were miraculously fed with manna, they had not arrived at the holy mount, but were in the desert of Sin. *This* was their eighth encampment; *that* was their twelfth. In order to refrain from labour on the seventh day, they than gathered on the sixth two omers of manna, which was twice the quantity of one day's consumption. When Moses assigns the reason for this, he mentions the Sabbath, not as any thing new, but as something to which they had been accustomed; "To-morrow is *the* rest of the holy Sabbath unto the Lord." It may further be remarked, that, notwithstanding the commandment in the text, and other arrangements in the Jewish law, for the service of the day, there is no particular mention of the observance of it for several years after Moses. But it is argued, if men had remembered the Sabbath day from the creation, why was it so formally ordained at the promulgation from Sinai? Now, would it not be equally as rational to argue, that it was not esteemed unlawful to dishonour parents, to commit adultery, to murder, to steal, to bear false witness, etc., previous to the Decalogue, because that, in that communication of the divine will, these crimes are formally forbidden? The truth of the matter undoubtedly is, that when Deity had sanctified the Sabbath, he informed man thereof; and, from Adam to Moses, those were not wanting who paid attention and reverence to the holy day. As men became more and more corrupt, the obligation to this, as well as all other moral obligations, were held less and less sacred. To revive their ideas of duty, and preserve among mankind a knowledge of his will, Deity, in his own time, benignantly vouchsafed to his people a written law. In this law, the religious and constant observance of the Sabbath was solemnly enjoined, and two additional motives thereto urged upon the Jews. "Remember that thou wast a servant in the land of Egypt, and that the Lord thy God brought thee out thence," therefore he "commanded thee to keep the Sabbath day." And likewise, "that thine ox and thine ass may rest, and the son of thine handmaid, and the stranger may be refreshed." Thus was the Sabbath established, and continued a day of rest, from the first pair of our race, to Jesus, the Emmanuel. At his birth, a new scene opened, a new era commenced. Then was the mystery, hidden from ages, revealed, and the whole counsel of God manifested. His religion was not to be the religion of a nation, but the religion of man. He came not, to deliver a single people from foreign servitude; but to rescue a world from tyrants, more merciless than Pharaoh and his officers; and from a slavery harder and more menial than the bondage of Egypt. Surely, if the Israelites were obligated to observe a Sabbath, in honor of him who broke the power which held them slaves, and gave them deliverance, Christians are bound to appropriate part of their time, as sacred, to the goodness which freed them, spontaneously, from the shackles of sin, and opened the prisons where death had confined them. But this is not all. The redemption effected by Jesus is styled in Scripture a new creation. And justly, my friends, may it thus be styled. Chaos itself did not exhibit more confusion, before the Creator converted it to order and beauty, than did the state of fallen man, before the Redeemer presented a spiritual system, far more wonderful, harmonious, and sublime, than that which we admire in the material world. As at the first creation, "the morning stars sang together, and the sons of God shouted for joy," so, at the second, the heavenly hosts exulted with reverence, and the inhabitants of the earth were bidden to rejoice. As it had been proper, that man should reflect upon the former glorious event, at every revolution of the period in which it was completed, so it was proper that that part of the week should be esteemed holy, on which, by rising from the dead, Jesus completed the latter. When the design of a Sabbath was thoroughly understood, the observance of any one day in seven, would perpetuate the memory of the first creation; and, by choosing that day on which Christ triumphed over death, we commemorate the greatest deliverance ever experienced by men, and secure the hebdomadal remembrance of the new creation. If it be asked, why the old Sabbath may not be preserved, and a new one appointed for the new creation? I answer, that the institution which commands men to appropriate a seventh part of their time to religion and rest, commands, also, that during the other six parts, they should manage faithfully their secular concerns. If it again be questioned, why the day first instituted should not be preferred? I answer, because the latter event is more wonderful, more interesting, and more glorious. In confirmation of this we find, that on the first day of the week, the disciples of our Lord rested; and assembled for religious worship and instruction. St. Paul, in many passages, proves, and declares, that we are not bound to observe the Jewish Sabbath, and the first day of the week is expressly styled in the revelation from God, "the Lord's day." Accordingly, the Christian Church, from the first moment of its existence, has consecrated this day, as holy to God and religion; and commands her sons to remember it, as the *Christian Sabbath.*

There is something of an awful holiness, of a solemn dignity, surrounding the Sabbath, when we consider the consecration of it as coeval with the existence of our race. How venerable its antiquity! How sublime the ends for which it was instituted! With what horror does the sensible mind recoil at the recollection of those, who would demolish, with worse than Vandal arms, this first and most gracious institution of God. My brethren, I must defer till another opportunity, to lay before you the distinct and most powerful motives which should induce you to remember, invariably, this holy day. But from the account which has been given of its nature and history, you may gather reasons, sufficiently engaging to fill you with a resolution, that you and your houses shall reverence the Sabbath of the Lord your God.

SERMON XIII.

ON THE SABBATH.

Exodus, xx. 8.

"Remember the Sabbath day, to keep it holy."

THESE words, many of you, my hearers, may recollect, were the subject of our meditation in the forenoon of the last Lord's day. When entering upon the discourse, I proposed to give you, in the first place, a history of the Sabbath. Secondly, the motives for remembering a Sabbath day; and thirdly, the most suitable methods of keeping it holy. To the first of these heads we paid full attention, and proved that the Sabbath began to be sacred at the time when the reason for consecrating it first existed; viz: when the Creator rested from his work, in which he had been engaged during the first six days from the beginning of the creation. We observed, that when mankind were grossly corrupted and alienated from all truth, Deity vouchsafed to his peculiar people a written declaration of his will, and enjoined upon them in one of his commands, the religious observance of this day. That the seventh day was dedicated to the Lord, from Moses to Christ, when man and all his concerns assumed another aspect. That a new creation was now to be commemorated; a new deliverance to be celebrated by man. That to unite a remembrance of the former with the latter event, the Church of Christ solemnized the day when the Lord completed his purposes of love; and has constantly observed the first day of the week, as the Christian Sabbath.

I now proceed to the second head of discourse, in which are to be shown the motives for observing a Sabbath. The first and most weighty of all motives is, that it is of divine appointment. It is not a human institution. It is not a mere matter of convenience. It is not left optional with us whether we will observe it or not. It is a positive command of that Lawgiver who rules supreme, and before whose judgment seat we all must stand. That the Most High had a right to frame such a law, no one will dare to question. That he did frame such a law, no one who has faithfully examined into the matter will presume to deny. That we are bound to live in obedience to his injunctions, no one who realizes the dependence of man and the supremacy of his Maker, can hesitate one moment to acknowledge. Now, however lightly we may think of it, every profanation, every wilful neglect of this holy day, is as likely to subject us to the punishment of transgressors as any other breach of God's sacred laws. We are as strongly bound to remember the Sabbath, as we are to refrain from stealing, murdering, bearing false witness, or breaking any of the commands of the Decalogue. It is expressly enjoined, "Remember that thou keep holy the Sabbath day;" and whoever by his conduct, his conversation, or even his careless indifference, forgets this day, implicitly revolts against the authority of his God. Every Christian, therefore, who feels that concern for the honour of his Maker which he ought to feel, must have his indignation excited, when he beholds this very day, sacred from the infancy of our species, and hallowed by the Sovereign of the universe, assailed and polluted by unthinking men; and treated with less reverence than savages would discover for religious institutions. If not its venerable antiquity, if not its usefulness to mankind, certainly the idea that it was instituted by the Creator, should restrain the arm of the sacrilegious assailant, and secure it respect from his dependent creature.

Again. But if the Sabbath were not a divine appointment, if it were only an institution devised and established by men for the maintenance of true religion, in this sense it would be entitled to our attention and reverence. So averse is corrupted nature from all religious sentiments, so alienated from a knowledge and love of God and of duty, that it is necessary to contrive expedients for enticing their minds to a contemplation of these things, and for impressing them with a sense of their solemnity and importance. By an observance of the Sabbath, a common respect is paid to religion; men are made acquainted with her character and loveliness; the mind, six days busied about secular concerns, is led to think upon nobler objects. That atheism which would be the consequence of no worship, and that superstition which would be the consequence of a worship always private are prevented; and a secure barrier is opposed to that general indifference to God and religion, which might possibly ensue if there were no fixed period at which man should pause from his worldly pursuits, and turn his attention to the one thing needful.

Every person who observes the ignorance and situation of man, must perceive the necessity of providing some means for communicating to him that religious instruction, without which he can give little significance to his life, and find but little hope in his death.

Ah, my friends, it is with this as with many others of the blessings we possess, we lose our sense of the value in the constancy of our enjoyment of it.

It is no extravagant assertion, that from this holy institution have accrued to man more knowledge of his God, more instruction in righteousness, more guidance of his affections, and more consolation of his spirit, than from all other means which have been devised in the world to make him wise and virtuous. We cannot fully estimate the effects of the Sabbath upon religion, unless we were once deprived of it. Imagination cannot picture the depravity which would gradually ensue, if time were thrown into one promiscuous field, without these *heaven-erected beacons*, to rest and direct the passing pilgrim. Man would then plod through a wilderness of being, and one of the main avenues which now admits the light that will illumine his path, would be perpetually closed. Considered, therefore, in this sense, the preservation of the Sabbath is of infinite importance.

But further, inadmissible as is the supposition, if the Sabbath were only a civil institution, if it could boast no higher authority than that of earthly powers, if the design in appropriating it to rest, worship, or instruction were altogether political, every friend to order, every friend to his country, every friend to mankind, must advocate its preservation and observance. The arm of secular power could never be strong, if the minds of men were wholly destitute of ideas of a God and a future state. As these ideas, and their consequent moral principles are more or less lively in the minds of a people, civil government will be more or less efficacious. Now, to have a day for publicly inculcating these ideas periodically observed, and revolving so frequently that the effects of the last are not erased from the mind before the return of the next, and, at the same time, leaving a sufficient interim for the discharge of the avocations, and the enjoyment of the pleasures of life, would be as advantageous an expedient as reason could devise. Besides, the effects of a Sabbath upon society are great, not merely in a civil but in a social sense. Members of the same community, on this day, meet to pay their addresses to their common Father and Friend. They see each other in a light highly engaging, and calculated to excite none but sentiments of affection. A variety of pursuits does not to-day distract their attention nor excite their jealousies, but they assemble, united in their intentions, prepared to join in the amiable acts of social worship. The royal Psalmist mentions it as one of the most pleasing circumstances which bound him to his friend, that they went up together to the house of the Lord. There is something in beholding people of all classes, dressed neat and clean, exhibiting a decorum becoming the rational character, going together into the sanctuary, like children into the presence of a parent, which, in a mind susceptible of delicate associations, excites indiscribable emotions of delight. The effects of the Sabbath upon individuals are still more important. The rich man finds in it a respite from his round of pleasures and pursuits, and an opportunity to collect his thoughts. The poor man finds in it a respite from those labours which are necessary to his subsistence, and, in our country, generally, enjoys on a Sunday a comfortable meal. The servant is happy in his Sunday attire, and in a relief from his weekly task; and even the *little ones*, forgetting their sports, take a pleasure in going to church. It relieves all descriptions of men from the cares of the week that is past, and invigorates them for the duties of that upon which they have entered. It forms habits of order in the mind, and introduces regularity into families. So much is this the case, that observation will generally sanction the assertion, that he who is punctual in his observance of the Sabbath, is generally regular in the management of all his concerns. Certain it is, that those families are the most regular in the arrangements, have the best domestics, and are most entitled to favour from heaven, in which a regard to sacred institutions is always paid, and an attachment to moral propriety steadily evinced. Such are the families which Deity delights to bless, for they resemble the households of the Patriarchs whom his soul loved. In a word, if the Sabbath were merely a civil institution, so beneficial are its influences upon all classes of men, that he can be no philanthropist who wishes its subversion; nay, who does not contribute to its support.

Again. Art thou emulous of the character of the grateful? Thou wilt "remember the Sabbath day." For gratitude pleads strongly for the observance of this institution. We find ourselves in this world, placed in a magnificent dwelling, furnished with innumerable varieties of good, all submitted to our use. Should we not, at times, turn our attention to the beneficent Architect who raised the stupendous building and placed us in it? We find deposited here for us a deed and title of eternal life, to be inherited by us when we shall have received the education for which we dwell in this building. Should we not, at times, turn our attention to the great Benefactor, through whose mediation this precious deed hath been obtained? To an ingenuous mind, there is something awful in the thought of living in a splendid abode, surrounded by comforts, and invested with privileges and honours without thinking of the Being to whom the abode belongs, and from whose munificence the comforts and privileges proceed. The consecration of a day to the remembrance of him must be pleasant as well as useful to the grateful heart. Base are our spirits, if, of this day, the vain idols of the world can deprive him! His goodness in vouchsafing to hallow this day, that of our highest relations and best privileges we may not be ignorant or unmindful, leaves our gratitude without a plea for its imbecility if the day pass with us as with those benighted mortals who know not that it is the Sabbath of God. For, Great Creator, when I contemplate thee, hallowing a stated time to bring back the recollection of thy children from the vanities of the world to thee, and their duty, and their eternal destiny, I behold an affecting manifestation of thy Fatherly care, which leaves them without excuse, yea, heinously criminal, if they neglect the gracious institution! How tender, how irresistible is the motive with which the Redeemer enforces the observance of his Supper: "Do this in remembrance of me." But in hallowing the Sabbath, what saith the Eternal God, the Author of all that we are and enjoy, but Observe this day in remembrance of me. Which, then, of his children can be willing to pollute it?

Thus, I have stated motives sufficiently powerful, to induce every good man to advocate the remembrance of the Sabbath day. I have entered thus largely upon this point, because it is an unhappy symptom of modern times, that this ark of the covenant, hitherto sacred, has been deserted by its friends and rudely shaken by its enemies. Frequently has it grieved the pious mind, to behold in our own country, but yet in its infancy, so solemn an institution so lightly regarded. The subversion of the Sabbath among Christians, is the subversion of all religion. When once the mind has become so callous to all sense of moral obligation, as to cease to venerate the institutes of heaven, religion is in it but an empty name. If, then, the felicity of our country, if the happiness of posterity can interest our hearts, let us strengthen our respect for this hallowed day.

SERMON XIV.

ON THE SABBATH.

EXODUS, xx. 8.

"Remember the Sabbath day, to keep it holy."

THIS sacred command has already afforded important matter for two discourses, and it again solicits your attention. We have already given a faithful history of the Sabbath, and have stated motives sufficiently powerful to induce every professor of Christianity, every believer in a Supreme Being, every lover of mankind, to hold it in remembrance as consecrated time. An interesting question now arises, how is it to be kept holy? what are the most suitable methods of remembering it? how far may it be used like other days, and in what is it different? The discussion of this point was reserved for that head of discourse upon which we are now about to enter; and which will close our observations upon this too much neglected subject. It is a point in which we are all concerned, and to which few have paid that attention which its consequence deserves. How they ought to spend the Sabbath is a question which men seldom ask. How they do spend it, is a question which the good man generally must answer with grief. For most men, alas! have run to an extreme, conceiving it necessary on this day to hang down their heads like bulrushes and to be masked in the austerity of monks; or else, converting it into a day for indulging themselves in indolence, pleasure, or dissipation. How, then, can your time be better employed than in listening to a statement of those methods of hallowing the Sabbath which are accommodated to human nature, conformable with the design of the institution, and coincident with the will of the Most High.

In the first place, the Sabbath is to be strictly observed as a day of rest. The avocations of life are to be suspended; we are to pause from our secular pursuits, to do no manner of work. No tonly we, but "our sons and our daughters, our man-servants and our maid-servants, our cattle, and the stranger who is within our gates," are peremptorily forbidden to labour on this holy day. By resting, we symbolically commemorate the rest of Deity, when he had completed creation, and that of the Messiah, when he had effected our redemption. By resting, the mind affords religion a hearing which she could not have, if its attention were engaged about worldly concerns. By resting, we advance the cause of humanity, and co-operate with the goodness of our God.

Sacred, my brethren, is the rest of the Sabbath. From its first establishment this was one appointed method of observing it. Jehovah frequently alleges it as a reason of his anger against his people, that they turned their feet from his Sabbath, and did their own pleasure on his holy day. And the good, the indefatigable Nehemiah, when he went up to Jerusalem to recover that city from the damages it had sustained from war's ruthless arm, had his spirit stirred within him, when he beheld some treading their wine-presses, bringing in their sheaves, selling their fish, and all manner of ware upon that day, which their God had consecrated to rest. It wounded the piety of the prophet. His bosom was fired with resentment. "I contended with them," says he, "and said, What evil thing is this which ye do, and profane the Sabbath day? Did not your fathers thus, and did not our God bring all this evil upon us, and upon this city? yet ye bring more wrath upon Israel by profaning the Sabbath." Such was the earnestness of the good man in the cause; and such must be the sentiments of every good man, when he beholds those occupations pursued upon this day, which are inconsistent with its nature and design. Whoever wishes to live in obedience to the command in my text, will not be unnecessarily employed himself, nor suffer those under his care to be unnecessarily employed in any occupation or pursuit, which may disturb that cessation from work, which is essentially necessary to the proper observance of the Sabbath. Here, perhaps, the question will arise in your minds, whether you may engage in no transactions of a temporal nature upon this day? He, to whom the day is dedicated, has declared for our instruction, "that he will have mercy before sacrifice." This being the case, all offices of humanity, all works of charity and love, either to those of our own species, or to the brute creation, may, and ought to be discharged upon this as upon other days. These works are in their very nature virtuous, and no after-arrangement, can render them displeasing in the eyes of heaven.

Further. The Saviour of the world asserted, when upon earth, that "the Sabbath was made for man, and not man for the Sabbath." That it was designed for the comfort of the creature, as well as for the glory of the Creator. Consequently, all those works may be innocently done, which are necessary to our subsistence and decent appearance. He, whose conduct should be our guide in all cases of doubt, never hesitated to do any thing upon the Sabbath which humanity or reasonable need required. A farther license than this we cannot safely take, and, surely, this is sufficiently liberal. It is equally remote from that hypocritical austereness which the Saviour reprimanded in the Jews, and those needless works, that willingness to do anything, indiscriminately, upon the Sabbath which, were he now upon earth, he would too often have occasion to reprimand, even in Christians.

But I hasten to observe, secondly, that though the Sabbath was designed for a day of rest, it was not designed for a day of indolence. There is a vast difference between that pious cessation from secular concerns which the command enjoins, and that lazy, lounging life which too many love to lead when this day arrives. The Sabbath is consecrated to religion as well as to rest, and the duties of public worship are essential parts of its solemnity. Deity never designed that this should be to man a day of idleness, but that the subjects it commemorates should fill his mind with devotion, and lead him to the discharge of religious duties. And how natural is the connection between contemplating the creation of the world by the Supreme Architect, and falling in reverence before his throne. How extremely natural is the connection between recalling to mind the redemption of our race and paying our homage to the great Redeemer. Accordingly, we find that the Sabbath and the sanctuary, on account of their alliance, are frequently joined together in Scripture. Before the birth of our Saviour, this day was always partly employed in publicly reading the Scriptures and worshipping God. When he came upon earth, that he might fulfil all righteousness, it was his invariable custom on the Sabbath to attend divine service in the Synagogue. So that it is evident, from the very nature of the institution, from the authority of custom, and from the unerring example of the Immanuel, that useless laziness on this day is highly criminal, and that assembling for the purposes of public worship, is an essential method of keeping it holy. Our world cannot exhibit a more lovely, heavenly sight, than that of a Christian society in "the still small voice" of devotion, unitedly worshipping their Father and God. When we carry the idea further, and reflect that the whole Church militant, the whole brotherhood of Christians upon earth, on this day assemble, and the Most High is, undoubtedly giving audience to their prayers and praises, can any, who have health and reason, avoid longing to join in the general devotion, or contentedly be absent from the grand community? Yet, alas! there are no less than three classes of character, each of which comprises many individuals, who, at best, are but inconstant in their attendance at the sanctuary. The first class is composed of those persons to whom the Sabbath is no holy day, who view religion and all its ordinances as chimeras, fit for weak minds, who, if they ever go to the sanctuary, are not led thither by an "hunger or a thirst after righteousness," but to try the preacher, to mingle with the multitude, or to pass away an hour or two, in seeing and being seen. Now, such characters exhibit living proofs of the depravity. For we cannot but conceive, that, by beings perfectly pure, the duties of devotion would be esteemed not only useful and pleasant, but in the highest degree honourable. If to be admitted to the presence of an earthly prince, is viewed by his subjects as the highest dignity they can receive, shall man lightly prize an admittance to the presence of his heavenly Prince; an intimate communion with his God? Do the pure spirits of heaven take pleasure in religious acts, and find their delight in worshipping their Maker; and shall mortals view these things as weak, superstitious, unworthy their attention? Blind infatuation! Proof convincing of the truth of man's fall! The fact is, these characters have no sense for the perception of the pleasures of public worship. They have no soil for the seed of the word. The things which they hear in the sanctuary are incompatible with their feelings and their wishes. Like the unhappy pair in Eden, their hearts are not in harmony with the voice of their Maker, and conscious of their nakedness, they shrink from his presence. There is another class of persons, who profess themselves religious, but who seldom join in the services of the sanctuary. These are they who have accustomed themselves to think that the duties of public worship are not essential to a virtuous life; that they can be devout at home, and there engage in pious meditations. Every one who has observed human nature in its various forms, must have observed that these persons are generally of a selfish disposition. They do not possess those feelings which make men love the countenance of man, which can contemplate a body of individuals as one, and which gives a zest to the acts of social worship. Such persons would do well to remember, that there are sins to be confessed, blessings to be acknowledged, and favours to be implored, by society as a body. They should bear in mind that the impotent who would be healed from their diseases, were to wait *at the pool*, till the angel moved the waters. They should consider, that at Zion, the Lord's blessing was to descend; that the foundation of social worship is laid in nature; that it was sanctioned by the practice of the Redeemer, and that it was tacitly inculcated in that promise of the Lord, that where two or three were gathered together in his name, he would be with them and grant their requests. There is a third class of characters, who are perfectly convinced of the importance of public worship, and yet are inconstant in their attendance at the sanctuary. These are they, whom the most trivial excuse of weather, of company, and even of dress, can detain from their duty to their God. That there are constitutions which cannot, and seasons when many persons ought not, expose themselves, every liberal man will readily allow. But are there not characters who can be kept from offering up their devotions to the Most High, in his sacred courts, by such circumstances as would not form the shadow of an obstacle to their visiting an earthly friend, or joining with a party in the pursuit of pleasure. Such persons cannot be said to remember the Sabbath. They do not live in obedience to the sacred command. Whoever would keep the Sabbath, must reverence the sanctuary, and not suffer himself to be needlessly absent from the duties of public worship.

In addition to the methods which have been mentioned, of keeping the day holy, we observe, thirdly, that the affectionate mother will find this an eligible opportunity of teaching to her children, and her children's children, the truths of that religion upon which she rests the anchor of her hopes. The Christian master will, on this day, acquaint his servants with those doctrines and precepts which are calculated to make men live the life becoming man, and to secure their felicity in the future state. The true Christian will, on this day, study the Scriptures; commune with his own heart; and put up his humble petitions in secret, to the prayer-hearing God. He will refrain from all amusements and engagements which do not comport with the solemnity of the holy day. At the same time, he will avoid that severity which makes man a slave to an institution designed for his comfort. After having faithfully discharged those services which are indispensably incumbent, he may spend the leisure moments that remain, with cheerfulness and joy, which the disciples of Jesus ought always to feel. Seated at the fireside, he may partake with his friends the innocent pleasures of social converse; or walking with Isaac, he may meditate in the fields; and join in the emphatic, though silent praise, which nature, through all her works, ascribes to God. Thus he will find the "Sabbath a delight; the holy of the Lord, honourable;" and even in the relaxation which his nature will require, find suitable methods of keeping it holy.

Thus, we have accomplished the plan which was projected when we entered upon this important subject. What now remains, but that each resolve for himself and his house, "to remember the Sabbath day to keep it holy." In so doing, we shall benefit ourselves, our country, and mankind. We shall derive joy from that declaration of the Most High, "Them that honour me, I will honour." And when time, and the divisions of time, shall be lost in eternity, we shall join "the general assembly and Church of the first-born," in celebrating that perpetual Sabbath, in enjoying that endless rest, which remaineth in heaven for the people of God.

SERMON XV.

ON THE SANCTUARY.

LEVITICUS, xxvi. 2.

"Reverence my Sanctuary; I am the Lord."

THE Mosaic dispensation consisted of three general divisions: its moral, its political, and its ceremonial institutes. The two last were adapted to the Jews as a nation, and specially accommodated to their time, circumstances, and necessities. These, at the promulgation of Christianity, were abrogated; for the dispensations of heaven then ceased to be confined to one people, and were extended to the whole human race. But the moral institutes of the Jewish code are, in their nature, unchangeable. Founded on the eternal principles of truth, they must for ever continue right and obligatory upon moral agents. These, Christianity did not abrogate; these, Jesus came not to destroy, but to fulfil. The Decalogue, if it do not express, implies all moral duties; and is a good summary of the virtues which are expected of man, considered as a rational being. Of these, an important one is contained in the words of my text; which, though originally delivered to the Jews, may with equal propriety be addressed to Christians. The duty which it ordains is implied in the fourth command; for it is essential to keeping holy the Sabbath day. Accordingly, in the very verse from which the words are selected, it is joined with the observation of the Lord's day: "Ye shall keep my Sabbaths, and reverence my sanctuary; I am the Lord."

In discoursing from the text, it is proposed to show, first, how the sanctuary is to be reverenced; and, secondly, the foundation and importance of this injunction of the Most High.

The sanctuary is reverenced when proper ideas are entertained of its nature and holiness. For the accommodation of his worshippers and the advancement of his glory, Deity commanded a sanctuary to be erected, that he might dwell among men. He took Moses up to Mount Sinai, and in awful state gave directions concerning the erection of the sacred dwelling. The first idea was that it should be a place where the Divine Presence should be manifested, where Deity should be met by the high priest in behalf of the people. There, by sacrifices and prayers he was to be honoured. There, by Urim and Thummim he was to be consulted in difficult cases. There the Sheckinah rendered the place supremely holy, for in it the Most High was visibly present. Thus sacred in its original was the sanctuary. It was the audience chamber and special residence of the Eternal God. In the gospel, his invisible presence is to be clearly understood; but still the sanctuary is the same in its nature and holiness. In it the people meet and worship their God, and Deity, though invisible, is specially present for the purpose of accepting their services. Though but two or three are together in his name, he has declared that he is there in the midst of them. In order, therefore, to reverence the sanctuary, we must not consider it as a mere place of resort, but view it as dedicated to God, and rendered holy by its appropriation. We must have a most respectful regard for the place, and have none but ideas of veneration towards it, as being the place where the Most High is worshipped, and where he expects to meet the faithful. This appropriate and sacred respect will be showed by not permitting the sanctuary to be dishonoured by any profane use of it; by keeping it in decent repair and cleanliness, and as far as in us lies, in a state of magnificence worthy of the Great Being to whom it is dedicated; and by those outward signs and tokens of reverence by which we can express without an idle superstition our respect for the Being, the dwelling-places of whose honour are the temples devoted to his service. The sanctuary is his house on earth. Our sentiments of it must be those of the pious Patriarch: "Surely, the Lord is in this place, and I knew it not; how dreadful is this place; this is none other than the house of God, and this is the gate of heaven."

After having proper ideas of the nature and holiness of the sanctuary, the next step towards reverencing it is to love to be in it, and to join in its services. When a place is consecrated to the worship of God, when he has promised to be there with a blessing, when he has proffered his word to be there as a fountain set open for sin and uncleanness, and has appointed a priesthood to minister between him and his people, when the priesthood of Christ is there enjoyed after his ordinance, to be wholly absent or but partially present comports little with a reverence for the sanctuary. The man who feels a respect for the house of the Lord will be detained from it by no trivial circumstance. He will be anxious for the honour of its proper offices. To him it will be a subject of anxiety and care, that its oblations should be statedly offered; that its altar should not be without its fire and its priest; that the smoke of its incense should constantly ascend, as is meet, from the habitations which men have devoted to God. He will not content himself with abstracted sentiments of the holiness and beauty of Zion; but will evince his reverence for the sanctuary by being always there when it is opened for devotion, and opportunity will permit. When there, he will find his purest delight in joining in the services of the temple; not with the empty sound of unfelt piety, but with the "still small voice" of devotion, giving utterance to the sincerity of the soul. In reverencing the sanctuary, he will reverence its services, and never think it irksome to be long or often in the temple of God. Did we possess that perfect respect for the Church and its institutions which the text inculcates, we should be always ready to adopt the language of the man after God's own heart, and say, "How amiable are thy tabernacles, O Lord of hosts! My soul longeth, yea, even fainteth, for the courts of the Lord; my heart and my flesh crieth out for the living God.

Yea, the sparrow hath found her an house, and the swallow a nest where she may lay her young, even thine altars, O Lord of hosts, my King and my God. Blessed are they that dwell in thy house; for a day in thy courts is better than a thousand."

Once more. It is essential to a reverence for the sanctuary that we strive not to bring thither our worldly thoughts and improper affections. When we are going to appear before any earthly personage whom we revere, do we not divest ourselves of all improper attire, and array ourselves in the garments of decency and comeliness? Shall we not, then, when we enter the courts of the Lord of the universe, divest ourselves of every improper appendage, and be clothed as becometh dependents, supplicants, and sinners. When about to present ourselves before any earthly dignity, do we not usually reflect where we are going, and free ourselves of all incumbrances which are foreign to our purpose? Ought we not, then, when expecting to present ourselves before the King of kings, prepare our minds for the solemn interview, and leave behind whatever may offend the Divine Majesty and interrupt the business upon which alone we should be intent? Surely, our God is entitled to as much courtesy as any of our fellows, and will not be satisfied with less respect than we pay to them! He expects when we come before him that we bring nothing with us but virtuous hearts, humble spirits, and minds established in the faith. No one who was in any respect unclean was permitted to enter the Jewish temple until he had undergone some established purification. Is it not incumbent, then, upon Christians to prepare themselves for the sanctuary; that they may not willingly carry into the sacred place their worldly cares and concerns, their temporal perplexities and passions? What can be more inconsistent than to profess a reverence for the sanctuary, and at the same time to rush into it thoughtless, without considering that it is the house of the Lord, and carrying in thither the "the lust of the flesh, the lust of the eye, and the pride of life?" Would we be obedient to the injunction in the text, we ought always before we go to the sanctuary, recall to mind the command of the Almighty to Moses: "Put off thy shoes from thy feet, for the place whereon thou standest is holy ground."

This leads me to observe, that in order to discharge the duty enforced in the text, we must be attentive to decorum; when entering the sanctuary, while continuing in it, and when returning from it. A due reverence for the sanctuary will lead the considerate man to be nicely attentive both to the time and the manner of his entrance. It will be done by the Apostle's rule, "decently and in order." He will be fearful lest he should mar the beauty of devotion by abruptness; and will realize how much the solemn scene of social worship is confused, by the movements which those must occasion who enter the temple after "the solemnities have commenced." He will, therefore, aim to be seasonably in the sanctuary; and will rather prefer sitting there awhile before the services are begun, to the unpleasantness of disturbing his brethren by an untimely entrance. While he continues there, he will possess the feelings and exhibit the deportment of the publican in the parable. He will consider that he is in the temple of the Almighty; and keep the object in view for which good men go thither. Awed by a sense of the Divine presence, his thoughts will not wander to the world's end. He will be still. With sober attention he "will hearken unto the voice of his word." With profound solemnity he will make his supplications and offer praise. No whisper of thoughtlessness, no air of folly, no frivolous indecency will render him a proof of the too common, though I fain would hope, unjust observation, that pride, curiosity, and fashion, are most operative in filling the sanctuary. On the contrary, he will be rendered steadily attentive and uniformly devout, by the emphatic declaration with which our church wisely opens her service: "The Lord is in his holy temple, let all the earth keep silence before him." Nothing can justify light or improper behaviour in the house of the Lord. It is shameful in itself; it is insulting to those who are present; it is an effrontery to the Majesty of heaven. A proper reverence for the sanctuary will imprint on the mind the pertinent admonition of Solomon: "Keep thy foot when thou goest to the house of the Lord, and be more ready to hear than to give the sacrifice of fools; for they consider not that they do evil." To the discharge of the duty enjoined in the text, a due decorum should be observed in retiring from the sanctuary. People should observe a distinction, between leaving a theatre and a temple; between retiring from a play and from social worship! There is a fitness of behaviour becoming place, as well as character. Far be it from religion to impose rigid restrictions; to tie up the limbs and every social feeling. She forbids not the sweet interchanges of civility and the amiable smiles of courteousness. But she suggests that when the services are concluded, the sanctuary is still the Lord's, and, consequently, that it is meet to observe a decent respect, so long as we are in it. A society thus uniformly acting in his house, each striving to contribute his part in support of the general reverence for the place, and all exhibiting one scene of devotion, regularity, and religious respect for the invisibly present Deity, must appear delightful to the angelic hosts, if they be conversant with the things of this world; and is doubtless as pleasing an exhibition in the sight of God, as any which he can behold among the children of men.

Having thus shown how the sanctuary is to be reverenced, I proceed to state briefly, the foundation and importance of the duty enjoined in the text.

This is briefly and fully assigned in the words, "I am the Lord." If we consider the nature of the Being to whom the sanctuary belongs, and whom we there meet, this is sufficient to fill us with awe. It is none other than the High and Holy One, who inhabiteth eternity! To be in his presence and not to feel a solemn reverence, to approach him in his house and not be impressed with profound respect, may justly excite his displeasure. It is a privilege that man should have intercourse with the Majesty of heaven; and he must pay the honour due to the holy name. Shall the earth tremble at his presence? Shall mountains quake in his sight? And shall not man be afraid?

Again. The authority of the Lord, as our Sovereign, renders an obedience to his law indispensable. One would think that a command like that in the text would not have been necessary for rational beings. There is something in a place dedicated to religion which seems of itself sufficient to inspire reverence and holy dread. But alas, the thoughtlessness of man lulls him into negligence; and his depravity has but too lately been proved sufficient to denounce Deity, and fill the sacred niches of his temple with atheists and monsters! Happy we! if we listen to this positive law of Jehovah, and by most sacredly reverencing the sanctuary, preserve a railing round its altar and cover its services with the protection of sincerity. This will be one sure way of checking the progress of irreligion; for a reverence towards the temple is one barrier to impiety.

Lastly. When we consider that we are sinners, that at best we must appear before the Most High covered with imperfections, ought we not to be filled with respect when in his holy temple? The four and twenty elders of heaven worship him not without casting their crowns at his feet. The celestial Cherubim chant not the perpetual *trisagium*, till they have first veiled their faces with reverential awe. The Son of God when he approached his Father in worship, bowed his knees to the earth. "Shall man," then, "who is a worm," shall "the son of man, who is a" sinful "worm," tread the courts of the Most High irreverently, or feel any but sentiments of profound respect when in the house of God! Be it ours, my brethren, to have and exhibit always a reverence for the sanctuary. Let us preserve for the temple of the Lord, an appropriate respect. So shall our worship be decent and acceptable; our conduct will be consistent with our character and situations; and we shall be better prepared for an admittance into the sanctuary above, where angels and archangels, and the whole company of heaven, in perfect felicity and eternal duration, will unitedly worship God and the Lamb.

SERMON XVI.

ON THE SANCTUARY.

PSALM, cxxxii. 7.

"We will go into his tabernacles; we will worship at his footstool."

THE sweet singer of Israel, the holy David, was not more distinguished by any quality of his heart than by his reverence and affection for the sanctuary. "Lord," says he, "I have loved the habitation of thy house, and the place where thine honour dwelleth." Separated from the sanctuary by civil occurrences, he could find in nothing, not even in the elevated strains of his private devotion, that pleasure he had tasted in the house of God. "How amiable are thy tabernacles, O Lord of Hosts. My soul longeth, yea, even fainteth, for the courts of the Lord. My heart and my flesh crieth out for the living God. Blessed are they that dwell in thy house, for a day in thy courts is better than a thousand." Restored to the privilege of assembling with the saints, with what pious fervour does he express his joy. "I was glad when they said unto me, let us go into the house of the Lord. Our feet shall stand within thy gates, O Jerusalem! We will go into his tabernacles; we will worship at his footstool."

It would be happy for themselves and the world, if all men partook of the Psalmist's love for the sanctuary and its services.

There is no duty of religion enforced by more affecting considerations, and attended with happier consequences, than this of public worship; a duty, of whose sacred nature, some sentiment has pervaded the bosoms of mankind in every age and situation. Man has everywhere possessed ideas of a superior power, and, under whatever forms he may have represented his gods to his mind, has deemed it proper to offer them public, social expressions of homage and adoration. It is a shame in the Christian world, which has the purest knowledge of the being and perfections of Deity, and the strongest motives to love and serve him; that the ways of Zion should ever mourn because any of her children come not to her solemn services! If, with half the interest which their temporal concerns excite, men would reflect upon the nature of public worship; its reasonableness and advantages, they would, with one mind, perceive it to be a duty which they cannot excusably nor safely neglect.

Consider yourselves, in the first place, in your social capacity. The interest and happiness of society do very much depend upon a general reverence for the Supreme Being, and a knowledge of future accountability. Free men from the restraints of religion, and leave them to the passions of nature, and the world will soon be converted into a scene of wickedness, debasement, and misery. But how is a general sentiment of religion to be preserved? Doubtless, one of the best means, perhaps that which is more conducive than any other to this desirable end, is the consecration of a part of our time to the holy purpose of recognizing the sovereignty of the Deity, and learning his will. There are many persons, who, from want of leisure, or from habitual heedlessness, would never turn their attention to the Author, truths, and obligations of religion were it not for the regular return of a period appropriated to this very thing. For this class of people, and they form a large part of the community, the establishment of the Lord's day is a most merciful and wholesome institution. There is a general, though it may not always be a definite or efficient sentiment of Deity and duty preserved by it, in the public mind, which, did all time lie in common, and no solemnities of public worship invite their attendance, would most undoubtedly be obliterated. Besides, it is the natural tendency of this duty to civilize the manners and the affections. Ideas of subordination are cherished when all feel their accountability to a superior power. Mutual regard and fidelity are promoted when all assemble together as brethren, before one common parent, with sentiments of humility and hope. Even the decencies of dress, and decorum of behaviour, to which public worship leads, do soften the character, and increase the courteousness of mankind. In your social capacities, then, you cannot but view the services of the sanctuary of sacred importance. But it should be considered that it is by the exemplary attendance of every one upon them, that will preserve respectability, and be productive of their effects. No man who regards the happiness of his family, the good order of society, and the improvement of his fellow beings, will unnecessarily absent himself from public worship. For if his neighbours should use the same liberty, and the example is contagious, the right the same; we might, too late, learn the value of this institution by the deplorable abandonment of it.

But I will dwell no longer upon this point. Powerful as it is, it is the least of the motives which should recommend public worship to your regard. Let me request you to consider yourselves, in the second place, in your relation to God. We cannot look into ourselves and observe, "how fearfully and wonderfully we are made," nor look around us upon the wonders and beauties which are everywhere displayed, without perceiving that we have a relation to an intelligent God. It results from our moral capacity, that the glory of this Being who hath given us existence, and so highly endowed and exalted us, should be the supreme object of our lives. Now he is glorified by our virtuous demeanour in the world, and by our private bosom acknowledgments of him, as our Lord and beloved Benefactor; but he is more especially and suitably glorified by us when we unite together to offer him, in the presence of each other and the universe, the devout homage of our hearts and lips. This is the greatest tribute we can bring him, a tribute which nature dictates and reason recommends. And methinks such an assembly must be contemplated with delight by the angels of heaven; yea, if there be one scene upon the earth more agreeable to the eternal Father than any other, it is, perhaps, the congregation of the saints, in the garments of humility and spirit of love, worshipping him in the temples which piety has consecrated to his name.

There are none in this assembly, I would anxiously presume, who doubt the existence of the Deity, or their dependence on him for life, health, reason, and happiness; "for the means," also, "of grace, and the hope of glory." But will you acknowledge such a Father, and have no communion with him? When he invites you to seek his face, will you refuse to come? Such conduct, even towards an earthly parent, would be considered as monstrous. Surely, none who would have the benediction of the everlasting Father, will be guilty of it.

There are general mercies, of which we are all partakers, which require a common acknowledgment. There are public evils to which we are all exposed, which we ought jointly to deprecate. We are social beings. The worship which we render to God must, to become us, be answerable to our nature. By our relation to him we are related to each other, and therefore do but imperfectly serve him, even by the best of our private devotions, if we come not with our brethren to the social worship of his name. This even nature dictates. The heathen and the savage neglect not the ceremonies by which their deities may publicly be worshipped. Our God deserves and requires as much at our hands. He gave the first pattern of the tabernacle. When the first temple was built, he filled it with his glory, and placed his name there. And upon Zion, a type of every place which should afterwards be consecrated to his worship, he promised his blessing, even life for evermore.

Once more. Consider the requirements of the religion you profess. What was the conduct of our blessed Lord with respect to public worship? For our example, his custom was to go into the synagogue every Sabbath day. What was the practice of the primitive Church, the happy few who had been often with him, and knew his will? On the first day of the week, they were always with one accord in one place, and "continued steadfastly in the Apostles' doctrine and fellowship, and in breaking of bread, and in prayers." What are the express or implied precepts of the gospel upon this subject? We are commanded not "to forsake the assembling of ourselves together, as the manner of some is;" but to exhort one another to this necessary duty. Why, indeed, did our Lord ordain holy mysteries, which are social in their nature, very forms of public worship? Why did he appoint a ministry in his Church, and promise to be with this ministry even unto the end of the world? Why, in the comprehensive and beautiful prayer which he has given us as a model for our petitions, did he altogether use a plural form? Are not these expressions of his will that his disciples should assemble together to preach and hear his word, and to worship the Father in spirit and truth? The genius of Christianity is, indeed, liberal. It frees us from the ceremonies of the law. It teaches that "the Sabbath was made for man, and not man for the Sabbath." But it does not relax the ties of moral obligation. They are eternal. By these a Sabbath is sanctified to God. And, surely, the Christian whom he has ransomed from death, and made an heir of everlasting life, has the strongest reason to bring the offerings of gladness to his house, and celebrate his marvellous mercies.

Let me urge you, further, to consider the advantages which belong to a constant attendance on public worship. It is pleasant and profitable. The purest and most exalted pleasure of which we are capable, is a communion with the Father of our spirits. In that beauty of holiness which the worship of the Christian temple exhibits, the devout soul can find more ravishing delight than in any earthly occupation. It is here he drinks of peace, and is refreshed with spiritual joy. Were he long deprived of the pleasures of God's house, he would be ready to cry out with the Psalmist, "As the hart panteth for the water brooks, so panteth my soul after thee, O God! My soul is athirst for God; yea, even for the living God; when shall I come to appear before God." But it is profitable as well as pleasant. We may reasonably conclude that the Most High will annex peculiar blessings to a devout attendance in his sanctuary. If individual and private prayers avail much at his throne, great must be the efficacy of the combined devotions of his Church? If the light of his countenance will anywhere be lifted up upon us, we may expect it in the places where he is specially present, to receive and bless his people. These sentiments are confirmed by facts. It was by his altar that Noah received the covenanted mercies of God. It was to the devout eunuch, whom no distance nor employment could deter from going to Jerusalem at the appointed feasts, that the joys of the Messiah were eminently given. It was to the good Anna who never absented herself from the temple at the hours of prayer, that the infant Redeemer gave a knowledge of himself, and the rich consolations of his kingdom. And it is to be feared that the catalogue is not small, which the recording angel will, at the last day adduce, of wretched beings to be consigned to perdition, whose departure from the sanctuary lost them the favour and the knowledge of God. If reason were silent, and experience afforded us no instruction respecting the advantages of an attendance upon public worship, we have the declaration of our blessed Lord, that "Where two or three are gathered together in his name, he is there in the midst of them."

Thus weighty are the considerations which oblige us to an attendance upon public worship. From this obligation there are some, no doubt, who are exempted. The really sick, the infirm through age, and those who are occupied in the works of mercy, are, doubtless, excused by the Deity for not coming into his tabernacles. But can all who stay from the sanctuary maintain these pleas? Let us, with all tenderness, but with that plainness which the subject requires, look into the reasons for their conduct.

In some is the sentiment that they learn nothing new when they go to church. But are they so perfect as never to need to be reminded of their duty, nor prompted to the discharge of it? Can their hearts be right who have so little relish for the truths of the gospel that it is tedious to them to hear them repeated? If God have given to any a knowledge of the whole counsel of his will, is not this an additional reason why they should conform to it, and magnify him in the assembly of the saints? The example of every one is claimed by religion for the benefit of others, even if his time could be spent as advantageously to himself at home, and those whose religious attainments have been really great, do generally manifest it by exhibiting this example.

There are others who are often detained from the sanctuary by the consideration that there will be no sermon. But, my friends, is it only to have your ears employed and your minds amused that you are called to the temple of the Most High? Is it not inducement enough to come hither, that you have sinned against the Almighty, and have need of his pardon; that you have been created, redeemed, and are daily preserved by him, and owe him your adoration and praise? Is it not an affront to your Creator, to prefer any object to the worship of his name; and can any sermon, even if it were clothed with an angel's eloquence, be so worthy of your attention as the sacred Scriptures which are read? Preaching is an important part of the employments of the sanctuary; but it is of secondary importance. Let sober reflection be indulged for a moment, and you will readily perceive that the leading object, when we go into the tabernacles of God, should be, to "worship at his footstool."

But may it not consistently with the restraints of candour, be further observed, that many persons are detained from the worship of the sanctuary by an indifference to it? The services are tedious to them. They prefer to do their own will, and seek their own pleasure on the holy day. The heat, or the coldness of the weather, or a lowering sky, neither of which would prevent them from pursuing their secular concerns, is sufficient to withhold them from the audience of the Most High. They stay at home, and a habit is formed which indolence persuades them is favourable to their ease. If any such are now hearing me, let me beseech them to give this subject the sober consideration it deserves. Can we be worthy of the favour of the Almighty if we are indifferent to the honour of his name? Do we deserve the blessings we enjoy if we refuse the easy return of our praise? Can we expect to be made wise unto salvation if we neglect the means of grace? Are we worthy or fit to be admitted into his temple above, if we find it irksome here, to adore and serve him? Those have certainly a solemn reason to be concerned for their spiritual state, in whom this indifference to the services of the temple exists. He hath said, and let all such lay his declaration to heart: "Them that honour me, I will honour; but they who despise me, shall be lightly esteemed."

It is among our most valuable privileges, a privilege which the best of us do but imperfectly appreciate, that we are permitted to tread the courts of the Most High. It is a privilege for which we shall be called to strict account; and dreadful will be our confusion, if, in the great day of retribution, the Almighty shall lay it to our charge, that we lightly regarded the services of his temple, and irreverently withheld ourselves from his presence when we were upon earth. Of your privilege, then, beloved, fail not to avail yourselves. Come to this sacred place whenever it is set open for the purposes of devotion. When you come, come to worship your God. Come with hands washed in innocency, and hearts intent upon glorifying your Father who is in heaven. Come thus, and you shall soon love the habitation of his house; you shall find it good for you to be here. From the humble confession of your sins, you will rise relieved; from the proclamation of your Maker's praise, you will sit down refreshed; from the supplication of his mercies you will go away satisfied. You will return to your homes, calm and happy in the consciousness of having done your duty; and the word of your God will, through his blessing, be productive in you, of peace, righteousness, and eternal life. "Blessed is the man whom thou choosest, and causest to approach unto thee, that he may dwell in thy courts: he shall be satisfied with the goodness of thy house, even of thy holy temple."

SERMON XVII.

ON THE LITURGY.*

PSALM, xlv. 13.

"Her clothing is of wrought gold."

OF whom speaketh the Psalmist this? Of the Church; whom David, with the eye of prophecy, saw in all that glorious beauty, in which, in the age of her maturity, she should be "brought unto the king," and enjoy the choicest demonstrations of his affections and favour. What was meant by her clothing in the Psalmist's mind, we may not be able indisputably to ascertain; but we shall not materially err, if we consider it as signifying those offices of devotion in which she is seen by mankind sublimely attired; and on the days on which he vouchsafes to give her a special audience, presents herself before the Lord her God. In this view of their import, the words of the text have been taken to introduce a discourse upon that excellent Liturgy, the public service of our Common Prayer,

* This discourse, differently arranged, was originally delivered in Charleston. It was, subsequently, preached, May 21, 1814, before the General Convention of the Protestant Episcopal Church, convened in Philadelphia, and published at their request. The following advertisement was prefixed: "When this discourse was preached, the time of the Convention was deemed by the writer too precious to admit of the delivery of the whole of it. The parts which were then omitted, are given in the publication, in the humble hope that they will be acceptable to his brethren; and render the discourse more practically useful to those who shall read it."

in which the Church is as truly seen by us as she was by the Psalmist, in a clothing of wrought gold.

Should I attempt, in a single discourse, to treat fully of the Liturgy of the Church, I should wrong the subject, and fill your minds and my own with dissatisfaction. It is a work for a volume. And the many excellent volumes in which its character is analyzed and its perfection developed, render unnecessary any efforts of mine to add to its celebrity or illustrate its praise. All, therefore, that I shall aim to do, will be to point out to you some of its most distinguished properties; properties, an acquaintance with which is indispensably necessary to enable us to know its excellence, and to use it in such a manner as will render it that pure and holy, that becoming and acceptable sacrifice which it was intended we should offer in it to God and the Redeemer.

That you may the more fully see the importance of the subject, allow me, before I proceed to the discussion of it, to recall to your minds the important truth, that the great, the chief object of our assembling together in the sanctuary is to worship God. Sermons have, in modern times, more admirers than prayers. But whoever considers the authority by which public worship is instituted, the reasons on which it is grounded, and the purposes for which it is designed, will perceive that the first business for which we come together into the temple is to acknowledge the Most High God our Redeemer; to recognize our relations to him, and pay him our homage; to seek of him the mercies and blessings which we need, and in acts of adoration and praise to celebrate his glorious name. Preaching is undoubtedly an ordinance of the Almighty; and so long as "faith shall come by hearing, and hearing by the word of God," must be an ordinance of very great moment to the salvation of men. But it is, nevertheless, secondary in nature and importance to that great, that leading, that most interesting duty of worshipping the "Lord in the beauty of holiness." This is the highest act in which our nature can be engaged. And the people who are furnished with the means of performing it most perfectly, are brought nearest to the angels in their privileges, and will, if they use them faithfully, be beheld in their public assemblies with most complacency by the Almighty. How important, then, the inquiry concerning the properties of that service which the Church has provided for us to perform, when we are gathered together in the courts of our Maker! What are these properties? I would call your attention to those which follow: that our Liturgy is social, that it is sensible, that it is spiritual, that it is complete, that it is well arranged, and that it is holy. Under these heads may be brought to view enough of its character to confirm our attachment to it. We may find under each of them instruction concerning its excellency, and direction concerning its use.

Men are social beings; and when they are assembled in the temples of the Almighty, their *natures* and the *community* of their blessings and wants require that they should offer a common worship. In order to do this a form of prayer and praise is necessary. Without it they cannot *associate* in the performance of the service. And he who is most averse to this idea will, upon reflection, perceive, that even extemporary prayers are forms to all who hear them, from which they cannot wander without relinquishing their part in the common business of the congregation. As a form is in the nature of the thing necessary, so *established* forms have, in all ages of the Church, been esteemed most conducive to the purposes of social worship. They were used by God's chosen people in the service of the tabernacle and the temple; they have the sanction of our blessed Lord; they were adopted by the Apostles and primitive Christians, and are found in the Church in every age, from their time to the present day. By such *stated* services the people know beforehand the sacrifice which is to be offered; they have it, as it were, in their hands; they *unitedly* bring it to the altar and lay it thereon; it is *their* offering as well as the priest's. Here, then, may be observed, the happy adaptation of our Liturgy to the social character which should appertain to the worship of the Christian temple. Whereas, it is not easy for us to conceive how—having no established service—we could assent to that which we had never contemplated, or offer that which we never possessed.

But further. That the service of the sanctuary may be, as it should be, perfectly social, the people should have in it an active part. In the prayers as well as the praises, with their bodies as well as with their spirits, they should all, after an orderly manner, be engaged, that the service may be most truly the service of all.

Conformably with this principle was our Liturgy constructed. The people have in it an active service as well as the priest; sometimes, as in the collects and the prayers, or adorations which have been offered, expressing their assent by an audible and devout Amen; sometimes, as in the versicles, echoing the petition which the priest has made, or enforcing it with new considerations; sometimes, as in the Litany, when the minister has offered the suffrage, taking, as it were, with holy ardour, the words out of his mouth, and uttering the deprecation or the entreaty; and sometimes, as in the holy hymns, the psalms, and the doxologies, responding in alternate verse the praises of God, the desires of men, the holiness and homage, the faith, and hopes, and charity of religion; thus exhibiting an humble imitation of the worship of heaven, in which we are told the celestial beings *cry one to another.* How admirably is this arrangement adapted to exhibit the perfection of the beauty of social worship! Allow me, then, to notice the importance, that, in order to the production of its due effect, the people should refrain, on the one hand, from repeating the parts which belong exclusively to the minister, as the Exhortations, the Absolution, the Commandments, the Benediction, and those prayers which are to be said by him alone; and on the other hand, that with pure hearts, and humble, yet audible voices, they should perform the parts which belong exclusively to *them.* The responses are a beautiful, very ancient, peculiar, and most useful part of the Liturgy of our Church. By the solemn performance of them, the people may keep their own attention engaged, may animate him who is ministering among them, and may kindle devotion one in another. Yea, if the little children were taught to pronounce with attention and proper solemnity these parts of divine service, it would add to the beauty and utility of public worship; and in our assemblies would be exhibited the verity of the inspired declaration, *out of the mouths of babes and sucklings thou hast perfected praise.*

To excite you to join diligently and with reverence in the service of common prayer, I need only guide your attention to the sublime extent of the application of its social character. It is not only in this house in which you assemble, that in all its parts it is sociably performed. The same prayers and praises, in the same words, are offered, perhaps at the same hour, with the same faith, by ten thousand tongues, to the same God and Father of all. From all Christian parts of the globe the Amen resounds, which you here utter; and the doxology is raised, in which you are here called upon to bear a part. It is not in this age only in which you live that this service conveys the devotions of Christians to heaven. In some of the ejaculations it contains, the first disciples breathed their praises and their wishes to the Most High. Its collects have, many of them, for many hundreds of years, been the vehicles of the public devotions of the Church. And upon some of its apostrophes has the last breath of distinguished martyrs trembled, whose piety during their lives was refreshed with its hymns and its psalms. It is not under the gospel dispensation alone that some parts of this service have been used to express the common devotions of the faithful. There are hymns in it which were sung by saints under the Mosaic dispensation, and in the use of the psalms particularly the Church of the New Testament is found in society with the Church of the Old; for in these sacred compositions, not the emotions of David's heart only were vented, but much of the worship of God's ancient people did consist. It is not only in the Church militant upon earth that this service, in some of its parts, is used. We have borrowed from the Church triumphant in heaven, their gratulatory anthem and their perpetual hymn, and have reason to believe that their voices are in concert with ours, when they sing the song of the redeemed. How sublime is this view of the communion and fellowship of the Church under the Mosaic and Christian dispensations, in different ages and in distant nations on earth and in heaven, in the use of some part or other of that holy Liturgy which it is our distinguishing felicity to have received from our fathers! Who would not wish, in the temple, to bear upon his lips those psalms and prayers in which "The glorious company of the Apostles," "the goodly fellowship of the prophets," and "the noble army of martyrs," have uttered their devotions to God! How dead must he be to the finest associations which can affect the mind, who is not animated to a devout and fervent performance of his part of the service of the sanctuary, by the consideration, that upon this same censer which the Church holds out to him, incense hath been put by those hands which are now extended before the throne of the Almighty, and that as its smoke ascended, those eyes were lifted up to heaven which are now fixed upon the visible glory of God and the Lamb.

This social property of our Liturgy forms its most prominent feature; and endears it to us as suitable to our nature, and friendly to the best feelings of the heart. Would to God, its beauty were noticed by every member of our congregations and commended by his practice to others. Pleasant and elevating is the scene which the Christian temple exhibits, when the priest and the people are as one, to make one offering unto the Lord; and from every mouth, from the infant of days, and from the old man who hath not filled his days, there arises the alternate adoration or the assenting Amen.

But this leads me to the second property of our Liturgy to be noticed, viz., that it is sensible. By this I mean that it has a body as well as spirit; that it is adapted to the nature of beings who have senses as well as souls. All worship to be becoming, must be suitable to the nature of those who offer it, as well as to his nature to whom it is offered. A worship wholly spiritual, would not be proper for man in his present state. It would be the act of but half of his nature. To be complete, all his faculties must be employed in it. With his body as well as his spirit he must worship; for each is a part of himself, each is the offspring of divine power, each is a partaker of the divine blessings, each is redeemed by the divine mercy, each needs the divine protection, and both are God's. Indeed it is difficult to conceive how, without corporeal acts, the important quality of sociality in worship, upon which we have already dilated, could be maintained. If the service be not sensible the signs must be wanting, by which alone men can manifest their association in a common work to the world, and to each other. Shall I be told that the spirit may be engaged when the body is still? It may. But the spirits of men cannot, in this present state, evidence to men what are their engagements, but by signs and deeds. If there be in the assemblies of the saints no sound of words and no consentaneous posture of bodies, there may be sincerity in the individual; there may be an insulated altar in every bosom; but the visible chain is wanting which should connect all together, and conduct the spirit by which one is animated, through the whole. On these accounts, mankind have been impelled by the dictates of reason, in every country, to invest their public worship with rites and ceremonies; and with an eye to these principles, the wise compilers of our Liturgy have rendered it a sensible service. They have adapted it to our state of being upon "this visible diurnal sphere," guarding with equal caution, against the impalpable reveries of the mystic, and the tedious mummeries of the formalist; on the one hand, avoiding to incumber the service of the sanctuary with such a mass of ceremonies as would obscure and overwhelm its spirit, and restraining themselves on the other hand, from affecting a worship so abstract and imperceptible as would not become man on the earth; and, indeed, we know not whether any such is offered in heaven. It is here, then, you will be struck with the importance of the audible voice with which the congregation as well as the priest are to celebrate divine service, that they may honour God with the best member which they have. Here you will perceive the propriety of using, to enliven and beautify the worship of the sanctuary, that faculty, which is given to men, of clothing their thoughts and their feelings, their faith, their hopes, and their love, in the ravishing charms of melodious sounds. Here you will discern the fitness of that decent attire, which the Church has prescribed for her priests; of that adoration which she expresses by the consecration to the honour of the Almighty of temples meet for his service; and of those "outward visible signs of inward and spiritual grace," which she has received in the sacraments from her Lord, and transmits as hallowed to posterity. Here you will see the reasons of those holy instructions which teach us to fall low on our knees when we confess our sins to Almighty God, or supplicate his mercies; and to stand upon our feet when we declare the articles of faith which we are resolved to maintain, or with elevated emotions, proclaim the greatness and the goodness whereby the Most High hath made us glad. These sensible acts, this employment of the faculties and posture of our bodies, the worshipping our Creator, how natural are they, how expressive, how becoming our condition in this state of being! To show you in what value they were held by those who were best able to estimate them, need I turn your attention to Solomon kneeling upon his knees, when he offers his prayer to God; and rising upon his feet and stretching forth his hands, when in the name of the Almighty he blesses the people? Need I bring to your view the congregation of Israel, the chosen and divinely instructed people, bowing their heads when they received the benediction of the Most High; and raising their bodies and voices when they magnify his name? Need I call to your recollection, the striking picture which the spirit of revelation hath given us of the inhabitants of heaven, veiling their faces and casting down their crowns, when they worship Him who sitteth upon the throne? Need I take you to Gethsemane and show you Jesus, the pattern of all that is perfect, thrice kneeling down before his Father, while he thrice utters the same earnest supplication? No; I need not. These, and other examples, are familiar to your minds. And whenever you have pondered seriously the import of prayer and praise, conscience has testified to you the wisdom of the rubrics which teach us to do likewise. They are but repetitions of rubrics of nature. Is other evidence of their fitness needed than that which is furnished by reason? You hear it in the voice of the Almighty himself, calling upon you in his holy word, *to glorify God in your bodies, and in your spirits, which are his.*

This leads me to a third property of our Liturgy, worthy of observation, viz: that it is spiritual. Important as it is, that our religious services should have a sensible form, this form would be of no worth if it were destitute of life. The audible voice is of no value, but as it expresses the thoughts of the heart. The bended knee is of no significance but as it represents the humbled soul. "God is a spirit; and they that worship him must worship him in spirit and in truth." And as a spirit, he is truly worshipped in the service of our Church. No image of the Godhead is contemplated by our minds. By no attempt to represent the Almighty to our senses is the divine nature dishonoured, and our own weakness betrayed. As the Great Spirit, who pervadeth all space and inhabiteth eternity, we address him, "whom, not having seen, we love; in whom, though now we see him not, yet believing, we rejoice with joy unspeakable and full of glory." The worship which is rendered to him is, too, in a high degree spiritual. In every part of it there is life. Within the beautiful and holy form, there is a *soul*, fraught with the treasures of divine truth, and pure as has been found on earth since the transgression of man. Is it said that it is cold? Where is manifested more fervent affection than in its addresses, or more intense devotion than in its litany and hymns? Is it said to confide too much in its exterior? The faith which it implies, is seated in the spirit; the blessings which it most celebrates and deserves, are spiritual; and it is skilfully contrived to engage *our souls* in the acts of it, and to carry them on a stream of sacred emotions, perpetually flowing to the foot of the mount of God. Is it said that it affords not scope for the feelings, which are sometimes kindled in the heart, when it approaches its Maker; nor freedom to the action of the soul, when the spirit of devotion comes upon it? Which of the affections or dispositions of man that is proper to be engaged in the worship of his Maker, may not find employment and vent for itself in the psalms, and in some or other of the collects? And in what production of the most rapturous being, has piety taken a loftier flight than in her favourite *Te Deum*, the hymn so eminently spiritual, so wonderfully sublime, that one can scarce forbear to believe that the lips which first uttered it, were touched with a coal from the altar of heaven? Is it said that it is formal? What faculty of our nature, meet for the work, is not brought into action in the due performance of the Common Prayer? Our souls, and all that is within us, our understanding, our will, and our affections, all in this service have their part and occupation; and he who engages in it as he ought, cannot fail to enjoy a very near communion with his God. In short, humility, and faith, and love, and gratitude, and sincerity, have all here a place, that they may come and adorn the worship of the sanctuary; and the propensity of our minds to wander, even when our tongues are engaged, is checked with the happiest skill, by those variations and acclamations, which now relieve, and now quicken attention; and by those sudden breaks and frequent apostrophes, which remind us of the nature of our work, and of the presence of the Almighty. It is true, all this may be overlooked or disregarded. In our temples, with all the spirituality of our service, there may pass from our lips an empty sound; our hands may offer an unhallowed oblation. But who that would worship the Lord his God as he ought, will not be careful to engage the powers of his mind and affections of his heart in this his highest duty? To what purpose shall we, as taught by the Redeemer, address the Deity as our parent, if we have none of the feelings which the idea of a father, of a father in heaven, of a Father who is God, ought to excite? With what benefit are we so often reminded, in the beginning and end of our prayers, of the attributes of God and mediation of Christ, if we do not exert that reverence and fear, that faith and hope, that affection and confidence which the very frequent recurrence of these great ideas was designed to inspire? Where is the propriety, when *we* have said, we trust with simplicity and sincerity, "The Lord be with you," in replying, "and with thy spirit," if the heart do not wish what the lips express? What honour can result to the Almighty, or what advantage to ourselves, from pronouncing the customary Amen, if we thereby assent to that to which we have not listened; or ratify that about which we are indifferent? Can we expect that the doxology of the tongue will be reported by the spirits that minister about the throne, if it be unaccompanied by the hallelujah of the soul? O, let us not separate the life from the form; the soul from the body of our excellent Liturgy! With its *sensible* let us combine its *spiritual* property; that thus we may offer to God a reasonable service. With us, who in this respect are so signally blessed, what apology can be found, if the Almighty shall have occasion to say of us, "This people draweth nigh unto me with their mouth, and honoureth me with their lips; but their heart is far from me."

But it is time for me to pass to another distinguishing property of our Liturgy, its comprehensivess, or fulness. Here was the labour, this was the difficulty, in compiling a book of Common Prayer, to provide for the claims and expectations of God, and for the conditions, and wants, and wishes, and duties of all estates of men; so that of such honour, as we unworthy creatures can render unto our heavenly Father, there should be no deficiency; and none of his worshippers be left without such instructions as they would need to receive; such oblations as it would become them to offer; and such supplications as they might wish to make. And when we consider how successfully the framers of our Liturgy have accomplished this, we must look upon it as among the most wonderful achievements of wisdom and piety which the world has known. They have recurred to the oracles of truth, and have brought the Old and the New Testament to stand daily, and always, as parts of the

Liturgy; that thus, it might be enriched with perennial sources of wisdom, and instruction, and peace. They have gone to the Jewish church, and have brought thence the wonderful psalms, and many hymns, which the spirit of God seems to have inspired his servants to indite for the use of his people. They have had recourse to the first Christians, and the first churches; to the fathers, and to their immediate descendants; and from their precious stores have obtained parts of the primitive Liturgies, venerable for their antiquity and holy simplicity. They have looked among the Christians of the Eastern and of the Western Empire; into the Greek church, and into the church of Rome; and from them have taken many most excellent prayers, versicles, and litany-suffrages, which they have rendered of great value and utility in the accomplishment of their work. To these rich materials they have added many productions of their own pious and enlarged minds; productions, which, in purity of language, sanctity of sentiment, and true character of devotion, are not inferior to the generality of those with which they are combined. From this mass of materials they separated whatever was gross, discordant, or unnecessary; and with the rest composed the service which enriches and adorns our Church. Thus, you perceive, that from the richest mines, there has, from time to time, been collected in large abundance, for the perfecting of the work, the choicest gold; and under the following head, which will treat of the arrangement of the service, will see, that the gold has been wrought into this clothing of the Church with exquisite skill and finished effect. At present, our concern is only with the fulness of the Liturgy.

Let us consider it with respect to the Being to whom its adorations are addressed. He is recognized and worshipped in his great characters of our Creator, Redeemer, and Sanctifier. His glorious attributes, as far as they are known to us, are all of them celebrated. That confession of sins, acknowledgment of dependence, thanksgiving for blessings, adoration of his greatness, supplication for his favour, and avowal of allegiance to him, and all those dispositions and affections towards the Deity which man should possess and manifest, are provided for in this Liturgy; and, conformably with the divine canon, God in all its parts is glorified, through Christ Jesus.

Consider it with respect to the beings by whom it is to be used. How admirably adapted to instruct the ignorant, and remind the well informed, in what they are to believe and do, is the *reading of the holy Scriptures* in order, throughout the year; the rehearsal *in the creed* whenever they assemble and meet together, of a summary of the truths which God has revealed to be embraced and cherished by them; and the declaration *in the decalogue*, of his will and pleasure concerning their conduct! Who that attends statedly upon this service can long be ignorant what is good, and what the Lord his God doth require of him! So full is it with respect to the truths of Christianity, that it has been well observed, a complete body of divinity might be easily framed out of the words it contains. With what felicity, also, are its prayers and praises so framed as to embrace, almost without an exception, the wants and the blessings of every human being! Is there a lust or passion, a vice or misery, an evil or danger common to mankind, which is not in it deprecated and deplored? Is there a grace of Christianity, a virtue which can adorn and bless the human character, a thing essential to life or godliness which is not celebrated in it, and devoutly sought? Is there a condition of prosperity or adversity, of joy or sorrow to which man can be brought, in which he may not find vent for his wishes in that eminently complete production, *the Litany;* and for his praises, in the thanksgiving and the psalms? As was the case with the food furnished for the Israelites in the wilderness, there is in this service, provision made for every man according to his necessities, and the necessities of his household.

But that which renders this property of our Liturgy very admirable, is the skill with which it is so framed as to be adapted to the use of all classes and orders of men. The high and the low, the rich and the poor, the old and the young, the ruler and the subject, the master and the slave, the saint and the sinner, may each find in it an oblation meet for him to offer, and a blessing worthy to be thankfully received. It may be used without perplexity by the mean and the ignorant, and by the wise and the mighty without disgust. The plainest may understand it; and it may entertain all the faculties of the most refined. With a felicity rarely to be found in any human production, its fulness is such, and so continued, that the prince and the beggar may use it together, and both find in it becoming devotion, instruction, and delight. It has been objected to it that it is too long. But when, with serious deliberation, we have considered the matter, we shall discover unexpected difficulty in selecting the parts with which we would most willingly dispense; and shall perceive, that no part can be removed from it without imparing its strength, disturbing its proportions, and diminishing its fulness.

From the fulness of the Liturgy we pass to the arrangement of its parts. A mass of materials, however great and valuable, can excite but little admiration, and be of but little utility till it is reduced to some form and order. It has been said, that order is heaven's first law. All the works of God, from the disposition of the parts which form the humblest flower of the field, to the disposition of the planets and stars which form the magnificence of unbounded space, are, doubtless, conformed to the principles, and exhibit to the eye, which can ken the whole, the beauty of order. And man, who was made originally in the image of God, and is taught in the gospel to aspire after a recovery of that image, should, in all his concerns, but especially in the worship which he renders to the Being who is the author of beauty and lover of harmony, observe and cherish order. Without this, the service he renders must produce a jargon with the very nature of the Being to whom it is addressed. In the prophetic vision which the Psalmist had of the Church, when in the age of her maturity she should be espoused to her Lord, he remarks, that "she should be brought unto the king in raiment of needlework," intimating not only that her attire should not be plain, coarse, or common, but that it should be costly, and adorned by the skilful, according to the unchangeable principles of art and excellency. We have mentioned, as a fifth property of our Liturgy worthy to be noticed, that it is well arranged; and if we advert to it, we shall find that the golden materials of which it is composed, are not thrown together in splendid confusion, but disposed systematically, and in such a way as to produce the great ends of arrangement, convenience, pleasure, and the best accomplishment of the effect proposed.

The parts of our service are so disposed as to produce a variety, which is at once convenient and delightful to the worshipper. The corruptible body too much presses down the mind; and the mind itself, in the present state, is too weak to be long continued upon the same stretch with much satisfaction. On this account, with wise adaptation to the infirmities as well as powers of our nature, and in humble imitation of the economy of the Great Creator in the production of his works, our Liturgy is rendered "*various;*

> that the mind
> Of desultory man, studious of change,
> ——————— may be indulged."

This variety is in a happy manner produced by the division of the service into many short prayers; whereby the thoughts and affections are concentrated a little while upon one subject, and then relieved by transition to another; excited afresh in each by the new address with which it begins, and resting a moment upon the Amen at the end. These frequent addresses direct our attention, each one of them, to a distinct attribute of God; and thus, in the course of the service, all the parts of the glory of his character with which we are acquainted, in grateful succession pass before us. Nor is it with an idle volatility that this transition from one attribute of the Deity to another is so frequently made; but every address is with great felicity adapted to the subject of the prayer which begins with it; a thing worthy to be observed, that when in the use of these various collects, we "pray with the spirit," we may "pray with the understanding also." Thus, when we are about to confess our sins, and implore the forgiveness of them, that we may be filled with that union of fear and hope which becomes sincere penitents before "the throne of the heavenly grace," we are directed to contemplate and address him before whom we bow, as an "*Almighty and most merciful Father.*" Thus, when about to beseech him at his holy table, to prepare us, by cleansing the thoughts of our hearts, perfectly to love him, and worthily to magnify his holy name, we look up to him as the Being "unto whom all hearts are open, all desires known, and from whom no secrets are hid." Thus, when in obedience to the instructions of the gospel, we are about to offer supplications for the rulers of the land, we address him as "the high and mighty Ruler of the universe, who doth from his throne behold all the dwellers upon earth." And in like manner, when, with the comprehensive benevolence of our holy religion, we are about to pray for all sorts and conditions of men, or to offer thanks for all the blessings enjoyed by us, and by all men, we, in the former case, approach him as "the Creator and Preserver of all mankind," and in the latter, as "the Father of all mercies." And all this in conformity with the example of our blessed Lord, who, in the inimitable prayer he hath given us, that we may be filled with the filial reverence and affection which we ought to feel when approaching God, hath taught us in the beginning of it, to call upon him, as "our Father;" and that we may have confidence in his power to do what we ask, hath reminded us, that he is "in heaven."

The variety, however, which so much enlivens and beautifies our service, does not consist wholly nor chiefly in the division of it into many prayers. However numerous the parts of worship may be, if they be all of the same kind, without change or variation of their nature, the mind would become satiated with the sameness and wearied with the repetition. The humblest penitent might be oppressed by prolonged confession, if no recollection of the promise of absolution gleamed upon his heart. The most devout suppliant would have his fervour abated if no recollection of past mercies animated his hopes, and no acts of praise enlivened his spirit. On this account it is that there are introduced into our Liturgy those changes of occupation, of subject, and of posture, which, by diversifying our business, render it more interesting. Indeed, variety in our acts of worship is not less answerable to the claims of the Almighty than to the necessities of man. "The Church, therefore, diversifies and variegates her service with friendly exhortations, humbling confessions, comforting absolutions, fervent prayers, hymns, and psalms of cheerful praise, and with the writings of the Prophets and Apostles; to a participation of the benefits of all which her children are admitted by the initiatory sacrament of baptism; as afterwards they are promoted to the stature of perfect men in Christ Jesus, by the repeated communications of his Holy Spirit in the blessed eucharist." In this view of it, our Liturgy is as a well furnished garden, in which are shades of the deepest verdure and flowers of the liveliest hue, waters flowing from perennial fountains to fertilize and delight, and seats, at which, at proper intervals, we may rest and be refreshed.

But I hasten to observe, that amidst all this variety there is a perfect order. The different materials are not thrown together without design. Every part is placed according to principles of fitness. Each has a relation to and dependence upon others. And the pleasing effect of the whole is the result of that happy union of order with variety which is the source of the beautiful in all the works of nature and art. It would be instructive and pleasant to contemplate the beauty of the arrangement in every part of the Common Prayer and administration of the Holy Sacraments. But to do it completely in a discourse is impossible. I must content myself with pointing out to you some of the most prominent features of the felicity of this arrangement in the services which we most frequently use. Attentive observation in your retired hours, will discover equal beauty and utility in the disposition of the parts of all the several offices, and many excellencies in the order of the *daily* service, which the lapse of time will compel me to leave unnoticed.

Interesting is the scene, when a congregation are assembled as a people whom the Most High hath redeemed, to worship him in his holy temple. How solemn the moment when they are about to present themselves before the Almighty! To collect their thoughts, and excite in them a due solemnity, the service opens with some passages of Scripture peculiarly impressive. To these follows an address, in which the Minister, while he sets before them the great purposes of their assembling together, aims chiefly to excite in them humility and confidence in "Almighty God, their heavenly Father," and invites them to accompany him with their hearts and voices to "the throne of the heavenly grace." After this decent preparation, they are ready to bow before his footstool. With what shall they begin? Angels, ye, first and last, utter only adorations! Spirits of the just made perfect, ye break forth at every approach to your Creator, in acts of praise! But sinful men—should they not first propitiate their Maker before they offer him any oblation? Accordingly, the first act of our devotion is the confession of our sins; a confession, so comprehensive, that under some one or other of its general clauses every fault with which a man can charge himself, may be included; and so very affecting that his heart must be dead to all religious emotions, who is not humbled by it before his God. To the pious penitent who has made this confession, how joyous would it be could he hear immediately from the throne of the Almighty, "Thy sins are forgiven thee!" This he cannot hear till Jesus shall personally present him to the Father. But, behold, for their comfort and encouragement, while they continue in the flesh, God "hath given power and commandment to his Ministers to declare and pronounce to his people, being penitent, the absolution and remission of their sins." This declaration, therefore, the Priest, rising from before the throne, makes to the people directly after their confession. And of the comfort of it, every Christian who is conscious that he "truly repents and unfeignedly believes the gospel," should with faith avail himself, to the quieting of his conscience and perfecting of his gratitude and joy.

Being now reconciled to God, according to the promises declared to our race in Christ Jesus, we, as children adopted anew into his family, extend our affections and lift our grateful eyes to him as "our Father," and address to him that summary of our homage and desires, in which he who purchased our forgiveness hath taught us to pray. Our spirits being relieved from the burthen of their fears, and revived by the tenor of this prayer which his Son hath authorized us to address to our Maker, we rise upon our feet, and, with hearts glowing with devotion, in a most ancient doxology, an animated hymn, and a portion of the sacred psalms, ascribe everlasting glory to him in language of inspiration celebrating his praise. This first part of the service, how beautiful it is! How proper the order, how natural and significant the transitions, how happy our minds when we sit down, how well prepared to listen to the instructions of God's holy word! A lesson is read from the Old Testament. At the close of it we rise, and cherish the flame of our devotion by celebrating in suitable hymns his character, and works, and grace. There is then read a lesson from the New Testament, and by this arrangement the Law and the Gospel, the Prophets and the Apostles, are brought, at a suitable time, to adorn and bless our service; and the important truth is inculcated, that throughout the Bible there is but one scheme carried on, issuing in the redemption of the world through Jesus the Son of God. To the lesson from the New Testament, there follow appropriate hymns, in which we express our adorations and joy. And then, having heard the Scriptures, we, in the presence of each other, of the world, and of God, with great propriety rehearse a summary of the truths which have been received from revelation; by our Amen, declaring our assent to them, and our resolution to maintain them. Knowing in whom we may believe, and what are our interests, and for how great mercies we are indebted to the Most High, we, after a reciprocation of holy wishes between the priest and people, venerable for the antiquity of its use, and for its Christian courteousness, prostrate ourselves again before the Almighty, and in a series of prayers engage in acts of supplication; in which spiritual blessings are magnified above temporal ones; the Church is regarded more than the world; the less is sought after the greater; and sometimes, as in the Litany, which was originally a separate service, but now is incorporated into the Morning Prayer, there is a regular transition from invocation of mercy to deprecation of evil, and from deprecation of evil to supplication of favours; in all which the concerns of the soul are remembered before those of the body; the concerns of the Church before those of the world; the concerns of the world, and the powers whom God hath ordained to rule it before those of individuals; and yet, there is not a thing needful for the body which is forgotten, nor an individual who may not find a petition adapted to his own case. As we draw towards the close of this service, we are called upon to exalt our gratitude to the highest point of fervour, and to expand our charity to the utmost extent. In a prayer for all sorts and conditions of men, we, as we would ask an alms for the dumb beggar, supplicate appropriate mercies *for all our race.* And in a general thanksgiving which burns with the holiest and most ardent spirit of praise, we honour God for all his mercies to us and to all men. An excellent summary from the pen of the pious Chrysostom, of all for which the Christian can be solicitous, follows; and the benedictory prayer, which the spirit of inspiration hath hallowed, closes the daily service.

I must forbear to enter at present upon the office of the communion. This is, perhaps, the most finished peace of devotion which exists in the world. In a hasty manner to speak of its excellence would not satisfy my admiration of it. Happily, its beauties are so striking and impressive, that they who use it need not to have them described. No good Christian can join in the celebration of this office, without discovering in it as high perfection of the beauty of holiness, as he can expect to behold upon earth.

It is objected to the arrangement of our Liturgy, that the many variations and frequent risings and sittings diminish its solemnity. But to those who have studied the principles by which it is framed, these changes have a lively significance; and while they are calculated to keep attention awake, give to the service a becoming character of activity.

It has also been objected, that the apostrophes and short ejaculations, which abound in our Liturgy, produce confusion, and are useless. But they are of precious value, as relics of primitive devotion; are, many of them important as connecting ligaments in the system, or powerful expressions in themselves of true piety. "In these connections," says an admirer of the Liturgy, "the wisdom of the Church hath imitated the skill of nature. For as in framing the body of man, nature has not only formed the limbs in proportion, and placed them in order, but has also fastened them with joints, which seem made no less for beauty than necessity; so, in composing the body of our Common Prayer, the Church hath not only framed the several offices of a due length, and ranged them in a just method, but has likewise united them with versicles, as it were with joints; which, though less regarded, are yet the no less beautiful than necessary parts of our Liturgy; so that we shall find as great comeliness and art in these connections, as there are in the compositions themselves."

After this manner, are wisdom and propriety displayed throughout the service, in the arrangement of its parts. The choice gold, which with so much care was collected for the foundation of it, is not thrown together in a promiscuous heap. It is "*wrought*;" and wrought with such skill, as to produce in the system all the charms and advantages which are found in what is significant, orderly, and beautiful. And the effect proposed in instituting the service, is by the arrangement most surely accomplished. The Church is enabled to present herself before her Lord, in a clothing suitable to her character and condition; and her Lord, when he beholds her in this good and glorious attire, "hath pleasure in her beauty."

The last property of our Liturgy, which we shall consider is, that it is holy. Without this quality, no offering can be acceptable unto God. Into his ancient tabernacle and temple, nothing that had the least impurity was allowed to enter. To his altar, no sacrifice that had any blemish was permitted to be brought. Upon the forehead of the priests, and upon the holy vestments, and upon all the utensils of the sacred place, was inscribed, "Holiness unto the Lord." And it is its most important commendation, that the service provided for us to offer in his sanctuary, is pre-eminently holy.

Shall I speak to you of its language? Much of it is the language of inspiration. All of it is grand and reverent. So pure and chaste is it, so free from imbecility and corruption, that perhaps there is no better standard of the excellencies of our tongue. If there be here and there and ancient phrase, or expression, this does not diminish, but rather adds to its solemnity. Who would exchange any part of the rich, majestic, and durable clothing of wrought gold, for the fripperies of modern decoration; the tinsel and gaudy affectations with which some would refine it?

Shall I speak to you of its doctrines and sentiments? They are purely Scriptural. The pattern of them was brought by Jesus from heaven. Nothing is there among them, which has not affinity with the sacred truths which God hath taught us to revere. They are holy, as the gold of the censers upon which the ministering spirits in heaven offer the prayers of the saints.

Shall I speak to you of its forms and ceremonies? There is nothing in them to debase the worshipper, or offend his God. No tarnish of pious fraud rests upon them. No stain of human vanity defiles them. They are simple, pure, significant; wholly calculated to give an expression of sanctity to the *manner*, that it may correspond with the *spirit* of the holy service.

Shall I speak to you of the object to whom it is addressed? He is the one only living and true God, in the Trinity of Persons, as he has graciously revealed himself to mankind, in the oracles of truth; the Being before whom the company of heaven "rest not day nor night, saying, Holy, holy, holy, Lord God Almighty, who was, and is, and is to come."

Shall I speak to you of its tendency? It is to inspire us with an abhorrence of impurity; to sanctify our thoughts, and elevate our affections; to beget in us holiness of heart and life. He who duly uses it will be made more pious and virtuous by it. As Moses, by long contemplation of the divine nature in the mount, caught a gleam of its lustre, with which his countenance beamed, so he, who shall long and constantly use this service, may, at length, in the temper of his soul and conduct of his life, be changed into its glory.

In short, when I speak of the holiness of our service, shall I err, if I say, that no sacrifice more perfect in this respect, hath been prepared to be offered to God, in this world, since the fall of man, except the sacrifice of his adorable Son? Let us bring to the use of it, dispositions and affections correspondent to its character; and we shall not fail to "worship the Lord with an holy worship."

I have now finished what I proposed to do, in treating upon the Liturgy of our Church. In reviewing what has been said, you cannot, my brethren, but perceive, that we ought to consider ourselves as highly distinguished by the Almighty, in that we are furnished with such a pure, pleasant, and acceptable service, wherewith to present ourselves before him in his holy temple. With what sacred care should we keep this treasure! Let us guard it vigilantly in its integrity, that those who come after us, when they shall look upon the Church, may not have occasion to say, "The gold of her clothing, how is it become dim! and the fine gold, how is it changed!" Wisely has our Church required of all who are admitted to her ministry a solemn promise which is made at their ordination, that they will conform themselves to this Liturgy in their official services. Let her clergy, then, under the influence of their vows, consider the care of its integrity as a part of their charge. Let not the hand of any individual disturb its proportions, or with additions or devices of his own, soil its beauty. In its excellent fulness, let it be preserved inviolate, and it will be to our Church an invaluable barrier against the whims, and errors, and dangerous speculations of innovating ages, and restless men. Then, should the Almighty, in awful retribution upon the world for their unfaithful use of the gospel of his mercy, permit a period to arrive in which the doctrines of Christianity shall be changed, and his Son, should he come, would scarcely find faith on the earth, this Liturgy will be as the ark of the ancient temple; in which posterity may find samples of the manna with which their fathers were fed; proofs, perhaps the only ones which will remain, of the substance and quality of that bread of life which came down from heaven.

SERMON XVIII.

ON PSALMODY.

2 Chronicles, v. 13, 14.

"It came even to pass, as the trumpeters and singers were as one, to make one sound to be heard in praising and thanking the Lord; and when they lifted up their voice with the trumpets, and cymbals, and instruments of music, and praised the Lord, saying, For he is good; for his mercy endureth for ever; that then the house was filled with a cloud, even the house of the Lord; so that the Priests could not stand to minister by reason of the cloud; for the glory of the Lord had filled the house of God."

"WILL God in very deed dwell on the earth? Behold, the heaven, and the heaven of heavens cannot contain him!" Yet we here find him, veiling himself in a cloud, and descending into the temple in all his glory, to testify by his presence, his gracious satisfaction in the choral hymns and melodious sounds, which, at the bringing up of his ark into his house, ascended unto him from a hundred instruments, and a thousand tongues. The scene is sublime. And, perhaps, among all the achievements for which music has been celebrated, we have here the greatest. In the temple just erected to the Almighty, King Solomon and his people are assembled. The whole company of the priests are in service. Singers in white, an unnumbered company, having cymbals, and psalteries, and harps, stand by the altar, and with them a hundred and twenty priests, sounding with trumpets. And it "came to pass, as the trumpeters and singers were as one, to make one sound to be heard in praising and thanking the Lord, and when they lifted up their voice with the trumpets and cymbals, and instruments of music, and praised the Lord, saying, For he is good, for his mercy endureth for ever, that then the house was filled with a cloud, even the house of the Lord, so that the priests could not stand to minister by reason of the cloud, for the glory of the Lord had filled the house of God."

The observations which these words will introduce, I am prompted to offer to your attention, by the laudable attempt which is now making, to reform the music of our Church; an attempt the motives to which are, I am persuaded, as pure as the end which it contemplates; and the accomplishment of which would greatly conduce to the beauty and perfection of our religious services. Much need will the speaker have of your candour and indulgence. Though an admirer of this heavenly art, he is unskilled in its principles and its practice, and cannot, therefore, be expected to rise to all the raptures which the contemplation of it by a proficient might justly inspire; or to descend to any of the particulars which relate to its scientific and happy performance. But he trusts he shall not be considered as going beyond his province, if he endeavour to show,

In the first place, why, or for what end, music is used in religious worship.

Secondly, what are the examples and authorities for it.

Thirdly, how it was performed by the first Christians.

And, lastly, after what manner we may best use it to our own benefit and the glory of God.

The aim of all that shall be said will be simply this, to excite your attention to the subject; and to engage you all to promote, as you are able, the improvement of this branch of public worship; which, as indeed may be said of every part of the service of God, if we perform it at all, we should endeavour to perform in the most excellent way.

Let us first consider, why music is used in religious worship? For what end it is introduced into the service of the sanctuary? For this, there can be no other unexceptionable reason, than that it is a very powerful and happy mean of exciting, or increasing, or expressing, our devout affections. It results from the constitution of our nature, that music, by a mysterious and potent agency, awakens the heart, concentrates the thoughts, and elevates the soul. There are chords in human nature which answer to its sounds. It touches, fixes, rules, relieves, delights the mind. The praises of God, the truths of religion, and the commendations of virtue, are, it would seem, most intensely dwelt upon, most deeply impressed upon the heart, and most agreeably expressed, when they are clothed with the accents, and followed through the windings of an engaging melody. "By reason," says a venerable father of the Church, "by reason of the proneness of our affections to that which delights, it pleased the wisdom of the Spirit, to borrow from melody that pleasure, which, mingled with heavenly mysteries, causes the smoothness and softness of that which touches the ear, to convey, as it were by stealth, the treasure of good things into men's minds; for this purpose were those harmonious tunes of psalms composed." This, then, is the end, for which music is used in religious worship; to assist our devotions, by an application to our affections of that, which has upon them a powerful action, to excite and direct them; by engaging us in an exercise in which sympathy has large scope, and every one acts upon the rest, to enable us to animate each other; to pour forth our praises and adorations in a way that is significant and edifying, delightsome and impressive. Should we suppose it introduced into the Church for any other purpose than this, we must first forget the sanctity of the place, and the business for which alone we here assemble.

A principle of so powerful action upon human nature as music is known to have, ought, unquestionably, to be applied to the promotion of the best objects which human nature can pursue. And hence, all nations have called to the aid of their religion and expression of their joy the measured hymn and the tuneful sound. Hence, too, we may infer the propriety with which instruments, designed for sacred use, are combined in our service with the human voice; for both have a tendency to the same end; the elevation of the soul and exciting and assisting of its devout affections. It may be added, that in the social performance of this exercise, there is necessarily in the concert, a perception and expression of unity which beautifully typifies, and in Christian bosoms may happily promote, that unity of spirit and affections which is so important a quality in the Church of Christ. And, moreover, as it is the glory of this art, to embrace and display only the principles of order and harmony, we may safely presume, that it is with great fitness and very acceptably brought into the service of that God, who is the lover of concord, and through all whose works order and harmony do eternally pervade. There is harmony in the movements of "the heavens," whereby they "declare the glory of God;" there is music among the spheres when they show forth "his handy work."

How far the end of introducing music in religious worship is actually accomplished, must depend upon many circumstances. But of its fitness and utility, who can doubt? Imagine a congregation assembled with sanctified affections, in the house of the Lord. They are conscious of the presence of God, their Creator and Redeemer; and their hearts glow with the love, their thoughts burn with the devotion which the contemplation of his perfections inspires. Penetrated with a sense of his goodness in having snatched them from destruction, each one is anxious to send from his heart a tribute of admiration and praise. The full-toned organ now breathes forth the majestic strain, consecrated to their feelings and to the words they are about to utter. From every part of the sacred place there rises, from unnumbered tongues, the glowing hymn, "Our God is good, his mercy endureth for ever." The voice of him whose brow is whitened with age, as he looks back upon fourscore years of divine protection and forward to a better world, lingers with delight upon the strain. The lips of the youth, whom education hath taught to adore the Divinity of the place, join, with sweet concord, in the strain of his sires. From every tongue, from the priest and the people, from the learned and the illiterate, from the rich and mighty, and from him that hath no other helper, resounds the peal, "Our God is good; his mercy endureth for ever." Methinks, if the Deity be present in his temple with his train, the hosts who compose his train would not disdain to join in the devotion, and the Almighty Father would condescend to listen to the creature's praise. Methinks, the fellow worshippers could hardly fail to catch new fervour from each other's song; and the unbeliever coming in, would fall down and worship.

Before we proceed to the second thing proposed, it may be well to remark, that, from the nature of the purposes for which music is introduced into our religious services, there arises an absurdity in making it a matter of mere entertainment, or of vain show; and also, that all kinds of music which have no tendency to aid and gratify devotion, ought to be banished from the house of God. Whatever charms such music may have, at suitable times and in proper places, it is unfit in the sanctuary.

Let us now consider, in the second place, some of the examples and authorities for making music a handmaid to religion. How long, or from how many worlds, praise has risen to the throne of Jehovah in tuneful sounds, we, beings of yesterday, and dwellers upon earth, are unable to ascertain. Probably, in all space, there are those who sing of his glory. The oldest anthem of which we have any account, was at the laying of the corner stone of this fair world, when "the morning stars sang together, and all the sons of God shouted for joy." Among the inhabitants of the earth, we may infer from such records as are left, it has been customary to call music to the service of religion and virtue, under the Patriarchal, the Mosaic, and the Christian dispensations. Man soon sought for himself the pleasure of forming melodious sounds. In a sixth person from Adam, we find Jubal mentioned, and honoured as the father of such as handle the harp and organ; nor can we doubt, that the dictate of nature, which has always led mankind to wed music with joy, especially when religion has owned the latter as her daughter, would induce them to bring the instruments and melodies with which they were delighted, to the assistance of their devotion in the Patriarchal age, when religious service seems very much to have consisted in adoration and praise. As we descend lower, we have surer information. In the very dawn of the Mosaic economy, music was engaged in the worship of the Deity. The most ancient song in the world, and one, than which there can be none more sublime and affecting, was a song to the Almighty, sung by the Israelites on the bank of the Red Sea; in which Moses and the people took the lead, and Miriam and the daughters of Israel answered them with timbrels and with dances. In the times of the tabernacle, when the ark of the Lord dwelt within curtains, hymns were appointed, and musical instruments provided, and singers set apart to thank and praise the Lord. The psalms of David, those wonderful compositions, which seem to have been breathed by the Spirit of God upon his harp for the use of the Church in every subsequent generation, were, most of them, as appears by their addresses and use, designed originally to be sung; and from the steps which the Psalmist took in providing for this part of religious service, it is incontrovertibly evident, that in his view, both the charms of poetry and the powers of sound should be employed to animate and aid the worshippers of God, and give grandeur to the service of his sanctuary. After the erection of the temple, it is, I presume, almost unnecessary to observe, that to "show themselves joyful before the Lord with trumpets and shawms," to "sing praises, to sing praises upon the harp unto their King," was, after their sacrifices, the most important part of the Jewish worship. Here were sung, in course, the psalms of David, with accompaniments of instruments consecrated to the use, and we have, in the text, a fine specimen of their manner, and an evidence of the approbation it obtained from Jehovah. A pause there was in the psalmody of the Jews. When they were carried away captive, they hanged their harps upon the trees, and faintly, if at all, sang the Lord's songs in a strange land. But at their return from captivity, the musical instruments which Solomon had provided for the service of the temple, were restored to them; the good and zealous Nehemiah re-established, with great care, the order of this part of divine service; and, at the time of the coming of our Lord, it was continued in the second temple.

If now we attend to the practice of the Christian era, we shall find this heaven-born art, the daughter of piety and delight, who has descended through so many ages, aiding and adorning the worship of the Almighty, still retained in the service of religion. It is among the precepts of inspiration that Christians should "sing and make melody in their hearts unto the Lord." Correspondent to the precept, has been the practice of the Church in every age. We find in the morning of Christianity, Apostles offering praise in social song. Pliny, in his famous letter to Trajan, describes the Christians chiefly as assembling to sing hymns unto Christ. And since the establishment of the gospel, I know of but one sect, and that of modern origin, among whose religious services psalmody has no place. But above all, that which conferred on music her highest glory, and entitles her forever to a place in the Christian temple, was the honour she received from the Son of God. The Author of our faith took her by the hand as she was yet lingering about the Jewish temple; he introduced her to his Church at the institution of his holy Supper; and from that day to this, she has been found in the Church in her purest and most exalted character. And who amongst us, whether skilled or unskilled in her mysteries, shall not here honour her for this? At the most affecting meeting they ever had, Jesus with his disciples sang a hymn.

Let us, in the third place, consider after what manner the first Christians performed this service. For the nearer we come to the model of the primitive Church in this, and in every part of faith and Christian duty, the nearer, in my estimation, we shall approach to perfection. It appears, then, from such an examination as I have been able to make, and I believe it is confirmed by the result of the most learned researches, that the psalmody of the first Christians was plain, simple, and solemn; and that the whole body of the church joined in the performance of it. Their tunes were, probably, easy and few, and the character of them such as expressed humility and love, and was calculated rather to melt than to enrapture the heart. Afterwards, as piety declined, it became necessary to re-excite and reanimate it by more striking music, and the whole congregation was divided into two parts, which sang responsive to each other. Inattention and indifference increased, for, alas! with how much difficulty is our frail nature kept engaged in the best services of God. We find in the fourth century, councils employed in devising means for reforming the music of churches; and precentors or choristers appointed to lead and instruct in this service such as were devoted to it. But it is evident from the sentiments of that age, and from the subsequent practice, that the end of this arrangement was to perfect the people in the art, and restore the simple primitive usage. The Church returned again to the plain song, in which every member probably, with modesty, according to the degree of his skill, bore his part of the exercise. The consigning of this service wholly and permanently to a separate band, if we except the practice of some Egyptian monasteries, was of more modern origin. The only difficulty is, to conceive how, in the primitive psalmody, as all are not singers, the inconvenience of dissonance was avoided. Probably they aimed more at the glory of God than at the gratification of a very fastidious ear. I will give you the evidence and account of the practice, in the words of St. Chrysostom, an ancient father of the Church: "Women and men," says he, "old men and children, differ in sex and age, but they differ not in the harmony of singing hymns, for the Spirit tempers all their voices together, making one melody of them all." Nor may we think that their music was lifeless and insipid. It was of such singing that the celebrated St. Augustin, addressing his spiritual father, exclaims: "O how I wept in the hymns and holy canticles, being enforced thereunto by the sweet voices of thy melodious Church."

I come now, in the last place, to furnish some brief suggestions how we may use this part of divine service to our own benefit and the glory of God. It is evidently desirable, that all the congregation should be able to unite their voices in the praise of God; and to this end the tunes should be few, plain, and calculated to move them to devotion. If any are utterly unable to sing, they should endeavour to make melody in their hearts; to send their thoughts to accompany the voices of the rest, in bearing to the footstool of the throne, the burthen of the hymn. Those who sing with but indifferent skill, should not forbear when they are able, to join in the exercise; and while the spirit is one, the affections one, and the psalm one, they may, it is presumed, in a moderate voice, avoid occasioning any intolerable discord, and add to the acceptableness of the service. With regard to the posture in which this duty may be best performed, for posture, in beings composed of body and spirit, is not a matter of indifference, I am told by those who are judges, that if performers stand while they sing, they sing both with more ease and more effect. And they who are not singers, should they rise with the rest, they might, by this act, express their union in the service. Indeed, as the example of Christ, the instruction of the Church, the practice of the pious of every age, and our own sober reflection teach us, that we pray most becomingly when we kneel; so standing appears to be the most suitable posture for praise. By the erection of the body we express the elevation of the soul; and also our respect for the Being whom we address. Should these brief hints be attended to, and what is of more consequence than all, the duty be performed with a single eye to the glory of our Creator and Redeemer, I cannot but flatter myself that they would aid the attempt to give new beauty, acceptableness, and effect, to this part of our public worship.

Let me first address myself to those of you who are singers. You are blessed with a talent above your fellows. Yours is a privilege which opens to you pleasures great, and peculiarly your own. It is a privilege which thousands would be glad to share. Shall no honour arise from it to Him from whom you have received it? What can be more ungrateful to "the Author and Giver of every good and perfect gift," than to refuse or neglect to employ in his service, those talents with which he hath blessed you, while you willingly employ them for the gratification of mortals like yourselves? "He that planted the ear," that wonderful organ, through which the delights of sound pass to the soul, and by which you are enabled to attune your voices to the concord of sweet sounds, "shall not he hear" the sweetest melody which your voices can utter, the most grateful hymns which your tongues can raise? If the Psalmist calls upon "every thing which hath breath, to praise the Lord," much more may we call upon you who, with breath, have the faculty of converting it to the production of significant and ravishing sound, to join in beautifying the services of God's temple; to bear for us our praises on the wings of your melody, to Him unto whom the angels sing.

Those of us who are unskilled in this art, may, I conceive, as well as the first disciples of our Lord, in due time be able to join without making excessive dissonance in the praises of our Creator and Redeemer. At least the rising generation may be accustomed to unite always in this part of the service; and the sons, if the fathers are unable, may be taught to bear for them this homage to the Most High. Other offices are appropriate. It is in this that the daughters of Zion should prophecy in the Church. It is thus, that in his temple, every man should speak of his honour.

To conclude. There is a brief address, which in an age when an attempt was making to restore to the Church a psalmody worthy of it, was provided by a celebrated council, to be given to those who were to take the lead in the work of reformation, and have the principal care of this part of the public service. The address might be given by a bishop or a presbyter, and it is not the less comprehensive and emphatic than the most finished charges of antiquity. It is contained in these few memorable words: "See that thou believe in thy heart what thou singest with thy mouth; and approve in thy works what thou believest in thy heart." This address, my brethren, allow me to impress upon you all. Vain is it to draw nigh to God with your lips if your heart is far from him. Vain is it to flatter yourselves that you draw near to him in your heart, if in your lives you dishonour him. But when the faith, the life, and the voice are in unison, sweet is the offering unto God. The sounds of your praise will reach unto heaven, and he who sitteth upon the throne will hear it with approbation and reward it with favour. Thus singing, your piety will be strengthened, your gratitude gladdened, your griefs relieved, and your affections raised; and you will be trained in the temple on earth, to join in the chorus which shall resound eternally through the arches of heaven, to the glory of the Being who there receives the homage of all perfect beings, and gladdens the hosts that worship him with eternal smiles.

SERMON XIX.

ON PUBLIC INSTRUCTION.

ROMANS, x. 14, 15.

"How then shall they call on him in whom they have not believed? And how shall they believe in him of whom they have not heard? And how shall they hear without a preacher? And how shall they preach except they be sent?"

OF the public means of grace provided by Almighty God for the birth, nourishment, instruction, accomplishment, and final salvation of the members of his Church, there remains one, my brethren, as yet to be treated of, in the course of Sermons which are devoted to these subjects; and to this one, you will permit me now to call your attention. It is that of public instruction, which is pressed upon our notice in all its importance in these words of the great Apostle of the Gentiles, which I have just read: "How shall they call on him in whom they have not believed? And how shall they believe in him of whom they have not heard? And how shall they hear without a preacher? And how shall they preach except they be sent?"

With us, there are three modes of instruction, each of which is a species of public promulgation of truth, having its distinct character and peculiar utility; by catechism, by reading the Scriptures, and by sermons.

The young have the tenderest care of the Church. For them is provided a particular system of instruction. And it is made a solemn and most interesting part of the duty of her ministers to feed these lambs. To this system of instruction, with such advantages of preparation as can be given them, they should be brought. For how shall these little ones learn to call with sincerity on their God and Redeemer in whom they have not believed? And how shall they believe in them, if of them they have never heard? And how shall they hear without instruction?

To the edification of the whole body of the Church is applied the public reading of the sacred Scriptures. Having discoursed to you at large upon their high character and utility, at the commencement of these discourses, I need here only observe, that we shall greatly err, if to the holy instructions which come through these channels we give less diligent heed than to those which come through any other. As means of public instruction, the Scriptures have advantage of all other compositions. If I speak of eloquence, lo! these are convincing, persuasive, powerful, "piercing even to the dividing asunder of soul and spirit, and of the joints and marrow." If I speak of taste, lo! these abound with the pure, the beautiful, and the sublime. If I speak of reasoning, lo! these are strong; and if of adaptation to the condition of the hearers, lo! every man from these may be "thoroughly furnished unto all good works." But that which raises the lessons which are read from the desk to a pre-eminence above all sermons which are heard from the pulpit, is this—that in the former are heard the words of God, in the latter, the words of fallible men. To the Scriptures, then, when they are read, should be given our most eager and devout attention. And let us not only hearken, but, as one with much emphasis has recommended, "apply what we hear; if examples, let these lead us; if precepts, let these teach us; if commands, let these bind us; if promises, let these encourage us; if threats, let these warn us; if mercies, let these comfort us; if judgments, let these awaken us."

But the means of public instruction more generally sought, and of more general use, and which was, probably, in the view of the Apostle's mind when he wrote my text, is preaching, or the declaring, explaining, and enforcing, by the ministry of men, of the Gospel of God. And the words of the Apostle bring to our view those points of this subject to which I am most anxious in this discourse to draw your attention. At first, the true end of preaching, to beget and cherish in the hearers a sound faith, upon the ground of which they may be led to call upon, obey, and confide in the God of their salvation. Secondly, the utility and importance of this means of grace; "How shall they believe in him of whom they have not heard? And how shall they hear without a preacher?" And thirdly, the qualification which should be found in every preacher, "How shall they preach except they be sent?"

Let us first advert to the true end of preaching. Is it, as it is frequently used, merely to entertain our ears, to exercise our minds with ingenious disquisition, or to promote the passing of an hour of holy time in a rational manner? Ah, no! The subjects on which we are to address you, admit not this supposition. The fall, the sinfulness, and helplessness of man; the incarnation of God for his recovery; the humiliation and crucifixion, the resurrection and ascension of his Redeemer; his feebleness without the assistance of the Holy Spirit, and his power with it; the solemn obligations of virtue; the transitoriness of this life; death, judgment, heaven, and hell; these are topics too momentous in their nature, too serious in their aspect to be made, in the discussion of them, mere occasions of entertainment. Unhappy is the failure of one of the most gracious provisions which the Almighty has made for the improvement of our race, if, when the fancy is gratified, neither faith is confirmed nor the heart made better!

Let me not be misunderstood. Far be it from me not to encourage the most assiduous care in bringing to the service of religion every power and charm of mind, imagination, and speech which may allure men to the contemplation of her holiness and beauty, and impress upon their hearts her blessed instructions. It is happy when, in any of her services, pleasure may be made her handmaid; and the opinion, that the aid of human accomplishments is useless in advancing her cause, if it have not been palmed upon the world by hypocrisy, is certainly the child of mistake. He who is emphatically denominated the wise man, sought to find out acceptable words. Prophets and Apostles present truth in a dress worthy of her majesty and beauty. And would I choose the figures of rhetoric which should be constantly by me to refresh and delight my mind, they should be gathered from the parables and comparisons of our blessed Lord. For not more truly of his doctrines than of the power of his speech and felicity of his illustrations, must it be said that "never man spake like this man."

But the great end of our Lord's discourses, and the end of every honest discourse of any of his ministers, is to lead men to the knowledge of God, and of the revelation of his mercy and will; to allure them into the paths of truth and goodness, and to conduct them therein, to the attainment of the object of all God's dispensations to our world, the salvation of their souls. Yes, my brethren, preaching has a higher object than the gratification of your taste. There are assigned to it more glorious purposes than the mere entertainment of your minds. It is its office to proclaim to you the only living and true God, and to make you acquainted with his character and laws, that you may believe, and, believing, may govern your conduct as becometh the offspring of such a Being—the subjects of such a King. It is its office to raise before you the cross, to show you the sacrifice upon it "which taketh away the sins of the world," and to entreat you to take of its blood and sprinkle it upon all your raiment, that when the destroying angel shall execute the vengeance of the Almighty upon a guilty world, it may be to you the token of everlasting preservation. It is its office to open for you the oracles of truth, and thence to bring to you the true knowledge of the foundation and excellency of every virtue; the motive by which it should be consecrated, and the extent to which it should be carried; and thence, also, to bring the probe which shall convict your hearts of sin. It is its office to go before you into the tomb with the bright torch which it receives from revelation; to disperse the blackness of darkness which hangs over its entrance, to show you the place where Jesus lay; to wipe away the tears which are falling upon the mouldering relics; and when the blood throbs at the heart amidst the horrors of the scene, to restore it to its sober, equal flow, by reminding you that Jesus is risen, and that this awful dominion, with its awful king, shall be finally overturned. It is its office to draw aside the veil which conceals from view the eternal world; to show you hell and all its torments, and beseech you to escape; to show you heaven and all its glories, and entreat you to enter. It may, it must divide its work. At one time it declares the doctrines of the Gospel, and at another the duties which spring from them. Now it dwells upon what is due to God, and now upon what is due to men. But the object of all is the renovation of your nature after the image of Him who created you; that having been redeemed from death, you may be restored to the liberty and glorious privileges of the children of God. This is the object of preaching, which renders it an institution worthy to have had the Almighty for its author. This is the object, by the pursuit of which alone, the faithful minister may answer the instructions and charges he has received, and conform himself to the example of those holy preachers, who were the earliest and most approved messengers of the Almighty to men. This is the object, without the attainment of which, the hearing of sermons, whatever pleasure it may afford, yields not the fruit which is valuable to them who hear. If this object be lost sight of, or fail, our preaching is vain, and your attention is vain also.

If, then, this means of grace be well adapted to the promotion of the object to which it is devoted, the second point will become clear and striking, namely, its utility and importance. Now, it must be acknowledged in the outset, that the effects of the preaching of the Gospel are fewer and less satisfactory than might reasonably be expected. For when we consider the strength of evidence which God hath furnished for the foundation of our faith, it may well surprise the judicious, that the ministers of religion should ever have occasion to exclaim, "Who hath believed our report?" And when we consider the importance of the interests involved in the discussion, and the evident adaptation of Christianity to the necessities and desires of man, it may well astonish the thoughtful that there should so often be occasion to renew the ancient lamentation, "Ah, Lord God! they say of me, Doth he not speak parables?" Much, we are sensible, of the inefficacy of preaching is to be attributed to our feebleness and manifold imperfections, unto whom is committed the word of life. For though this "ministry of reconciliation" be a treasure of inestimable value, yet, alas! you "have this treasure in earthen vessels."

It is worthy of consideration, also, whether some of the reasons why the great truths of the Gospel which are so often inculcated, do not always produce their proper effects, may not be found in the disposition of mind with which they are sometimes heard, and the quality of life by which the hearing of them is frequently followed. Allow me to instance in a few particulars. Are they always heard with a docile disposition? Our blessed Lord most strongly inculcated the importance of this disposition, yea, its absolute necessity, to an obedient reception of his Gospel, when he took a little child and set him in the midst of his disciples, and said, "Except ye become as little children, ye shall not enter into the kingdom of God." It was the predominance in their bosoms of very different qualities which, when it was given to the humble fishermen of Galilee to know the mysteries of the kingdom of God, caused all these things, in the view of the haughty Pharisee, and of the carnal Publican, to be done in parables.

Again. It may be inquired, whether the measure of knowledge or grace which at any time we have received, has been faithfully used? Or whether, because we have as yet received but one talent, we have, with culpable indolence and timid apprehension of our master's austerity, wrapped that talent in a napkin, and buried it in the earth? For it is a principle of the economy of the divine government in the spiritual world, which is not without its analogy in the natural world, "that from him that hath not shall be taken away even that which he seemeth to have."

Further. With the same intent it may be inquired, whether men, when they hear sermons, do supplicate the blessing of the Almighty to accompany his word? Man's natural life is not sustained "by bread alone," and the viands which a gracious Providence furnishes for him, but by the attendant will of Him who hath appropriated them to their use. In like manner, the means of spiritual life are inefficient, if they be not sanctified by benediction and prayer.

But after all the abatements which must be made on account of the deficiencies of preachers and negligence of hearers, there will remain a sufficient sum of good resulting from this means of grace, to convince us of its utility and importance. Considered as the appointment of the Most High, it must be adapted to the purposes for which he hath ordained it. Considered as the instrument by which the altars of Paganism were overturned, and their gods driven into non-existence by the first Apostles of our blessed Lord, and Jews and Gentiles gathered by them into one fold, it is worthy of our admiration. Considered as a mean of enlightening and civilizing mankind, the evidence of historic fact attests its importance. It was in the ages in which preaching was rare, that superstition spread her pall over the human mind. And it is in countries and ages in which it has been enjoyed in an enlightened and holy character, and regular appearance, that the manners of men will be found softened, their minds instructed, their morals purified, their faith rational, their hopes constant, and their departure from this life more peaceful and resigned. Shall I err if I add, that considered with regard to the condition and dispositions of the mass of mankind, it is a mean of religious instruction, without which, many under the clouds of ignorance would become the prey of perdition, and for which we all have cause to be grateful to Him that hath ordained it. How many of our fellow-beings are there, who have neither opportunity nor capacity to discover and open for themselves the fountains of truth, and who would perish in their thirst but for the streams which they find in the sanctuary! How many more are there, who, immersed in the business, encumbered with the cares, or surrounded with the beguiling pleasures of life, would have their minds wholly estranged to all consistent views of God and goodness, but for the weekly exercises, which, with the consideration and care of a parent, God has provided for them in the Christian world. And have we not all, as members of a Christian family, cause to be grateful, that God hath committed unto men to be constantly exercised, "the ministry of reconciliation," whereby his word shall perpetually be dispensed, and portions of the bread of life distributed to every one of the household in season.

I know not where, but in the Church of God, this mode of religious instruction is enjoyed. Paganism hath manifested no such concern for the instruction of its votaries. It was worthy of the free, liberal, and compassionate spirit of the gospel, that its author should have provided, by the appointment of a priesthood to wait continually on this very thing, for the instruction in their faith, their duties, and their privileges, of all his followers unto the end of the world. And when I consider the special obligations to gratitude which this kind provision for us begets, the incalculable advantages which we may derive from it, and the expectation from us of superior attainments in knowledge and virtue which it authorizes, I discern a solemn import of which we should never lose sight, in that pertinent injunction of our Lord, "Take heed how ye hear."

We have now, my Christian friends, finished the consideration of the public means of grace, upon which, in a succession of discourses, our thoughts have, for some time past, been fixed. We have contemplated the Scriptures, the foundation of all our religion, and have considered their inspiration; their completeness, their use, and our felicity in possessing them. We have pondered the necessity and utility of rites and ordinances in a religion designed for men; and the advantages of a priesthood for the regular and valid administration of them. We have bestowed much thought upon the Sacraments of Christianity, Baptism and the Lord's Supper; and have endeavoured to investigate their nature and obligatoriness, the qualifications with which they should be received, and the obstacles which at any time impede the observance of them. We have adverted to the institution of the Sabbath, and from its history, the divine command, and divers other considerations, have deduced our obligation to hallow it; and inquired concerning the proper methods of keeping it holy. We have contemplated the propriety of erecting sanctuaries for the worship of God; and have shown both how and why they should be reverenced. We have dwelt with pleasure upon the excellencies of the Liturgy, which the Church, under the special goodness of God, hath provided for our use; and have attempted to bring to notice and practical utility, some of its most striking and important properties. Upon psalmody we have bestowed a discourse; and have endeavoured to show the principles upon which it is introduced into the service of religious worship, and how it may be best used to our own benefit and the glory of God. And to-day we have contemplated the several methods of public instruction, particularly preaching, of which we have wished to ascertain the proper end, and have remarked the utility and importance of it. I have been induced, my brethren, thus long and fully, to address you upon these means of grace; by a conviction, that as bread and the viands which God hath bountifully provided for us, are the means of sustaining our natural life, so these are the means of our sustenance and growth in grace, and advancement to the stature of perfect men in Christ. When I look abroad, and observe the declension of piety in some, the progress of irreligion in others, and the extension of fanaticism and false religion among more, I fear these evils are to be traced to a departure from the simplicity of the gospel; a want of holy and constant adherence to the way, which, with wise and kind accommodation to our nature and present condition, God hath marked out for us to walk in. In discoursing upon these diverse and important subjects, I have often lamented my want of skill, more fully to illus-strate and more powerfully to enforce. But I know that God is able to bless the endeavours of the humblest of his instruments, to the advancement of the cause in which he condescends to employ them.

My brethren, beloved in the Lord, upon a topic more important than this, to your advancement in virtue and your everlasting happiness, I could not have addressed you. It hath pleased our heavenly Father, after ample demonstration, that "the world by wisdom knew not God"—"by the foolishness of preaching to save them that believe." The instructions which this ordinance opens to you were not obtained but by the incarnation of the Son of God. To procure the influences of the Holy Spirit, to render these instructions efficacious, and the fruits of them acceptable to the Almighty, your Redeemer shed his blood. For the right use of every sermon which you hear, you may justly be called to account; and, it is most probable, that such as shall be the measure of your seriousness and care, in laying the word of God to your hearts, will be the measure of your faith and virtue here, and of your happiness forever. Hear then his word with meekness, and receive it always with pure affection. And God grant, that every seed of his word which shall, in this place be sown, may be productive, as he shall see fit, of its thirty, its sixty, or its hundred fold; that in the great day of retribution, when for the means of instruction which so highly distinguish us above a large portion of our race, we shall be all called to account, you may each one be able to say, Lord, thy pound hath gained two, or five, or ten pounds; and hear the ravishing words from the lips of your Judge, "Well done, good and faithful servant, enter thou into the joy of thy Lord."

SERMON XX.

ON ADVENT.

St. Matthew, xxi. 5.

"Tell ye the daughter of Zion, Behold, thy King cometh."

THE Church is frequently spoken of in Scripture under the title of the daughter of Zion. For this, there are obvious reasons. Zion was her pristine abode. She dwelt, most especially, upon that hill where the Lord promised his blessing. There she stood collected, and there she went forth in her strength. There she received her richest dowry, and her costliest jewels; and there she sent out the distribution of her choicest gifts. There she met her Lord; and thence, she is one day to hear the consummation of her renown; the loftiest celebration of her glory, and beauty, and victories.

But, though from the holy mount she hath taken one of her titles, there is nothing restrictive in the appellation. She is the same in every age, in every country, and in every place. Whether she wait at Bethel or at Shiloh; whether she tremble at the foot of Sinai, or rejoice on the sides of Zion; whether she be confined to Jerusalem, or extended over the whole earth, the Church is one, and her head one, and her faith one, and the ground of all her hopes, and services, and expectations one, and the same forever. And wherever she be dwelling, in whatever region of the earth she can be found, at this season of Advent, there is not a message with which she can more suitably be addressed, than this in the text: "Tell ye the daughter of Zion, Behold, thy King cometh."

If we contemplate some of the leading purposes for which, under this character, the Head of the Church cometh, we shall find in this annunciation, matter of great joy and serious reflection.

In the first place, the King of the daughter of Zion came to destroy her enemies; sin, and death, and hell. Subject to these is every descendant of Adam; and under the awful consequences of this subjection must have for ever remained, if help had not been laid upon one mighty to save. For this purpose was the Redeemer sent forth by the Father. The end of his coming was, to take away the sins of the world, and be death's destruction. The sins of every true member of the Church he taketh away by the most precious sacrifice of himself, to satisfy the justice of heaven. And by his own death, he hath virtually destroyed death, and him that had the power of death; that is, the devil; and hath brought life and immortality to light for all them that believe. This is the mighty conquest achieved by Christ in our behalf; which commenced when he "bare our sins in his own body on the tree," and will be completed in the day of the final consummation, when death shall be "swallowed up in victory." For this deliverance of his captive offspring, which God, in his great mercy, desired, the the Son of God was invested by him with all power in heaven and on earth. And "he must reign till he hath put all enemies under his feet. The last enemy that shall be destroyed, is death; for he hath put all things under his feet." "The sting of death is sin, and the strength of sin is the law;" but to the nations that are saved, there is given victory through their Lord Jesus Christ. Of this victory, every living member of his Church partaketh; for them hath he purchased with his blood. "Rejoice greatly, O daughter of Zion," saith the Prophet to whom the Evangelist in the text alludes, "shout, O daughter of Jerusalem, Behold, thy King cometh unto thee, he is just, and having salvation."

Another object of the advent of Messiah the Prince, was to gather together the children of God into one kingdom; for the coming of which, in its completeness and universal establishment, we are taught to pray daily in the Lord's prayer; and which, on account of its excellency, is styled sometimes in Scripture, "the kingdom of heaven." To this end Christ hath died, and rose, and revived, that he might be Lord of the dead and the living. God hath set him as his King upon his holy hill of Zion. And this is the Almighty's great decree: "Desire of me, and I shall give thee the heathen for thine inheritance, and the uttermost parts of the earth for thy possession."

It was one of the first acts of this King after his appearance in the flesh, to break down the wall of partition between Jews and Gentiles, and of both to make one. And unto the Church, on the promulgation of tidings of salvation, the Gentiles were immediately seen flying, according to the beautiful simile of the Prophet, as "doves to the windows." The fulness of them is to come in. All nations shall fall down before him; all people shall do him service. "He hath on his vesture a name written, KING OF KINGS, AND LORD OF LORDS." The events of our day show us the extension of his kingdom, and the gathering to him of the people. To the occurrences in the east, one can hardly refrain from applying the prophetic words, "I am sought of them that asked not after me, I am found of them that sought me not."

But though the wall of partition is broken down, God hath not cast away his people. The inscription on the cross, though Pilate meant not so, shall yet be fulfilled: "THIS IS JESUS THE KING OF THE JEWS." "He came" first "to his own, and his own received him not," and, therefore, are scattered among all the nations of the earth. Yet they shall return; and "look on him whom they pierced;" and "every tongue shall confess that he is Lord, to the glory of God the Father."

This, then, is a most interesting object of the advent of Christ; to enlarge the border of the Church; to extend the participation of the sure mercies of God; to open the kingdom of heaven to all believers; to make known the mystery that the Gentiles should be fellow heirs, and of the same body with God's ancient people, and partakers of his promise in Christ by the gospel; to bring both Jews and Gentiles into one fold under one shepherd, giving them his peace; that thus, the Church of the living God might be as extensive as the families of men; and in him, the true and most eminent seed of Abraham, all the nations of the earth be blessed.

And this leads me to observe another object of the coming of Christ, viz: to administer the government of his kingdom; promulgating its laws; dispensing its blessings; and protecting and ordering the subjects of it. "His kingdom is not of this world." It is that spiritual kingdom which God hath had in the world in all ages. Its entertainments are not meat and drink, but righteousness, peace, and joy in the Holy Ghost. In it are found, not they who go about to establish their own righteousness, but they who have submitted themselves to the righteousness of Christ. To it resort, not they who never heaved a sigh under the burthen of sin and misery, to which they are heirs, but they who "labour and are heavy laden," grieved and wearied, and seeking rest. Into it are welcomed, not the self-complacent and vainglorious, but the poor in spirit, the humble and penitent, who hunger and thirst after righteousness, and desire forgiveness. In it abide not the unbelieving and disobedient, but they who, with confidence in the word of the Most High, lay hold of his great and needed mercies in Christ Jesus, and are led by the contemplation of them, to love him and all his creatures, and to endeavour to perform all such good works as are acceptable in his sight. For these, his true and proper subjects, there are secured and deposited in his kingdom, the pardons of sin, the instructions and assistances of the Holy Spirit, and the titles and deeds of eternal life.

To deliver us from our enemies, to establish his kingdom and promulgate its laws, and to proclaim and evidence the certainty of his great salvation, he once hath come in person to our world. But he remaineth not visible in the administration of its affairs.

"For the kingdom of heaven is as a man travelling into a far country, who called his servants and delivered unto them his goods." With his Church he hath left his word and his sacraments, by which, through the agency of his ministers, the members of it are built up in the faith of his gospel, and nurtured for the regions of glory. Nevertheless, "the government is upon his shoulder." Of all power in his Church, he is the source; of all the gifts of his people, he is the author, of all their attainments, he is the strength.

When he ascended up on high, he, as their King, took possession of heaven; whence he dispenseth the gifts of the Holy Ghost to those who ask it; and where he is preparing mansions for all those who love his appearing. His throne is established in the heavens. He sitteth on the right hand of God; and hath the keys of death and of hell. All nature is subject to his control. The devils, he hath subdued. The elements, and the hearts of men, he hath in his hands. And ten thousand times ten thousands of angels minister unto him. In this plenitude of power which the Father hath given him, he looketh upon his Church, and upon every sincere member of it, and with undiminished affection for those whom he died to save, causeth all things to work together for their good.

After a long time, at the end of the world, this King, who hath travelled into a far country, to take possession of his and his people's inheritance, returneth. From his state of exaltation, Christ shall come again, in glorious majesty, to judge the quick and dead. He returneth to execute vengeance upon his adversaries; concerning whom he will say in the great day, "Those mine enemies, who would not that I should reign over them, bring them hither and slay them before me." But, for his faithful adherents he returneth, to take them to his better country; to the mansions he went to prepare for them; that, changed and glorified, they may be presented faultless before the presence of the Father, and be forever with their Lord. With his servants is yet left the message: "Tell ye the daughter of Zion, Behold, thy King cometh;" just, indeed, as at the first, and bringing unto thee salvation; but "riding" now "upon the heaven in thy help, and in his excellency on the sky."

Such are some of the great ends of the advent of the Redeemer. And now, brethren, "what think ye of Christ?" Who is this King and Head of the Church? "This that cometh from Edom, with dyed garments from Bozra? This that is glorious in his apparel, travelling in the greatness of his strength?" "Who is this King of glory?" "The Lord of Hosts;" the everlasting Son of the Father, the Creator and Upholder of all worlds, he, O daughter of Zion, he is this King. "The Lord of Hosts;" "The mighty God;" the only begotten Son of the Highest; he is this King of glory.

In announcing to you the approach of the festival of his nativity, the Church, in some sense, repeats the message, ."Behold, thy King cometh;" meek, for he shall be presented to you as a babe lying in a manger; "and having salvation," for he shall meet you at his holy table with the pledges of pardon and eternal life. How should we meet him? With faith in him as our Deliverer, and songs of "Hosanna in the highest," with that gladness of heart, which caused the multitude to cut down branches from the trees and strew them in the way, and that sense of our happiness in his salvation, which will fill us with benevolence to every fellow being. Take with you faith, and hope, and charity, and come to his temple, to offer him your homage and your gifts; and the celebration of his first advent may prepare you for the great day of his second coming.

SERMON XXI.

ON ADVENT.

ST. MATTHEW, xi. 3.

"Art thou he that should come, or do we look for another?"

THERE is no part of the economy of our Church more proper and excellent, than the appropriation of the four Sundays preceding Christmas, to the preparation of our minds for the celebration of that festival. The portions of Scripture, which she has appointed to be read during this joyous season, set before us the necessity of a Saviour, the nature and end of his mission, some principal prophecies relative to his kingdom, the annunciation of Gabriel to his mother and her cousin, and the birth and testimonies of his forerunner John. To further the object contemplated in this arrangement, no passage of Scripture can be more suitable for our meditation at our entrance on these days of joy, than that question of the Baptist which he sent to Christ, "Art thou he that should come, or do we look for another?"

The words will very naturally lead us to consider in the first place the singular and important truth, that before the nativity of Christ, there was an expectation of some personage that should come, great and greatly to be honoured.

And, secondly, that the Author of our religion was "he of whom Moses and the Prophets did write," and for whose appearance the whole world was waiting.

The traces of the tradition of the promise first made to man, that a Redeemer should be born of a woman, were never wholly effaced. We discover it in innumerable transactions and sentiments of the oldest families of the earth, whose history is preserved in the sacred volume; for which we can in no way satisfactorily account, but by referring them to a desire, that, of them or their descendants the promised seed should be born. Remains of it are evident in the wish, and the hope, expressed by many of the most ancient and respectable philosophers, that the gods would, one time or another, send a teacher into the world, who should remove the darkness which bounded their researches, and instruct them in many things, which it evidently concerned them to know. As the time approached for the advent of the Messiah, expectation looked more earnestly; and, whether it may be attributed to tradition, to inspiration, to what the Prophets had promulged, or, which is most likely to all these causes at the period when Jesus Christ was born, the eyes of expectation were fixed upon Judea. How far this was the case in the Gentile world, is evident from the testimony of two of the most eminent profane historians. One of them* says: "There was an ancient and general opinion, famous throughout all the eastern parts, that the fates had determined, that there should come out of Judea, those who should govern the world." The other† declares, that "a great many were possessed with a persuasion, that it was contained in the ancient books of the priests, that, at that very time the East should prevail, and that they who should govern the world should come out of Judea." These testimonies are very decisive. Many others of a similar nature might be adduced from the expressions of the heathen poets and the observations of other writers. But I conceive these are sufficient to confirm our assertion. I cannot, however, forbear to observe, that the conduct of the Magi, related in Scripture, evinces the existence of the sentiment in Persia and Arabia, where they are supposed to have resided; for with what readi-

* Sueton. Lib. viii. c. 4. † Tacit. Hist. Lib. v.

ness and certainty, when they saw the star in the east, did then hasten towards Judea, to seek the extraordinary personage who was born King of the Jews.

While the rays of expectation were thus scattered throughout the heathen world, among the Jews, a nation ancient, distinct, and taught of God, they were strong and collected. A Messiah, a great personage to come, was a grand object of Jewish hope. They all looked for such a character. Led by the instructions of their ancestors and by their sacred writings, it was part of their common belief, that some one should be born among them, who should be unequalled by any one before or after him, in greatness and in glory. So essential a part of their religion was this, that they still retain it, and, having rejected the true Immanuel, according to their predictions of their Prophets, are yet looking for his appearance. But the time at which Christ was born, was the period when they universally expected him. Tradition and their Scriptures had alike led them to this period, and innumerable evidences render it indisputable, that here they took a stand and were "waiting for the consolation of Israel." If it had not been for such an expectation, would multitudes, just about that time, have declared themselves Messiahs, and, with their flimsy pretences, have obtained followers? An age, when science, the detector of art was at its acme, what could have made it advantageous for imposture? An age, when every thing was unfavourable to the introduction of a new religion, why should it have abounded with false Christs? If it had not been for such an expectation, would the jealousy of Herod have been excited by the visit and business of the wise men from the East? Holding his power by the will of the Roman emperor, what had he to fear from a Jew? Naturally bold and confident, why should he have dreaded a rival in a babe? Yet, he immediately collected the priests, demanded of them, not when, but where the Christ should be born, and, to relieve his jealousy, dooms all the male children of Bethlehem and its neighbourhood to bleed. Indeed, the Jewish rabbies inform us, that there was instruction received in the ancient school of Elias, a source to them of certainty, that at the end of the second two thousand years the Messias should come. There was also a computation made by a number of Jewish doctors, previous to the birth of Christ, the result of which confirmed the tradition from the family of Elias. These, together with the plain and common interpretation of those prophecies, which related to the time of the appearance of the Messiah, fixed their attention on the age when Christ was born, and held them in full expectation of a deliverer. If this be not conclusive, there is a passage of their historian Josephus, with which I shall close the evidence of this singular and important truth: "The Jews," says he, "rebelled against the Romans, being encouraged thereto by a celebrated prophecy in their Scriptures, that, about that time a famous prince should be born among them, who should rule the world."

Thus, then, we arrange our ideas upon this point. The gracious promise to the first human pair, that "the seed of the woman should bruise the serpent's head," was never wholly lost. In the heathen world, like the original sentiment of a God, it became faint, and was corrupted. But still, a glimpse of it sometimes appeared, especially in the mind of the studious and virtuous sage. In the family of Abraham it was kept alive. At intervals it was renewed and unfolded. When the Jews were separated from all other people, and formed into a nation under a theocracy, the Prophets of the Almighty repeated the promise more and more explicitly, till, like the dawn, obscure at first, and opening gradually, it expanded into full light; and all observers saw that in the east the sun should presently appear. There was a full expectation of a personage great and greatly to be honoured, when Christ was born; and John sent no unmeaning nor untimely question to him in the text, "Art thou he that should come, or do we look for another?"

How singular and wonderful was this expectation of an extraordinary person to be born into our world! It could have come only from God. Would he have raised it without intending it should be answered? Would the Most High sport with the minds of his creatures? No! It was intended by way of preparation. It was high presumptive evidence in favour of any one who should appear with plausible credentials.

Let us, then, hasten to the second thing proposed, and show that the Author of our religion was HE, "of whom Moses and the Prophets did write," and for whose advent the world was waiting.

The first evidence of this which we will notice, is that he perfectly answered the purposes for which he was expected in the Gentile world. The ground on which they hoped for an instructor from heaven was their utter inability satisfactorily to ascertain their duty, or answer the queries of the mind respecting man's extinction or immortality. They wanted instruction in their duty. Of God, and the economy of his government, they had but imperfect knowledge. Of virtue and the chief good, they could gain no full, indubitable ideas. The systems of different teachers opposed each other. And when virtue appeared clear and indisputable, nature was so frail that they fell before they reached it. But the Author of our religion has removed all these difficulties. Need any one now be ignorant of the true God or of his attributes, and the nature of his government? Need any one continue doubtful what is the measure of right, or wherein happiness consists? Is there one virtue undefined, or one vice unreprobated, to which he is exposed? Can any disciple of Christ have his mind puzzled like the minds of heathen sages, about his duty, the wonders that surround him, and the chief good? When he feels in doubt whether the Deity is placable, and will assist his frailty, need he despond, or be at a loss how to seek for the means and use them, which will enable him to do what is required of him? Every point of duty is clearly and certainly made known by him, who, coming from the bosom of the Father, understood his will, and infinite in wisdom, knew what was in man.

Further. The extinction or immortality of man, was an interesting subject, upon which reason could discover nothing certain. It was of all points most important, and excited the greatest anxiety. But the most which heathen philosophy could do was to maintain a dubious hope. Nothing but certainty upon this subject could give satisfaction to the mind which nourished the desire of information from heaven. The Author of our religion, anticipating the anxiety of nature, has placed this matter beyond dispute. He "has brought life and immortality to light;" and familiarizing our minds with a rational account of death, teaches us how he is subdued, and that we are destined for future glory. What he taught, he exemplified; giving us, in his own resurrection, a sure earnest that we shall be raised to life. "Do we," then, "look for another?" What can another do which Jesus hath not done? Can there be a greater atonement offered for the sins of the world? Or greater demonstration given by God that he hath accepted the atonement? Can there be a purer morality preached, a more excellent path opened for human beings to walk in? Can the tomb be more joyfully enlightened, or the kingdom of heaven more satisfactorily opened, consistently with the nature of our probationary state, and with the existence of the veil with which God, in his infinite wisdom, thought fit to separate the visible from the invisible world?

Another evidence that the Author of our religion is he who should come, is that he, and he only, exhibited the fulfilments of the predictions upon which the Jews grounded the expectations of a Messiah. Here a field opens before us of vast extent and various productions. To notice every thing in it which has reference to the point at hand, would require more time than we can spare; I shall, therefore, confine myself to the principal prophecies which respect the time and the consequences of the Saviour's advent. These are more explicit, and their consequences carry conviction into our minds more forcibly than any others.

There are three memorable predictions which point to the time when "the desire of all nations" should come. The first, venerable for its author and its age, is that of good old Jacob, upon his death-bed: "The sceptre shall not depart from Judah, nor a lawgiver from between his feet until Shiloh come." The Jews, and all paraphrasts, take this prediction of the Patriarch to mean, that the civil authority should not depart from the house of Judah, nor the Jews cease to be governed by their own political laws, till the time of the coming of the Messiah. Now, about the period when Christ was born, the first foreign governor was set over Judea, as a province, by the Roman authority; and not long after he had finished his ministry, the Jewish polity, with their city, was destroyed, and the people dispersed into all countries of the earth, where, to this day, they continue, without confederation or power, and subject to the government under which they happen to live. Surprising coincidence between the prophecy and events! Surely, in Christ Shiloh is come!

Again. Daniel declared, that the time from the giving of orders to restore and build Jerusalem to the end of the Messiah's ministry, should be seventy weeks. That is, according to prophetic arithmetic, four hundred and ninety years. Now, if from the time at which our Lord closed his ministry upon the cross, which was in the nineteenth year of the reign of Tiberius, the Roman emperor, we count backwards four hundred and ninety years, it brings us to the seventh year of Artaxerxes, in which very year Ezra received orders to repair to Jerusalem, make arrangements for rebuilding it, and restore the oblations of the temple. Here are a most definite prophecy and exact fulfilment; and it is remarkable, that computations made by Jewish doctors before Christ was born, place the termination of Daniel's weeks just about the time when he was crucified.

There remains one other remarkable prediction for ascertaining the period of the true Messiah. It is the declaration of the Almighty to Zerubbabel and Joshua, who regretted that in point of magnificence and tokens of divine favour, the first temple far excelled the second; that "the desire of all nations" should come, and that the glory of this house should be greater than that of the former, and that in it he would give peace.

This appeared so plain, that it was a prevalent sentiment among the Jews that their deliverer should come while the second temple was standing. He did so; and preached in it the gospel of peace, and by his presence filled the house with the divine glory. Shortly after, it was reduced to the ruins in which it has since remained; and one of their rabbies, who saw it razed to the ground, declared that the time of the Messiah was past. Thus minutely does the advent of Christ correspond with the time for his coming who was expected; and thus did the Jews contribute to the establishment of the cause which they were labouring to subvert.

The Jews having committed themselves, by declaring that to be the time of the Messiah, which elapsed while they were rejecting Christ, soon afterwards argued that his advent was deferred because of the sins of the people. Strange that the conduct of men should derange the counsels of the Most High! That He should not foresee what would be the situation of things at the time which he fixed and promulged for sending his Son into the world! While we are amazed at the incredulity of those to whom the Messiah presented himself, let us adore the depths of the wisdom of God; for when we review what was previously written concerning him, it must be a powerful confirmation of our faith, "that blindness did, in part, happen unto Israel."

Which leads me to observe, once more, under this head, that the situation of the people to whom he was promised, is now, and has been for sixteen hundred years, what the Prophets foretold it should be after the days of the Messiah, and unfitted for giving birth to any other who can answer the descriptions of the promised seed. As was predicted, they have rejected Christ. As was predicted, they have since been scattered through the earth. As was predicted, they remain unparalleled in the history of nations, a distinct people. And, as was predicted, they seem reserved for that restoration and fulness of dominion which is to crown the second advent of our Lord. In this situation, it is not easy to conceive how we may look for another who shall answer the description of the promised seed. Where, now, is the lineage and household of David, of which Immanuel must spring? Who, now, inhabit Bethlehem, the town of promise, and where is the Jewish crown to which the Messiah shall be heir? Where, now, is the second temple in which he shall appear; and where the hitherto unalienated sceptre to depart from Judah when Shiloh comes? Where, now, is the idolatry which, when he comes, the Messiah shall find in all the earth, when the Author of our religion has introduced the knowledge and worship of the true God? Where, now, are the sacrifice and the oblation which Messiah the Prince is to cause to cease? And who after Jesus can have any thing to add to render the moral law complete? What spirit more holy can be poured out from on high than that which hath been shed abroad by Christ; and how shall another challenge to himself the praise of taking away "the face of the covering cast over all people, and the veil that is spread over all nations?" The work is done which Messiah was to perform, and consequently the time of his appearance is past. What Jesus hath done, forbids us to wish, and the state of the Jews and other consequences of his coming, forbid us to look for another. With more than the ground of Philip's faith we may adopt this declaration: "We have found him of whom Moses in the law and the Prophets did write, Jesus of Nazareth, the son of Joseph."

The last evidence which we will notice, that the Author of our religion is he, "of whom Moses and the Prophets did write," and for whom the world was waiting, is the positive testimony which he brought with him, and to which he himself appealed. At his entrance upon his ministry, he declared himself to be the Messiah, the person of whom the Scriptures testified. This he sufficiently proved to ingenuous observers, by descending from the family, being born in the place, enduring the hardships, leading the life, doing the works, and suffering the death which the Prophets had foretold. But while he thus answered, in every point, the description which had been given of the Saviour who was to come, he confirmed his right to that character by fair and full displays of divine power. Miracles are the most natural and satisfactory credentials which a messenger from heaven can be supposed to bring. Such they were always considered, and as such, it was declared that they should accompany the Prophet who should come into the world. When the Saviour found himself rejected by his own, that they would not receive him as the Messiah, he pointed them to his works, arguing that if they would give no credit to the words of one, who came under all the circumstances, and with all the marks by which the prophetic spirit had described their deliverer, they ought to perceive that his declaration of his character was attested in his miracles, by the power of God. If I do not "the works of my Father, believe me not; but if I do, though ye believe not me, believe the works, that ye may know and believe, that the Father is in me, and I in him."

The miracles which the Saviour wrought possessed every character of credibility which could be required. They were wrought in evidence of a doctrine worthy of God. They were wrought at no particular times, and in no set place, but before the eyes of anybody, in the public streets, whenever occasion presented. They were such as were beyond the reach of any powers of nature, like instantaneous cures of mortal diseases, and raising of the dead. They bore marks of divine beneficence, in that they were promotive of the happiness of men. There was no collusion, for in performing them Christ was alone. There was no aim at profit or honour, for they subjected their author to hatred, persecution, and death. Above all, to give them a twofold force, they were exactly those which it had been declared, for hundreds of years before his birth, the great personage who was to come should perform. "Behold," says Isaiah, "your God will come, he will come and save you. Then the eyes of the blind shall be opened, and the ears of the deaf shall be unstopped; then shall the lame man leap as an hart, and the tongue of the dumb shall sing; the Spirit of the Lord is upon me, because he hath anointed me to preach good tidings to the meek, he hath sent me to bind up the broken-hearted, to proclaim liberty to the captives, and the opening the prison to them that are bound, to proclaim the acceptable year of the Lord." So that the miracles of our blessed Lord are, of themselves, sufficient evidence that he was the extraordinary character who should come; and he gave a satisfactory answer to the Baptist's inquiry in the text, when he replied to the disciples who brought it, "Go, and tell John those things which ye both see and hear: the blind receive their sight, the lame walk, the lepers are cleansed, and the deaf hear, the dead are raised, and to the poor the gospel is preached."

You have seen to-day, Christians, that God at no time left himself without witness of his benevolent purposes towards his human offspring; that from the beginning the promise of a Redeemer was given to them; and that at the time of his coming, all men were in expectation; and their attention turned toward Judea; that the Author of our religion combines in himself and exhibited to the world all the characteristics of the Messiah who was to come into the world; and that we should indulge an expectation as unreasonable and perverse as it would be vain, if we should "look for another." How plain, then, our duty; to receive and honour Jesus Christ, as the bearer of God's mercies, and will; to enlist ourselves under his banners, and conform to his instructions; looking for and hasting unto the day of his second advent, with full confidence, that they who shall have lived according to his gospel, will then be received to the fullest joy which God hath designed for those who love him.

SERMON XXII.

ON CHRISTMAS-DAY.

JOHN, iii. 16.

"God so loved the world, that he gave his only begotten Son, that whosoever believeth in him should not perish, but have everlasting life."

THE deluded worshipper of the sun waits in the morning, prepared, we are told, with many ablutions, to prostrate himself before his god, and adore him at his rising. With how much more exalted joy; with how much happier worship are we Christians assembled to-day, to hail at his dawn that "Sun of righteousness," which, through the tender mercy of God, is rising upon our disordered world with everlasting "healing in his wings!" The sun of the visible world rises but to set; this that we worship, shall never go down. That sun affects only material natures, and dispels for a time the darkness which was spread over temporal scenes; this shines to give joy to the souls of men, and disperses forever the darkness which covered eternal concerns. That gilds only the surface of life; its beams reach not into the valley of the shadow of death; this brightens the tomb; it brings that life and immortality to light which cheers the secret chambers of the bosom. The material sun is destined one day to have its fires extinguished forever; but this, when earth and the skies shall have passed away, is ordained to endure as the light of the celestial world, and to it angels and men shall everlastingly bow, as to the brightness of the Father's glory and image, or manifestation of his Person. How pregnant, then, with joy is the day of the rising of this glorious luminary upon our benighted world! It is the commencement, to us, of the years of the right hand of the Most High. Patriarchs saw it at a distance, with the eye of faith, and were glad. Prophets have celebrated its coming. "The morning stars have sung together" at its dawn; "and the sons of God have shouted" in heaven "for joy." And we, if we are not still lost in the dreadful slumbers of the spiritual night, we shall be abroad from the chambers of darkness, contemplating and adoring this glorious regent of the spiritual day.

I can think of no passage of Scripture which more fully, plainly, and affectingly unfolds the truths with which our hearts and minds should, at this time, be impressed, than these words from the gospel of the beloved disciple: "God so loved the world, that he gave his only begotten Son, that whosoever believeth in him should not perish, but have everlasting life." Here is brought to our notice a most wonderful gift from God to the world; even the gift of "his only begotten Son." Here is suggested to us the end or purpose of this wonderful gift; "that whosoever believeth in him should not perish, but have everlasting life." Here is declared to us the motive which actuated the Almighty to this most gracious and amazing deed; he "so loved the world." Topics these, without a right understanding of which we can have no adequate conception of the greatness of the event we celebrate; nor celebrate it with any just degree of gratitude or joy.

Let us, then, in the first place, consider this extraordinary gift; the only begotten Son of God. Christ is said to be the Son of God, on account of his wonderful conception in the womb of the virgin. "The Holy Ghost shall come upon thee," said the angel; "and the power of the Highest shall overshadow thee; therefore, also, that holy thing which shall be born of thee, shall be called the Son of God." He is also invested with this title, as "the first born among many brethren," who are the children of God, being children of the resurrection. But it is in a higher and more wonderful sense that the text presents him to our view. The phrase is peculiar and appropriate. You will observe, he is styled "the *only* begotten Son" which implies, that in nature and character, and mode of subsistence, there is no other such Being in the universe. After the manner in which Christ stands in this relation to the Father, God hath no other Son. You will notice, further, that he is said to be "the only *begotten* Son." Other beings are created. They are formed by the hand of God. They are merely the offspring of his power. But unto the Son God hath communicated his own nature and perfections, his own life and glory. He is of "one substance with his Father;" "begotten, not made." Let me also recall to your minds the sublime account of him which you have just heard in the gospel of this day; that he "was in the beginning with God," that "all things were made by him;" and that "without him, was not any thing made that was made." From this it appears, that he had existence before all worlds; that he was eternally begotten of the Father; that as the Prophet saith, "his goings forth have been from of old, even from everlasting;" that like his great type, the wonderful Priest whom Abraham met in the valley of Shaveh, he is without "beginning of days, or end of life." And now, if God only hath eternity; if the substance and perfections of God belong only to God; if to create, be the prerogative of God; if God only can be the image of himself, it is evident that the Son hath received of the Father a divine nature; that he is "God *of* God," and "very God *of* very God."

The manner in which the Son is derived from, and subsists equally with, the Father, I attempt not to explain. For in this respect, "who," indeed, "shall declare his generation?" It is not for us, who do not comprehend our own existence, nor the existence of the moth which we crush under our feet, to scan the existence or the operations of God. It is sufficient for us to know from that source, from which alone we can know any thing of the divine nature with certainty, that God hath, in all time of his own existence, such a Son, the second person of a Trinity, in which, with infinite perfection and happiness, the divine unity exists; and that this Son is the object of his utmost affection, and possessor of all his perfections and glory. "In him dwelleth all the fulness of the Godhead bodily."

But how, then, is this divine Person said to be given to the world? Amazing condescension! Mysterious event! He is given, to empty himself of all the glory which he had in the bosom of his Father, and, for our sakes, to be made man. He is given, to take upon him the human nature, with all its infirmities and sorrows, but sin. He is given, to be born of a woman; to come into the world a helpless babe; to sojourn here in the humblest condition of life; and to die a painful and ignominious death. Yes; in the babe at Bethlehem, God is incarnate. In this Son of Man, whom we find to-day lying in a manger, and shall behold ere long, stretched upon the cross, a divine Being tabernacles in the flesh! He, who before all worlds was the object of the Father's love, is surrendered to bear all the tokens of the Father's vengeance. He, who from everlasting was "in the form of God," and allowed to think himself "equal with God," is sent to take our nature upon him, and, as a man, to dwell among the children of men. A virgin hath conceived, and brought him forth, and his name is called IMMANUEL. The enraptured Prophet, having this mysterious union of the two natures in view, six hundred years before it took effect, broke forth, as if it were then present, in that blissful strain: "Unto us a child is born, unto us a Son is given, and his name shall be called Wonderful, Counsellor, the Mighty God, the Everlasting Father, the Prince of Peace." And the holy recorder of my text, closes his sublime account of the person of the Son, with that memorable passage, in which the Prophet and the Evangelist are found celebrating the same thing; "The word was made flesh and dwelt among us; and we beheld his glory, the glory as of the only begotten of the Father, full of grace and truth."

But, surely, it is for the accomplishment of no ordinary business, that God thus sends his Son into the world, "in the likeness of sinful flesh." Surely, it is for some great and most gracious purpose, that one of the Holy Three leaves the abode of glory, and is found on earth, "in fashion as a man." And this we shall indeed find to be the case, if we now proceed to consider the end of this wonderful gift; "that whosoever believeth in him should not perish, but have everlasting life." These words do most clearly imply, that but for the gift of the only begotten Son of God, the human race were exposed to perish. This was not the case in their original condition. Whatever comes from the hands of God, cannot but be perfect in its kind, and altogether holy. Man, when he came from his Maker, was innocent as the angels of heaven, and designed for happiness and immortality. But "how art thou fallen," thou "son of the morning!" We find an awful change in his nature, and a dreadful alteration in his condition. Instead of innocence, he is the slave of sin; how much so, let his deeds and his conscience testify. Instead of the favourite of his Creator, he is the child of wrath; how really so, let his sorrows and mortality speak; let the curse under which he groans declare. Who that observes his ignorance of his Maker, his stupidity and brutishness, the uncleanness of his life, and the hopelessness of his death; where the light of revelation hath not dawned upon him; or the motions of the Spirit within him are quenched; can forbear to sigh at the thought, that the parent of the race to which he belongs, was once made after "the image of God." The account of this awful change is contained in the mournful record, that "by one man's disobedience, sin entered into the world, and death by sin, and so death passed upon all men, for that all have sinned." Brought by transgression into this dreadful condition, alienated from the love of his Maker, his life forfeited, become carnal in his views, and vicious in his inclinations; to raise himself from this low estate, to recover himself from this awful condemnation, was utterly beyond man's power. He had become a debtor to the law in a sum which he never could have paid. He was offensive to the Almighty for a guilt which he never could have expiated. He was enslaved to sin with bonds and chains, which he never could have broken. He was doomed to death by a sentence, which he never could have commuted nor repealed. Left to himself, his body must have passed to irretrievable corruption, and his soul to everlasting depravity and misery. In this chilling view of the condition of our race, how joyous is the assurance, that God hath given his only begotten Son to ransom us from it. This is the great and most gracious work upon which he comes into our world, even to bring salvation and eternal life to all them that believe. "Thou shalt call his name Jesus, for he shall save his people from their sins."

Anxiously we shall inquire how this is done; and we can be satisfied only by adverting to the offices which he fulfilled in the flesh. He came as our great High Priest, anointed by God, to make atonement for sin, by offering himself in the body, once for all; and thus to turn away the vengeance of the law, and reconcile the Almighty to his apostate creatures. He came as our most Holy Prophet, on whom the Spirit of God rested, to preach to us in the Father's name, the glad tidings of this redemption, and by his instructions and example, to restore the paths of righteousness and guide our steps therein. He came, too, as our omnipotent King, to take upon his shoulders the new and most merciful government of peace; to protect and defend us from the power of our enemies, sin, death, and hell; to dispense to us from that inexhaustible treasury which God hath committed to his disposal, all spiritual succours; and to crown us, after the manifestation of our fidelity and obedience, with the joys and honours of his eternal kingdom. These are the offices in which prophecy promised him. These are the offices which he fulfils in the flesh. These are the offices in which the dignity of his person, and the perfection of his obedience, render him acceptable to the Father, and all-sufficient for our salvation. And these are the offices in which, if we turn not our backs upon him, but receive and embrace him and comply with the terms of his gospel, he will not only snatch us from the perdition to which the first transgression exposed us, but will exalt us to everlasting life. "Behold the man," saith Zechariah, "whose name is The BRANCH; and he shall grow up out of his place, and shall build the temple of the Lord; and he shall bear the glory, and shall sit and rule upon his throne; and he shall be a priest upon his throne, and the counsel of peace shall be between them both." "This is his name," saith Jeremiah, "whereby he shall be called the LORD our righteousness." "In whom," saith the Apostle, "we have redemption through his blood," even "the forgiveness of sins." "As many as received him," saith the Evangelist, "to them gave he power to become the sons of God, even to them that believe on his name."

But I must haste to call your attention to what indeed should never be out of your minds, the motive which actuated the Father to this wonderful gift;—he "so loved the world." You will observe, that the Son is said to be *given* unto us; which plainly indicates that there was no claim in the receivers, neither obligation upon the giver. It is entirely to the free and disinterested compassion and goodness of God, that we are indebted for this great salvation. For on the part of man, where was the least shadow of claim to this wonderful mercy? He had rebelled against his Creator. Under an easy and equitable law he had forfeited his life. And who can limit the degree of sinfulness to which his depravity tends? Alas! it has been found sufficient to despise the humiliation to which his Saviour condescended for his ransom; to dash back the cup of mercy upon his Maker and prefer the servitude of iniquity. Had the Most High then left him to the fruit of his own devices; nay, had he erased him utterly from amongst his works, who could have laid any charge against the righteousness of God? And on the part of the Deity, what constraint of wisdom or interest could have caused our preservation? All angels that fill heaven are his; and so, for ought we know, are the inhabitants of a thousand worlds. What are we, and what is our origin, that we should by our being add anything to his glory; or by our service to his happiness! "He speaks and it is done;" and were we removed for ever from the creation we have blemished, in the place we occupy, beings of surpassing innocence would, at his fiat appear. Nay, from everlasting to everlasting, without aid or benefit from any of his creatures, he hath in himself the utmost plentitude of glory and bliss. Nothing, therefore, but that benevolence which induced him, for the communication of happiness, to give existence to the creatures; nothing but that ineffable love which makes him the fit object of the entire affection of every intelligent being, could have actuated him to resign the beloved Son of his bosom for the recovery of our ruined race! He saw the unhappy condition into which his erring children had brought themselves by transgression; he saw and pitied them. He desired to rescue them from impending destruction. His own Son he would give, to make atonement for their guilt, by the sacrifice of himself; his own Spirit he would give to renew them in righteousness; his own nature he would permit to be united with theirs, that the dignity they had lost might be restored, and man be begotten again to the love of his Maker! In this way he would commend both his justice and his mercy to all the objects of his government; and a beloved part of his family be brought back from the paths of perdition to the enjoyment of that happiness for which he created them. In the moment, therefore, in which he passed upon man the doom which immutable truth required, he consoled the hopeless offenders with the promise of a deliverer. And when the fulness of time was come, the period which his wisdom had chosen, he sent forth his Son to appear in the flesh and fulfil his gracious pleasure. It is difficult to conceive in what way God's love to the world could have been so strongly manifested. What could he have given us that was dearer to himself; what could he have given us of which we were more unworthy; what could he have given us that would be, to us, a source of such felicity? "Made of God unto us wisdom, and righteousness, and sanctification and redemption;" he is both the pledge and security to us sinful beings, of the remission of sins and eternal life. But we strive in vain, to rise to a full apprehension of the greatness of this mercy. We may perceive the benefit; we may rejoice in the bliss; but we must say, with the great Apostle of the Gentiles, that the love which produced it, "passeth knowledge."

Thus, I have endeavoured to set before you some of the great truths with which our hearts and souls should, at this time, be impressed; the exalted nature and character of the Being who is given unto us, the only begotten Son of God; the blissful end and fruit of this gift; our ransom from destruction to everlasting life, and the gracious motive which actuated the giver—his tender love to our sinful world. And, my brethren, if into this stupendous dispensation "the angels desire to look," we, whom it so nearly concerns, ought not to hear it with unprofitable attention, nor to celebrate it with transient praise. The time would fail me to speak to you of the gratitude and love which you owe to the Father, and to his Son Jesus Christ; to show you the danger and heinousness of neglecting this great salvation through heedlessness or unbelief; and to enforce the obligation devolved upon you by the incarnation of the Son of God, both to respect yourselves and love one another. These are inferences which I must leave to be deduced by you in your retired meditations. And to the discharge of your present duty you need not any exhortation. The choral hymn of the angels has not yet ceased to sound in your ears. Your hearts yet beat with joy at the message, that "unto you is born this day, in the city of David, a Saviour who is Christ the Lord." Come, then, to the manger, and behold the babe. "Kiss the Son, lest he be angry, and so ye perish from the right way." Let not the wise men of the east be alone in their homage to your infant Redeemer; but bring ye your gold, your frankincense, and myrrh—your gold in charity, your frankincense in praise, and your myrrh in a devout commemoration of his death, at his sacred table. And may he smile on our feast; may we have joy and peace in believing; may we go on our journey of life filled with the comfort which springs from this blissful assurance, that he who "spared not his own Son, but" freely "delivered him up for us all," will, we may reasonably hope, "with him freely give us all things."

SERMON XXIII.

ON CHRISTMAS-DAY.

NEHEMIAH, viii. 10.

"Go your way, eat the fat, and drink the sweet, and send portions unto them for whom nothing is prepared: for this day is holy unto our Lord: neither be ye sorry: for the joy of the Lord is your strength."

SOLEMN, and extremely interesting was the scene which occasioned this animated passage of holy writ. After a long and dreary captivity, the people of Israel were returned to Jerusalem, to the city, the distinctions, and the hopes of their fathers. At the season when the feast of tabernacles was wont to be celebrated, they gathered themselves together as one man, both the men and the women, and all that could hear with understanding. To this anxious multitude, long scattered and deprived of their spiritual privileges, the Book of the Law was now produced; and they received anew, at the mouth of his Prophet, the covenant and statutes of God. It was an august spectacle. They wept for the scene, and the complicated emotions it excited, softened into tenderness the most hardened heart.

But what is this scene, compared with that which the Christian Church is, this day, assembled to commemorate! In one, a single people is recovered from a temporary captivity; in the other, the whole human race, from the captivity of sin and death. In one, the ransomed are returned to an earthly and perishable Jerusalem; in the other, they are brought to a city which hath foundation, whose builder is God, and whose glory shall not pass away. In one, the law is renewed which is "the ministration of condemnation;" in the other, the Gospel is promulgated, which is "the ministration of righteousness," pardon, and peace. In one, the messenger of the covenant is a frail mortal, and his attendants a few mortals like himself; in the other, he is the "Wonderful, the Counsellor, the Mighty God, the Everlasting Father, the Prince of Peace;" and his attendants are the Prophets of all ages "since the world began," a multitude of the heavenly hosts, and a chosen angel of the Lord. In one, the people wept with mixed emotions of sadness, gladness, and fear; in the other, the tears which are shed are tears of ecstacy, flowing from the transports of the soul, while it contemplates a God incarnate for its salvation!—Verily, to the Jewish Church, rejoicing in the returning favour of the Most High, the lively exhortation of the Prophet is not more pertinent than it is to the Christian Church, called forth this morning to celebrate the birth of the Redeemer.—"Go your way, eat the fat, and drink the sweet, and send portions unto them for whom nothing is prepared: for this day is holy unto our Lord: neither be ye sorry: for the joy of the Lord is your strength."

Christians, indulge me with your attention, while in the sequel of this discourse, I endeavour to set before you, in the first place, what that joy is, in Christ Jesus our Lord, which anciently consecrated this day to him, and renders it a day of gladness and festivity to his people. And, in the second place, to illustrate the value and importance of this joy, by showing you its power and blessed influence upon the disciples of the Redeemer in the most interesting relations and aspects in which man can be contemplated.

In the first place, it is the joy which springs from a knowledge of the reconciliation of God to his sinful creatures, by which our lives are saved from destruction, and we are brought into a condition to enjoy his presence and favour. We are by nature the children of wrath. The unhappy transgression of the first progenitors of the race, alienated them and their offspring from the love of the Almighty, and subjected them to sin and its wages, death. Created in purity, invested with happiness, but little lower than the angels in honour and joy, they rashly trampled upon the law which was given them, and forfeited all their privileges. Had the penalty been executed which they had awfully incurred, man must have been doomed to the hopeless dissolution of his body, the departure of the Spirit of God from his soul, and the everlasting exclusion of both soul and body from the presence of his Maker and the realms of light and bliss. But at the moment when the arm of justice was raised to strike the awful blow, the adorable Redeemer intervened, caught the falling victims from their ruin, and graciously became the propitiation for their sins. Between death and the offenders this prevailing Intercessor stood. By covenanting with the Father to come into the world and do his will, he turned away the wrath of heaven; and now, once, in the fulness of time, hath he appeared in the flesh, to put away sin by the sacrifice of himself. By being made man, fulfilling all righteousness in our nature, and offering himself in his own immaculate perfection, a sacrifice for us upon the cross, he satisfied the demands of the divine government, and accomplished that redemption by which we live; and live rich in the favour of a reconciled God. "As by the offence of one, judgment came upon all men to condemnation; even so by the righteousness of one, the free gift came upon all men unto justification of life." "Thou shalt call his name JESUS," said the angel who announced his incarnation; "for he shall save his people from their sins."

Again. The joy which we have in our Lord is such a joy as arises from the possession of a perfect revelation of the character and will of the Most High, and consequently, of our interest, duty, and destination. Miserable, before the coming of Christ, was the state of this lower world. "Darkness had covered the earth, and thick darkness the nations." Over the picture of human nature, encompassed as it was with ignorance, vice, and misery, in the night of heathenism, the pious philanthropist as he looks, will sometimes have his face covered with blushes, and sometimes bedewed with tears. Men were utterly unacquainted with their Maker. They were sunk in the deepest ignorance and grossest pollutions. Idolatry reigned, and, with it, necessarily prevailed, a general depravation of morals, and a total want of those spiritual excellencies and comforts which exalt and bless the human character. Some few sages, indeed, shed by their researches a dubious light upon the paths of life. But they were like the scattered and glimmering stars of a cloudy midnight. They could neither impart the warmth, nor give the light which the wretched traveller needed. Their occasional twinklings only rendered the general darkness more apparent and impressive. It was not till the rising of the Sun of Righteousness, that this blackness of darkness began to be dispersed from the earth. By his gospel, we are made acquainted with the true God; in the glorious unity of his nature, and endearing perfections of his character. Our origin, duty, chief good, and destination are satisfactorily explained. Means are provided in the instructions of God's word, and help of his Spirit, for assisting the feebleness of nature in recovering its pristine excellence and beauty. And we are assured of a righteousness which shall supply our deficiencies, through which our sincerity shall be accepted instead of that innocence we have lost; and our obedience, for that perfection to which we are unable to attain. We no longer are left to err in vision, and to stumble in judgment. The Almighty hath, as it were, with a sunbeam, marked out the paths in which we are to walk. Through his tender mercy "the day-spring from on high hath visited us," to give light to them that "sat in darkness and the shadow of death," to guide our feet into the way of peace.

Further. Our joy in the Lord is the joy which springs from the well-grounded hope of inheriting heaven and immortality. By the coming of the Redeemer, that dominion of death is destroyed which kept the living in terror, and seemed to threaten to hold the dead in eternal bondage. Anxiously had nature looked into the tomb. With a heart overcharged with emotions, she endeavoured to look beyond it. But all she could with certainty discover, was mouldering relics of what man had been. Amidst these she stood, listening in anxious awe, if, from unseen forms any sound might be heard of departed beings still in existence. But there seemed none to answer, neither any that regarded. Hope whispered to her, listen more intensely, for that the spirits which had animated these relics yet did live. Again, she paused; again, she called; again, she hearkened; but all was solemn stillness. She turned from the tomb, clinging to the consideration that no voice had been heard unfavourable to her wishes. She looked back upon it, yet longing after immortality; but it was "a land of darkness, as darkness itself; and where the light was as darkness." But before the power of Immanuel, this kingdom fell. He "overcame the sharpness of death, and opened the kingdom of heaven to all believers." Through his most blessed gospel, we have the comfortable assurance from him who holds the keys of life and death, that when the waves of this troublesome world have subsided, we shall find a haven where there shall be no more storms, nor fears, nor death, and the tears shall be wiped from all faces. "Forasmuch as the children were partakers of flesh and blood, he, also, himself, likewise took part of the same; that through death he might destroy him that had the power of death, that is, the devil, and deliver them who, through fear of death, were all their lifetime subject to bondage."

Once more. Our joy in Christ Jesus our Lord is confirmed and increased by our knowledge of the greatness of the character and dignity of his person, whereby we have the strongest evidence of the divine mercy towards us, and the fullest confidence in all these glorious things which he hath achieved or promised for us. It was not a conspicuous individual of our own nature, who, in the form of man, accomplished our salvation. No. No mortal had strength and worth sufficient for the work. How, indeed, should one give to God a ransom for his brother, who needed the redemption of his own soul! It was not some chosen individual of the higher orders of created beings. No. "He took not on him the nature of angels." Unto the angels the Most High hath not put in subjection the world to come. Nay "when he bringeth in the first begotten into the world, he saith, And let all the angels of God worship him." Who, then, was the glorious deliverer, who has performed such services for our fallen race? It was none other than the only begotten Son of the Father; the second Person of that ineffable Trinity, which mysteriously exists in the unity of the Godhead. It was none other than that pre-eminent Being, who was "in the beginning" and "was with God," "without whom was not anything made, which was made;" who is the object of the worship of heaven, and though found on earth in "the form of a servant," had, in his glory, "thought it no robbery to be equal with God." Yes; in the Author of his salvation, the Christian beholds the heir of all the Father's power, and the image of all the Father's perfections. "The Word was made flesh, and dwelt among us, and we beheld his glory, the glory as of the only begotten of the Father, full of grace and truth."

From the transcendent nature, and exalted character of the Redeemer, arises the fulness of the Christian's joy. The dignity, righteousness, and spotless purity of him who offered himself upon the cross, in our behalf, furnishes a peaceful assurance of the sufficiency of the atonement, and of the greatness of the Almighty's love. Coming from the bosom of the Father, and having all the "fulness of the Godhead" dwelling in him, his doctrines, we may be satisfied, are true, his precepts perfect, and his promises sure. Having exalted our nature, by assuming it to his own divinity, and taken it with him to the right hand of the Throne, he has hereby given us the most certain pledge that he will not leave his redeemed to perish in the grave; but will make them partakers of the glory and happiness which he had with the Father before the foundation of the world.

That "God" should thus be "manifest in the flesh;" that he

who had existed from eternity should condescend to be born of a woman; that he, who made the worlds, should take upon him a human form, and commence, in a manger, a life which would be spent in poverty, and terminate on the cross, is, without controversy, a great mystery! But it is a mystery of joy; a mystery into which the angels delight to look; a mystery at which it becomes not those to cavil who are benefited by it; and to whom nature teaches a lesson of diffidence and docility in that, to their feeble powers, everything which they see and know, is mysterious. Received in faith, upon the word and authority of God, it gives us the most joyful and affecting evidence of the Almighty's benevolence towards our race; and is calculated to beget in us a noble trust and steadfast reliance upon his great and unchangeable mercy. "He that spared not his own Son, but delivered him up for us all, how shall he not with him also freely give us all things." "If, when we were enemies, we were reconciled to God by the death of his Son, much more, being reconciled, we shall be saved by his life."

Such, my hearers, is the joy which we have in our Lord; and to set before you its value and operation in all the extent of it, would require far higher powers than your preacher possesses. It was in the contemplation of its greatness and results that the enraptured Isaiah broke forth into that most animated apostrophe of which we have record: "Sing, O ye heavens; for the Lord hath done it; shout, ye lower parts of the earth; break forth into singing, ye mountains, O forest, and every tree therein; for the Lord hath redeemed Jacob, and glorified himself in Israel."

Thus great is the joy which we have in our Lord; and I cannot do justice to the subject nor to the occasion which has brought it under our consideration, without hinting to you some of the most obvious senses in which this joy is our strength.

It is the foundation of our encouragement in approaching our Maker. For what are we of ourselves that we should presume to look up to the holy and infinite God? Rebellious children!

worms of the dust! "dead in trespasses and sins!" Without the merits and mediation of our Advocate, we might well be anxious, with our dismayed progenitors, to hide ourselves from the presence of the Almighty. But Jesus is our peace! We, who were afar off, are now brought nigh by the blood of Christ. Through his worthiness we have boldness of access to the Father of our spirits, and hope for his love and heavenly benediction. For by this messenger from heaven, "we have not received the spirit of bondage again to fear; but we have received the Spirit of adoption, whereby we cry, Abba, Father."

Again. This joy which we have in the character, instructions, and achievements of Christ, animates us in performing the duties of life. Arduous is the ascent to that holiness unto which we are called. While we are encumbered with the infirmities of the flesh, who asks not for encouragement; who halts not on his way? Our assurance of pardon upon repentance, our satisfaction in the instructions we have received, the influences of the Spirit from on high, and the alluring power of that crown of life, which God, "the righteous Judge," shall one day give to the faithful, form together the only talisman which can dissolve the difficulties in virtue's way, and render the discharge of our duties our satisfaction and joy.

It is our strength in bearing up under the troubles and adversities of this transitory world. Vain is the expectation of the thoughtless to laugh out of countenance the miseries of life. Fallacious is the attempt of the stoic to despise its troubles. We need an internal source of joy; a tie which shall connect us with God and a better world, in order to enable us to possess a rational and happy equanimity, amidst the disappointments and sorrows of this changeable state. And speak, ye sincere followers of the Lamb, tell us how truly, in this respect, the joy of the Lord is your strength? What but the power of the Redeemer have you found sufficient to enable you to walk without sinking, upon the unstable and agitated waves of this troublesome world? Is it not owing to the instructions and hopes, the pardon and promises of his Gospel, that when we see you "troubled on every side you are not distressed; when perplexed, you are not in despair; when cast down, you are not destroyed; when chastened, you are not killed; when sorrowful, you still rejoice; when poor, you make many rich; when you have nothing, you seem to possess all things?" Yes. This is the influence of the joy which we have in Christ Jesus our Lord, upon the troubles of life. Let the winds of adversity howl; let the storms of misfortune rise; let the clouds of sorrow obscure all external joys, that peace of the Redeemer which he hath left with his disciples, gives a sunshine and serenity in their bosoms which nothing but the withdrawing of his countenance can interrupt. It is "the peace of God, and passeth all understanding." The world can neither give it nor take it away.

Once more. This joy is our comfort in the approach, and will give us victory in the conflict with our last enemy, death. By our knowledge of remission of sins through the achievements of the Redeemer at his first advent, "the sting of death" is taken away. By our assurance that we shall not always be holden by him, our horror at descending into the chambers of his prisons is abated. Peacefully we can submit to be bound by this mighty monarch. Resignedly we can surrender ourselves to be conveyed into his gloomy cells; when the Son of God, who for our deliverance was thus bound and thus buried, hath by his resurrection broken these shackles; and by his passage from the grave thrown everlasting light into these cells; and by his word hath left us to expect that "unto them that look for him he will appear a second time, without sin, unto salvation."

Which brings me to observe, in the last place, that the joy which we have in Christ Jesus our Lord, is the principal source of composure and hope when we contemplate the final judgment. For when we look forward to the winding up of this present state of things, and the coming of God to judgment; when we realize in thought that solemn account which every one shall give of himself unto God; when we contemplate the terrors of that final scene, when "the heavens shall be wrapped together as a scroll, and the elements shall melt with fervent heat, and the earth and all that is therein shall be burnt up;" what, under the consciousness which we have of innumerable imperfections, even in our best attainments, can allay the fears of the humble, and enable them even to look for this coming of the Lord with joyful expectation, but the knowledge that He who shall judge the world is also the Saviour of them that believe. In that great day, Jesus will be specially manifested as the strength of his people. To the wicked and unbelieving, his coming in his glorious majesty will be unspeakably dismaying; to his saints it will be the day of their complete redemption—the fulness of their joy. Supported by the hope of salvation, they are not sorrowful when they ponder the future advent of their Lord, but are enabled to say with meekness and faith, "Even so, come Lord Jesus, come quickly."

Such being the foundation, the greatness, and the perpetuity of the joy which we have in Christ Jesus our Lord, and so mighty and invaluable its efficacy, with what propriety is the day of his manifestation in the flesh consecrated to gladness in his Church. Let your hearts overflow with gratitude to the God who devised, and to Immanuel who accomplished your great salvation. In whatever ways are innocent and holy, manifest "your joy and peace in believing." With undissembled praise, unite your hallelujahs with those of the heavenly hosts, and let your hymns of gratulation penetrate the clouds. Come, in an especial manner, "eat the fat and drink the sweet" at the rich banquet which the Redeemer himself has provided for you at his own sacred table. There, press to your hearts the symbols of the body which he took upon himself, and graciously offered in expiation of your sins. There, too, take the pitch of your gladness; and while, in the spirit of the text, you with virtuous moderation indulge in grateful festivity, evidence the enlargedness of your joy by your desire to have all men happy, and by contributing liberally unto those "for whom nothing is prepared." This day is holy unto our Lord. Let there be no limits to your exultance but those which modesty assigns. Let there be no restraints upon your cheerfulness but those which sobriety ordains. Let the graces of the Christian life, unitedly, preside at this Christian festival. Come faith, and bend our knees before the incarnate God. Come hope, and spread above us the many-coloured bow; the enlivening token of the Almighty's covenant with the earth. And thou, the fairest daughter of heaven, the favourite virtue of the Redeemer, sweet charity, come; come, and render our adorations acceptable to our King; come, and make glad the poorest of his brethren with thy benevolent deeds; come, and begin in our hearts that work of love which shall be perpetuated under the smiles of the Almighty, in his glorious kingdom, when faith will be swallowed up in vision, and hope be forgotten in the full fruition of the promises.

SERMON XXIV.

ON CHRISTMAS-DAY.

ISAIAH, xliv. 23.

"Sing, O ye heavens; for the Lord hath done it; shout, ye lower parts of the earth; break forth into singing, ye mountains; O forest, and every tree therein; for the Lord hath redeemed Jacob, and glorified himself in Israel."

THE seraphic Isaiah was honoured with the clearest and most blissful views of the birth and achievements of the Messiah. To him it was shown, that "a virgin should conceive and bear a Son, whose name should be called Immanuel; that is, God with us;" and throughout his prophetic life, his spirit appears to have been constantly elated with the contemplation of the certainty, wonders, and joy of Immanuel's advent and reign. Borne forward on the wing of inspiration, to the period when the unparalleled child should be born; when the adorable Son should be given; when, by his various acts as our Prophet, Priest, and King, he should proclaim himself "Wonderful, the Counsellor, the Mighty God, the Everlasting Father, the Prince of Peace," the holy seer is rapt into ecstacy; and, in the text, breaks forth in the most natural and animated apostrophe to which transport ever gave birth: "Sing, O ye heavens, for the Lord hath done it; shout, ye lower parts of the earth; break forth into singing, ye mountains; O forest, and every tree therein; for the Lord hath redeemed Jacob, and glorified himself in Israel!" The heavens, the earth, the inanimate creation, mountains forests, trees, everything of which he could think, are personified by the prophet in his rapture, and called upon to exult at the glorification of God in the redemption of his people. And if ever it becomes us, my friends, to feel as the transported prophet felt, and join in the exultance which he wished to excite, it is on this joyful day, consecrated from a very early age of the Church, to the commemoration of the nativity of the great Redeemer. In the spirit of the text, and of all the services of this day, yea, and of the notes which have resounded from angels' lips, through the arches of heaven, and been responded for ages at this festival, by the Church upon earth, I would renew the declaration, that there is born unto you a Saviour, and call upon you to be filled with holy joy. And to this purpose, permit me, in the ensuing discourse, to set before you, in the first place, the reasons why you should be glad, and rejoice in this festival of the nativity; and, secondly, to state to you the most suitable methods of expressing your joy.

The propriety of being filled, at this festival, with grateful joy, will appear in an affecting light, if we consider, in the first place, the fruits of the event it celebrates. What are the consequences to us of the incarnation of the Son of God? What ends were contemplated in this extraordinary occurrence? They were our redemption from death; our instruction in righteousness; and the exaltation of our nature to new and most glorious honour and expectations.

A leading and invaluable benefit of this event, is our redemption from destruction. Created in innocence, man was designed by his Maker for life and felicity. He fell. Deep and dismal was the abyss into which he was about to sink; even deep and awful as everlasting destruction from the presence of God. The merciful promise, that "the seed of the woman should bruise the serpent's head," caught him upon the brink of ruin, and upheld him in life. And in the birth and achievements of the Messiah, this promise was fulfilled. Though the event was not accomplished till four thousand years after the creation, it operated retrospectively to the date of the mortality of man. But for its efficacy, we all had perished in Adam. To it we owe the ransom of our race from the sentence of perdition; virtually, a second gift of life, with the prospect and means of immortality. Slain was the Lamb, in the council of heaven, from the foundation of the world; by the anticipated efficacy of his blood, guilty man was delivered from the condemnation of death; and now in the end of the world, he appeared in the flesh, to put away sin by the covenanted sacrifice of himself.

But this is not all. Another fruit of this glorious event, is our instruction in righteousness. After man fell, his understanding became darkened, and his moral sense was corrupted. He nearly lost all knowledge of God. Scarcely could he determine what was duty. Ignorance, vice, and misery usurped the earth; impenetrable darkness obscured his path; gloomy uncertainty enveloped his destination. He did not more need a priest to absolve his life, than a prophet to instruct his mind. And one great end of the Messiah's mission was to discharge this prophetic office. To it we owe that renewed knowledge of the nature and will of God, which is so essential to our happiness and safety; that acquaintance with our duty and prospects, which is so important to the wise management of life; and those improved sentiments of religion and virtue, which alone can smooth the asperities of the present existence, and give worth and loveliness to the human character. There are, indeed, persons, who, without acknowledging any master in Jesus Christ, affect the praise of civil, social, and personal excellence. But it is happy for them that they live in an age when Christianity has rendered the amiable duties familiar and respectable. They are unconsciously benefited by the diffusion of that instruction which they profess to despise. Like erratic orbs, they shine with light borrowed from the same glorious sun from which their eccentric whirl keeps them forever wandering. Man is, by nature, ignorant and vicious. It is to revelation, shining in full lustre upon some regions, and in untraced coruscations upon others, that we owe, whatever of pure religion, sincere virtue, or exalted hope, he possesses. The instructions brought by the Messiah, through whom the paths of wisdom are defined, and strength is proffered to enable us to pursue them, form the only system of pure and satisfactory, efficacious and consoling truth with which the world has been blessed. And not till the period shall arrive when his name shall be known, and his gospel obeyed from the rivers to the ends of the earth, can be realized again, the reign of goodness, order, and peace; and the extent be perceived in which the tidings of his birth are joy to all people.

Still more, a capital fruit of this event is, the exaltation of our nature to new and most glorious honours and expectations. In his primeval state, man was but the connecting link between the animal and angelic world. And after he fell, how dreadful was his debasement! Gone from him was all claim to connection with the Almighty, and all title to the felicities of Paradise and immortality. But by the redemption which is in Christ Jesus, we are begotten anew to the noblest relations and most delightful hopes. "When the fullness of time was come, God sent forth his Son, made of a woman, made under the law, to redeem them who were under the law," for this amazing purpose, that we, lost and abased creatures, "might receive the adoption of sons." In virtue of this adoption, the only begotten of the Father, whom all the angels of God are commanded to worship, is not ashamed to call us brethren. In virtue of this adoption, God hath sent forth the Spirit of his Son into our hearts, authorizing and enabling us to cry unto him, "Abba, Father." In virtue of this adoption, there are given unto us exceeding great and precious promises, whereby we are partakers of the divine nature. In virtue of this adoption we are made "heirs of God, and joint heirs with Jesus Christ," in the expectation and final possession of purity, immortality and eternal bliss. In virtue of this adoption, we have a Head and King, to whom the Father hath committed all power in heaven and earth, that he may preserve and protect us in our present state, educate us in the church for the rank and condition which await us; defend us from every spiritual adversary, and bring us by the gate of death, through which we must pass, to a participation of his own glory and happiness in his heavenly kingdom. All this exaltation, all these hopes, are implied in that memorable declaration of the Evangelist, that to "as many as received" the Redeemer, "to them gave he power to become the sons of God, even to them that believe on his name." And what worth, what honour is conferred on our nature by this adoption! What hope, what expectation, what assurance of grace and immortality, does it beget in the bosom of every man who is a partaker of the heavenly calling! The exaltation is so stupendous, that it "fills the sober with amazement." The expectations are so august, that they humble the faithful by their greatness. "Lord, what is man, that thou art mindful of him, or the son of man, that thou so regardest him?" "Thou madest him lower than the angels, to crown him with glory and worship."

But I am encroaching upon what I wish kept distinct, and contemplated by you, in the second place, as affording additional reason for joy and gladness, viz: the character of the person who is born in our nature, and becomes the author and bearer to us of such inestimable benefits. Who was the Personage by whom our nature was assumed and redemption wrought? What Being came to expiate our sins; to dispel the deepening shades of ignorance and vice; and to raise us in the scale of being, even above the point from which we had fallen? Was it a man; some conspicuous individual of the species, who would himself be benefited in the general blessing? No. The most perfect of the sons of men, had not strength nor worth sufficient for the work; and how could one stand forth as the Saviour of a race, who, if he inherited only Adam's nature, must, himself, have needed salvation? Was it some higher created being; some generous spirit from the host of heaven, who compassionately sought our good? Not angels' love could have been adequate to the humiliation and sufferings of Christ. Not angels' purity could have paid the ransom required for man's life. And, "verily, he took not upon him the nature of angels," but these holy spirits are his attendant servants in the mighty work. What being then was it who was born of the virgin; and how were the benefits we have been contemplating accomplished and made sure? Behold, no less than the Deity became incarnate, to accomplish man's salvation! The mystery we celebrate is "God manifest in the flesh." For, verily, as you have heard in those sublime portions of Scripture, the epistle and gospel which have just been read to you, he, who as at this time was born of a woman, was "in the beginning, and was with God, and was God." Emanating, eternally, from the Almighty, and therefore styled the only begotten Son, he was "the brightness of the Father's glory, and express image of his person." Being the wisdom and the power of God, the active form and sensible demonstration of the Most High, it was he who "laid the foundations of the earth, and of whose hands the heavens are the work;" who, when they have waxed old, "shall fold them up as a vesture, and cause them to be changed; but who, himself, is forever the same, and his years shall not fail." This adorable Person, whom these and other inspired declarations of his nature and character compel us to contemplate, as "GOD OF GOD, LIGHT OF LIGHT, VERY GOD OF VERY GOD," he it is, who hath taken our nature upon him, and become our Redeemer from death, our Instructor in righteousness, and the Founder of our exaltation and hopes. In the fulness of time, at the period appointed by infinite wisdom, as most expedient, he left the regions of glory; was born unpolluted in human form, of a virgin mother, and dwelt among us, both God and Man. To cheer the lowest vales of life, and teach humility; to mark with contempt the vain pomp of the world, and commend the modest and resigned virtues, his chosen parents were indigent; he appeared at his birth in a manger; and though "foxes have holes, and the birds of the air have nests," he had not in his humiliation "where to lay his head." To give the utmost completeness to his instructions, he dwelt many years among us, exhibiting in his lectures and life, the knowledge and the model by which, through his grace, we may frame ourselves unto perfection. That he might "bear all our griefs and carry all our sorrows," he tasted every evil excepting sin, to which flesh is heir; and, finally, to expiate our offences and bring in for us an everlasting righteousness, he offered himself a sacrifice upon the cross, of worth adequate to the claims of justice, and of efficacy unbounded in the Father's sight. It was thus our salvation was accomplished by God the Son, "being found in fashion as a man, and humbling himself unto death, even the death of the cross." In the infant Jesus, you behold the "Word" of the Most High made flesh. The world is honoured by a visit from its Maker. He comes like the sun, to chase darkness from the earth, and shake healing upon the nations from his wings.

Now, the nature and high character of the Redeemer, together with the benefits of his advent in the flesh, render this day the epoch of their greatest felicity to the human race. When the patriarch saw it with the eye of faith, even at a great distance, he rejoiced and was glad. When the prophet contemplates it in holy vision, as already come, he calls upon heaven and earth to behold with admiration, and shout for joy. When the angels usher it in, their songs are wrought up to rapture by the view of our bliss; and the skies are rended by them with affectionate gratulations. Indeed, on this day, "mercy and truth are met together," the Law and the Prophets present themselves, saints and angels are assembled, God and man are united, to manifest, proclaim, and extol the wonderful goodness of the Creator, and the singular honour and happiness of his human creatures. And who, amidst the grandeur and the transport of the scene, can avoid partaking of the general glow? Who among the sinful offspring of Adam has not cause to leap as a hart at the tidings of redemption; especially when assured that his Redeemer is mighty, even the Holy One; and his Intercessor the beloved Son, in whom the Father is ever "well pleased?" What heir of the ignorance and infirmities of men should not welcome to his bosom with transports of gratitude, instructions from on high, concerning his origin, his duty, and destination; especially when they are brought to him, not as in unhappy regions to heathens, by erring sages, nor, as in times past, to the fathers, by imperfect prophets, but by the Son of

God, whose lips are full of grace, and unto whom, alone, of all beings, the spirit of truth is not given by measure? Where is the penitent child of mortality, borne down by sin and sorrow, and the fear of death, whose ears should not be ravished with the tidings of his adoption to a new sonship by the reconciled God; and with the consequent promise of grace and immortality? An event so wonderfully calculated as the birth of Christ, to give joy to faith, and confidence to hope, where is it to be found in the annals of the world? Here, in the incarnate Son, is the richest pledge, the strongest assurance which the Almighty has given, perhaps, which he is able to give, of his compassion, love, and desire of our salvation. This pledge is the Christian's encouragement in approaching the throne of the Most High. It is his support in discharging the duties of life. It is his consolation under the adversities to which heaven may see fit to subject him. It is his strength in death. Soothed is his spirit in every condition, by the inspired reflection, he that "spared not his own Son, but delivered him up for us all, how shall he not with him also freely give me all things." Rich source to the guilty children of men, of hope and peace! Blest pledge of mercy from the everlasting Father to the frail sojourners in this vale of tears! Transcendent mystery of godliness, by which, consistently with all the requirements of truth and holiness, apostate man is restored to God, and God and heaven are restored to apostate man! "Sing, O ye heavens; for the Lord hath done it; shout, ye lower parts of the earth; break forth into singing, ye mountains; O forest, and every tree therein; for the Lord hath redeemed Jacob, and glorified himself in Israel!"

From the contemplation of the reasons why we should be glad, let us proceed to consider what are the suitable methods of expressing our joy.

In the first place, then, we should call upon our souls, and all that is within us, to bless and adore Almighty God, the Father, the Son, and the Holy Ghost, for contriving and accomplishing this stupendous mode of ransoming us from destruction, and restoring us to the joys of light and grace, and expected immortality. Our hearts, to-day, should be altars to the Most High. Faith should be the ministering priest in every bosom. The sacrifice we should offer, is pure and fervent adoration, thanksgiving and love. And from the angelic hosts we may take the words which should consecrate our devotions: "Glory to God in the highest."

Again. We shall becomingly attest our grateful joy on the birth of the Redeemer, by availing ourselves of the benefits of his mediation. That for which we are sincerely glad, we shall love to think of, to use, to apply to the ends for which it is estimable. How unmeaning is our festivity, how empty these tokens of joy, how absurd our engagement in the services of this day, if we are not acquainted with Christ in his spiritual power, and devoted to him as our Lord and dearest friend! Are you, my brethren, washed, are you sanctified in the name of our Lord Jesus, and by the Spirit of our God? Are you striving for the faith and hope set before you in the gospel, able to say to its blessed Author, with his fond disciple, "Lord, thou knowest all things, thou knowest that I love thee." Without this, your joy and praises are but a solemn mockery in the face of heaven. To the ears of your God they are "as sounding brass, and a tinkling cymbal." O, "kiss the Son, lest he be angry," and ye be cut off from your portion of his joy. Embrace and obey him, with pure hearts fervently, lest he be incensed by your neglect of his blessings, and so "ye perish from the right way."

Once more. We should express our joy by expanding our souls with love and good will towards our fellow beings. Sweet is the aspect of benevolence. Honourable is her name and character. She is related to joy, and meet to accompany the happy whenever at devotion, in procession, or at the festal board, they celebrate their felicity. So natural is it to have the heart overflow with kindness to all about us, in times of distinguished blessedness, that courteous congratulations and distributions of gifts have prevailed at such seasons, even among heathens. But especially in the Church, is benevolence lovely. She is worthy, supported by faith and hope, to preside among Christians on this holy day. The event they celebrate is the most wonderful display of love. Through the love of the Almighty they are made rich and happy beyond expression. And their love to the Author of their bliss they can in no way more acceptably show than by showing it to his poor disciples. Whenever you come forth with joy to welcome and honour your Redeemer at his birth, bring with you charity. She is the grace upon whom, when he lifts his eyes, he never fails to smile.

Finally. Our grateful joy should be expressed by uniting in the celebration of the consecrated feast of love. To haste with the shepherds to the manger, and behold the infant Jesus, is not in our power. To go with the wise men to Bethlehem, carrying him homage and gifts, we are not permitted. But on the altar of God we may find the tokens of his presence. There, we may pay him our vows, and receive to our bosoms the figures of the body and blood which he assumed, and offered for our salvation. And where, at this feast, should the Christian seek him but at his holy table! Who, amidst the tidings of mercy and peace which are gladdening all heaven and earth, can refrain in his gratitude from hasting with an oblation to the altar of God, his exceeding joy!

Thus, I have shown you, why your hearts should overflow with gladness at the celebration of the Redeemer's nativity; and what are the most suitable methods of expressing your joy. Sacred, beloved, is this present time, to the improvement of all that has been said. Be not deterred from this special exercise of elevated affections by those who would invidiously say that the coming of Christ ought always and constantly to be remembered with joy. For this very reason do you keep this feast, that you may be reminded and assisted to joy in the God of your salvation throughout your lives. Let not the ardour of your devotions, nor the exultance of your spirits, be damped by any envious assertion, that this was not the season of the Messiah's birth. On this day did the good St. Chrysostom and the holy St. Augustine, whose discourses have come down to us, celebrate the event in the early centuries, declaring it to be the custom of primitive times. On this day, hath the Church, for ages, come forth in the best garments of gladness to receive and adore her new-born King. And if it were otherwise, vain would be dispute, inasmuch as the event sanctifies the day, not the day the event. If our souls are filled with hallowed rapture by the annunciation from the oracle of truth, that "unto us was born this day in the city of David, a Saviour, who is Christ the Lord;" and we express our joy by unfeigned ascriptions of adoration and praise, to the Father, Son, and Holy Ghost, for this unspeakable gift, by co-operating with the Almighty in this work of love, availing ourselves through faith and obedience, of the benefits of this great salvation; by expanding our affections with love and beneficence towards our fellow-beings, especially the poor "who are of the household of faith;" and by going to the altar of God with an oblation of gladness, and there receiving, with fervent gratitude and humble adorations, the symbols of the body and blood, which for our salvation his Son assumed, doubtless we shall keep an acceptable feast to the Most High. The Redeemer will behold and record our love. And the recurrence of the day may be rendered by him instrumental in preparing our souls for his second Advent, when he shall come in all the majesty of the court of heaven, to be glorified in his saints, and admired in all them that believe.

SERMON XXV.

ON THE CIRCUMCISION.

Luke, ii. 21.

"And when eight days were accomplished for the circumcising of the child, name was called Jesus."

THERE is no part of our Saviour's life uninteresting, or that will not yield instruction. The Church, at this season, presents us with the account of his circumcision; in which he began "to fulfil all righteousness," to bear our sins in his own body, and to shed his blood for us. With the history of this rite your Bibles have doubtless made you acquainted. My object, therefore, in the following discourse will be to make some reflections upon the Saviour's compliance with it, that may, with the divine blessing, be instructive and useful.

In the first place, why was he who was born free of sin, and had come to introduce a spiritual system, made subject to the rite of circumcision? The law required a perfect obedience. By it, therefore, no flesh living could be justified. To walk without transgression was not in the power of fallen man. If the law had had its course, destruction must have come upon every subject of it, for it could never have "made the comers thereunto perfect." The object of the incarnation of the Son of God was the salvation of the human race. To accomplish this, one office was to bring them under a new and more gracious covenant, in which a spotless perfection should not be required of feeble man; but faith, with its fruits, repentance and love, be made the condition of his acceptance with God. In order to this, it behoved the Saviour who appeared for the world to become our righteousness in honouring the law, and, by his perfect obedience to all its precepts, to abolish its force and condemning power over every transgressor. Circumcision was a rite instituted by God when he renewed his covenant with Abraham, the venerable father of the faithful; and may not improperly be styled the legal baptism. As a part of that law which he would abolish by fulfilling it, it became him to submit to this rite. Not for himself; the significancy of the ceremony in him was lost. He needed not to be purified or made a new creature. Spotless perfection belonged to him without this compliance with a hallowed ceremony. But for us he was circumcised; for us he was baptized; for us he exhibited entire legal obedience, that he might bring us under the tender, merciful, encouraging covenant of the Gospel, by fulfilling for us "all righteousness." For the Jew he satisfied the law, that he might deliver the believers of that nation from the curse which rested upon them in consequence of their inability to keep the whole law, to which they were debtors; and for us he satisfied the divine requirements, by a spotless obedience in our nature, to all the commandments of God; that, "as by one man's disobedience many were made sinners, so by the obedience of one, many might be made righteous."

The circumcision of our blessed Lord was necessary to obtain him a hearing among his own people. The Jews looked upon every uncircumcised person as unclean. Our Saviour could have had no access to them without submitting to this ceremony of their religion. To manifest himself of the seed of Abraham; to satisfy, in this respect, the requirements of his nation; to substantiate his pretensions to be their Messiah, and deprive them of what would have been an unanswerable plea for rejecting him, he graciously condescended to endure this painful rite. He needed not the sign of the "righteousness which is of faith," who had the perfect "righteousness of the law;" he needed not the seal of the covenant of mercy which God made with the faithful, being not an object of mercy, and himself very God. But as that seed of Abraham, in whom all "the nations of the earth should be blessed," he would take that mark by which Abraham's seed were known; and, by thus complying with the Jewish ordinances, remove what might have been an insuperable obstacle to the success of his ministrations among them. How amiable does our Lord appear, in thus accommodating himself to the usages of his countrymen for the better accomplishment of their salvation! What an example has he set us of the excellency of submitting to privations and pains in advancing the happiness of our fellow-beings! Did Jesus bear the marks of a humbling rite in his own most precious body, that his own when he came to them might not be offended in him? And shall not we yield to all innocent compliances with the habits and feelings of others which may facilitate our usefulness to them, and bear with contentment the labours and crosses, the self-denials, expenses, and cares which may be necessary in promoting their salvation or their happiness? Who shall refuse to descend to the walks of the poor that he may benefit the poor, when the Son of God became a Jew that he might save the Jews? Who shall refuse to resign the pleasures of a day, the charms of an opinion, the value of a temporal right, for the advancement of his fellow-beings in knowledge, faith, and goodness, when, for the satisfaction of his countrymen, in ministering to their salvation, Jesus was circumcised!

Again. The institution of this ceremony, and the compliance of the Saviour with it, suggests to us the propriety and efficacy of visible rites and sacraments. Here was a seal of a covenant established by God. It was to be a token for distinguishing the faithful; a sign of cleansing from pollution, and an assurance of blessing from Jehovah. Without some visible rite it is hardly conceivable how this or any church could be preserved distinct. Some sacrament is necessary; and, if necessary, obligatory upon every one who would support the church for which it is hallowed, and enjoy all its privileges. Accordingly, all systems of religion have had their rites, their mysteries, and their symbols. While the law stood, the Saviour honoured its ceremonies that were of sacred institution, and when he abolished circumcision, with the power of the law, by the introduction of the glorious Gospel Church, ordained baptism in its stead, to be the sign of discipleship and the assurance of adoption by the Father. What circumcision was to the Jews, baptism is to Christians. Both were of divine appointment. Both were significant of incorporation into the Church of God. Both required faith, represented purifying from the defilements of sin, and implied consequent self-denial, holiness, and obedience. Circumcision was obligatory upon every Jew who could receive it, and baptism is obligatory upon every Christian by whom it can be obtained. Special promises were annexed to circumcision, and special graces to baptism; and as the former was not rendered less sacred by neglect or abuse, so the latter cannot be lessened in its holiness and importance, because some who have been baptized have been bad men, and others have been good without it. Of circumcision, baptism takes place, and if the wilful neglect or abuse of that was attended with fatal consequences, much more of this.

Which leads me to observe, once more, that in the circumcision of the Saviour we are strikingly taught the propriety of submitting to all the precepts and institutions of the revelation under which we live. He was made under the law. Consequently the law had authority over him. With singular truth he might have asked, Can I be benefited by this rite, and by these simple ceremonies? With peculiar force he might have inquired, What connection can there be between these outward forms and my spirit; what efficacy can they have upon my heart? With more propriety than any mortal, he might have said, I can be safe and perfect without all these. But he did not stop to scruple their utility. He did not find fault with their nature. They were ordained by the Being who established the law under which he lived. This was sufficient for him. He wished not to contest divine authority, nor judge the wisdom of its arrangements. He was circumcised because it was enjoined by Jehovah upon the children of his people. Through life, he exhibited the same humble obedience. He kept the Passover, he observed the Sabbath, he went up to the feasts; he neglected no precept of the revelation which he knew came from God, and was of authority till superseded by his new and better dispensation. In this conduct of his life, the Saviour has set an example excellent in itself, and fit for his disciples to revere. It points to us the necessity of obeying every precept and observing every rite to which his Gospel gives the seal of divine authority. When we behold him receiving circumcision, asking baptism of John, because it became men "to fulfil all righteousness;" going up to Jerusalem to the feast, eating the pascal lamb; how wrong, how lamentable is the neglect of baptism and the sacramental supper by his followers? Is it because these rites are simple they are disregarded? This is to imitate the rashness of Naaman, who, scorning to wash in Jordan, would have retained his leprosy, and in a rage have left the Prophet who had recommended the easy remedy. Is it because they think they may be as good without them, and as safe? This is taking a ground which the all-perfect Son of God was too modest to assume. Is it because they cannot see how there can be efficacy or importance in these institutions? This is judging without knowledge, and arraigning the wisdom of heaven. In short, whether men may be saved without these means, how they effect what is attributed to them, whether they are the best which might have been selected, are points with which we have nothing to do. They are quite foreign to our business. The questions which concern us are, whether Christ instituted baptism and the eucharist; and if he did, whether his injunctions are binding upon us or not? On this plain ground, every man may easily form a just determination concerning the propriety of observing all the precepts and the institutions of the revelation under which he lives. His observance of them should be a simple act of faith and obedience, by which he should testify both to God and to men.

My brethren, in calling your attention to this event of our Lord's life, the Church exhibits him, as you have seen, accommodating himself graciously to the usages of his own people for their salvation; fulfilling for us "all righteousness," and leaving to mankind a declaration of the propriety and importance of observing the rites and ordinances of that dispensation of God under which they live.

Let us adore his condescension and love. Even in his infancy, he bears the griefs and carries the sorrows of his people. A week only elapses from his birth, in the helplessness and tears of human infirmity, when his blood begins significantly to be shed for the redemption of the human race. O kiss this Son, who as at this time was given you; "made under the law," that he might "redeem them who were under the law;" delivering his people from carnal ordinances, by his own fulfilment of them; and introducing them to a spiritual life.

Let us learn, also, to observe the sacraments of His Church, who, for our sakes, submitted to the sacraments of the Jewish Church, that he might bring in for us a better covenant. What believer will refuse to be baptized! What Christian will neglect to observe the Supper of the Lord, who properly considers, and consistently celebrates the act of the Redeemer in submitting to be circumcised! From the manger he instructs us. In this event of his infancy, Jesus says to you, "Thus it becomes us to fulfil all righteousness."

Finally, let the name which was given him when he was circumcised, induce you both to obey and confide in him forever. "His name was called Jesus." He "was so named of the Angel before he was conceived in the womb." The hosts of heaven knew it should be his name, and on account of it, felicitated the world when he was born. It signifies Saviour. What peace in the sound! He was a Saviour in his infancy, for then his blood began to be shed for his people. He was a Saviour upon the cross, for then his blood was fully poured out for their iniquities. He is a Saviour in heaven, for there his blood is pleaded in expiation of their offences; he "ever liveth to make intercession for them." His name is the "consolation" of his people. Amongst the weary travellers through this sinful state, it "is as ointment poured forth." They think of it, and are refreshed. Jesus! It is "a name above every name," which God hath given him. He is known by it in heaven. And to what name shall the feeble knees of men on earth so devoutly bow; what name shall the tongues of sinners so gladly confess to the praise and glory of God the Father! Disciples of Jesus, take up his cross; and go on your way rejoicing. "Your help is in the name of the Lord." "Thou shalt call his name Jesus, for he shall save his people from their sins."

SERMON XXVI.

ON NEW-YEAR'S DAY.

EPHESIANS, V. 16.

"Redeeming the time."

THE precept which touches a fault common to all men, and points out its remedy, is worthy of attentive consideration. The waste of time; the prodigality of being; the strange inconsistency of lamenting the shortness of life, and yet suffering many of its moments to elapse without obtaining from them any service, is more or less chargeable upon every one of our race. Where is the man who has justly appreciated and properly applied every part of his past existence? Where is the man against whom there has not been entered on the books of heaven, by some hour, some day, some year, that is gone, a charge of neglect, default or abuse? We look in vain for him among the descendants of Adam. All men have perceived the ungracious rapidity with which time comes and is gone; and many men have moralized upon his flight; but to have rightly estimated each hour as it passed; to have spent life without waste or loss of any of its parts, is yet unattained by mortals. Hence arises the value of the sacred maxims which teach us the true economy of time; and here is founded that solemn claim upon the attention of every man which that passage of Scripture has that I have just read; "redeeming the time."

Literally to comply with this exhortation of the Apostle, is not in our power. Sooner may we stop the revolutions of the orbs of heaven, and arrest the sun in his course, than recall the years that are past, the days that are gone, or even the moment which but now is vanished. Once gone, they are gone forever; until we find them in the eternity of God, at the day of judgment, giving testimony to our fidelity or witnessing against us. But we may review our past lives, and mark our faults, our follies and deficiencies. We may observe in the years that are gone, the snares in which we have been taken, and the spots where we have fallen; the temptations by which we have been seduced, and the paths which have led us from the way of life. We may consider how much time we have misimproved; what part of our Christian work remains undone; how imperfect our attainments are; how utterly disproportioned to the opportunities we have enjoyed. We may seize the present time, and look forward to the future, with a holy resolution to double our diligence; and by increased fidelity, make some atonement to our Creator for past prodigality, and some return for his mercy in still prolonging our being. By thus quickening our pace in our Christian course, and increasing our industry in every good work, we may, in some sort, retrieve the losses of past time, and make up for our former tardiness and waste of life. This is the duty to which the Apostle exhorts; and a very solemn duty it is, upon us erring and accountable beings. To the discharge of it we have as strong motives as can ever affect the human mind.

Time, in itself, is the gift of God, produced for us by his continual agency; and therefore, not to be wasted or abused. It is by the power of the Deity that we are upheld in being. He is active in continuing us in life. From him we received the years that are past; and it is he who gives us to call the present time our own. An end he contemplates in all his operations; and the end of this is his glory in our improvement and felicity. If, without profit to ourselves, and glory to him, we bring our days and years to an end, what do we but squander a treasure which the Most High God has been active to bestow. There is something in this thought, of the Supreme Being measuring out to us, from his own eternity, the portions of life which is sufficient of itself, to render us careful of every moment of our being, and, if any part of it have been spent by us to no proper purpose, anxious, by future fidelity to redeem it.

Again. The importance and magnitude of the business of life gives infinite value to every moment of it. Is it to pass a few years here, to catch such joys as we can find; to meet such sorrows as we can hardly sustain; and then to sink into eternal death, that we are born? Or is it to undergo the trials of a probationary existence; to become acquainted with God, and do his will, and form ourselves, by his grace, for enlarged being in a better state; to pass through death, if we rightly improve the dispensation under which we live, to eternal life and joy? Which is most consistent with the character of God? Which is according to the faith of your holy religion? Which is most readily believed by your reason and your conscience? Evidently, to exercise faith and exhibit obedience; to purify our nature, and to acquire divine habits, with a view to an immortal existence beyond the grave, is the primary object of our present being. How vast an object; and how momentous! Immortality to secure! Holiness to perfect in the fear of God! And is life too long for the work? "Verily, every man at his best estate," will find much to do. They who are farthest advanced in the course of duty, count not themselves to have apprehended. How anxious, then, should we be to redeem the periods of life that are gone, if we are behind hand in our business, and have neglected the service which they were prepared to afford.

Once more. We should be moved to obey the Apostle's exhortation, by the solemn consideration that we are accountable for our time. Life is the first, the greatest, and the most wonderful talent with which we are entrusted. Nor is it given to us merely for our sport. It is something which we are to use to our own benefit, and our Maker's glory. How we have employed it; what profit we have derived from it; to what purposes we have applied its precious periods; how we have served with it our God, our fellow beings, our country, our friends, and our own souls; what we have gained, that we can preserve; what we have acquired, that we can show to our Maker, we shall hereafter be called upon to declare. Every moment, as it is measured to us, is charged to our names in the chancery of heaven, and for it, we shall one day be required to account. Are we ready to answer for the portions of life that are gone? Can we account, satisfactorily, for the years we have already received and spent? The golden opportunities we have enjoyed, having God's word for the light of our paths, and his holy Spirit waiting to assist our infirmities; having the Son of God for our example, and the promise of immortality for our encouragement; having his Sabbaths constantly recurring, to remind us of our duty; and his sacraments constantly offered to strengthen and refresh us; these golden opportunities, have we vouchers to produce that they have been justly appreciated, and faithfully improved? I wait, trembling, for the reply. Alas! too many of our days have gone, we know not how, nor where; and some of them, we are conscious, we have squandered. We have passed from stage to stage of our being with but little improvement of our knowledge, or our faith; and even many of the truths, many of the virtues, many of the opportunities of improvement which have caught our attention, have been to us like the sweet flowers of nature to the traveller's eye; we have looked upon them, and hasted away. But our inadvertence will not alter the government of God. For our time, we must one day give account; and, by a standing principle of the divine equity, "to whomsoever much is given, of him will much be required." If, then, there be any way of retrieving what we have lost, and making good what we have wasted, how eagerly should we avail ourselves of it. And merciful is our God, that he permits us to cancel, with future fidelity, the deficiencies of past life. It is his voice speaking in the Apostle, that exhorts us, by a careful economy, and faithful use of the years which are yet allotted us, to redeem those which we have spent to little purpose; perhaps, have entirely lost.

And this leads me to observe, further, that we should be engaged to this duty, and excited to very great fidelity in it by a sense of the goodness of God in yet prolonging our days. We live. But what claim have we to survive those who are gone down to the chambers of the dead! Are we better than they! When the Almighty has walked through his vineyard, has he found more fruit upon us than he did upon them? Might not, then, the breath before which they faded, have justly lighted upon us? And oh! if it had, should we not have been found by our Lord, unfaithful stewards of many of the years that he has given us upon earth? "It is of the Lord's mercy that we are not consumed." That he yet spares us, that our lease of life is still prolonged; that, notwithstanding our unfaithfulness, he measures out to us new portions of time, and defers to call us to account, should make us tremblingly solicitous to regain what we have lost, and atone for what we have abused. When the day and means of grace are continued to us, while so many of our fellow men have been gathered to the dust, thankfulness should excite us to increased fidelity; it would be ingratitude of the most heinous degree, not to "walk circumspectly," "redeeming the time."

Finally; we should be induced to an immediate compliance with this Apostolic exhortation, by reflecting upon the uncertainty of life; and that the longer we defer the duty, the more complicate and arduous will be the task. There are but few persons who are not sensible of the importance of retrieving, in the future, the neglects and miscarriages of the past. Most men, when they allow themselves to think, perceive the wisdom of breaking from the shackles of vice! and resolve, that they will make the arrangements, and attend to the duties which may promote their eternal peace. But, the misfortune is, like the infatuated Felix, they forever postpone this weighty concern to a more "convenient season." By and by, when they have gained enough of honour, and of wealth, and can withdraw from the business and pleasures of the world, they intend to do all that they have left undone, and devote themselves particularly to the most serious business of life. Oh, fatal delusion! This more "convenient season," is like to-morrow; forever coming, and forever distant. Could they assign it a certain period; could they fix it to a future year, what hold would they have upon the days that must intervene? A thread, which the least blast may break; a hair, which the passing gossamer may snap. To build on distant days, when the young, as well as the old, lie in the grave; when the robust, as well as the feeble, wither like grass; what is it but to rely on the stability of a wave, or to trust to the gilding of a western cloud. Besides, if life should be prolonged through many years, and the period at which we promise ourselves we shall redeem lost time should arrive, the work will constantly increase as we advance, and our strength as constantly diminish. Will the task be more easy and pleasant when we have a long run of squandered years to redeem? Shall we be more adequate to the work when overtaken by sickness, or enfeebled by age? Can we most wisely and effectually balance our accounts in that period, "when the sun and the moon shall be darkened, and the clouds will return after the rain?" No, my friends, no! The present time alone is certain. And sufficient unto the future, if we ever reach it, will be the cares and duties thereof. Enough, especially for the hour of sickness, will be the pains of disease; and enough, for the evening of life, will be the infirmities of age. It is while our faculties are healthy and strong, and our opportunity sure, that we should attend to the main business of life. When a man sees his brethren falling around him, and considers that upon his own conduct depends his everlasting happiness or misery, to defer to hearken to his Maker's voice, and "walk in his laws which he hath set before us," is a high pitch of human folly, and a dreadful evidence of human perverseness. Gracious God! when eternal happiness is at stake, that man, amidst all the evidences of the uncertainty of life, should defer his duty to a future period! Behold; while he is thus deferring, a dart from the hand of death strikes him; and he is summoned to account for his time, while he is despising the forbearance and long-suffering of God, and neglecting to redeem it. "Make no tarrying," says the wise son of Sirach, "to turn unto the Lord; and put not off from day to day; for suddenly shall his wrath come forth, and in thy security thou shalt be destroyed and perish in the day of vengeance."

How many, and how weighty are these motives, to the duty of redeeming our time. Does it not, my brethren, appear to you, too solemn a duty to be cursorily thought of, or carelessly discharged? It is a duty to which we are particularly prompted, at this present moment. With noiseless step, and unwearied speed, Time has been spoiling us of another grand portion of life; and, through the goodness and forbearance of God, we are entered upon another new year. Let us look back upon the year that is gone, and see how much of it we have to redeem. Have we improved the blessings we have enjoyed, and the dispensations of Providence we have witnessed? The services of the sanctuary, the sacraments of the Church, and all the means of grace, whereby our merciful Creator would renew us after his own image, and fit us for his presence, have we availed ourselves of them, and been made better by them? Has the new year found us fitter for heaven than the old one did; stronger in faith, more free from vice, nearer to God, and having less wasted time to redeem? Are we better, as well as older; nearer to heaven, as well as nearer to the tomb? These are inquiries which we ought all to make; and if to them our hearts can give an affirmative reply, let us indulge that modest joy, which it belongs to the faithful followers of the Lamb to indulge. Let us go on to perfect holiness, and our God will prosper us. But if our hearts put a negative upon these inquiries, let us pause; let us consider the importance of time; the solemn magnitude of the true business of life; our accountability to our Creator for the years he allots us; his goodness in yet prolonging our probation, and the utter uncertainty how long we may be spared among the living. Let us endeavour, by future obedience, to atone for the manner in which we have spent our former years. Let us resolve that, through the grace of God, the year upon which we have entered, shall not be brought "to an end like a tale that is told;" but shall carry, as it elapses, to the author and owner of all time, good testimonies of our fidelity and improvement. Perhaps, my friends, before the sun shall return to the place from which he has just commenced his annual course, your probation will be finished, and you will stand at the bar of God. Oh! be induced, "while it is called to-day," to secure to yourselves the approbation and favour of your God. Let your loins be always girded, and your lamp burning; let your feet be always shod, and the staff of God's word in your hands. That if he should come this year, to call you to your account, he may find you waiting for him, with the vouchers of your fidelity in your hands. "Blessed," I say unto you, "is that servant whom his Lord when he cometh, shall find watching."

SERMON XXVII.

ON NEW-YEAR'S-DAY.

St. Luke, xii. 7, 8.

"Then said he unto the dresser of his vineyard, Behold these three years I come, seeking fruit on this fig-tree, and find none: cut it down; why cumbereth it the ground? And he, answering, said unto him, Lord, let it alone this year also."

I HAVE selected this passage of holy writ, not with a design to enter into a disquisition concerning its original respect to the Jewish nation, but, rather, to apply it to ourselves, as suggesting many pertinent and useful reflections to *us*, who, through the good providence of the Almighty, have just been brought to the commencement of a new year. God grant, that it may be to you, my brethren, a year of blessings, in yourselves, in your families, in your Church, and in the concerns of your common country. As far as a wise improvement of our time is calculated to bring down upon us the favour of heaven, it will, perhaps, be promotive of our happiness, to attend to the truths which are offered to our consideration in this beautiful parable of our blessed Lord. We may, alas, consider ourselves as too justly represented under the figure of a fruitless fig-tree; and whatever was the design of Christ, when he spake the parable, it will very naturally furnish us with admonition and instruction.

In the first place it may be used to remind us, that we owe our existence and the prolongation of our lives to Almighty

God. The fig-tree was planted by him who owned the vineyard. Though we were born of our parents and seem sustained by the nourishment we take, yet, our bones could have been formed in the womb, and the secret, subtil spark of life, could have been kindled, in these bodies of clay, only by that Being who is the source of all life, and accomplishes what he wills by an unfailing omnipotence. His hand, too, upholds us in being. We live by his power, constantly exerted to continue us in life. Let him withdraw his arm, and instantly we are no more. "If he set his heart upon man, if he gather unto himself his spirit and his breath, all flesh shall perish together, and man shall turn again unto dust." We are God's by every right which can give him a property in us. He has, too, and asserts, an unlimited freedom to do what he will with his own. When he pleaseth, he saith to the dresser of his vineyard, concerning any tree which he had planted, "Cut it down;" and "who can stay his hand, or say unto him, what doest thou?" You will, therefore, consider yourselves as wholly indebted to the Most High, for the life you have received, and will attribute it entirely to his help, that you continue unto this day. The years roll on, and multitudes are constantly carried with them to the abodes of oblivion. To what power do we owe it, that we survive the wrecks of the years which are past, but to that invisible, Almighty power, which gives to time both his victims and his wings.

Again. We may consider the parable as suggesting to us, that God expects from us every year the proper fruits of the being and advantages which he has given us. "Behold, these three years I come, seeking fruit on this fig-tree." In our germen state, in the days of our infancy and childhood, he has protected us. We have grown up under his care. While we were yet tender, his insensible hand often averted from us the wind and the blast; and the drops of dew, which he begat, descended silently upon us. He expects, that in our youth we be ornaments and not blots upon his creation; and that when we are come to years of maturity, we consider the station he hath assigned us in the scale of beings, appreciate faithfully the advantages, mercies, and honours, which he has bestowed upon us, and bring forth, according to our abilities, correspondent fruits. And when we advert to our condition, great has been his favour towards us; ample the endowments we have received. He has given us more understanding than the beasts of the field; "and made us wiser than the fowls of the air." We are exalted to be rational creatures; capable of knowing our Creator, of enjoying the pleasures of intelligence; and of giving a direction and meaning to the actions of our lives. He has instructed us fully in the ways of righteousness. We know what is good. Our duties and all the excellencies which beings of our faculties are capable of acquiring, are clearly manifested to us. We have received from his love the Son of his bosom, to be an everlasting propitiation for our sins; and, through his merits, the kingdom of heaven is set open, the joys and glories of immortality are offered to all believers. Having thus qualified us for attaining high degrees of spiritual beauty and achieving excellent deeds of virtue, he justly looks that we should bring forth fruits answerable to his exertions in our behalf. To be thus endowed, and yet to be cumberers of the ground! To be upheld in being by the power of God, and yet to be useless to ourselves, useless to our families and useless to the world! To be enriched with the blessings, both of "the upper and nether spring," and yet to bring no glory to our Maker and no accession of virtues to his moral creation! Surely, this would entitle us to the utter neglect of God. What, then, shall be said of those, who consume the years after years which are given them, in wickedness and unbelief; who, instead of bringing forth fragrant and wholesome fruits, beautifully represented in the parable by the fruit of the fig-tree, yield, in their vices and infidelity, a noxious poison, odious in itself, and fatal, like the effluvia of the fabled Upas, to everything within its reach! Verily, it could attach no imputation of blame to the character of the Most High, if, anxious for the perfection of his works, and desirous of exhibiting to all the subjects of his moral kingdom, evidences of the infinite holiness, and justice of his government, he should, at any time, say to the dresser of his vineyard, concerning such, "Cut them down; why cumber they the ground?"

But, great is the forbearance of God! The text brings to our notice and admiration his patience and long-suffering, in waiting for our fruitfulness. "Behold, these three years I come." It is happy for the erring race of men, that the judgments of the Almighty seldom follow immediately upon the offence. He is a lenient and merciful God. Infinitely indulgent, and anxious that none of his creatures should perish, he comes not only one year seeking fruit, but year after year, unwearied by our barrenness. Again and again he prolongs our probation, if haply his forbearance, his goodness, or any of the means he uses, may cause us to produce the virtues and graces which he planted us in his vineyard to bear. And in how many ways does he endeavour, to correct the waywardness of our nature, and to execute in us the love of righteousness and holiness. He reveals himself to us in the works of creation, assuring us by them, that he is good and worthy of our affections and fear. He comes to us in the whispers of conscience, checking us at every entrance of the paths of vice. He approaches us in the ministry of his word, laying open the guilt of our hearts before us, moving to embrace the offices of the Mediator, and imparting to us knowledge and strength. He descends as the dew upon our hearts in the silent influences of his Spirit, to renew in us the virtues which are decayed, and to revive those which are perishing. He comes to us in the dispensations of his providence, pruning us with the hand of affliction, hardening us by conflicts with the gales of adversity, and suppressing our attachment to the things of this deceitful world, by a thousand evidences of their transitoriness and vanity. And even in the flight of time a voice is heard, calling, in language which none but the deaf and the rash can disregard, "That thou doest, do quickly." But, notwithstanding this patience and long-suffering, this careful cultivation and benign influence of God, sterile are the hearts of men. It is melancholy to reflect, how many human beings there are, fluttering amidst the vanities and deceiving themselves with the follies of life; whose removal, should it come suddenly, would take from the earth no Christian virtues and cause no joy in heaven. The best of us, in reviewing our lives, shall find little cause to solace ourselves with our fidelity. We have consumed our days in vanity. "We have brought our years to an end as a tale that is told." One year has been given us after another, through the same indulgent mercy, yet we have not obeyed the voice of the Lord God to make our hearts perfect towards him. Still he waits to be gracious. He still defers to terminate the day, or to withhold the means of grace. Full often when the lives of men have been prolonged, beyond the lives of their contemporaries, yea, when they have been brought to the hoary limit of human existence, full often, when all the means of fertility have been ineffectual upon us, and justice might well call for our excision, he listens to the entreaty of the kind dresser of his vineyard, our prevailing Intercessor, and grants the trial of another year. "Let it alone this year also."

But, though this is a merciful, it is a most solemn indulgence. It brings me to remark, that there is a period beyond which the Spirit of God will not strive with man. It implies an awful limitation. It is an observation of the wise man, that "because sentence against an evil work is not executed speedily, therefore the hearts of the sons of men are fully set in them to do evil." Too true a picture of the presumption of our race. By a strange calculation, because we have already wasted so much time, we trust that we have much more to waste. That very forbearance of God, which should lead us to repentance, through our perverseness confirms us in sin. The years which are gone, have left us among the living; we have not yet felt the fatal consequence of deferring to do good; we therefore go on thoughtlessly in the same evil way, trusting that the years to come will be as those which are past; yea, "and much more abundant." "But," says the wise son of Sirach, "say not I have sinned, and what harm hath happened unto me? For the Lord is long-suffering, he will in nowise let thee go. Make no tarrying to turn unto him, and put not off from day to day: for suddenly shall the wrath of the Lord come forth, and in thy security thou shalt be destroyed, and perish in the day of vengeance. Imperfectly has he considered the qualities which must enter into the character of a perfect being, who, from his past experience of forbearance and impunity, goes on still in his imperfections, presuming upon the mercy of God, and repaying his patience and long-suffering with continued unfruitfulness. There is a degree of obduracy at which the heart becomes reprobate. There is a stage of iniquity at which intercession ceases. There is a year to every man which must be his last. The joyful indulgence, "Let it alone this year also," implies in itself the solemn and weighty consequence which is afterwards expressed—"If it bear fruit, well; but if not, then after that thou shalt cut it down."

We have now seen the impressive truths which this beautiful allegory is calculated to suggest. The present is a season when they should be brought home to our hearts. We have just finished another year. If, in the course of it, our God have looked upon us, how fruitless have we been found. Oh, if indeed we have at any time brought forth fruit, how little, how imperfect, how far short of what he might justly have expected! Have we sorrowed for our sins; and when we have sorrowed, have we not transgressed again? Have our defects been all corrected, and all our vows and resolutions fulfilled? When called to attend on the ordinances of God, have we gone to them; and when we have been to them, have they produced in us increased faith and righteousness, more perfect purity and peace? Have the tempers and desires of our souls been refined, and in the acts of our lives, have we done what we could for the glory of God and the benefit of our fellow-men? "He that was unjust, is he not unjust still; and he that was filthy, is he not filthy still?" The thoughtless unbeliever, does he not yet walk in the comfortless and dangerous paths of skepticism; and he who had glanced a finger beckoning him to an acquaintance with God and with the beauty of holiness, has he not, after half resolving to obey it, looked for it no more? If so, are we sure that we are not of the number, concerning whom it had been said in the councils of heaven, "Cut them down;" but for whom "the dresser of the vineyard," our compassionate and prevailing Intercessor has entreated, "Lord, let them alone this year also." And, ah! in granting his request, may not the Almighty have annexed the solemn condition, "If they bear fruit, well; but if not, then after that thou shalt cut them down." I tremble at the thought, that any who hear me should be in this case, and be found in the course of the year barren and unfruitful, under the forbearance and cultivation of God. My brethren, you are planted in the vineyard of the Lord of Hosts. His ministering servants are employed by him to foster your life and protect your growth. The dews of his Spirit are sent down from on high to refresh and invigorate you. "The Sun of Righteousness" shines constantly upon you, to impart to you life and strength, and abundant fertility. And if clouds of sorrow at times gather over you, they are gathered by him to shade some tender grace, or to check some perverse inclination; and the rains which descend from them, even these are designed to add to your freshness, and to the number and the soundness of your fruits. Under these advantages, great is the product of piety and virtue which Jehovah may justly expect you to yield. And is it possible, that this year may be the last in which he will come, seeking his fruits? How awful the thought! How precious the moments, which will fly with swift and noiseless wings, notwithstanding they are charged with such important issues. Here, at the threshold of the year, consecrate yourselves anew to the service of God. Give to each day as it passes its devotion and its duties. Grow every day in grace and in the knowledge of the Lord and Saviour Jesus Christ. Be pure from sin, and in very deed servants unto God, that ye may "have your fruit unto holiness, and the end everlasting life." Then, when the Almighty walks through his vineyard, he will behold you with complacency. Your emblem shall no longer be found in the unfruitful fig-tree, but in those trees seen in prophetic vision, which are called "trees of righteousness, the planting of the Lord, that he might be glorified. To "the dresser of his vineyard," God will never say, concerning these trees, "Cut them down;" but at the proper time, when they shall have been fitted for the purpose in this nursery of the world, take them up carefully, and free them from all unsound and uncomely appendages, and let them be transplanted, to flourish forever, into the garden by the river of my kingdom in the heavens.

SERMON XXVIII.

ON THE EPIPHANY.

ISAIAH, lx. 3.

"And the Gentiles shall come to thy light, and kings to the brightness of thy rising."

AT the season of the Epiphany did these words begin to receive their fulfilment. Led by a star, there came soon after the nativity, Magi from among the heathens, to worship, at his rising, "the Sun of Righteousness." These were the first Gentiles who rendered homage to the Head of the Church. By some they are believed to have been royal personages, and thus to have accomplished exactly the ancient prophecy in the text. Be this as it may, at the promulgation of the Gospel, the wall of partition between Jews and Gentiles was broken down; God's purpose was declared, to make all men partakers of his promises and mercy; multitudes of the heathens flowed into the Church, whose kings and princes became its protectors; and at this day, the Gentiles are the inheritors of God's most precious gifts, having for a while taken place of the Jews, through the blindness which hath happened to the latter, because of their unbelief.

The rejection of the Jews and calling of the Gentiles is styled by the sacred writers a mystery. And a mystery it is, the depths of whose fitness and utility we shall be unable to fathom, till we come to the place of the Redeemer's glory, and contemplate with enlarged powers, the manifold wisdom of God.

Some views of the subject, however, it becomes us to take; for all the dispensations of God are good and instructive, designed to display his perfections to the world, and to lead men, if they will be humble and docile, to a knowledge of his name, and an admiration of his work.

In the first place, we are not to think the Deity unjust, in leaving the Gentiles a long time in the darkness of heathenism. Is there unrighteousness with God? God forbid! Their blindness was the consequence of their transgression. God made man upright and just. In the morning of the world he revealed himself fully unto him, and he gave him a law whereby he might have lived. He foolishly transgressed, and became subject to sin. A spiritual and moral blindness justly ensued; and having voluntarily departed from his Maker, his heart became more and more alienated, till he plunged himself into the deepest abyss of idolatry and iniquity.

God, however, left the Gentiles at no time without sufficient manifestations of his Being and presence. If they had felt after him to find him, he was not far from every one of them. The wonders of his hands surrounded them. His works, if pondered with attention, proclaimed his unity and glory. "The invisible things of him, from the creation of the world, are clearly seen, being understood by the things that are made, even his eternal power and Godhead; so that they are without excuse."

The Holy Ghost, also, did frequently strive in the hearts of the heathens. This blessed Spirit, which the mediation of the Son hath purchased for the children of men, lifts his "still, small voice" in the bosom of every man. Whatever attainments in true wisdom or virtue we find in the heathen world, all was the fruit of the assistance of that blessed Spirit by which we are sanctified. His motions enabled them to show "the work of the law written in their hearts, their conscience also bearing witness, and their thoughts the meanwhile accusing or else excusing one another." And had they yielded to his gracious influences, he would, no doubt, have led them to God and virtue. But they preferred their carnal inclinations and depraved lusts. They resisted and quenched the Spirit. And God, surely, was not obliged, in justice, to preserve them, supernaturally, from the consequences of their wickedness. No creature can claim anything of him as a right; much less sinners the interference of his mercy.

In many ways also, there was some communicated knowledge of God diffused, in all ages, among the Gentiles. Though they were so wretchedly ignorant of him, they might have been better informed. He had selected a peculiar people to preserve in the world a knowledge of himself and of his will. This people was known to all nations. The wanderings of the Patriarchs in the first ages, carried a knowledge of the true God among the Canaanites, the Egyptians, the inhabitants of Mesopotamia, and many countries of the East. The captivities of the Jews, under the Mosaic dispensation, brought the divine name and character among the Assyrians, the Medes and Persians, and many polished neighbouring nations. The dispersion of the tribes, and indeed, the commercial intercourse of the Hebrews with other nations, must have introduced the mention of the true God among the inhabitants of Europe, and Asia, and of all places whither they went. The prevalence of circumcision among some heathen nations, and many parts of the mythology of others, are, to this day, vestiges—defaced vestiges, of the course of truth; monuments of opportunities afforded all men to become acquainted with the true theology. But, as the sacred writers observe, and as profane writers prove, they were "vain in their imaginations, and their foolish heart was darkened. When they knew God, they glorified him not as God, neither were thankful." They "changed the truth of God into a lie;" hankered after idols and sinful pleasures, "and worshipped and served the creature more than the Creator." And forasmuch "as they did not like to retain God in their knowledge, God," in just and awful vengeance, "gave them over to a reprobate mind," and "suffered all nations to walk in their own ways. Nevertheless, he left not himself" at any time "without witness, in that he did good, and gave them rain from heaven, and fruitful seasons, filling their hearts with food and gladness."

Again. The righteousness of God, in the rejection of the Jews, is worthy of observation. To act in conformity with the requirements of justice, is not to act inconsistently with mercy. The Jews had been a highly favoured people. To them pertained the adoption, and the glory, and the covenant, and the giving of the law, and the service of God, and the promises; theirs were "the fathers, and of them, as concerning the flesh, Christ came, who is over all, God blessed forever." Of a people so distinguished, the Most High might justly expect an eminent degree of holiness and fidelity. But their inconstancy and insincerity, their idolatries and impurities, had many times brought upon them his displeasure and vengeance. Still he favoured them. Still he fulfilled his promises. His loving kindness he never took utterly from them, nor suffered his truth to fail. In the fulness of time, he sent to them his beloved Son, the bearer of the blessings he had promised to the fathers, the Messiah, whom it was their nation's most glorious privilege to produce. But how did they receive this author of salvation, for whom their prophets had directed them to look? How did they receive this Son of the Highest, who came to them with the fulness of the blessings of the Gospel of peace? They were unbelieving and contumacious. They despised their Redeemer. "Dead in trespasses and sins," they could not open their eyes upon his spiritual power and glory. They were carnal in their affections and hopes. They were obstinate and rebellious in their hearts. Proud and presumptuous in their descent and privileges, going about to establish their own righteousness, and to justify themselves by external observances of the law, they scoffed at that righteousness of faith, by which Abraham and all the worthies were justified, and held in contempt the adorable Immanuel, in whom alone we have salvation, even the remission of sins. Though informed of his character and the time of his coming; though he was the end of the law for righteousness to every one who believed; though he united in himself all their types and prophecies, and exhibited the most stupendous evidences of his authority; though God had done everything to turn their hearts to him, and designed for them the highest mercies and most glorious privileges in him; they despised his humility and purity, and, after embittering his life with most unjust persecutions and impious mockeries, caused this most gracious Messenger of heaven, this blessed Saviour and Minister of reconciliation, to be barbarously crucified. In this they filled up the measure of their iniquities. And God, willing to show his wrath upon the impenitent and unbelieving, and to make his power known to all people, visited them with the awful judgments which befel their nation. He expected of his people fruits answerable to their privileges. They were filled with contumacy and sin. His word they had polluted. His beloved Son they had crucified. Therefore the hedge of their vineyard he hath taken away, and the wall thereof he hath broken down. "The wild boar out of the wood doth root it up, and the wild beasts of the field devour it." He hath laid it waste that it is not pruned nor digged. With dreadful vengeance he hath commanded the clouds that they rain no rain upon it. Let those who hope for the mercy of God, while they obstinately reject his counsels in the Redeemer, consider their fate, and learn from it the certainty that he will avenge his Son of all his adversaries; that he will not fail to recompense his enemies.

But in what part of the divine government is not judgment connected with mercy? "Behold," says St. Paul, writing upon this subject to Gentile converts, "behold the goodness and severity of God; on them who fell, severity; but towards thee, goodness, if thou continue in his goodness." The calling of the Gentiles was, indeed, an infinite display of compassion in the Most High. Who can speak the greatness of the mercy, which brought the nations that had polluted his glory and their own nature, and lay in darkness and the shadow of death, to a knowledge of himself, and a participation of grace and pardon and everlasting life. "He was found of them who sought him not; he was made manifest to them that asked not after him."

In this economy of his government, God has most strikingly displayed to the world, both the freedom and the extent of his grace. We see him bestowing his mercy where in his sovereign wisdom he sees fit; and perceive that the greatest sinners may be partakers of it, if they will comply with the conditions upon which it is offered. The Gentiles, by embracing the Gospel, have attained to the hope of salvation, though they were buried in ignorance and sin; while the Jews, who rejected the counsels of God in Christ Jesus, and sought their justification in the deeds of the law, have come short of the felicity they desired. Herein is the sovereignty, and justice, and unlimited goodness of the Almighty manifested. While the rejection of the Jews shows his wrath upon the perverse and unbelieving, the calling of the Gentiles makes known the riches of his glory, or the vessels of mercy which he had afore prepared unto glory.

It is worthy of observation, that God foreknew, from the beginning, by whom his Son would be received, and by whom he would be rejected; and this wonderful restoration of the Gentiles to favor, in the kingdom of the Messiah, was proclaimed by prophecy in many a sublime strain, in all ages of the world. Who that ponders the primitive promise, that in the seed of Abraham "all nations of the earth should be blessed;" who that hears old Jacob declaring in remote time, that unto Shiloh should "the gathering of the people be;" who that catches the strain of Hosea, "I will call them my people that were not my people, and her beloved that was not beloved;" who that listens to the enraptured Psalmist as he sings, "The kings of Tharsis and of the Isles shall give presents; the kings of Arabia and Saba shall bring gifts. All kings shall fall down before him; all nations shall do him service;" who that hearkens to the seraphic Isaiah, uttering upon his heaven-tuned harp, these wonderful strains; "To him whom man despiseth, to him whom the nation abhorreth, kings shall see and arise, princes also shall worship;" for "I will give thee for a light to the Gentiles, that thou mayest be my salvation unto the end of the earth;" who that recollects these, and many other predictions, and then turns his eyes to the wise men coming from the East, with gold, frankincense and myrrh, to worship "the Sun of Righteousness" at his rising, and considers the subsequent recovery of the Gentile nations, from their idolatry and ignorance, to a pure religion and elevated hopes, and this, through the preaching of the gospel by a few friendless and illiterate men, without the aid of wealth or power, and in opposition to all the prejudices and inclinations of the age; who, that ponders these things as he ought, can avoid applying to the flight of the Gentiles into the bosom of the Church, the words of the king of Israel: "This is the Lord's doing, and it is marvellous in our eyes."

But, there remains to be observed, in the last place, a yet more wonderful part of the economy of God. Behold the Jews; "a people scattered and peeled," and plucked up by the roots, yet living, and preserving their distinct character. Since their rejection of the Messiah, the strong bands of their nation have been dissolved, and they are dispersed in all parts of the world. Everywhere they are associated with other people; but nowhere are they assimilated. Though they do not exist in any place as a corporate body, they are preserved a distinct people throughout the whole earth. Other people are soon blended with those with whom they live. Other nations are soon lost in their conquerors. But, unparalleled fact! the Hebrews, though scattered by the Most High, and divested of all civil polity, are, to this day, preserved, an unmixed and peculiar people. They are a monument of the truth of Scripture. They are a monument of the authority of Christ. They are a monument of the vengeance of the Almighty upon the faithless generation by whom his Son was rejected and crucified. But let no man despise them. They are still the people of God. That they should reject the Messiah, and for a recompense be rejected of God, the prophets foretold with wonderful precision; but they have also foretold, that though in his wrath he has hid his face from them, he will, with great loving kindness, gather them. As touching the Gospel, they are enemies for our sakes, but as touching the election, they are beloved for the fathers' sakes.

We behold them reserved, doubtless not in vain, but for the accomplishment of glorious purposes. Though now "broken off" from the stock of the goodly olive-tree, into which, of God's mercy, we have been "graffed," "they also, if they abide not still in unbelief, shall be graffed in, for God is able to graff them in again." Our duty is, to derive from their situation a confirmation of our faith, and an assurance of the truth and holiness of God. And verily, if any man will not be convinced by this standing miracle, this daily testimony of the truth of Christianity, "neither would he be persuaded, though one rose from the dead." With tenderness and awe we should consider their situation, and with brotherly love, offer frequently the prayer of faith, that God would hasten the time, when his people shall say of their Redeemer, "Blessed be he that cometh in the name of the Lord."

I have dwelt so long upon the topics which the subject brought into view, that but little time remains for the practical remarks which it suggests. The manifestation of Christ to the heathen world, and this season in which the Church commemorates it, are peculiarly interesting to us. Remember, that we were Gentiles, "aliens from the commonwealth of Israel, and strangers from the covenants of promise." But now we are partakers of the best mercies of the Most High. Great should be our gratitude to him for "calling us out of darkness into his marvellous light." Let us be what our Christian privileges obligate us to be; let us "walk as becometh the children of light." There is nothing of absolute, unconditional decree in our election to the blessings of the Gospel; for unless we continue in goodness, we "also shall be cut off." Look to the quarter of the globe which first came to the brightness of the Saviour's rising. Ignorance and superstition have extinguished the light of the Gospel, and the Koran of Muhammed supplies the place of the Oracles of the Living God. And to what must we ascribe the melancholy change? The people were departed from the love of Christ, and held the truth in unrighteousness. Should we corrupt our faith, or dishonor it by iniquity, great will be the cause to fear that our light also will be obscured. Let every one, then, be induced, by his own individual piety and virtue, and by the Christian education of his family, to assist his country in retaining the favour of the Head of the Church; if, haply, from her land, which is now blessed with the light of the Gospel, the golden candlesticks may not be taken away. And, while we rejoice in our happiness, let us cast our eyes upon the multitudes of our brethren who are yet benighted; "having no hope, and without God in the world." While their situation teaches us our own felicity, let it induce us, with holy and humble devotion, to offer, frequently, the prayer which the Church hath taught us, that God would have "mercy upon all Jews, Turks, infidels and heretics; and take from them all ignorance, hardness of heart, and contempt of his word; and so fetch them home to his flock, that they may be saved among the remnant of the true Israelites, and made one fold, under one Shepherd, Jesus Christ," our most blessed Lord and Saviour. Amen.

SERMON XXIX.

ON THE EPIPHANY.

MATTHEW, ii. 9, 10, 11

"When they had heard the king, they departed; and, lo, the star, which they saw in the east, went before them, till it came and stood over where the young child was. When they saw the star, they rejoiced with exceeding great joy. And when they were come into the house, they saw the young child with Mary his mother, and fell down and worshipped him; and when they had opened their treasures, they presented unto him gifts: gold, and frankincense, and myrrh."

IN one of the sublimest prophecies which the Scriptures contain respecting the advent of the Messiah, the Almighty is introduced as addressing his Son in these memorable words: "It is a light thing that thou shouldest be my servant, to raise up the tribes of Jacob, and to restore the preserved of Israel; I will also give thee for a light to the Gentiles, that thou mayest be my salvation unto the end of the earth." The fulfillment of this glorious declaration commenced, as at this season of the Epiphany, when Christ Jesus was first manifested to the Gentiles as their Lord and Saviour, and received the first fruits of their faith and devotion. I purpose, therefore, to set before you, as proper topics for your attention, at this time, the manner in which this manifestation was made; the conduct of those to whom he was manifested, and the consequences of the manifestation. Subjects these, in which are involved some of the most interesting wonders of the divine economy, and from which we may derive some important instructions.

The manner of Christ's manifestation to the Gentiles, is first to be considered; and this, we are told, was by the appearance of a star, discerned by wise men of the East; and by them understood to indicate the birth of an expected king and deliverer. This star was supernatural; appearing and disappearing as the occasion required; and never setting like other luminaries of the skies, but resting, in a glorious hour, "over the place where the young child was." Holy St. Chrysostom, in a discourse upon the Epiphany, which has come down to us, supposes, that it was an angel in the form of a star, traversing the skies as the guide of the wise men to the new-born King. Others have imagined that it was a new star, or extraordinary meteor, created in honour of the Saviour's nativity, and made the herald of his birth to the inhabitants of distant lands. The most probable opinion is, that the Shechinah, or glory of the Lord, which shone round about the shepherds on the night of his nativity, was also seen distinct and elevated in the heavens by the vigilant astronomers of the East, and that to selected individuals, of both Jews and Gentiles, the same wonderful appearance announced the birth of the Saviour of all nations. Easily we may imagine it seen at a distance in the heavens, in the form of a star, as, anciently to the Israelites, in the figure of a pillar of fire. The wise men saw it, and set out in pursuit of him whose birth it indicated. When it became needful for their guidance, lo, it again appeared, to their exceeding joy. It now went before them, their wonderful and most welcome conductor, till it came near the humble mansion where the Redeemer lay. There it rested: there it stood: at once an assurance to these faithful visitors of the certainty of the place, and the majesty of the Infant Jesus. But, whatever opinion we may choose of the nature of this star, who can avoid admiring, amidst the humiliation of Christ, the accompanying attestations of his extraordinary character. While he is wrapped in swaddling bands on earth, the heavens declare his glory. He sleeps in a manger; but a star, as a diadem of divinity, is suspended over his head. It led the wise men to seek and honour him as a king. It shadows forth to us the glorious office which this neglected infant may challenge to himself, even to be the "light of the world." It recalls to our minds the august figure under which he once proclaims himself, "the bright and morning star."

Before we proceed to the consequences of this extraordinary manifestation of Christ to the Gentiles, it is meet we should bestow some attention upon the conduct of these distinguished visitors of our blessed Lord. Under the character of wise men, we are to consider them as belonging to that order of men among the eastern nations, who gave themselves to the study of philosophy and sciences, particularly, of the appearances and laws of the heavenly bodies. They were called Magi. Of them, were sometimes kings and priests; and always, they were of high respectability and influence. The sign which the Almighty gave them on this great occasion, was kindly and wisely taken from objects and exhibited in scenes with which they were habitually conversant.

They might, too, be naturally inclined to give to the appearance of this new object in the heavens the significance it was designed to bear. For it was a prevailing superstition in many heathen countries, that a new star indicated the birth of an extraordinary person, and that they should be great who were born under its influence, at its appearance. In this view, God may be considered as condescending to the weakness of men, and using a thing which is not, to illustrate and advance "things that are."

Still, you will ask, what connection is there between the appearance of a star and the birth of Christ, or of any other man, that it should lead the wise men so earnestly to seek, so explicitly to inquire for "him who was born King of the Jews." Here we must remember, that there prevailed at that time throughout the world, an expectation of an extraordinary person who should come from Judea. This is testified to us by profane and sacred historians, and by occurrences at the time, which, without the prevalence of such an expectation, would be utterly inexplicable. That the Magi had received this traditionary expectation, and were also acquainted with the grounds of it, is in a high degree probable. Through neighbouring nations, the intercourse of the Jews would naturally promulge this leading and flattering article of their faith. The captivities, too, of the tribes of Israel, and afterwards of Judah, could hardly fail to diffuse through the regions of the East, a knowledge of their prophecies, and, especially, of this cherished hope, this consoling promise of their peculiar religion. Balaam, too, had travelled through some of those regions, and sojourned in others; and from his lips, though a Gentile, came the prediction, "I shall see him, but not now; I shall behold him, but not nigh; there shall come a star out of Jacob, and a sceptre shall rise out of Israel." Above all, Daniel had dwelt in some of these countries, and his prophecies, it is reasonable to believe, had been known in many of them; and who could be acquainted with the books of this learned prophet, and not be open to the liveliest impression, which a current expectation of an extraordinary person, to appear among the Jews, could make. From some or other of these sources, the wise men unquestionably had become possessed of the tradition then so widely diffused, that about that time an extraordinary king should be born in Judea, who should rule the earth. When, therefore, they beheld the new and extraordinary star shining over the holy land, they would inquire what it portended, and might well infer from it, that the expected King of the Jews was born. Of this also we may be sure, that he, who gave this sign in the heavens, would render it effectual to all the purposes for which it was given. God has as easy access to the minds, as to the senses of men. By message to the wise men, or by vision, or by the secret movements of his Spirit upon their souls, he could inform them of the cause and significance of the phenomenon they beheld. And since by the last method, most of the means which he uses for our spiritual instruction, are rendered effectual, we may safely conclude that his holy Spirit, influencing the minds of these contemplative and inquiring sages, strengthened and confirmed their apprehension of the portent of the star, and urged them on to the journey, which should accomplish, strikingly, many of the prophecies, and bring them to behold, and, as an earnest of the future homage he should receive, to adore, at his birth, the Deliverer of men.

In the readiness of their faith, in their zeal and perseverance, in their humility and reverent devotion to Christ, these forerunners of us Gentiles, it behooves me to remark, are both our example and reproof. Roused by the appearance of a star, they come from a distant land to find and adore the "King of kings," "the Prince of Peace." We have in the sure word of prophecy, a light shining in a dark place, to guide our minds to the same great Deliverer, and in the gospel and sacraments of God, we may find, and embrace, reverence and obey him. But how slow of heart are we to examine and follow the one; how backward to embrace and rejoice in the other. Fearless of the danger of proclaiming to a corrupt king the birth of a rival, and regardless of the taunts of men, they demand at Jerusalem where Christ is born; and when they have heard the reply, they instantly depart, undetained by the allurements of the city, or the gaieties of the court, from prosecuting their journey to render homage and oblations to the great Messiah. Easy is it for us to inquire of "the law and the testimony," all things concerning Christ. But how damped are our inquiries, how restrained our professions, by a regard to the opinions and sneers of men. And when "we have found him of whom Moses and the prophets write," when the Scriptures, or the ministers of the sanctuary, have pointed us to Jesus, how apt are we to loiter in the city, to be fascinated with the pleasures and vanities of the world, even when the Spirit of the Most High hath shined in our hearts, and is ready to go before us till he brings us to the place where we may behold the Redeemer, surrounded with the glories of heaven, and enjoy his presence for ever. When the wise men had worshipped the infant Jesus, they opened their treasures and presented unto him gifts; such gifts as were most significant for them to offer, and most honourable for him to receive. "*Myrrh*," says some one, "as to a man who was to be delivered to death and the grave for our salvation; *gold* as to a king whose kingdom shall have no end; *incense* as to a God who was made known to them that sought him not." With such gifts to approach him in his infancy, is not in our power. But we may offer him the oblations of our lips. We may own and adore him as our Redeemer, our King, and our God. We should "present" unto him "our bodies a living sacrifice, holy and acceptable unto" him, "which is our reasonable service."

And that we may be excited thus to do, let us now proceed to consider in the third place, the consequences of this manifestation of Christ to the Gentiles. We behold, at his birth, both Jews and Gentiles in the persons of the wise men and the shepherds, brought together unto Jesus. Both render homage, and the homage of both is received. Here, then, they are made one; and the middle wall of partition is broken down between them." We see here a demonstration of the comfortable truth, that "there is no difference between the Jew and the Greek; for the same Lord over all is rich unto all that call upon him."

From the time of Abraham it pleased God to select unto himself a peculiar people; to them to give his revelations, and covenants, and the knowledge of his mercies; and to suffer all other nations to walk in their own ways. And, alas, their ways became most wretchedly dark and desolate. Ignorance and stupidity, idolatry and vice, darkness and corruption, overwhelmed all people. Depravity carried them into the dismal state in which they had "no hope, and were without God in the world." To the Jew seemed confined the revelation of the Creator's will and the knowledge of the creature's salvation and destiny. But the conducting of the wise men unto the Messiah was the commencement of the disclosure of what St. Paul, justly calls, "the mystery, which from the beginning of the world had been hidden in God;" viz: that the Gentile should be fellow heirs, and of the same body, and partakers of his promise in Christ by the Gospel. And who are these, that have have flown unto the Church as "doves unto their windows;" these, that have come out of darkness into marvellous light; these, that have seen the salvation of God and compose the greater part of those inhabitants of the earth, who rejoice in the knowledge of his mercy and worship him in spirit and in truth? They are successors of the Magi; converts and subjects from the Gentile world. They are people, who were once "aliens from the commonwealth of Israel;" having no part in the adoption and the glory, in the oracles of truth, the service of God and the knowledge of eternal life. They are beings who were once strangers to the covenant of promise; unacquainted with the ransom for their sins; groping in darkness for the wall; dwelling in the regions and shadow of death. But now, through the blood of Christ, they who were afar off are brought nigh. The end of the mystery, of which this was the opening, will be conversion of all Gentiles, in God's good time, from the ignorance, idolatry and hopelessness, in which they have lived, to the knowledge of their duty, to the worship of the true God and the blessed hope of everlasting life. The coming of the wise men to worship the Redeemer was the pledge unto him, that heathenism should forsake her thousand polluted altars, and cast off her countless polluting delusions, and fly to the truth which he should diffuse, and to the altar and hopes which he should establish. In this event God embraced, as it were, all nations "in the arms of his mercy," and extended the limits of his Church to the ends of the earth. The language of the wonderful star was Peace; "peace to them that are afar off, and to them that are nigh." While it designated the place where the Redeemer lay, it was at the same time a symbol of his glorious character; "a light to lighten the Gentiles," and God's salvation to the ends of the world.

Nay, more; this calling of the Gentiles shall be, ultimately, instrumental in bringing the Jews to the faith of the Redeemer. God hath not cast away his people. They are yet beloved for the fathers' sakes. Though scattered, you behold them preserved; and the Apostle intimates that, by the calling of us Gentiles, they shall finally be provoked to "jealousy;" that, as we have "obtained mercy through their unbelief, even so they now have not believed," that, through the mercy we have found, "they also may obtain mercy." "Blindness in part" hath at present happened unto them, till the fulness of the Gentiles be come in." But they have not stumbled that they might fall; they have not been cut off from the goodly olive-tree, that they might perish. But, "if they abide not in unbelief, shall be graffed in" again; "for God is able to graff them in." In his time, he will, through the instrumentality of the Gentiles, gather the tribes of Jacob, "and restore the preserved of Israel." "And so all Israel shall be saved." "For he hath concluded them all in unbelief, that he might have mercy upon all." This is, indeed, a mystery, into the reasons and fitness of which we shall not be able fully to penetrate, till the consummation of all things shall declare to us the wisdom and equity of God. At present, we must wrap up our wonder in the language of St. Paul: "O, the depth of the riches both of the wisdom and knowledge of God! how unsearchable are his judgments, and his ways past finding out."

In improving this subject, let me first beseech you, my brethren, to consider and be thankful for your own condition. Remember that ye are of the nations who were Gentiles, and rejoice with grateful joy, that the "day-spring from on high hath visited you," to chase away "the shadow of death, and to guide your feet in the way of peace."

Let me, in the second place, exhort you, by a pure faith and holy lives, to secure your privileges. From some countries which were once enlightened by the Gospel, alas, the light is departed, and they are fallen from their felicity to the debasement of Muhammedan corruption or Pagan delusion. The cause of their calamity was the inconstancy of their faith and pollutedness of their lives. "Thou standest by faith. Be not high minded, but fear." Remember that God's favourite people "were broken off" from the olive-tree of his planting, because of their "unbelief." And if he "spared not the natural branches, take heed that he spare not thee."

Once more. Let me entreat you to look upon the multitude of heathens upon whom the light of the Gospel hath not shined. While their dark, degraded, dismal condition excites your gratitude for your Christian felicities, let it prompt you, if you have means or opportunities, faithfully to use them, for extending to the benighted heathen the instructions and hopes in which you are happy. Means and opportunities, have you none? Yes. You may give them your prayers. And what Christian will neglect to do this, when he considers that peace cannot be among men till it is shed upon them by the Redeemer; and that "Jerusalem must be trodden down of the Gentiles, until the times of the Gentiles be fulfilled."

Which brings me, in the last place, to observe, that upon God's ancient people, our elder brethren, we should bestow the look and the wishes of an holy and anxious regard. "If the fall of them have been the riches of the world, and the diminishing of them the riches of the Gentiles, how much more their fulness." They are kept yet to acknowledge the Messiah whom they have rejected. They are reserved to be the crown of our Lord's rejoicing, the consummating triumph of his word and power. He came to our earth to be not only "the light which should lighten the Gentiles," but also "the glory of God's people Israel." Let us, then, as our Church teaches us, offer our prayers for "all Jews," as well as "Turks, infidels, and heretics;" that God would "take from them all ignorance, hardness of heart, and contempt of his word; and so fetch them home to his flock, that they may be saved among the remnant of the true Israelites, and made one fold, under one Shepherd, Jesus Christ, our Lord."

SERMON XXX.

ON THE EPIPHANY.

ST. JOHN, viii. 12.

"I am the light of the world."

AMONG the most beautiful and important things which our eyes behold, is the effect of light upon the earth. When it dawns in the east, and the sun rises in its splendour, the whole face of nature assumes a new and joyful aspect. It dispels the darkness and the chilliness of night. Creation is awakened to new life by its beams. "Man goeth forth" cheerfully "to his work and to his labour till the evening." The beauty of every object is shown, and their uses and relations manifested. Earth and the skies are enlivened, and the glory of the Creator is sublimely proclaimed.

By a very striking metaphor, this principle of nature, upon which our knowledge, our joys, our life, so much depend, is used in the sacred volume to represent to us in figure the Saviour of the world. Its fitness for an emblem of the Messiah could not escape the notice of those whose minds were enlightened, and whose bosoms rejoiced with the knowledge of his character and offices. Prophecy had scarcely opened the organs of her blissful vision, when a star was seen coming out of Jacob, and the light of the Lord in which we should see light. And when upon her harp she sent forth, in its most rapturous tones, the proclamation of his coming, she sang him as a light to "the people who walked in darkness," and as a shining upon them who "dwelt in the land of the shadow of death." His harbinger's errand was to give knowledge of the tender mercy of God, whereby "the day-spring from on high hath visited us;" and when piety first discovered him in the early temple, she hailed him as "a light to lighten the Gentiles, and the glory of Israel." There is, indeed, no language by which his greatness and our interest in his coming can be more happily expressed. All the inspired writers, as it were with one mind, conceived of him under the sublime imagery of a luminary shedding light and life, knowledge and joy upon mankind; and he himself invites us to contemplate him under this figure, in those emphatic words of his own, "I am the light of the world."

The situation of mankind before his rising; his wonderful appearance in the fulness of time; the realized and expected effects of his coming, are topics which the words very naturally suggest to our consideration; and while an attention to them will show the peculiar propriety with which the glorious Being, whose visit to our sphere we are assembled to commemorate, is styled "the light of the world;" it may also lead us to such reflections as will be pertinent to the joy and solemnities of this day.

The Scriptures represent mankind as in a state of deplorable ignorance and wretchedness before the appearance of the Messiah. If we advert to their religion, morals, and expectations, we shall be convinced that the picture is not too deeply shaded, but that the world was indeed overcast with clouds, and filled with blindness and debasement.

Dreadful was their ignorance of the Supreme Being, and consequently of all rational worship and correct views of life, into which men sunk during the night of heathenism. Nothing can surpass the crudeness of their ideas of the Deity, and the absurdity of their sentiments towards him. We look among them in vain for any knowledge of the true God. Here, the material sun was mistaken for him, and honoured with a frantic worship and human sacrifices. There, some departed mortal was raised to divinity, and his anger deprecated or his kind influence sought by the most monstrous cruelties and pollutions. Here, some consecrated animal received the adorations of degraded man. There, he prostrated himself devoutly before some idol which his hands had made, or some grosser divinity which his very vices had enthroned. In no country was there a pure theology. Religion, even in the most polished age and nation, was at best a complication of absurdities. We find at Athens, where reason attained its greatest lustre, an altar "to the unknown God;" and the best of heathens and greatest of philosophers, who, amidst the errors of polytheism, had refined, in some degree, his sentiments of the divine nature, was there put to death by his countrymen, as guilty of impiety. How totally must the understandings of men have been darkened, when, upon the subject with which every thing is dear, ennobling, or joyful in the intelligent world is connected, they were so grossly ignorant. How dismally wretched must have been their state, when none could guide them to the pure and benevolent author of their existence; but "the glory of the incorruptible God was changed into an image made like to corruptible man, and to birds, and four-footed beasts and creeping things."

Proportioned to the correctness of the ideas which they have of the Supreme Being, and the purity of their reverence towards him, will always be the elevation of the morals of mankind. We may not, therefore, be surprised that before the promulgation of the Gospel, they were ignorant of holiness and enslaved to sin. Their sense of right and wrong, and all their affections were corrupted. Of a uniform, satisfactory, efficacious system of morals, by which they might regulate their conduct, and attain the true perfection and happiness of their nature, they were utterly destitute. What, though a few endeavoured to raise themselves to some degree of moral excellence! They differed from each other. By the brightest light which they could kindle, they were unable to guide their own steps; and it was a light which their fellow-mortals never felt obligated to regard, which they oftentimes contemned. They, therefore, can be considered only as coruscations of the night, unsteady and transient, rendering the general darkness more awfully apparent, and vanishing without any essential influence upon the morals of the people. The multitude grovelled in their vices. They were "dead in trespasses and sins." There was nothing to elevate, to purify, to direct their affections, to enlighten their consciences, or to give energy and efficacy to the expiring struggles of virtue. Guided in this moral darkness only by corrupt inclination, they sunk into a depravity, over the picture of which, should I exhibit it to your view, you would blush for humanity, and, with the great Apostle who drew it, cover it with your tears.

But with this dominion of sin, was connected the dominion of death. If men reflected at all upon their conduct, they could not but be conscious that they fell short of their duty. If they reflected soberly upon their condition, they could not but be sensible that they were the children of wrath. But in what way, as sinners, they could appease the unknown Deity, whom nature taught them to fear, whether he would in any way be reconciled to transgressors, how they should make atonement for their offences and propitiate his smiles, they were miserably ignorant. In the hour of superstitious dread, they might come before their imaginary gods "with thousands of rams" and "ten thousands of rivers of oil." Under the confused apprehension of a judgment to come, they might offer "their first-born for their transgressions, the fruit of their bodies for the sin of their souls." But what could this avail? Where was the voice to assure them of pardon? Where were the means of certain acceptance with God? They found themselves subject to the law of death. Of their inability to deliver themselves from this awful dominion they could not doubt. The wise and the ignorant, the virtuous and the vicious, were hitherto his mute and helpless prey. Whether the invisible power would raise them from the dust; whether their "corruptible" would ever "put on incorruption," and their "mortal" be clothed with "immortality," were questions enveloped in obscurity. With trembling solicitude they looked into the tomb; but all which they there beheld, was melancholy evidence of its monarch's undisturbed sway. If they attempted to look beyond it, feeble were their conceptions of immortality; absurd and groundless were their notions of heaven. The measure of their wretchedness was filled by the awful consciousness that, from this perplexed life they descended into "a land of darkness, as darkness itself, and where the light was as darkness."

Among the Jews, it must be confessed, the case was somewhat different. But how small a part of mankind was that nation. They, too, were perpetually prone to idolatry and iniquity. Their religion was but a system of shadows, which the multitude very imperfectly understood; and the law far from delivering them from the power of death, was itself "the strength of sin" and the ministration of condemnation. How destitute they were of that spiritual life which is the light of men, may easily be inferred from their rejection of the adorable Messiah, because he did not answer their carnal expectations. "The light shined in darkness, and the darkness comprehended it not."

In a word; from the original apostasy, man was enveloped in the gloom of ignorance, sin, and death. A forlorn traveller, he wandered, either in perplexity or stupidity, through a dreary state, without virtue or happiness, without God or hope. In the solemn language of Scripture, "darkness had covered the earth, and gross darkness the people."

Such was the unhappy situation of the world, before "the Sun of Righteousness arose, with healing in his wings." The time when he should appear was appointed by the Father; and every preparation was made to obtain him the attention and homage of mankind. From the fall, a vast system of types and symbols had been put in operation, that the faithful might be assisted in their conceptions of his authority and offices, and behold, with wonder, the hand of God conducting the accomplishment of the same gracious purpose in all the periods of time. Prophets, like the planets of night, while yet the Sun was unseen, glowed with his beams, and, in harmonious concert, proclaimed the certainty of his existence, and instructed the devout to be waiting for his appearance. The time when he should come had been precisely foretold. So well were the predictions understood, and so decidedly applied to a Messiah, that as the period of his coming drew near, all men were in expectation. At length, "the night was far spent; the day was at hand." Reason now stood at her zenith, in her proudest lustre, and all men saw her insufficiency to conduct them to their Creator or to holiness, or to the sure expectation of everlasting life. "The sceptre" was now about to "depart from Judah," and "the lawgiver from between his feet," which Jacob had anciently declared should not take place, "till Shiloh came." The second temple was shortly to be razed, never to be repaired, in which Haggai had proclaimed the glory of the Lord should appear. The "seventy weeks" were nearly numbered, which Daniel had ascertained should elapse, from "the commandment to restore and build Jerusalem, unto" the time of "Messiah the Prince." The Baptist was now on the horizon, in pre-eminent brightness, as Isaiah and Malachi foretold, announcing, like the morning star, the near approach of "the Light of the world." At this eventful period, when the world had slumbered its appointed time, and attention stood turned to the East, in expectation of a glorious appearance, "the Sun of Righteousness" rose upon the earth, "to give light to them that sit in darkness and in the shadow of death, to guide our feet into the way of peace."

It has been objected by cavillers, if such a light was prepared for the world, why were mankind so long left in darkness, and why are its beams so partially distributed? But does it become us, with our finite powers, to scrutinize the wisdom of the arrangements of God! What are we, short-sighted beings of a day, that we should presume to judge of an economy which may have a thousand reasons that we have not knowledge to discern; and a thousand relations that we have not capacity to comprehend? When thou art conscious, O skeptic!

that thou possessest all wisdom and virtue, and needest no instruction from thy Maker; when thou art ready to retire from the light of yonder material sun, and bury thyself in the dens and caves of the earth because it may not rise at the hour which thou wouldest choose, nor shine equally, and at once, upon all the nations of the globe, then turn thy back upon the Sun of the spiritual world, because thou art not satisfied with the partiality of his course, nor with the time of his coming. But, till then, be thankful for his light, and guide thy steps by his beams. It is surely enough for us to know, that he came at the time appointed by the Father. The devout mind will discover, in the equal duration of the patriarchal and of the Mosaic economy, before the Christian dispensation, an evident adoption of an order, whose significance and end it may not yet perceive, and will be fully persuaded, that the future economy will harmonize with the past, and the time of the Redeemer's appearance be finally manifested to have been appointed, like all the dispensations of the Almighty, with infinite wisdom and equity. Much more than to cavil at the councils of the Most High, does it become us to consider what are the realized and expected effects of the coming of the Messiah.

And, in the first place, men are no longer in the dark with regard to the Supreme Being, and his intentions towards them. His nature and perfections are revealed. The purposes of his government are disclosed. They are taught how they may worship him acceptably, and find peace in his service. He is manifested as their Everlasting Father and friend, anxiously reconciling a guilty world unto himself, through the gracious intervention of his beloved Son. Happy in a knowledge of his divine unity and unbounded mercy, they are no longer left to the absurdities of idolatry, nor to the awful dread of an unknown deity; but are enabled to elevate their souls to the true and only God, and with filial confidence to cry unto him, "Abba, Father." The appearance of his Son in the flesh, is the great proclamation of his care for mankind, and they are assured by it of his readiness to grant unto them, through this

Redeemer, remission of their sins, and the gift of the Holy Ghost.

But further; by the appearance of this "light of the world," the moral sight of mankind is purged, and the path of duty made plain before them. It is the office of light, to exhibit things in their proper character, to give to the beautiful their hues, to show the relations of the various, to enable man to choose what is good, and admire the excellency of the works of God. By the Sun of the spiritual world, the beauty of holiness is illustrated; the virtues are shown in their true characters and relations to each other; the soul is awakened from its state of delusion, and enabled to choose what to practice, what to cultivate, what to admire; and a general light is thrown upon all the situations and events of life. No longer need the children of men wander in the mazes of doubt, inquiring, anxiously, what is good, and what the Lord their God doth require of them? By the moral information which the Saviour hath diffused, and by the Spirit which he sends into the hearts of the obedient, they are enabled to walk with safety, satisfaction, and happiness, amidst the devious roads and perplexing difficulties with which they are surrounded. Their path is as the shining light; and by that increase of brightness which attends progressive holiness, it "shineth more and more unto the perfect day."

But, above all, by this "light of the world," the darkness has been dispersed which hung over the final destiny of men. Heaven has been opened to the view of the faithful. They have received anew, the adoption of sons, and to this adoption appertains the pardon of their transgressions, the immortality and pleasures of the Father's house. The awful dominion which death maintained over the human race, was founded upon sin. This foundation the Son of God was sent to destroy. "In the end of the world he hath appeared, and put away sin by the sacrifice of himself." This done, he hath commanded the king of terrors to resign his sceptre; he hath rolled back the clouds which rested upon the tomb; and, to the gazing eyes of the anxious children of mortality, hath exhibited beyond the confines of this transitory world, "a better country, even a heavenly." "Thou shalt call his name Jesus," said the angel to his virgin mother, "for he shall save his people from their sins." He "hath abolished death," saith the voice of inspiration, "and brought life and immortality to light."

In short, to redeem men from destruction and bring them back to God, to virtue and to immortality, was the end of the manifestation of the Son of God. Effulgent in all the Father's perfections, "being the brightness of his glory, and the express image of his person," he was peculiarly qualified to be set in the spiritual firmament as that "light" which should "lighten every man that cometh into the world." Before the brightness of his shining, all other lights have had their lustre quenched, and hidden their diminished heads. Whatever there is of pure religion and elevated morals in the world; whatever consoling hope we have of the pardon of our God, and his grace and favour; whatever prospect there is of a restoration to man, of peace, dignity and the divine likeness; whatever beams of comfort come to the chambers of anguish, and to the bosom of grief, from the well grounded assurance of immortality and a better world, all are the effects of that "light" which "the Son of Righteousness" hath diffused. It is by the power of his beams alone, that the face of our desolate nature can be, in any degree, renewed. And only when they have had full course and operation, shall "the wolf lie down with the lamb, and the leopard with the kid; and the calf, and the young lion, and the fatling together; and a little child shall lead them." As yet all nations feel not his blessed influence. The analogy of the divine operations would lead us to expect that his course would be progressive, and our knowledge of the corruption of the human heart, should prevent us from being surprised, if men "prefer darkness rather than light, because their deeds are evil." But moving on like the sun in the heavens, in the greatness of his strength, he is unaffected by the mists which rise from the earth to obscure his lustre, and laugh to scorn their impotence, who hail him, only to tell him how they hate his beams. Upheld and guided by the power of God, he shall not rest till all nations have seen his glory. Prophecy, whose exact veracity hitherto is a sure pledge of the future fulfilment of her predictions, assures us that "in returning and rest," the Jew shall "be saved," and that the fulness of the Gentiles shall come in;" that under the benign influence of this "light of the world," "the wilderness and the solitary place shall be glad, and the desert shall rejoice and blossom as the rose."

But I strive in vain to set before you, the effects of the coming of the Messiah in their full extent and vast importance. It requires a position which would command a view of the number and glory of the redeemed, and a ken which would embrace eternity. Far short of this knowledge we must all remain, till the period of the consummation of the work of this adorable Being, "Who of God is made unto us wisdom, and righteousness, and sanctification, and redemption."

It is the glorious nature, and blessed influence of this "light of the world," which renders the day of his rising a day of gladness and festivity. You are assembled, I trust, to commemorate the event, with none but the feelings of Christians. As such, the first effects of your contemplations will be, an overflow of praise to God, and joy for mankind. What stupendous love has our heavenly Father manifested in giving such a source of eternal light and life to his fallen creatures! What a change is wrought in their condition and expectations, by the prospects which "the day-spring from on high" hath opened! Great should be our thankfulness and joy. The peal with which heaven rang on the morn of the Nativity, should animate our hearts, and to the song of the angels, "Glory to God in the highest, and on earth peace, good will towards men," we should respond with our utmost devotion, Amen; hallelujah.

But, while we rejoice in the rising of the Sun of our Righteousness upon our benighted world, we should be individually grateful that we are of the number who now behold his beams. What tidings so glad have ever reached your ears, as the tidings of a Redeemer's birth! How valuable is the knowledge, that we are rescued from the doom of transgressors, and that "if we sin, we have" a prevailing "advocate with the Father," in his own beloved Son. How precious is a clear information of the way, and a certain promise of the means, by which we may please our God, and arrive at the true end and perfection of our nature! How ravishing is the assurance that the sceptre of death is broken, and that the hours which are bearing us from this world, are bringing us to immortality and heaven. Verily, blessed are our eyes that they see, and our ears that they hear. If you have soberly considered the unhappy condition of those of your fellow beings who know not the gospel; if you have properly estimated the joy which you have in Christ Jesus, and your privilege in being brought out "of darkness into his marvellous light," you will be ready on this day, with the enraptured Seer to exclaim, "How beautiful upon the mountains are the feet of him that bringeth good tidings, that publisheth peace; that bringeth good tidings of good, that publisheth salvation; that saith unto Zion, Thy God reigneth."

Finally. It should be our study, to reflect in our lives the lustre of that glorious Being by whom we are enlightened. In acts of humility, piety and benevolence, we should put on the Lord Jesus Christ. To all the appointed means of instruction and grace, we should give heed, "till the day dawn, and the day-star arise in our hearts." Being made the children of God and of the light, it should be our principal care to walk answerably to our Christian calling, and as becometh the children of light. To no purpose do we admire the adorable condescension of our Saviour, in taking upon him our nature, and being born of a Virgin, unless we are penetrated with his humility and obedience, and induced to copy it into our lives. In vain do we solace ourselves in the beams of that love, which brought him from the bosom of his Father, for our salvation, unless our bosoms are warmed with his benevolent spirit, and we are kind and compassionate to our fellow beings. Cold in our sense of his goodness, and imperfect our return, if we do not rejoice in every opportunity to eat of his bread, and drink of his cup, as he hath appointed, "in remembrance of him." In vain do we come to his light, and rejoice in the brightness of his rising, unless we "cast away the works of darkness," and, in all things, "walk honestly as in the day." Impressed with a sense of the distinguished excellence, with which the Church under her peculiar advantages should appear, the prophet calls to her, "Arise, shine, for thy light is come, and the glory of the Lord is risen upon thee." And, doubtless, the moral scene would be grand, harmonious and happy, as the order of the spheres, if every Christian shone in the brightness of the common Lord, and reflected his beams in every direction. Be it yours, my brethren, to imitate the Being you admire. The deluded Pagan who worships the material sun, offers not his homage without many ablutions. Look to it that your hands be clean, and your hearts pure, when you come to prostrate yourselves before that Sun, whom it is no idolatry to adore. So shall you render an acceptable service to the Redeemer, in celebrating his gracious appearance among men, and it shall fit you for the eternal commemoration of his love in that "city," which hath "no need of the sun, neither of the moon to shine in it; for the glory of God" doth give it perpetual day, "and the Lamb is the light thereof."

SERMON XXXI.

ON THE TEMPTATION.

MATTHEW, iv. 1.

"Then was Jesus led up of the Spirit into the wilderness, to be tempted of the devil."

THE Church, from her earliest days, has set apart the season in which the Saviour was tempted as a time of special thoughtfulness, humiliation, and prayer. In happier times than the present, in point of religious regularity, it wrought abundantly the peaceable fruits of repentance, and obtained a pious observance. A revival of the ancient zeal, without its superstition, or its intolerance, is devoutly to be wished, but is hardly to be hoped. If Christians at the present age are induced in the Lent season, to present themselves frequently before the Lord, and to turn their thoughts upon such subjects, as may promote contrition for the past and future rectitude, it is as much as can be expected. This easy observance of holy time is reasonable; and its tendency is, to produce good fruits.

Among the subjects which are meet for attention, at this season, that which it commemorates is a principal one. The temptation of the Saviour has been esteemed a very instructive, yet mysterious part of the gospel economy. Very many different opinions have been adopted concerning it. Some have objected to it; some have thought it attended with inexplicable difficulties. But all that it concerns us to consider, may, I apprehend, be reduced to these two general heads; the end of the Saviour's temptation and the circumstances of it. To these let me now invite your attention. They are serious and instructive points, and deserve to be well understood.

Why, first, was the Saviour exposed to the assaults of Satan; why did he endure the abasement in the wilderness?

We may justly view it as one end of this surprising occurrence in the Saviour's life, that he who was to be the sacrifice for sin, should be shown to be without sin. The law required for the Passover a lamb without blemish. This was typical of the spotless purity which should be found in "the Lamb of God," who should "take away the sins of the world." The High Priest who offered the Jewish atonenent, needed expiation for himself; the sacrifice was made for him, as well as the people; it was offered every year continually, and could never have effectually put away sin. That the Saviour might offer himself, once for all, and by the sacrifice expiate the guilt of man, it was necessary that he should owe nothing on his own account to the law, but be a pure and spotless Being. In the temptation he passed the trial. It was a furnace in which, if there had been one particle of dross in his nature, it would have been ascertained. But he came out of the fire which he submitted to endure, unsullied and all perfect, a lamb of infinite value, for its infinite purity. As such, he was worthy to be accepted of the Father; as such, our obligation to him is rendered the greatest possible; and that he, as such, was made the price of our redemption, should fill us with abhorrence of vice.

Again. It was desirable, that as the Adam who involved us in ruin, fell a victim to the artifice of the prince of darkness, the heavenly Adam, who was to restore us to life and blessedness, should triumph over the adversary and foil his arts. When man transgressed, he brought upon himself the tyranny of the tempter. The rebel angel exulted in his subjection. Temptation was the weapon of his success with the sons of men, and in his shrewd management of it, he placed his glory. To free us from the dominion as well as the punishment of sin, was a grand object of the gospel dispensation. The Saviour appeared, not only to save us from the death that awaited us, but to break the yoke which held us in bondage. Before his advent, the power of Satan was great over men; from possessions he had power over their bodies. Oracles and soothsayings attest his influence upon their minds. It was therefore necessary, that the Captain of our deliverance should break his power and destroy his haughty triumph over fallen man. To have redeemed us, and left his sceptre unbroken, would have been a less glorious work, than crushing the rebel power that had beguiled man from God, and held him in ignominious servitude. Evincing himself every way adequate to the salvation he had undertaken for us, he met the foe; he withstood the bold assault; he put the fiend to flight, and, "as in Adam all" fell, "so in Christ" all triumphed. Perhaps this was the period to which he in his life alluded: "I beheld Satan fall as lightning from heaven." If so, it was the foundation of that joy with which his disciples said to him, "Lord, even the devils are subject to us;" and of that promise, by which we were assured, that against his "Church the gates of hell shall never prevail."

Another reason for the temptation which Christ submitted to endure was, that it behoved him to be made in all things like unto his brethren, and to leave them a full and perfect example. It is one considerable part of the calamity to which the fall reduced us, that we must meet such trials; that we must withstand such conflicts; that, with our prospect, the vigilance required is greater. Adam had but one alluring object to withstand. His offspring have thousands. No man, I believe, is insensible how much his nature suffers from its liability to many and strong temptations. It is, undoubtedly, a just consequence of the first deviation from rectitude, founded upon that principle of the divine government, upon which the strength of the faithful is increased, and the difficulties of the negligent multiplied. "To him that hath shall be given; but from him that hath not shall be taken away even that which he hath." The adorable Redeemer chose to share all our griefs and taste all our sorrows. The conflicts of virtue with the foe are not among the least, and how these conflicts might best be managed, man needed to be taught. Infinite abasement! The Son of God consented, in order to "bring in for us an everlasting righteousness," to be, like us, assaulted by temptation. In his resistance, we see that man is not necessarily subdued by the greatest trials. He may resist till the tempter shall flee. The Saviour's example and triumph are, in this point of view, of inestimable value. The vicious they deprive of the blasphemous plea, we are delivered to do all these things; and the good man they furnish with an encouragement, without which he might halt and sigh on his difficult way, and perhaps despair. Life is, indeed, a wilderness. Innumerable temptations assault our frailty. They take us often in our feeblest hours. But with "the Captain of our salvation" before us, we are inexcusable if we yield without resistance. With his success recorded for our instruction, we cannot honourably compromise with evil, or be less persevering than the foe.

Once more. It was a principal object of the Saviour's temptation, that we might thus be made happy in the knowledge of a High Priest and Judge capable of feeling what our difficulties are, and making that tender allowance for our frailty which the best men need. "In that he himself hath suffered, being tempted he is able to succour them that are tempted." Destined to be our Judge hereafter, as well as our Saviour already, nothing can more comfort us under the apprehension of his coming, than that he was in our nature, has a sympathy for all its sufferings, and knows the arduousness of the conflict which his disciples endure. Our Intercessor in heaven, as heretofore our visible High Priest, nothing can more inspire us with affectionate confidence in his offices than the assurance that "he can be touched with the feeling of our infirmities," and know, from experience, what are the graces which he needs ask for us of the Father. To give us hope in the expectation of such a Judge, and joy in the intercession of such a Mediator, the Redeemer partook of all the trials of humanity, even of the strong and complex temptations with which our adversary, the devil, seeketh to destroy. By this we are made sensible that the laws he has enjoined us are not severe, formed without regard to our weakness and exposures. It teaches us to trust, that acquainted with the struggles which those must have who resist evil, he will adjust his gifts to their necessities. And it fills us with the composing thought, that he who shall come in majesty to allot our final doom, will be one sensible of our frailty and difficulties, and capable of judging us with infinite mercy and truth. "We have not an High Priest who cannot be touched with the feelings of our infirmities; but was in all points tempted as we are, yet without sin. Let us, therefore, come boldly unto the throne of grace, that we may obtain mercy, and find grace to help in time of need."

The other point proposed, as completing all that it concerns us to consider upon this subject, now solicits our attention, namely, the circumstances of the event whose end we have ascertained.

These are many, and of an instructive nature. We shall take them without reference to the order of time, and, in our explication of them, be guided by the best authorities.

In the first place, we observe, the character of the being who assailed the Son of God. It was the devil, emphatically styled *the* Tempter. By this being, mentioned in Scriptures under different names, we are ever to understand the head of apostates from God; the contriver and finisher of all mischief. That angels and invisible beings are permitted to have interference with the affairs of the world, is a doctrine to be found in the ancient traces of tradition, and explicitly taught us in the word of God. These spirits are good and bad. While the hosts of God encamp around us for our protection, the arch-fiend who left his holy state, goeth "about, seeking whom he may devour." No more is revealed to us of the history of these invisible beings than is sufficient to inform us that there are fallen ones among them, and that we are obnoxious to their malignity. Debased themselves, seeking by the conduct of other beings to apologize for their own vileness, envying the happiness of the upright, they seek to sully the pure, and have bent their arts for the destruction of man. The prince of these powers of darkness, too successfully, alas, assailed the innocence of Eden; and wishing to blast the mean of restoration, he attacked the great Redeemer in the wilderness.

Here, it is questioned, whether the tempter knew that the person whom he assaulted was the Son of God. Considering the temptation as a part of the plan of redemption and instruction adopted by God, it to me appears a matter of no consequence whether he did or did not. But, says the objector, if he did, how foolish the story; the subtle fiend would never have attempted where he could not have expected anything but defeat and disgrace. There is more of sound than sense in this remark. Bad men, whose understandings are perverted, and whose malice is intense, often essay the most foolish projects; and it will be difficult to conceive any thing too bold or extravagant for the devil to undertake. On many accounts, however, it is probable that the tempter only suspected, but was not indubitably certain of the high character of Christ. Both his suspicions and his doubts seem to be expressed by his repeated address, "If thou be the Son of God." That the invisible spirits did not wholly comprehend the mysteries of the redemption which God designed to effect for man, is evident from many passages of Scripture. "Which things the angels desire to look into." "That now unto the principalities and powers in heavenly places, might be known by the Church the manifold wisdom of God." But, that man was to be redeemed, and that it was for this purpose Messiah was born into the world, they clearly understood. Witness their carols on the night of his birth, and the joy which the Saviour assures us they feel in heaven when one sinner repenteth. Of this knowledge, it is probable, the tempter partook. He had observed the prophecies, for, a genuine deceiver, he could quote Scripture to conceal his baseness. He had seen the movement of Christ's birth, and heard the acknowledgment of him by angels, sages, and men. He therefore could not but have had some conception of the office and business of Christ, if he was ignorant of his character. Finding him hungry in a wilderness, his suspicion of his high dignity as the Son of God wavered. He madly thought to prove him. The moment was favourable. If he could draw him into sin, he should triumph over the Being who was intended to "bruise his head," and confirm the mischievous work he had accomplished in the garden. Thus thinking, he entered the wilderness, and doubtless, in some friendly form and beguiling air, accosted the lonely Saviour.

This appears to be the truth of the case. The father of mischief, the chief of apostates, he who was thrust from heaven, and had ruined man, in deceitful form assaulted Christ. Of his divinity, he had suspicions. Of his designation to recover man, he had no doubt. He thought by one mad effort to try him, if, haply, he might again defeat the conditional counsel of heaven, as it respected the happiness of the human race.

And what may we infer from this circumstance, of the event. First, a confirmation of the humanity of Christ. The Godhead, his divine nature, was unapproachable by temptations; especially by such as were borrowed from earthly scenes, and addressed to worldly desires. The ancient heretics, who denied the humanity of Christ, were quite as inconsiderate, though not so impious as the modern ones, who deny his divinity. They must have forgotten the hungering of the Saviour, and neglected to advert to the truth, that the Godhead cannot be tempted. In this incident we have a proof that he was made like unto us, that he partook of the nature of her who bare him.

From this circumstance of the Saviour's temptation, we may also learn, that to such trials and assaults the best men are liable. The Author of our hopes was made perfect through suffering. The adversary was not distanced by his excellence. He endured the conflict with inducements to evil. He waged the warfare with sin. Let none of his disciples, then, expect to be exempt. Can they be so faithful as to merit no chastisement? Can they be so good as to need no trial? Can they be so perfect as to be above the reach of the prince of darkness? Let them, rather, expect to have severe trials allotted them, and, while they stand, "take heed lest they fall."

Lastly; from this circumstance we learn the great malevolence of the Tempter. This was sufficiently seen at the fall of man. Terrible must be that malice, which could set its eye upon innocence and happiness like that for which our race was formed, and seek to destroy it. But when we behold the chief of the "principalities and powers" with whom, St. Paul says, we "wrestle," assaulting the very son of God, and endeavouring to overthrow the deep and gracious counsel of redemption, nothing can give us a stronger sentiment of the turpitude and malignity of him and his fallen race. Heinous must have been the apostacy which could render an order of angels so depraved. It should keep us ever awake against his insidious wiles; and alarm us at the depth of depravity, to which a nature become sinful, and given to itself, may sink. "Be sober. Be vigilant, because your adversary, the devil, as a roaring lion, walketh about seeking whom he may devour."

SERMON XXXII.

ON THE TEMPTATION.

MATTHEW, iv. 2.

"And when he had fasted forty days and forty nights, he was afterward an hungered."

HAVING, in a preceding discourse, ascertained the ends of the Saviour's temptation, and considered the nature and views of the Tempter who assaulted him; I now would turn your attention to another illustrious circumstance;. one that, by churchmen, should be well understood. It is the fast which Christ observed in the wilderness, previous to the open attack of the adversary. All three of the Evangelists who have recorded this incident of the Saviour's life, inform us that he continued fasting for "forty days" before the commencement of the temptations which they relate. St. Matthew's words, as being the most explicit, I have placed at the head of this discourse. "And when he had fasted forty days and forty nights, he was afterward an hungered."

It will first be asked by our minds, why the Son of God fasted at all? He had no sins to expiate by this penance; nor had he any unruly desires to restrain by this self-denial. Why, then, did he withdraw from the gay scenes of life, and subject himself to this fast? Let us adjust our ideas of this attendant circumstance of his temptation, and then we may discover reasons to satisfy the mind.

By his fasting, we are not to understand the mere abstinence from food, or denial of gratification to craving appetites. He was not "an hungered," till the forty days were ended. He felt no wish, nor want, for sustenance during that time. His fasting, therefore, did not consist in a restraint put upon the cravings of nature. It is rather to be considered as signifying a withdrawing into retirement, that he might give himself to serious meditation, earnest prayer, and the most ardent devotion. To assist him in these, he became wholly free from the indulgences of life, sought the wilderness, and was absorbed in pious reflections and acts. This seems to be the true idea of his fasting. Indeed, the word is often used in the sacred volume to express humiliation and prayer, in conjunction with abstinence; and the latter, considered but as a help to the former. In this sense, there are purposes in virtuous life, for which it is necessary. The Saviour used it the night before his selection of his disciples. He declared, that one kind of miracle was not to be effected without fasting and prayer. We find innumerable instances of the use of it by the servants of God, to his acceptance, and their benefit. Mere abstinence itself can have no merit. Unless it be necessary to assist our devotions and virtue, it is idle to afflict our souls. But in conjunction with humiliation and prayer, as their assistant, it is of high commendation in the word of God. If, with this idea of fasting, we follow the Saviour into the wilderness, we shall see satisfactory reasons for his miraculous fast.

The reasons appear to be reducible to two: that he might prepare himself for the mighty work in which he was about to engage; and, to qualify himself to withstand the temptations by which he was to be assaulted.

One object of the Saviour's fasting was, to prepare himself for the mighty work in which he was about to engage. He had just received baptism of John, and the Holy Ghost had proclaimed him the Messenger of the Most High. He now was to enter upon his ministry. A work of such solemnity and magnitude was not to be undertaken lightly nor rashly. It was a work in which infinite interests were involved; in which he had much to do and much to suffer. Impressed with its magnitude, he withdrew. In solitude he sought the Father. He gave himself to fasting, meditation, and prayer, that he might come forth with strength, and be prepared for the mighty business in which he was to engage. Thus had the prophets and saints done before him. Thus did he before he chose and delegated his disciples. The Father had declared, that a fast which did not consist merely in afflicting the soul, was by him approved. The Saviour, therefore, exemplified in his fast the dictates of religion and reason, and, in this example, instructed mankind to forbear to enter upon sacred or important functions, without serious reflection and communion with God.

But, it may be considered as another reason of the Saviour's fasting, that he would be in the best condition to meet the temptations by which he was to be assaulted. We read, that it was for the purpose of being tempted, that the Spirit impelled him to go into the wilderness. It was impossible that, as Immanuel, he could be overcome by the Tempter. But, in his moral life, he conducted wholly as man, that he might be our perfect pattern. That circumspection, self-examination, serious reflection, and humble prayer, which constitute the substance of the fast which the Lord hath chosen, are the best preservatives from vice and folly. "Watch and pray, lest ye enter into temptation." To teach his followers, who he knew would be exposed to vice, how best to strengthen themselves against her assaults, he, as a man, prepared himself for the temptations which awaited him by this timely fast. By collecting himself in retirement, and seeking strength of the Most High, he was well qualified to meet and vanquish the foe, and, in this point left "us an example that we should follow his steps."

But, notwithstanding these reasons do away the difficulty, with which we conceived why the Son of God fasted at all; notwithstanding they show us the perfection of our exemplar, and an admirable wisdom in the selection of the time, there arises another question relative to this conduct of our Lord.

Where was the necessity of his fasting "forty days?" The purposes which have been mentioned, might have been accomplished in a shorter period. Indeed, in this prolonged fast he cannot be our example. Nature is not equal to it. In him it was miraculous. Why, then, the unremitted solitariness and fast of Christ for "forty days?"

This question will unfold to us one of the chief beauties of the divine dispensations. "Known unto God are all his works from the beginning." They are all connected. Harmony pervades the whole. In the economy of nature it is delightful to trace the analogies between different parts, to see one operation leading on another; to observe in the less, true emblems of the greater, and to mark, how all parts together form one august whole. In the economy of grace, most analogous to that of nature, it is not less delightful to study the connection of remote parts; the gradations by which the uniform, sublime whole, is unfolded. Types, ordinances, prophecies, form links by which most distant events are connected, and, doubtless, when our souls shall contemplate the reasons and completion of the whole scheme, they will behold a more affecting display of the divine character, than even the august system of nature exhibits.

This seemingly strange circumstance of the Saviour's fasting for no less nor greater time than "forty days and forty nights," acquires wonderful propriety and use, when viewed in conjunction with previous events, in the divine dispensations. When Moses, the promulgator of the Law, was preparing in Mount Sinai the two tables of commands which he was to give to the people, it is related of him, that "he was there with the Lord forty days and forty nights, and did neither eat bread, nor drink water." He fasted that his people might be forgiven, and received into divine favour; he was engaged in close converse with the Lord, who alone was with him in the Mount, and, having been miraculously sustained in life without means, he would descend to the people with a convincing attestation of his authority.

When Elijah, the restorer of the law and recoverer of the

people from idolatry and ruin, was qualified by Deity for his arduous work, we are told, that he went through the wilderness "in the strength of" one refreshment "forty days and forty nights." Thus assured of the divine power, with, or without means, to strengthen and support him, he pursued his rout "unto Horeb, the Mount of God;" and, having received the instructions of Jehovah, entered upon the delegation of officers and the reformation of the people.

These two most eminent of the instruments of the Almighty, in conducting his divine dispensations, were illustrious types of Christ. And as they each were in the wilderness "forty days and forty nights," without eating or drinking, preparatory to their work, it behooved him, whose authority was greatly to be attested, by his uniting in his life a wonderful fulfilment of innumerable prophetic types, to observe a similar fast. Why the term "forty days and forty nights" was preferred at first, we are unable to determine. The Jewish rabbins have some vague conjectures about it. But it is best to refer it to the choice and inscrutable wisdom of God. If we consider that the waters of the deluge were "forty days and forty nights" coming upon the earth; that forty years the Israelites did penance in the wilderness; that forty stripes were the appointed punishment for malefactors; that forty days were allowed the Ninevites to repent; that forty years from the ascension of the Saviour impenitent Jerusalem received her punishment; that Moses, Elijah, and Jesus Christ fasted, each "forty days and forty nights," we must admire the uniformity of the divine economy, and believe that this period was not without reason so singularly distinguished. It chiefly concerns us, however, to dwell on the fulfilment of the ancient types in Christ. This will satisfy us, why he fasted for this particular space of time. As Moses and Elias, by being thus sustained miraculously, were assured of the divine sufficiency for their aid, so Christ, in like manner, was animated to meet his temptations, and to fulfil his ministry by the assurance of the power of the divine, to sustain his human nature without the use of food or rest. As their miraculous sustenance attested their mission, his qualified him to enter on his work with high authority. By his fulfilment of remote types which, under the law, foretold in figure his advent and offices, we have a resistless proof, that it is he "of whom Moses and the Prophets did write;" in whom all the arrangements, symbols, and mysteries of the divine economy, meet their explanation and significance. When we thus see the connection between the parts of revelation, from the first communication from Jehovah, to the promulgation of the gospel; when we behold little matters rising into consequence as emblems of greater ones, when we observe all tending to form one complex, yet uniform, one stupendous, yet clear system, we cannot but infer, as we do from the harmony, design, and order of the works of nature, that one is the author and one the end of the whole; the Author, God; the end, his glory; in the happiness of his creatures.

SERMON XXXIII.

ON THE TEMPTATION.

MATTHEW, iv. 2.

"And when he had fasted forty days and forty nights, he was afterward an hungered."

UPON the subject of the Saviour's temptation, which has already occupied much of our attention, we come now to consider the particular enticements which the Tempter used, and our exemplar withstood. From the contemplation of them many useful hints will arise, for they were such temptations as are common to man, most insidiously adduced, and powerfully urged.

When the Messiah had ended his fast, so timely, proper, and significant, the fast of "forty days," the sacred records inform us "he afterwards was an hungered." Here some may stop to wonder that the Son of God should be capable of being hungry; especially after enduring, without wish or need for food, a fast of so long duration. But if he had suffered hunger before the forty days and nights, his fast, as to its typical and miraculous nature, would not have been complete; he would not have derived from it so full assurances, and its uses, to us, would have been curtailed. And if he had continued free from hunger, after nature was restored to her usual course, and the divine power withdrawn, which sustained her without the usual or any means, we could hardly have believed him man. He had taken upon him our nature, with all its natural infirmities, liabilities to pain and mortality. Without continual nourishment, this nature fails, and craves, and feels, indescribable torture. He then, after passing forty days and nights without taking any food, must, if he were human, when the miracle which had supported him ceased, have felt all the worriment of appetite haunting for nourishment with unmanageable cries. Besides, to wish and want for lack of food, to suffer pain, is one of the dire consequences of the first trangression. Before the fall, if man felt the smallest inclination to solace his palate, he anywhere stretched forth his hand and gathered salubrious food. Nature, the moment she indicated a wish for sustenance, was gratified. Hunger, that most wearisome of bodily sensations, that feeling which every man dreads, and no one who has not felt its tortures, and witnessed the horrid expedients to which it has sometimes driven men, can well express. Hunger was not known in Eden. It is an ingredient in the bitter cup, which fallen Adam devolved upon mankind, to be their portion while they continue in his nature. To drink the dregs of this cup, to carry all our griefs, was a determination of the Saviour's love. That he might be in all things like his brethren, and by enduring all the painful consequences of sin, open to man that heaven whose inhabitants "shall hunger no more, neither thirst any more," nor be liable to any more death, the Son of God, though "all the beasts of the forest" were his, and "the cattle upon a thousand hills," submitted himself to endure the pains of hunger. In a lone desert, without one visible creature to commiserate and assist him, nor any apparent possibility of immediate relief, his sensations of hunger must have been excessively keen. This species of humiliation and distress he experienced in as great a degree, as any of the race whom he came to relieve, even the most destitute wretch, in the humblest vale of poverty. But as he was led into the wilderness to be tempted, his experience of this kind of human misery, at the particular time, answered a useful end. It gave an opportunity to the tempter, of making the trial of his obedience under the greatest advantage. And, accordingly, it was while Christ was suffering the pangs of hunger, in a most dismal, barren place, that he determined to accomplish his purposes.

"And when the tempter came to him, he said, If thou be the Son of God, command that these stones be made bread." Never was a temptation more advantageously timed, or cunningly urged, than this. Christ was experiencing uneasy sensations for want of food to satisfy the cravings of nature. He had no immediate prospect of relief. The wilderness was barren and uninhabited, save by ferocious beasts. Insidiously the tempter argues, Surely, if thou art the Son of God, it is strange thou shouldest be left thus destitute. Thou must have power to convert these stones into bread, and, certainly, thy necessities will justify the act. Either thou art unable, and a poor outcast from God, or thou canst relieve thyself as I advise, without incurring his blame who placed thee in this situation. How many enticements to wrong can be gilded with plausibility by a depraved mind! But the Saviour discovers in this seemingly just and friendly expostulation, a temptation to gross sin. It would lead him, without his Father's will, to endeavour, unnecessarily, to prove his Sonship, and to relieve his necessities by unauthorized means. The former was to distrust the truth, and the latter the good providence of God. To render Christ guilty of this distrust, to shake his faith in God, and in his own character, was the object of the tempter's first proposal. Had he succeeded in this, the foundation of duty, of worth, of strength, of everything excellent in Christ would have been destroyed, and by this one blow the enemy would have defeated the counsels of heaven, and destroyed the last, best hopes of man. Recurring to the real source of wisdom and truth for his defence, the Saviour, with infinite dignity, replied, "It is written," the word of God, the only proper rule of conduct, declares, "Man shall not live by bread alone, but by every word that proceedeth out of the mouth of God." By recurring to the Scriptures, he instructed us that they are the only proper rule of belief and life, and by recurring to the Old Testament, he taught us that whatever was morally right in the Jewish dispensation, as distinct from their ceremonial and political institutes, is binding upon Christians, and of perpetual obligation.

It is remarkable, that the passage to which the Saviour alluded, is a declaration to the Israelites, respecting the gracious appearance of the Most High for them, when they were an hungered in the wilderness, in which they sojourned forty years. Moses, recounting to them the events they had witnessed, reminds them that the Almighty "humbled them, and suffered them to hunger that he might prove them, and know what was in their hearts, whether they would keep his commandments or no." And that when they were hungry, and unable in the wilderness to obtain food, his providence came to their relief, in a miraculous supply of such bread as neither they nor their fathers had known, "that he might make them know that man doth not live by bread only, but by every word that proceedeth out of the mouth of the Lord, doth man live." They were first left to hunger and then satisfied, not with usual means, but by a supernatural supply, that they might be impressed with this grand, eternal truth, that the providence of God should be man's trust in every exigence, by whose blessing alone food has power to sustain us, and who can by any other means, or with his word alone, as effectually uphold us in being.

From this passage the Saviour chose the reply with which he foiled the first attack of the adversary. It met and answered all he had advanced. Infinite and incessant are the truth, and goodness, and power of the word of Jehovah. It is this word which gives to everything its being and its efficacy. This had declared him his Son; this had placed him in a situation of hunger; this could relieve him when it was fit, and without this no substance whatever could nourish or affect him. To have attempted a miracle, then, without his Father's will, to prove his character or to relieve his wants, would have been indicative of disbelief and distrust in the word of God. To have done it solely at the instigation of Satan, without prospect of any benefit. was incompatible with his divine nature, and would have been an aggravation of the fault. He might justly have answered, Confirmation of my character as the Son of God I need not for myself. None else are here to witness it but yourself, and on you it would be lost. But he deigned not to consider the suspicious suggestion with which the tempter introduced and urged his expostulation. The thing he advised was in itself wrong and ineligible, and nothing could make it right or necessary. He, therefore, spoke immediately to the advice, and instructing while he repelled his foe, answered to this effect: I am, indeed, distressed with hunger; it is an allotment to human nature; the Almighty can convert it to some good end; could I, without his will or blessing, obtain bread, it would be useless or injurious; he can supply my wants, and in his own good time will come to my relief; "It is written, man shall not live by bread alone, but by every word that proceedeth out of the mouth of God." The answer was as complete as the temptation was insidious, and the tempter, confounded, urged his first expostulation no more.

Having now seen the point at which the tempter aimed his first assault upon Messiah, namely, his faith in the truth and good providence of God, we will pause and observe the instructive lesson it conveys. It has already been observed, that the temptations which Christ encountered, were such as are common to men. With us, as with our Lord, the tempter's first effort and wish is, to excite our distrust in the promises and providence of the Most High, and thus destroy the foundation of all goodness and peace.

There are two ways in which men are most liable to fall into this most dangerous temptation. The first is, when they are led to believe that they are outcasts from the Almighty, utterly excluded from his care, and reprobated from the beginning to misery. There are some, whose adverse fates, whose gloomy imaginations, whose terrible apprehensions of the requirements of the Most High, or whose unfortunate choice of books and company, have rendered them victims of this despondence. When those who strive to believe, and live according to the requirements of the Gospel, thus droop under the thought that they have not, and can have no interest in the care and mercies of God, we can in no way account for it, but that they are urged into this distrust by the adversary, who endeavoured in this way to destroy the integrity of Job, and with a similar temptation tried the Redeemer of the world. Such should consider that the proffers of happiness depend not on their feelings, but upon the infinite and unchangeable love of the Most High. They should reflect that the offers of peace and joy are general, made to all, not excepting any but those who choose to except themselves. Let them seek and cultivate a sincere faith in Christ, and endeavour in every duty to walk uprightly; and then, if distressed with the thought of being irrevocably and unconditionally cast off by the Creator, and reprobated to eternal misery, let them consider it as suggested with evil design by the enemy of man's happiness and his Maker's glory, and recurring like their Saviour for an instrument of defence to the storehouse of all truth, repel the insidious suggestion with, "It is written;" "Him that cometh unto me, I will in nowise cast out." Can the sad victim of despair in this way gain no gleam of comfort? Does it seem strange, if he may hope, why the thought which depresses him has such hold of his mind? Let him look up, and behold even the Immanuel urged by the grand seducer, to infer from his dismal condition when hungry in the wilderness, that his Father had abandoned him, that he could not be the Son of God. If, notwithstanding this, he can see nothing but displeasure and wretchedness for himself, let him resolve, as the safest experiment he can make, and the most prudent conduct he can pursue, to comply with this advice of a venerable divine of our Church, to the unhappy children of despair: "In thy strongest encounter, wait still on Christ till he comes, and commit thyself in well doing into his hands, as into the hands of a faithful Creator; say with Esther, I will go to the king; if I perish, I perish; it may be he will reach out his sceptre graciously, and I shall live; but if I must needs perish, I will perish under the wing of my Lord and husband." This advice is inimitably tender and judicious. Would heaven it were followed by every human being! All men would then be indeed saved; for none who shall be found under the wing of the Redeemer can possibly be lost. They only shall perish who, when with the most affectionate entreaties he would have "gathered them, as a hen gathereth her chickens under her wings, would not;" but gave themselves to follow their own devices, and to walk after the counsels of their own minds.

Another, and more common way, in which men are led to distrust the good providence of God, is when they are filled with dissatisfaction with their condition, and are prompted to the use of any unlawful means. If they are urged into any wrong, thinking that their necessities will justify it; if they aim at the attainment of any good by sinful means; if they neglect with patience to pursue the paths which Deity has marked, and resolve to accomplish their wishes by their own devices; or if, in their necessity, they look anywhere for help but to the Almighty, then are they guilty of that to which the enemy tempted Christ. Dreadful is your situation; loud are the calls of nature; you must and ought to live and do well by yourself; your situation will justify it, are arguments which have led to many a nefarious act. Those who are influenced by them might with equal rectitude in time of hunger be led to despise the care of Providence, and induced to command stones to be made bread. It is Machiavelian morality; it is among the basest of atheistical principles, that "the end will justify the means." Nothing which is in itself wrong, can, by adventitious circumstances, be made right. Our duty is to consider all means as efficacious only through God's blessing, and to seek them conformably with his will. In whatever situation we are placed, we should not have our assurance of his constant agency shaken, nor, in a fit of despair, murmur at his allotments, and think by our own expedients to forego his time. Are we pressed by most urgent reasons, the support of, the safety of, reputation; the care of a family; the cause of benevolence? If we cannot accomplish these or any objects without deviating from rectitude, it is better with virtuous resolution to risk the issue with the providence of God. He appointed no means to be improperly used; it is not by bread alone, but by his word we live; he can, therefore, come to our relief, in ways unexpected and gracious. With Christ, then, we should not prefer our own efforts to the power of his providence. Safe is our reliance on him to the last emergence; for if he smite the flinty rock, water shall flow to refresh the thirsty, and he can rain manna from heaven for his faithful people, when hunger seizes them in the wilderness.

SERMON XXXIV.

ON THE TEMPTATION.

MATTHEW, iv. 5–11.

"Then the devil taketh him up into the holy city, and setteth him on a pinnacle of the temple, and saith unto him, If thou be the Son of God, cast thyself down; for it is written, He shall give his angels charge concerning thee; and in their hands they shall bear thee up, lest at any time thou dash thy foot against a stone. Jesus said unto him, It is written again, Thou shalt not tempt the Lord thy God. Again the devil taketh him up into an exceeding high mountain, and showeth him all the kingdoms of the world, and the glory of them; and saith unto him, All these things will I give thee, if thou wilt fall down and worship me. Then saith Jesus unto him, Get thee hence, Satan; for it is written, Thou shalt worship the Lord thy God, and him only shalt thou serve."

ALREADY we have considered the end of the Saviour's temptation, and among the circumstances of it, the character of the tempter, the fast which Christ endured in the wilderness, and the nature and issue of the enemy's first assault. Rebuffed, as we left him, in his attempt to draw the Messiah into a distrust of the truth and good providence of God, he framed another scheme of an opposite nature. Though vanquished, he did not desist from his purpose, but pursued it another way; and, on the Saviour's firm confidence in his Father, grounded his second attack. It is thus that the best principles and motives, by being wrongly directed, are converted into causes of error and transgression.

The nature, and issue of the second temptation, and the instructions it contains for us, now solicit our attention. The aim of it was to excite him who would not distrust, to presume upon the word and power of God; and because he placed no reliance in the efficacy of means without the divine blessing, to scorn the appointed use of them, and cast himself against nature and reason, without any effort or precaution of his own, upon the misconstrued promises of the Most High.

To give opportunity and plausibility to this temptation, the sacred historian relates: "Then the devil taketh him up into the holy city, and setteth him on a pinnacle of the temple." Upon the mode in which Christ was brought to this situation, there have been many inquiries, and many opinions. Some expositors, of high character, have supposed that the whole temptation was transacted in vision, and that the tempter only raised in the mind of Christ an illusive scene of Jerusalem and the temple. But the narratives of all the Evangelists evidently give to the transaction the face of reality; and the supposition of an ideal management is, at least, arbitrary, if not unnecessary. Other writers have understood that the evil spirit, by the permission of the Most High, had power over the body of Christ, and conveyed him from the wilderness to the temple, miraculously through the air. This opinion is the most general, and commentators who advance it, are of the most respectable authority. But there is another solution proposed by an eminent divine, and adopted by many, which, though it has not the greatest number of advocates, is to me, I confess, the most satisfactory. It is this; that the tempter, being in some friendly form, is said to take Christ up into the holy city, as a man is said to take his neighbour to any place, when he pursuades him to accompany him thither; and to set Christ upon a pinnacle of the temple, as in common language we are said to seat a person, when we conduct him to his seat; or to place him when we lead him to his position. The word rendered in the translation "taketh," is used, by the best profane writers, to express the act of a person when leading a companion from one place to another. It often, too, has this signification in the sacred volume; and this use of it, is indisputable in one passage, which is very analogous to the text. When the three favoured disciples were conducted by their Lord up a mountain, that they might witness his transfiguration, it is written, then "Jesus taketh Peter, James, and John his brother, and bringeth them up into a high mountain." It will not be here supposed, that they were supernaturally carried by Christ, but that, going himself, at his instigation, they accompanied him to the spot, which he had selected for the august display of his character. In like manner, without the difficulties of conceiving the scene of this temptation to be only imaginary, and without the uncouthness of the idea of the Son of God transported in the hands of the devil, through a long tract of air, we may naturally, and in strict conformity with the usual and almost invariable sense of the phrase in the original text, suppose the tempter to have attended Christ from the desert, to the holy city, invited him into the temple, and conducted him up to its battlements. This seems to be an adequate and natural way of explaining how the Saviour was taken by his adversary to the holy city, and placed in the situation upon the temple, in which the text represents him. It is objected, how, then, was he tempted in the wilderness? He was there forty days tempted; none of the Evangelists say that the wilderness was the only scene of the three particular assaults, which they have recorded. Nor is this objection avoided, by supposing him conveyed in any other way, to the pinnacle of the temple. It is also objected to this solution, that St. Luke, after relating the temptations, says, "Jesus returned in the power of the Spirit into Galilee." He does so. But, he must be considered as meaning that, he returned from the place where the tempter left him. This was on the summit of the exceeding high mountain, where he repelled the last assault, respecting which, there is no certainty that it lay in the wilderness; and, indeed, that mountain does not, to which tradition, at this day, points as the place where the Messiah withstood the allurement of the kingdoms of the world, and the glory of them. A greater difficulty arises from the distance between the wilderness and Jerusalem, which, upon the smallest calculation, could not have been less than twelve miles. This is, indeed, a considerable distance for our Lord to have travelled, situated as he was. But, of opinions, which all are attended with some difficulties to finite minds, a wise man will ever adopt that which has the fewest and least.

But I urge not the opinion, nor dwell longer upon the criticism. You will pardon the introduction of it. It originated from a desire to show to the thoughtless scoffers at this part of his life, in whom we believe, that it may, without force or sophistry, be so explained, as to appear neither so wonderful as to be incredible, nor so strange as to be ludicrous. After all, more time, perhaps, has been spent upon this point than it required. I preach to believers; to whom it is of less consequence to know in what way the Saviour was conveyed to the battlement of the temple, than how he converted his situation into a place of triumph.

Christ had repelled the first temptation with his full assurance of the power and goodness of God. Having brought him to the lofty battlement on the top of the temple, the tempter's second aim was to draw him into sinful presumption, by inducing him to cast himself down headlong, that he might thus prove the readiness of the Most High to save him, and publicly evince himself the Son of God. To enforce his expostulation, this father of hypocrites, as well as liars, this most subtle seducer, feigns a reverence for Scripture, and, impiously imitating the wisdom of Christ, urges his temptation with, "It is written." What cause of shame to those, who, deeply interested in the sacred volume, are yet utterly ignorant of its contents! What a plain lesson to all, to "judge no man" to be certainly right and good, because he is well versed in the sacred volume, and can quote holy writ upon all occasions. The best things may be abused. Even Scripture may be perverted by the wicked. "If thou be the Son of God, cast thyself down, for," says the tempter, "it is written, He shall give his angels charge concerning thee, and in their hands they shall bear thee up, lest at any time thou dash thy foot against a stone."

It is the unceasing artifice of the enemy to make men err by urging them to extremes. If they are not prodigal, they may be covetous. Though they fly the pleasures and dissipations of the fool, they may sink into the selfishness and austerity of the monk. Though they do not despair under the threats and frowns of the Most High, they may become arrogant in his promises and smiles. So subtle is vice, so beset are we with evil, that our very speed in recoiling from one error, may hurry us into another. How few of mankind do we behold travelling on steadily in the path, equidistant from all extremes, where virtue generally sojourns, and peace is found. The temptations of the Saviour were such in their nature, as are common to men. He had just withstood the most powerful solicitations to distrust; while full of confidence in the truth and good providence of God, the tempter hopes to seduce him into presumption. The Most High is able to preserve thee, he has promised to do it; "cast thyself down." But the Author of our religion was too calm and considerate to vibrate to extremes. The velocity with which he avoided evil, was under his own control. He knew the narrow line where virtue borders upon vice. It was a vain expectation that he would not distinguish between faith and vanity, between trust and presumption. His regard for the Scriptures undiminished by the abuse of them, he recurs again to the treasures of truth, for a weapon of defence; he finds it in the reproof of Moses to those who, in the wilderness, demanded miraculous tokens that Jehovah was with them; and he at once repels the subtle deceiver with, "It is written, Thou shalt not tempt the Lord thy God." This passage from the records of revelation showed at once, that, great and infallible as are the promises and power of God, no one may safely expose himself to danger, for no other purpose than to be miraculously preserved; nor urge him to anger by seeking to try the extent of his goodness, and to extort from him unnecessary evidences of his providence and power. While the answer rectified the Scripture the tempter had perverted, and gave him his rebuff, it keenly reprimanded him for the work in which he was engaged. Vexed with reproof, as well as disappointed in his wishes, he could not defend his expostulation, but hoped, alas! like the infatuated Balak, to accomplish his nefarious project, by trying, yet again, in another place.

Such was the second triumph of our Lord. The instructions which we derive from what has been said, are the exact counterpart to those inferred from the nature and issue of the first temptation. That, cautioned against despair, and the use of unlawful means; this, against presumption and the neglect of those means which are appointed. If we take hold of his promises, we presume ourselves his elect; and that nothing we can do can injure our future fate; or if, under the cover of relying on the mercy of the Most High, we are careless how we live, assuring ourselves that the angel of the covenant must preserve us; if we demand unnecessary miracles, try vain experiment, or expose ourselves boldly to danger, to prove the being and truth of the Most High; if in the pursuit of any end, temporal or spiritual, we neglect the means he has ordained, yet throw ourselves upon him, and expect his help, what do we in all these things, but cast ourselves down, because, "it is written, he will give his angels charge over us?" Our business is, to be regular in observing the order which Deity has established in nature and in revelation; to depend, indeed, for all things upon his blessing, but not to seek to snatch it from his hands, but to obtain, in the channels in which he has appointed it to flow, humbly to strive for our own safety, expecting no supernatural aid from him, till we have used the powers he has already given us. Around the good man, thus holding the virtuous tenor of his way, the heavenly hosts do indeed encamp, his safeguards and his friends. He will experience more than the fulfilment of all the promises of heaven.

SERMON XXXV.

ON THE TEMPTATION.

MATTHEW, iv. 8–12.

"Again the devil taketh him up into an exceeding high mountain, and showeth him all the kingdoms of the world, and the glory of them; and saith unto him, all these things will I give thee, if thou wilt fall down and worship me. Then saith Jesus unto him, Get thee hence, Satan; for it is written, Thou shalt worship the Lord thy God, and him only shalt thou serve. Then the devil leaveth him, and, behold, angels came and ministered unto him."

AMONG the allurements which beguile mankind, ambition and pleasure hold out the strongest. Power and fame, wealth and gratification, are objects of such infatuating influence upon the minds of men, that they can even blind them to the worth of virtue, and entice them from the path of duty, without persuasion. These dangerous seducers may boast more triumphs in behalf of vice than all the others employed in her service. To these, the tempter resorted when he had twice failed in his malignant attempts upon the Author of our salvation. More indefatigable than better beings, in a worse cause than they have to promote, this deceiver is not discouraged by ill success. Temptations seldom come single. By varying them, and urging them in succession, he thought to exhaust the virtue and vanquish the resistance of the Son of God. He had endeavoured to excite him to a distrust of the truth and good providence of his Father, but had failed. Finding Christ filled with immovable faith in his Father's power and love, he thought to draw him into heedless presumption. Here, too, he was rebuffed, and his defeat brought with it vexatious reproof. Still, if he could with dazzling promises persuade the Saviour to yield to him one offering of that worship and service which is due only to the Most High, he should both provoke the Almighty to anger, who hath said, "Mine honour will I not give to another," and exult in the homage of him who was designed to "bruise his head," and save mankind. But how should he beguile the circumspect Jesus into idolatry like this! He remembered that ambition and the love of pleasure were powerful principles in the human breast. By aid of these he had seduced the first human pair. These, too, had brought him full many a victim from among their deluded descendants. Haply, they might be found in the bosom of this Person, and decoyed to his purpose by splendid allurements and weighty bribes. Accordingly, he expends his utmost power in gilding his bait; from his store of lies he selects the most imposing, and of every circumstance which can promote his design, he takes advantage. What a satire is his enterprise, activity, and perseverance upon the supineness of men, in nobler and more profitable business! "Again," says the Evangelist, "the devil taketh him up into an exceeding high mountain, and showeth him all the kingdoms of the world, and the glory of them; and saith unto him, All these things will I give thee, if thou wilt fall down and worship me." Insolent spirit! that durst indulge such boldness and depravity. But it shall serve to burnish the character of Messiah, and to teach the best men that they may be tempted to heinous crimes. "Let him that thinketh he standeth, take heed lest he fall.

We left the Saviour, in our last discourse, triumphant upon the pinnacle of the temple. In the same way in which he was taken thither by the tempter, no doubt he was taken to the top of the mountain. The reasons which led to the conclusion in the former case, that the mode of conveyance was natural, and not miraculous, are equally applicable to the latter case. As when Abraham is said to take two of his young men and Isaac his son to the place of which God had told him, we understand only that he induced them to go with him, and as when Christ is said to take his disciples with him to Jerusalem, we suppose no more than that he conducted them thither, so it seems most natural, unexceptionable, and conformable with the use of the words, when the tempter is said to take our Lord from the holy city to the top of the mountain, to understand that he conducted Christ thither, who was induced to accompany him, by the impulses of the Spirit, which at first led him into the wilderness to be tempted.

What mountain it was which the tempter chose as best suited to his design, it is not easy to determine. The Scriptures do not name, and but cursorily describe it. It was an exceeding high mountain. From this circumstance, some have supposed it was Mount Ararat, on which the waters of the flood first disappeared, and the ark rested. But this lay quite in a distant part of the world; and there can be no reason for going so far for a mountain, when such lofty ones, with such august prospects, may be found in Palestine. Others have supposed that it was Mount Calvary, ever memorable for the place of the crucifixion of our Lord. But Calvary was not a very high hill, and answers not the description in the text. Various other mountains, famed for some Scripture events, have been conjectured to be the same with that in the text; but the greatest number of expositors have resorted to the renowned Pisgah, from which Moses took his view of the extent and glories of that promised land, which, alas! for his inadvertence, the anxious prophet was not permitted to enter. There is a mountain, which tradition has, to this day, consecrated as the scene of this temptation of Christ. It may be seen distinguished on the maps of the Holy Land, and is mentioned by the most reputable of modern travellers. This mountain, however, answers not to Pisgah, nor to any of those which have been mentioned. It is situated on the skirt of the plain of Jericho, about five hours' moderate travelling from Jerusalem. There are on its sides the ruins of caves and huts, in which piety, shrouded in zeal, once passed an obscure life, but which now gives a shelter to the wild Arab, who profits by Satan's expedient, exacting of superstition no small tribute, when she would take the view from its awful summit. This mountain, all travellers describe as exceeding high, and in allusion to Christ's temptation, the name it bears is Quarantania. Whether this be the real mount or not, I profess not to determine. It may, however, be generally remarked, that more credit is due to ancient tradition than to modern conjecture. But this benefit we may derive from having dwelt thus long upon this obscure, and perhaps unimportant point; it gives collateral confirmation to our belief. When places renowned for great or singular events are from the time distinguished, and through successive generations pointed at, by tradition, as memorable for those very events, our confidence in the historian who relates them is strengthened; and thus, even superstition is rendered serviceable to truth. Does it not increase our satisfaction in the life and works of Virgil, the Roman bard, that from the age when he is said to have lived, the classic genius was wont to tread lightly over Mantua? Does it not support our faith in the destruction of Pharaoh and his host in the Red Sea, that the place where they were overwhelmed when pursuing Israel, has been for ages, and to this day is called "The Pool of Destruction?" It justly, then, may confirm our belief in the history of our Lord, that desolate as is the country, and inhabited by heathens, the traveller yet hears at the foot of Quarantania the triumph of Christ upon its lofty summit, and finds almost an accurate account of his life, written by tradition, in the dust of the spots where the events of it happened.

But we must return to the evangelical narrative. When the tempter had brought our Lord to the top of this exceeding high mountain, he showed him, says the historian, "all the kingdoms of the world, and the glory of them," and saith unto him, "All these things will I give thee, if thou wilt fall down and worship me." Here, the first inquiry of our minds will be, in what sense the tempter showed "all the kingdoms of the world?" From the round form of the earth, it is impossible they should be brought into one view to any person upon it; and if they could, no human eye would be adequate to the extensive survey. There are but two ways worthy of notice, in which this difficulty has been solved. One is, that the tempter presented to the Saviour's view, only an airy picture of the magnificence, wealth, and pleasures of "the kingdoms of the world," something fictitious, which he was permitted to form for the occasion, and which had all the effect of reality upon Christ. The other is, that the words rendered in our translation, "all the kingdoms of the world," being often used in a partial sense, here signify the kingdoms round about, and that the tempter, having taken the Saviour to a very lofty eminence, caused him at once to behold a most delightful prospect of Palestine, which was "the glory of all lands;" its cities, palaces, riches and magnificence; and rendered them yet more alluring by high-wrought descriptions of glory and power which could not be seen, and of honours and pleasures which would attach to him who should have them in possession. Of these two expositions, the latter seems to be the best, and every way satisfactory. That the Greek phrase, which we translate "the world," is very frequently used when the whole globe is not meant, is undeniable. Thus, Augustus is said to have decreed "that the whole world should be taxed;" intending only the dominions under the Roman empire. And Jehovah is said to have promised to Abraham that he should be heir of the world, meaning the land of Canaan. If, then, we suppose the tempter to have placed Christ upon a mountain, from which he would at once be struck with the ravishing prospect of Judea, its pomp, extent, and riches; to have pointed out to him the Roman provinces and the neighbouring territories, we shall do full justice to the original expression, without either forcing the passage or finding ourselves perplexed. Upon a commanding situation, the prospect would at once strike the eye, and the observer might well be said to see them in a moment or instantaneously. And as power and glory seem to require to be described to the imagination rather than placed before the sight, so the word "showeth," is very frequently used, to convey the idea of description. When thus the difficulty may be solved, and the narrative so explicitly gives to the fact the character of reality, I see not the necessity of resorting to an airy picture. There seems something forced and unnecessary in it; and if we admit it here, what event in Scripture may not be declared to have been figurative or fictitious? Indeed, upon this supposition, I see not the necessity nor use of selecting an exceeding high mountain, nor of carrying Christ to the top of it. An illusive scene could have as well been exhibited in a valley or upon a plain. Besides, in interpreting this passage, and in all our labours, we have the example of our Creator and Preserver, never to resort to supernatural expedients for the attainment of any end, which may as well be accomplished by natural ones.

But whichever way the tempter showed the Saviour "the kingdoms of the world, and the glory of them," certain it is, he presented him with such a view as he thought sufficient to inflame his ambition, to infatuate his desires, and to prepare him to grasp greedily at the dazzling offer; "all these things will I give thee, if thou wilt fall down and worship me."

Idle! exclaims the thoughtless scoffer at sacred writ. Can any one suppose the evil spirit would be so stupid, as to expect that this or any man, would believe he had these things, and the glory of them at his disposal, or that the Son of God could in any way be induced to fall down and worship him. Opinions hastily adopted are often wrong. Sound judgment is the result of serious examination. If we consider the narrative candidly, and compare it with sentiments at the time prevalent, we shall perceive that, notwithstanding the scoffs of those who love no revealed truth, this was as plausible and deeply insidious a temptation as could have been devised.

In all nations, some traces may be found of a belief in tutelary beings, who watched and managed the affairs of countries unseen, and had each his particular province. That the idea of guardian angels over the kingdoms of the earth, as well as over favoured individuals, was among the Jews, is indisputable. It had no little sanction in their Scriptures. We read of Michael and Gabriel holding conference about the fate of Daniel's people, as well as of the angels of the little ones, beholding the face of the Most High in heaven. If, then, the tempter, who has all along been supposed to have disguised himself under some friendly form, feigned himself the guardian of the kingdoms which he showed to Christ, this lover of lies might, with the most plausible assurance, declare they were at his disposal, and this seems the probable ground of the words with which St. Luke relates he vouched his promise; "For that is delivered unto me, and to whomsoever I will, I give it."

Further. The Jews were almost universally impressed with the sentiment that the Messiah would be a temporal prince, vested with all temporal pomp and power. This they gathered from the sublime, prophetic, but misconstrued descriptions in the sacred writings, of the extent of his kingdom and duration of his reign. With these passages of Scripture, the evil spirit was probably acquainted, whether he understood them or not, as well as with others which he quoted. He, therefore, well might think the kingdom of the Jews, with all temporal power and glory, were the most alluring objects he could hold out to Messiah. In all human bosoms, there are passions which these may kindle into a ruinous flame. Are there not men whom ambition for empire, and thirst for fame, wealth, and pleasure, could induce to worship God, reason, Muhammed, or anything else, which the attainment of their object required? Of this powerful sway of these passions, the tempter had often availed himself with great success. How natural then for him to think that if this were the Messiah, of whom the Jews mused, and he were in any point vulnerable, nothing would be so effectual as a proffer of "the kingdoms of the world, and the glory of them."

As to the condition that he should do him homage, the most venerable patriarchs, prophets and men, had felt sometimes impelled to prostrate themselves before good angels. The Saviour had not yet discovered to his adversary that he knew him; therefore he might hope that his friendly appearance would justify the condition, and the greatness of the gifts and glory which he promised, induce the Messiah to do him worship.

Thus we see that, far from being unlikely or stupid, this temptation was the most specious and powerful which this subtle deceiver ever devised. It prompted to the most debasing sin, and the motives were disguised under the most insidious plausibility. It was the tempter's strongest effort, and no doubt, with all the horrid hopeful anxiety, with which he watched the determination of our frail mother, while he invited her to pluck the forbidden fruit, he now expected the homage, and the ruin of the great deliverer of our race.

Look well to it, Satan; is thy net strong; hast thou spread all thy most alluring baits? Vain blasphemer! It had been better for thee, if thou hadst before desisted! Till now, the Saviour had willingly endured, and calmly replied. But the last daring suggestion excites his holy wrath. His resistance strengthens; he discovers to the tempter that he well knows his vileness; and with becoming spirit bids him quit his presence. "Get thee hence, Satan;" but first know, that thou wert base in withdrawing thy allegiance from thy Maker, and art baser in labouring to seduce others from their duty. Right it is, and commendable, and it is enjoined by the rules of eternal truth, that all creatures give their homage, affection, and obedience to Him only who made them; the Almighty. "It is written, Thou shalt worship the Lord thy God, and him only shalt thou serve." Quick as the lightning falls from heaven, when he found himself known, the fiend disappeared; owning, and trembling at that authority, which he had been labouring to subvert.

Thus was the triumph of our blessed Lord complete. Tempted in all points like as we are, yet, adorable perfection, "without sin." But what instruction is there for us in the nature and issue of this temptation? The other two were such as are common to men, and furnished useful lessons; but have we here anything for our direction? Much, and of great importance. This, too, was a temptation which we, in some sense, may endure. It is not indeed, probable, that the tempter will, in visible form, take us to a mountain, and proffer us the kingdoms of the earth, and their glory, if we will worship him. But into the same seducement, in effect, he incessantly strives to draw mankind, by very similar means. When ambition displays the pomps of station, the emoluments of power, the gaudy wreath of fame urging us to pursue them at the expense of duty, benevolence and truth, what does she but say, "All these will I give thee," if thou wilt devote thy life to my gratification. When fortune sets before us her glittering gold, her splendid edifices, her train of sycophants and slaves, her cloak that covers every deficiency, urging to sacrifice to the attainment of them, honesty, humanity, piety, and peace, what does she but say, "All these things will I give thee, if thou wilt fall down and worship me?" When pleasure spreads her sensual joys, her luxurious gratifications, her enticing amusements, her ease without care, urging us to neglect for them the worship of God, the duties of our stations, and the care of the one thing needful, what does she but say, All these shall be thine, if thou wilt become my votary, and spend thy time and powers in my service. If we comply with these, or any of these enticements, we are then guilty of the crime in which the tempter would have involved our Lord; for what are ambition, wealth and pleasure, when they would lead us into wrong, but prostituted ministers of vice. Every man who sets his heart wholly upon any earthly object, devotes himself to the gratification of any passion, or dedicates life solely to the pursuit of temporal good, regardless of God, and his requirements, in a real sense worships the creature, and is guilty of idolatry. Respecting the undivided devotion which Deity exacts, it is most strictly certain that he who is not with him is against him; and it is remarkable that the votary to pleasure is pointedly said to have his god in his belly, and the covetous is expressly styled an idolator. Besides, happiness is the substance of all the promises which ambition, fortune, and pleasure hold out to us, if we will relinquish all other allegiance and serve them. If we comply with the impious condition, are they able to give us this happiness, and make their promise good? No more than the prince of iniquity was, to give "the kingdoms of the world and the glory of them," to the Son of God. When they have made us dupes, they will leave us wretches. Our interest and our wisdom, then, lie in learning from the example of the Saviour, the value of resistance. By withstanding the allurements of temptation, and abiding faithful to God and the word of truth, the Messiah eventually obtained all power and glory, which he might have lost for ever, if he had sought them at the hand of one, who, with great shows and much fair speech, enticed him. In like manner if we resist steadfastly every solicitation to alienate our affections, worship and obedience, from the Creator and his laws, we shall assuredly obtain the full reality of that happiness, with false promises of which the notorious seducers, of whom we have been speaking, would delude mankind. "It is written," and from him, the great I AM, before whose word the heavens and earth shall fail, "He that overcometh, shall inherit all things."

SERMON XXXVI.

ON REPENTANCE.

1 JOHN, i. 8, 9.

"If we say that we have no sin, we deceive ourselves, and the truth is not in us. If we confess our sins, he is faithful, and just, to forgive us our sins, and to cleanse us from all unrighteousness."

THERE is, perhaps, nothing on earth, on which so much of man's best interests depends, and to which the angels of God look with such lively concern, as the repentance of the children of men. This was the burthen of the most earnest admonitions of the Prophets. This was the substance of the preaching of John the Baptist. The Apostles of our Lord began their Gospel with the invitation to repent. Yea, the great end of the incarnation and death, and resurrection and ascension of the Son of God was, that repentance and remission of sins should be preached in his name, among all nations.

Brought, my brethren, to the commencement of that holy season in which the Church, sorrowfully conscious of the imperfection that is in man, has, from her earliest days, invited her members to a more particular exercise of penitence, humiliation, and religious reflection, I am desirous of bringing this subject to your view; not as it respects the Pagan, who, in his repentance, is to turn from his dumb idols to serve the living God; not as it respects the Jew, the Turk, the heretic, or the infidel, who, in their repentance, are to turn from their rejection of the Messiah, and the perverseness of their own minds and wills, to a reception of Jesus, and of the law of the spirit of life, which is in him; but as it respects the Christian, encumbered, so long as he continues in the flesh, with the infection of a sinful nature, and the consciousness of an imperfect life, and a part of the perpetual business of whose vocation it is to confess his sinfulness to Almighty God, with full purpose of amendment of life. The words I have read to you, present a comprehensive view of the subject. They are spoken by the disciple whom Jesus loved. They are spoken by him, with a view of his own condition, and of the condition of all the fellow disciples of our Lord. They are spoken by him of Christians, and with an intent to beget in them those very dispositions, and an attention to those very duties, for the cherishing and perfecting of which the season of Lent is consecrated. "If we say that we have no sin, we deceive ourselves, and the truth is not in us. If we confess our sins, he is faithful and just, to forgive us our sins, and to cleanse us from all unrighteousness."

Here are exhibited to you the ground and occasion which all have to practice repentance, in the certainty of their sinfulness.

And here is presented to your view, the great inducement to repentance, in the certainty of its efficacy.

Under these two views of the subject, we shall find all that we are concerned to know of the doctrine concerning it; except, that it will be necessary, before we advance to the consideration of them, to adjust our ideas of the nature of repentance.

Briefly, then, it implies a conviction of our sinfulness in the thoughts, words, or deeds, by which we have, at any time transgressed the will of God, and a hearty contrition for the same; a penitential acknowledgment unto God, of our sins, with a renunciation of them, and earnest desire, resolution, and endeavour to be freed from them, and imbued with the opposite virtues. And such deeds of restitution, satisfaction, atonement or amends for any, or all of our offences, as we may be able, at any time, to make. To distinguish it from the compunction of the devils, for they, in their chains and torments, regret their iniquities, it must proceed more from a love, than a fear of

God; it must be less a sorrow that we are endangered, than that our Creator, Redeemer, and Sanctifier, has been offended. To distinguish it from the remorse of Judas, for he is said to have repented, it must be mixed with confidence in the mercy of the Being to whom the confession is made; the awe must be pious, and not selfish; the fear filial, and not base, which the conviction produces. Indeed, it springs from faith. It is nursed by hope. And when it speaks, it speaks with the feelings of a child to the ear of a father. Christian repentance is sorrowful, but not distracted. It is not more a turning from the wrath of God, than a turning to his love. The companion whom it seeketh is, moreover, charity.

Such is that repentance, which, after the idiom of the Scripture language, in which a duty is often expressed by some leading branch of it, is signified in the text by confessing our sins; and this not unhappily; for no man will confess his sins who is not conscious of them; nor will any person confess them unto God, who does not "believe that he is," and desire his forgiveness; nor will they be humbly confessed at all, except by those who wish to be freed from them; to whom, in the fine language of the Church, "the remembrance of them is grievous, the burthen of them is intolerable."

Let us, now, proceed to consider the ground and occasion which all have for the practice of repentance, in the certainty of their sinfulness. However humbling the doctrine may be, it is nevertheless true, that "the Scripture concludes all men under sin." "How," says Job, "should man be just with God?" "There is no man," says Solomon, "that sinneth not." "In many things," says St. James, "we offend all." "All have sinned," says St. Paul, "and come short of the glory of God." "If we say that we have no sin," says St. John, "we deceive ourselves, and the truth is not in us." "There is none good," says our blessed Lord, "but one, that is God." The whole scheme of the Christian religion; all its provisions; all its purposes; all its promises; proceed on the supposition, or rather the assertion, of the sinfulness of man. It "is a faithful saying, that Christ Jesus came into the world to save sinners," and this saying is "worthy of all men to be" thankfully "received," for this reason, that "all have sinned."

This doctrine of the Scripture is very explicitly professed by our Church, in the confessions, which are found in all her offices for the use of all her children; and when she says in her articles, that the infection of nature, which "is engendered of the offspring of Adam, doth remain, yea, in them that are regenerated;" and again, that sin was not in Christ. But all we, the rest, although baptized, and born again in Christ, yet offend in many things, and "if we say we have no sin, we deceive ourselves, and the truth is not in us."

But the evidence of this doctrine, most convincing to every man, is to be drawn from his own observation and experience. In vain shall we look, in this region of infirmity, for a faultless character. They who approach nearest to God, are, perhaps, most sensible how far off they are from him. Such, indeed, is the purity of the divine requirements, and such, the frailty of our nature, that there is enough in man, in his most holy state, to require the sacrifice and mediation of his Saviour, to reconcile him to God. Even "if we walk in the light, as he is in the light," and have "fellowship one with another," still, we shall need "the blood of his Son to cleanse us from all sin." Examine your best deeds. How inconstant are they; how alloyed with worldly feebleness and selfish considerations. Consider your omissions of duties, which have the nature of sin. How numerous, how often repeated, how frequently without excuse. Look into your hearts; and call the passions which are there, into review before you. Are none of them inordinate and sinful? Is there not among them, if not obtrusive, yet lurking in some secret corner, and occasionally showing itself, pride, or anger, or envy, or covetousness, or lust, or hatred, or vainglory? Look into your minds; and examine your thoughts. Are they never vain, irregular, sensual, uncharitable, or malevolent? Observe your deeds and habits. Is there no sin which most easily besets you; no vice which you spare, as Saul spared the king of Amalek; no sloth, no unfaithfulness, no neglect of the happiness of your neighbour; no intemperate, no peevish, no criminal indulgence? Try your piety. Is it never enfeebled by listlessness, nor sullied by the accompaniment of unfriendly sentiments towards your fellow beings? Prove your faith. Does it never waver; is it always used? Test your obedience. Is it universal? Take the picture of the life of Jesus Christ. It is not overwrought. It is, what every man would be, if he were perfect. Compare with it your own lives. Ah, dear Lord, it is thus, by the standard thou hast given us, we detect our deficiencies! When we look upon the features of thy character, and then look upon our own, we see little in ourselves to give us complacency; we lay our hands on our mouths, and our mouths in the dust, and "cry, unclean, unclean."

Now, amidst these sins and imperfections, of which, in some degree or other, all men are conscious, that which escapes observation, but which my purpose obliges me to press upon your notice, is the solemn consideration that in the sight of the pure God, and under the operation of his holy government, any of these sins, much more many of them, is sufficient to subject us to his displeasure, and to incur his dreadful condemnation. "The soul that sinneth," it is the language of his law, "the soul that sinneth, it shall die." "The wages of sin," it is the declaration of his Gospel, "the wages of sin is death." "Whosoever shall keep the whole law," it is the decision of inspired wisdom, "whosoever shall keep the whole law, and yet offend in one point, he is guilty of all." So that under the law of God, which the morality of Jesus does not destroy, but rather renders more strict, more spiritual, more complete, the situation of every transgressor is awfully perilous. Unless he be extricated from the dangers to which his transgressions expose him, by availing himself of those means of extrication which our heavenly Father hath most graciously provided in the Gospel of his Son, it cannot be otherwise than that his transgressions should bring upon him anger and wrath, and final destruction.

What, then, are these means? Repentance, springing from faith, and producing its proper fruits is the chief. To the accomplishment of our salvation, it would seem to be necessarily indispensable. For without departing from iniquity, it is not easy to conceive how any can be free from misery, since these are, in the nature of things, so inseparably connected, that he who chooses the one must choose the other. Without turning from sin unto God, and manifesting at least a desire and endeavour to be conformed to his will, it is not easy to conceive how any can be holy; and "without holiness no man shall see the Lord." Here, then, you may perceive the ground and occasion which all Christians have to cherish and exercise that true repentance which the Church teaches them, whenever they assemble and meet together to beseech God to give them; to seek earnestly for that forgiveness of sins, for which their compassionate Lord, aware of the imperfections which would always be found in them, hath in his own most holy prayer taught them, daily, to pray. Repentance is, to every, even the most perfect saint, essential to his salvation and peace. Nor can any considerate Christian neglect to fly to it with eager haste and unwearied assiduity, who considers what is further offered to your view in the text, the certainty of its efficacy.

Shall I, if I repent of my past sins, assuredly obtain forgiveness? It is a question which reason answers not. The solution of it depends upon the will of God. And blessed be his name, he has given us such satisfactory information concerning it, that the repentance ceases to be Christian which is not accompanied with a belief in its efficacy. The expressions in the text are singularly marked and forcible. They set before us on its proper foundation, this doctrine of Christianity, than which I know of none more full of comfort for the frail inhabitants of this sinful world. Let us ponder the great truths which they contain.

Repentance cannot mend the broken law of God. It can found no claim to favour or reward. Nor is it certain that it would comport with the wisdom or stability of any government, that violators of its laws should, on account of their sorrow for what they had done, be always pardoned. Yet, says my text, "If we confess our sins, he is faithful and just to forgive us our sins, and to cleanse us from all unrighteousness." What! is God in justice bound to receive us when we return to him? Is the Most High obligated to forgive us when we truly repent? Herein is disclosed the wonderful mystery of his mercy. He hath bound and obligated himself. Foreseeing the condition into which we should fall, our merciful Father provided a way in which the requirements of his justice might be satisfied, and yet sinners be forgiven; in which "he might be just, and yet the justifier of those who believe in Jesus." He gave his Son, who, "by his one oblation of himself, once offered, hath made upon the cross a full, perfect, and sufficient sacrifice, oblation, and satisfaction for the sins of the whole world." When, therefore, the penitent believer returns to God, he finds that the penalty which was his due, his Saviour hath sustained; that the debt which was charged against him, his divine surety hath paid. And the just God, he is confidently assured, will not twice exact that which his love doth but once require. The everlasting Father, moreover, hath promised to the Son, as the reward of his obedience and sufferings, that "he should see of the travail of his soul; and also, to all those "who truly repent and unfeignedly believe his Gospel," the pardon and remission of all their sins. And he "is not a man that he should lie, nor the son of man that he should repent. Hath he said, and shall he not do it, or hath he spoken, and shall he not make it good?" All who truly repent and come unto him by faith, he will give unto his Son, in the fulfilment of his promise, and unto them, also, he will give eternal life. In faithful and just adherence to the covenant of mercy which he hath made with our race, in Christ Jesus, unto every penitent Christian, God will "forgive his sins, and cleanse him from all unrighteousness," with the blood of the sacrifice which he hath provided for the purpose. Sooner shall heaven and earth pass away; as soon may the veracity and equity of the Deity fail, as repentant believers fail to obtain from him the pardon of their sins, and all the unspeakable benefits of the mediation of his Son, Jesus Christ, their Lord.

"That we, through patience and comfort of the Scriptures, might have hope" of this efficacy of repentance, God has caused to be recorded for us many impressive and animating examples. When the people of Nineveh humbled themselves for their sins, and turned every one from the evil of his ways, that great city was spared from its doom. Whenever his chosen people returned from their wanderings unto him, he returned unto them, and they rejoiced in his smiles. It was for his repentance that David was forgiven. He had violated in a heinous manner God's laws. But when he perceived his guilt, he, with a broken heart cried, "I have sinned." And God, as he was assured by the mouth of his Prophet, "put away his sin." It was this that restored Peter to favour. He had, in an evil hour, denied his Lord. But when he thought thereon, "he went out and wept bitterly." And Jesus remembered him, as soon as he was risen, and committed to him the care of his sheep and the keys of his kingdom. It was this that obtained for the woman of Jerusalem, who had been a sinner, the protection and peace of the Son of God. When she knew his power and offices, she turned and came to him. With deep contrition she lay at his feet, and did "wash them with her tears;" with affectionate devotion, she "wiped them with the hairs of her head." And "her sins, which were many, were forgiven her; for she loved much." The whole company of the saints who have passed into heaven, were subject to like passions and infirmities with ourselves. They were saints, not because they had no unrighteousness, but because they were cleansed from it. They are taken unto God and the Lamb, not because they never had offended, but because they faithfully and entirely, and constantly performed the conditions of the new and gracious covenant into which God had brought them, through the death of his Son; of which conditions, repentance "from dead works to serve the living God," was a perpetual and very important one.

Will it be said that these examples are instances of singular mercy and special favour? And that the inference of the efficacy of repentance from the faithfulness and justice of God, is too refined for common utility? Let it then be considered that the certainty of its efficacy has been declared fully by that Sovereign on whose will it depends. We have the most comfortable and satisfactory assurance of it in innumerable declarations, which, that we might have strong consolation, who flee for refuge to "the hope set before us," our heavenly Father hath in his word vouchsafed to make. "Come now and let us reason together, saith the Lord: though your sins be as scarlet, they shall be white as snow; though they be red like crimson, they shall be as wool." "When the wicked man turneth away from his wickedness that he hath committed, and doeth that which is lawful and right, he shall save his soul alive." "The sacrifices of God are a broken spirit; a broken and contrite heart, O God, thou wilt not despise." "Whoso confesseth and forsaketh" his sins, "shall have mercy." "I have no pleasure in the death of him that dieth, wherefore turn yourselves and live ye." "Blessed are they that mourn, for they shall be comforted." "Repent ye, therefore, and be converted, that your sins may be blotted out, when the times of refreshing shall come from the presence of the Lord." "I dwell in the high and holy place, with him also that is of a contrite and humble spirit, to revive the spirit of the humble, and to revive the heart of the contrite ones." The passage at the head of this discourse is as full and plain as it could have been made; and in the parable of the prodigal son, wherein, whatever were its first application, is represented what I trust is constantly occurring in the intercourse of God and his human children. As soon as the prodigal came to himself and bewailed his conduct, and arose with humility and affection to return to his father, while "he was yet a great way off, his father saw him, and had compassion, and ran and fell on his neck, and kissed him." He heard his confession, and gave him a garment to cover and adorn him, from his own wardrobe. He commanded his servants to "put a ring on his hand, and shoes on his feet." And all his family were called upon to rejoice at the recovery of a son who was lost.

My brethren, you have now seen the necessity which we all have for repentance, and the certainty of its efficacy with our God. How important is this duty. On this grace depends our favour with God; our peace; our final salvation. Except men repent, they perish; if they turn unto God he will heal them, and they shall live. On this account it is that such earnest entreaties are used in the Scriptures, to move men to the performance of his duty. On this account it is that the angels of God are represented as rejoicing "in heaven, over one sinner that repenteth." On this account it is that the Church annually sets apart so large a portion of time for the more certain and complete accomplishment in us, of this most necessary and momentous work. Be induced, then, Christians, to consider your ways and turn unto the Lord your God. Learn from what has been said, to utter in future with increased humility and sincerity, the meek confession which is made here in the temple, whenever "we assemble and meet together." Go often with true penitent hearts to the holy table, seeking the tokens and pledges of forgiveness, be penetrated with a sense of your necessities as sinners; disdain not to stand there, weeping at the feet of your Lord, if haply he may say to you, "Thy sins are forgiven thee; go in peace." Use to the purpose to which it is devoted, this holy season; by examining your ways, humbling yourselves before God, and turning to him with new and more lively resolutions of obedience. Consider that the path of repentance is the only path to heaven. To induce you to use it, remember that it hath been opened for you at the expense of the sacrifice of the Son of God; that it is washed with his blood. Is it rugged at its entrance? Be not deceived by a partial appearance. It is the path of peace. Enter it and walk in it daily; it will improve as you advance. The further you proceed in it, the further you will leave behind you the infirmities and miseries of your condition; till at length it shall conduct you to the borders of that country, of whose felicity it is not the least ingredient, that there shall be in it no sin.

SERMON XXXVII.

ON THE PASSION.

Ecclesiastes, iii. 4.

"A time to mourn."

WE enter to-day upon the most solemn week of the Christian year. The Church is clothed in her sackcloth. All her services are services of sorrow and deep humiliation. Day after day, we are called upon to attend our Saviour through the several stages of his passion, till we leave him in the grave numbered with the dead. It is a week which might be rendered to the faithful, productive of the happiest attainments; and I crave your attention while, with a view to restore to it that devout observance which its objects claim, and it anciently received, and to render your attendance on the services of it gratifying to your spirits, and fruitful of their proper effects, I offer to your notice some reasons for observing the Passion Week, drawn from the institution of it, and some also drawn from the dispositions and advantages which the observation of it is calculated to produce.

In the first place, the institution of it is respectful to our Saviour. The world owes its redemption to his blood. The time in which he offered himself for the sins of men was the most awful in the annals of this globe. Nature marked it. The earth shook. The sun was darkened. Rocks rent. The graves were opened. In a series of sufferings, at which heaven and earth were amazed, the Son of God expiated the offences of man, and restored him to favour with his Maker, and to the hope of eternal life. The seasons of great and beneficial actions, have, at the periods of their revolution, been generally distinguished with suitable observation. Is it not due to the great Saviour of our race, when the part of the year returns in which he endured the heavy "stripes by which we are healed," to pause from the bustle of life, to recur to the scenes of his sufferings, and indulge in the emotions which they are calculated to excite. That he is not insensible to such expressions of our respect, we may infer from his own institution of an ordinance for "showing forth his death till he comes." The particular time in which he suffered could hardly have needed a command for its consecration to the remembrance of him. For who can reflect that, at this time, the great Benefactor of the human race was making that sacrifice of himself which redeemed them from perdition, and not go to his Church to listen to the narrative of his sorrows, and bend the knee to him in gratitude and adoration!

Again. With respect to ourselves, this institution is proper, to impress us with a lively memory of our Saviour's sufferings. Amidst the blandishments of pleasure and distractions of business, the sufferings of the Son of God are too early forgotten. It is almost impossible to have his cross constantly in view. His humiliation and his agony give place in our minds to those cares and pursuits which are inseparable from our existence. But unless his death be properly impressed upon us, it can hardly produce in us its proper effects. It is therefore useful, if indeed it be not necessary, at stated times to retire from the common occupations of life and meditate upon the acts of his Passion, as we do sometimes upon the deeds and sorrows of our departed friends. And what time so suitable for the purpose as that in which his Passion was sustained, and his life terminated? When may we so well be at the foot of his cross as in the week in which he hung upon it? Here, in this week, Christians, with other emotions than Pilate felt, "behold the man!" They behold him "bearing their griefs and carrying their sorrows," and sustaining "the iniquities of them all." They see him in the guest chamber oppressed in spirit under the prospect of being betrayed, and offering himself in the eucharist in the presence of his disciples for the remission of their sins. They accompany him to Gethsemane, and witness the agony in which he sustains the wrath of God; his fervent prayers; his sweat of blood. They go with him to the judgment hall, and see the humiliation and shame to which he is subjected; the mockery of the multitude; the scourgings of his body; the piercing his temples with the crown of thorns. They ascend Mount Calvary; they behold the cross erected, and see their Saviour extended upon it; they hear him cry as he drinks from them the bitterest dreg of the cup of their deserts, "My God, my God, why hast thou forsaken me!" He dies. Can there be devised a more effectual way of impressing upon them the acts of their Redeemer's Passion? Can it fail to produce some effect upon their memories, their faith, their dispositions? It may be, that in their return to their intercourse with the world, the vividness of the impression may be much diminished. And "He who knoweth whereof we are made; who remembereth that we are but dust," will, we may humbly hope, pardon the unavoidable operation of the innocent concerns of life, upon the religious feelings of those who manifest their desire by stated recurrences to the sources of inspiration, to have in remembrance his marvellous deeds. But still it is probable there will abide in their minds some distinct impression of what the Saviour hath endured, from which, under the influence of the dews of heaven, may spring up some sense of the correspondent obligations. They, surely, will be more likely to be affected by the sufferings of Christ, who, with proper affections, attend the services of the Passion Week, than they by whom it is disregarded. On this account, it was observed with great strictness by the primitive Christians; from whose practice I would derive a further reason for attending devoutly on this institution.

In an adherence to those usages of the ancient Church, which have not been rendered useless by the changes of time, nor shown to be pernicious by the abuse of them, there is, probably, the likeliest way of attaining to the highest effects of the Christian religion. The earliest Christians, influenced by those feelings of their nature which man has manifested in every age and nation, commemorated the great events of the Saviour's life at the times when they happened. The week of his Passion was with them a week of great devotion. They called it "the holy week," and spent it, particularly the four last days of it, in much humiliation, and fasting, and public and private meditations, upon the sufferings and death of the Redeemer. Their penitence was deeper and their faith stronger than ours; and their superiority over us in these respects, may doubtless be attributed, in some degree, to the happy use they made of this and other institutions of the Church, which were founded on principles of human nature, and adapted to promote their growth in grace, and in the knowledge of our Lord and Saviour Jesus Christ. From the first ages down to this present time, this week hath thus been kept holy; and you will esteem it a felicity that, in your Church, the observance of it is retained; and you may be induced to bestow on it your devout attention, if you now proceed to consider some of the dispositions and advantages which the due observance of it is calculated to produce and cherish.

And, in the first place, a disposition suited to this week, and likely to be promoted in us by the scenes which it commemorates, is humility. This is the most important of Christian virtues, and in the collect which is used on the first five days of the week, the production of it in us is represented by the Church as one end of the Saviour's Passion, and made the object of her repeated prayer. And, if anything will humble the heart of man, it must be the recollection of that helplessness and wretchedness of his nature, which made the death of the Son of God necessary for his redemption. If anything can render man ashamed of pride, and make him desire to possess a meek and lowly heart, it must be to behold his Saviour in the scenes through which he passed in the time of his Passion. Behold, thousands of angels minister unto him; yet he "washes his disciples' feet!" "In him dwelt all the fulness of the God-head bodily;" yet he "withheld not his face from shame and spitting!" Lord of all; heir of heaven and earth; yet he endures reproach; he suffers injury and wrong; ignominy and sorrow; he humbles himself, "even to the death upon the cross;" he bears the cross on which he will offer himself, to "take away the sins of the world!" Who of his disciples can follow the Son of God through the stages of his Passion, and not have the pride of his heart reproved, and all the vain dispositions of his nature made to bow before humility? Christians, consider the importance of this grace to your peace, your virtue, your enjoyment of the favour of God; and you will perceive it advantageous to be conversant with the scenes in which it is so impressively taught, so transcendently exemplified.

Another fruit of a right understanding of the Passion Week, is penitence. He, who looks at the cross, can hardly fail to be grieved by his sins. It is in the sufferings and death of our Redeemer, that the strongest motives to repentance are found. The observance of this institution, in the first ages, was mighty to produce among Christians humiliation and fasting for their past offences, and earnest devotion of themselves to "newness of life." Their penitential services were multiplied, they put sackcloth upon themselves, and went mourning; they confessed and bewailed their transgressions, while they commemorated the unparalleled sufferings of the Son of God, by which they were redeemed. And scarcely is it possible for the believer, who comes to this "Lamb of God" to put his hand upon him, that he may be saved, to avoid confessing over him the sins which oppress him, and lifting his eye to heaven, that he may sin no more. It was, indeed, anciently, the penitential week. And we should do well in our use of it, with more than ordinary sorrow, to bewail the corruption of our nature, and imperfection of our lives; to "rend our hearts" before the cross, and "turn unto the Lord our God," while the agonies with which our sins were expiated by him, are presented to our view.

Another fruit, which a devout observance of this week is calculated to produce in us, is patience. Man is placed here in the midst of innumerable evils; and the school in which he may learn patiently to bear them, is the best to which he can be sent. And, virtue of heavenly origin, offspring of faith and hope, which came from above, where shall we behold thee in thy heavenly beauty but in thy attendance upon Jesus Christ, in the week of his Passion and death! "He is led as a lamb to the slaughter, and as a sheep before her shearers is dumb, so he openeth not his mouth." Patience is by him. Her hand holdeth upon the skies. Her lips are still. She looketh, sometimes to heaven, and sometimes she casteth her eyes meekly upon the agents of wrong; the instruments of sorrow. There is seen in her suppression of the rising sigh, her desire to be still; and when she speaks, it is only to say: It is God. Nowhere can the children of men see so much of the nature and beauty of this virtue, as in the week of the Saviour's Passion. He hath exhibited her perfect work. As they accompany him in his sorrows, they may learn to bear their own. Familiarity with his griefs, and with the manner in which he sustained them, will soften the temper, and beget in them an emulation of his gentleness. The things of this life will lose something of their importance, when he is seen willingly renouncing them all; and when he passes through the trials of calumny and pain, of treachery, agony, and death, with such meek composure and pious resignation, they may catch something of his spirit from him, and learn how to endure. Happy, upon all minds, must be the influence of the scenes of our Lord's Passion, but especially so upon children, whose dispositions are forming, and who, on this account, should attend the services of the Church in the holy week.

Again. We are commanded, when we stand praying for any favour from God, to forgive; and are taught that, if "we forgive not men their trespasses, neither will our heavenly Father forgive our trespasses." And where shall such inducements to the cultivation of this important and most difficult virtue be found, as in the scenes of the Saviour's Passion? We should come to them, that we may see and admire this temper in all its perfection, and be incited to possess ourselves of it, by the powerful consideration drawn from his love to us. When we see him washing the feet of him who betrayed him; feeding the disciples who he knew would desert him, with his body and blood; praying for, and affectionately encouraging the Apostle, who, he foresaw, would deny him; laying down his life for the salvation of his persecutors, and praying for his murderers in the agony of death, that his Father would forgive them; it is impossible, if we be conscious of any hatred or malice in our hearts, but that we should doubt, whether the "same mind be in us which was in Christ Jesus." The grandeur of this virtue, as it is seen in him, may excite our admiration of it, and while we behold how much he hath done and suffered for us, who were his enemies, our hearts will be more open to the inspired inference from it, that we ought to forgive, and love one another.

I add that, an attendance on the services of Passion Week, is an excellent preparation for receiving the sacrament at Easter. The dispositions of humility, penitence, submission, and forgiveness, which the Passion of the Saviour is so peculiarly calculated to produce in us, are dispositions which ought always to be carried to the holy table. And when will the Christian's faith be so strong; when will his remembrance of his Redeemer's death be so lively and thankful; when will his love and gratitude be so sincere and ardent, as when he hath been with him in the mazes of his sorrows, beholding him coming from Jerusalem "with dyed garments," and hearing of all the sorrow with which, for our salvation, he gave himself to be afflicted in the day of God's "fierce anger."

Finally. We should keep this week, and attend its services, that we may learn how to die. It is appointed unto us all to pass through the vale of death. To do it well and happily, should be our most anxious desire. From the conduct of our Lord, in the week of his Passion, we have a perfect example. There is a majesty, a transcendent decency, a holy propriety, a peace, in the death of Christ, which renders it worthy to be studied by all mortals. In his care to finish truly the work which his Father had given him to do; in his final instructions of his immediate family, the twelve, whom he had chosen; in his preparation of himself by prayer, and the celebration of the Passover; in his patience and entire resignation of himself concerning what he should suffer, to the will of God; in his provision for his mother, and forgiveness of his enemies; and in his humble commendation of his spirit at the last, into the hands of his Father, we see the lineament of a perfect character, brightening in trial, and consummated in death. As "never man spake like this man," nor lived like this man, so never man died like him. If we attend the scenes of his Passion, with a view to the regulation of our temper and conduct, when we shall be departing out of this life unto the Father, it will be good for us to have been with him in them; as his precepts teach us how to live, his Passion, haply, may teach us how to die.

These, brethren, are some of the considerations which should commend unto you the observance of the Passion Week. If Solomon, in his day, thought there was "a time to mourn," surely the Christian will find it in this sad, this holy, this affecting week, of the sufferings of our dear Redeemer. When you hear of the desertion of him by his disciples, and the denial of him by Peter, I doubt not you are ready to say, If we had been there, we would not thus have done. Be not ashamed, then, to be by his cross, in the season of his sufferings; with his mother, and the amiable women who followed him, and the disciples whom he loveth; if, haply, in reward for your fidelity, he may specially manifest to you his resurrection; and thus enable you to be promulgators to others, of the tidings of his salvation, and in the fullest sense, partakers, in the day of his power, of "the joy of your Lord."

SERMON XXXVIII.

ON THE PASSION.

MATTHEW, xxvi. 18.

"The Master saith, My time is at hand; I will keep the Passover at thy house, with my disciples."

THE part of the gospel history to which we are brought at this season, is stupendous and solemnly interesting. We are entering upon scenes by which the heavens and earth are affected; upon scenes filled with pathos and surprising providence; upon scenes which involve the eternal destinies of man. All is great; all is amazing; all is mournful, in this week of the Saviour's Passion. Jesus, the Son of God, who for our redemption came down from heaven, makes the important arrangements for his departure from our world; falls, betrayed by a disciple, into the hands of his foes; is "taken from prison and from judgment," to the agonies of the cross; expires under a weight of unspeakable sufferings, and slumbers among the dead! We attend the various occurrences in their sad succession; looking through the gloom to the joyous dawn when we shall hail him risen from the tomb, and in holy commemoration keep the great eucharistic feast.

In this eventful period of history, we find the Saviour prescient, collected, and altogether lovely; and not the sublimity of his precepts, nor the purity of his life, does more strikingly display the excellence of his character, or more strongly endear him to our hearts, than the dignity and wisdom with which he anticipated his approaching fate. A very affecting and instructive specimen we have in the lesson read to you this morning, from which I have taken my text. "The first day of the feast of unleavened bread the disciples came to Jesus, saying unto him, where wilt thou that we prepare for thee to eat the Passover? And he said, Go into the city to such a man, and say unto him, The Master saith, My time is at hand; I will keep the Passover at thy house, with my disciples." My design, in the following discourse, is to give these words of our Lord a particular consideration, sure, that the observations they may suggest will not be impertinent to the solemnities of this holy week, and hoping that, under the divine blessing, they may not be altogether useless.

In the first place, we notice the precise foreknowledge of his crucifixion, which the words discover Christ to have possessed. From his first entrance upon active life, he seems, indeed, to have had in his mind a full knowledge of all the events which should be accomplished in him; and kenning with prophecy's highest skill, the exact point of time of every occurrence, declares at one period that "his hour is not yet come;" and at another that "his time is at hand;" to-day, that he can perform safely amidst his foes the work of him that sent him, and "that after two days, he is to be betrayed to be crucified." At the time when the solemn declaration in the text was made, he was undisturbed in the midst of his disciples. His enemies were then busy in preparations for their great Paschal feast. The rulers had determined that he should not be taken during that feast, "lest there should be an uproar among the people." Under these circumstances, that he should in the course of one day, be betrayed, arrested, hurried through the forms of trial, and expire on a cross, was, in itself, in the highest degree improbable. It was at once the consequence and evidence of his intimacy in the bosom of God, that he knew, to an hour, the fulness of time when he should bear the sins of many, and declared it frequently to his followers with such confidence and composure. "Father, the hour is come." "All ye shall be offended because of me this night." "The things concerning me have an end." "Verily, I say unto you, that one of you shall betray me." "Thus shalt thou say unto him, The Master saith, My time is at hand." In these and several other passages of a similar import, a prophetic consciousness is manifested whose explicitness and dignity would suggest what their fulfilment establishes; that in the counsel of redemption the Author and the Father were one.

This foreknowledge of the time when he should suffer, leads us to remark the voluntariness with which our blessed Lord endured the cross. Though the Scriptures speak of God as sending his Son to be the propitiation for our sins; as appointing and giving him to be our mediator, yet we are ever to consider it as the free choice, the unconstrained desire of the Son, to bear our griefs and carry our sorrows, and give his life a ransom for us. Ineffably benevolent in his nature, having by his omniscience, a clear foresight of the glory which would redound to the divine government by the redemption of man, being necessarily coincident in his views and wishes with the whole Godhead that dwelt in him, the Father's will was his will; the Father's counsel was his counsel. And in regard to his manhood, apprized, as he evidently was, of the time and manner of his death, it should seem easy for him to have avoided it; and by withdrawing himself from the scenes and instruments marked out in prophecy for its accomplishment, to have renounced the offices and sufferings of Messiah. But instead of this, knowing his time was at hand he waited for it. Everything in his discourse and conduct was like an unrestrained surrender of himself. Though in the moments of extreme agony he prayed that if it were possible, the bitter cup might pass from him, it was not absolutely and without care for the consequences; for if it was his Father's will he preferred to drink it. Knowing all things that should come upon him, he quitted not his place nor his work, but rather, having in the elements of the Supper first offered himself symbolically, went forth to meet his cross.

This free will, with which Christ became a sacrifice for man's transgression, he was careful to inculcate upon the observation of his followers. He speaks of coming into the world, and of leaving it, as things of his choice; of giving his life a ransom for many, as a voluntary act. "No man taketh it from me, but I lay it down of myself. I have power to lay it down, and I have power to take it again; for as the Father hath life in himself, even so hath he given to the Son to have life in himself."

The same doctrine is explicitly taught by all the writers upon the subject in the Old and New Testament. Nothing like compulsion is conceived in the humiliation and death of the Redeemer. To have obliged him, innocent as he was, and omniscient, to bear against his will the heavy punishment of sinful, inferior beings, would not have appeared consistent with the Father's character, and might have diminished the merit of his atonement. Though the Father, therefore, gives or sends him, there is nothing of force. It is the result of mutual wishes and stipulations. The Son's delight was to make himself an offering for the salvation of our race, and, in the travail of his soul, he was satisfied.

This voluntariness of the Saviour's sufferings, it is important for you always to remember. It forms the consideration which so greatly magnifies his benevolence. It furnishes the motives of that grateful love which we owe him. It opens the ground upon which active philanthropy is most strongly commended to his followers. And it constitutes the unanswerable vindication of the Gospel, against the objections of those who stumble at the supposition that a just and holy God should lay upon an innocent victim the iniquities of us all.

Once more. We may remark, in the passage before us, the wisdom and dignity of our Lord's conduct when his departure from life was at hand. In the first place, he reflected upon it. Sorrowful as it was to be, he did not shrink from the contemplation of it. He gave it a timely consideration. It was the great end for which he was born. It was the act of his being, upon which more depended than words could express. He was to suffer, and to enter into glory; and an event of such pregnancy, to be rightly conducted, required and deserved preparatory attention. He therefore thought of it much. As it approached, it more constantly occupied his mind, and appeared in his conversation. He finished the work which was given him to do. He made every arrangement for the important hour. Such, and so frequent were his reflections upon it, that it could not take him by surprise, nor come too soon. What an example for every man living! When is the period at which any of us may not say, "My time is at hand?" But do we often reflect upon it? Are we prepared to meet it? Do we not put far from our thoughts the day of our death, and leave the principal business of this probationary life to be accomplished at a more convenient season? We may learn from the conduct of our Lord, often to anticipate in our minds our departure from this world to the Father; and if we would entirely imitate his example, much good might arise to ourselves and others from such anticipation.

For we further observe that, to a consideration of his expected end, he added those arrangements which were proper and important. Among these, his tender disclosure of his approaching crucifixion to his little band of disciples, will arrest the attention of every feeling reader of the Gospel. His interview with them, as exhibited from the thirteenth to the eighteenth of John, is one of the most affecting pieces of scene and dialogue that the human mind ever contemplated. He informs them that he is about to leave them, and of the awful issue of the treachery by which his death would be effected. In tender precept, and impressive illustration, he instructs them how to behave when he shall be gone. He reasons with them of the necessity of his departure, and how it should turn to their benefit. Consoling their sorrows, guarding them against the world, its seductions and trials, instructing them in every excellence, and leading them in his blessings to look for happiness in heavenly things, he rises in his troubles, and is loveliest in his saddest hour. How interesting and impressive when, to teach his disciples humility and kindness, he rises from supper and washes their feet. Who can behold unmoved, the affecting scene, when oppressed with regret, with concern, with the weight of the afflicting truth, he declared to them that one of them would betray him. How solemn and paternal does he appear when instituting and celebrating the great Christian sacrament, of which I shall presently speak. What more affecting than his language; his blessing. "Little children, yet a little while I am with you;" "love one another." "Peace I leave with you, my peace I give unto you; not as the world giveth, give I unto you. Let not your heart be troubled, neither be afraid." And again: "These things have I spoken unto you, that in me ye might have peace. In the world ye shall have tribulation; but be of good cheer, I have overcome the world." The time would fail me to quote all the excellent instructions and wise arrangements of our Lord, which the consideration that "his time was at hand," prompted him to make. Yet, long could I descant upon his transactions towards his disciples, his beloved family, in this close of his life. For I consider it as holding out to you, and to every good man, an unequalled example, a perfect model by which you may form your own conduct when your departure shall be drawing near. Here, you may learn to set your houses in order before you die, and to make every arrangement which may be necessary to the quiet, and conducive to the comfort of those whom you may leave behind. Here, you may learn to gather your family around you, with the voice of affection, to reconcile them to your departure, and with the counsel of wisdom, to instruct them concerning their lives. Here, you may learn from the example of Christ, that peace is better than pleasure, to leave to your offspring; and that the last injunctions which should tremble upon the parental lip are, to have trust in God, and to love one another. Sweet scene, when the head of a household, having timely made all other arrangements, spends his last hours in pointing others to heaven, and breathing upon his family the blessings of religious peace! Sweet scene! It is consoling to survivors; it is elevating to the human character; it must be beheld with pleasure by the Deity himself.

But I am reminded by my text, and brought by these remarks to notice a peculiarly striking trait of our Lord's conduct, when he knew that his sufferings were at hand. I mean his concern to eat the Passover. "The Master saith, My time is at hand; I will eat the Passover at thy house, with my disciples."

The Passover was the great ordinance of the law under which he was born. It was instituted by the Almighty, for his people to commemorate their deliverance from bondage, and favour with Jehovah; and as it led them to contemplate the greatness of his mercy and power on whom they were dependent, it must have been, to the serious Jew, a source of comfort and satisfaction. It was now, the thirteenth day of the month Abib, in which they were to make ready, and the even of which was the commencement of the fourteenth day, when they were to eat the Passover. Our Saviour had uniformly walked in all the commandments of the law, and this ordinance, of strong obligation and solemn significance, he had observed with undeviating regularity. Now, indeed, he knew, that before the sacrifice of the lamb would be over, he, of whose own blood its purple stream had for ages been an emblem, would be offered upon the cross. But for his disciples' sake, and for his regard to divine institutions, he would not, even in this hour of sorrow, abate one jot of his obedience. The houses of the Jews were, at this season, common to strangers. It is probable, however, that Christ sent his disciples to a man whom he knew, and had disposed to receive them, that under his roof they might make the usual preparations. They did accordingly; and there, with the twelve, he spent the last evening of his life, celebrating the appointed Paschal feast. If there were nothing more, this care of our Master to "fulfil all righteousness," and his observance of this ordinance, when the sorrows of death approached, hold out a mirror to every Christian, in which he may see a striking and beautified image of his duty. But in him who had no sins to cover, and no blessings to secure, there must have been something of mighty import, to have occasioned the earnest declaration, "With desire have I desired to eat this Passover with you, before I suffer." If we attend to the transactions of the evening, we shall find that this was, indeed, the case. It was at this last meeting with his friends, that he abolished the typical ordinance which was about to be fulfilled, and instituted in its stead, with bread and the cup, that sacrament whereby his death, of which the sacrifice of the Paschal lamb was only a shadow, should, in all ages, be shown forth until he comes. This was, probably, one cause of his anxiety to eat this Passover with his disciples. He now gave them to understand that they were henceforth to commemorate a greater deliverance than that which freed them from Egyptian bondage; that, as he had done, they, and all Christians to the end of time, should do in remembrance of him.

When we consider our Lord, first observing the ordinance which was yet in force, and then instituting upon it the Christian Supper, his example in the former, and his authority in the latter, furnish his disciples with a double motive to observe his holy sacrament. When I contemplate him, longing to be with his disciples at this Passover, that he might change it into a joyous memorial of his death; when I see him employing the last hours he should spend with them, in celebrating this Christian feast; when I hear him saying to his followers, Eat ye all of this bread, which is my body; drink ye all of this cup, which is my blood; when I ponder the import of this sacrament, its uses, the affecting circumstances under which it was ordained, and the claim of its Author to our entire obedience, I see not how any, who, with godly sincerity, are his disciples, can ever abstain from it. In every period of life, peaceful is the reflection, that we have endeavoured to "fulfil all righteousness," "to walk in the commandments and ordinances of the Lord blameless." And when the sorrows of death compass us around, and the pains of dissolution are getting hold upon us, memory can present no more pleasing recollection than that we have eaten of that flesh, and drank of that blood, of which, whosoever partaketh righteously, hath eternal life abiding in him. In that trying period, when our time is at hand, we should learn from the example of Christ, to seek in our Passover, the holy viands which may support us under the terrors and pains which most men apprehend, and many endure, in passing through the valley of the shadow of death. Trying is the hour, and what can be more consoling to the departing spirit, than the pledges of the Redeemer's love; what more animating than the holy mysteries whereby God hath sealed to us the pardon of our sins, and the precious promise of everlasting life.

But, finally, we must not omit to notice, among the acts of our Saviour when his end approached, his retirement after finishing his purposes, to devotion and communion with the Most High. With the world he had done. His Father alone could support him in the hour which was at hand. All of business, all of duty, all of preparation that remained, was between him and his God. Withdrawn, therefore, from all interruptions, he seeks the Almighty, and gives himself to ardent prayer. And in this holy occupation Jesus continued, till the commencement of the outrages upon him. Powerful comment upon the precept of his gospel, "is any afflicted, let him pray." Here, for the present, we shall leave him; but not, I trust, without learning from his example, the wisdom of betaking ourselves from the world and its phantoms, to the Father of our spirits, when we find our end approaching. Surely, it is time to have done with the pomps and vanities of life, when we are on the borders of eternity. Surely, it is time to draw near to God when we are losing our hold upon every thing else. It is communion with our Maker that will preserve in us a sense of our connection with him. And it is the tie which connects us with him, that will bind to the soul its most precious amulet, the hope of immortality. Happy, then, are they whom death, when he comes, finds in communion with their God. Appalled at their devotion, he drops the poison with which he was envenoming his shaft, and, instead of taking, resigns to heaven his prey.

Thus I have set before you some of the instructions suggested by this interesting passage in the gospel of the day. I might enlarge; but already I have trespassed too much upon your patience. One closing observation forces itself upon your minds; that our blessed Redeemer hath taught us how to die, as well as how to live; that in all the successive scenes of his Passion, he hath left us an example, that we should follow his steps.

SERMON XXXIX.

ON GOOD FRIDAY.

JOHN, i. 29.

"Behold the Lamb of God which taketh away the sins of the world."

I AM to address you, my brethren, to-day, upon the most solemn subject which can ever be contemplated by man. It is not to the character of any important virtue that I am to call your attention, but to Jesus Christ, the source and example of all virtues. It is not in the sweet periods of his life, when he is feeding the hungry, instructing the ignorant, and healing the sick, that I am to set him before you; but in the hour of his crucifixion, when he is nailed to the accursed tree. Here is no glorious light from heaven as on the morning of the nativity; but the sun withdraws his shining, and the heavens are shrouded in gloom. Here are no multitudes of the heavenly hosts, uttering their joyful acclamations; but in the darkness of the skies, imagination pictures angels and archangels hovering in amazement over their suffering Lord, and all the hosts of the Almighty meditating, in mute astonishment, the issue of the stupendous event. Here is no peaceful scene; no pulse of joy shot through the bosom of nature at the descent of her God; no shepherd returning with joy, nor wise men approaching with gifts; but horror reigns! The earth quakes; rocks are rent; the dead are moved; a wonder-struck multitude, who had gone out as to a common spectacle, are returning, smiting their breasts.

To set this event before you in all its magnitude, requires other eloquence than mine; lips touched like Isaiah's, with coals that have been taken from the altars of heaven. For myself, when I contemplate God, "found in fashion as a man," and humbled to "the death upon the cross," for the redemption of our sinful race, I am overwhelmed by the greatness of the mystery! It is a "depth of the riches both of the wisdom and knowledge of God," which human thoughts are unable to fathom! We know not its relations and influence to other worlds. We know but in part the measure of its importance, and the extent of its consequences to this. And the circumstances of it, the emotions it should excite in us, the fear, and gratitude, and faith, and obedience it should beget in us, who is able adequately to describe? All I can do is to stand with you at the foot of the cross; to wonder with you, and adore; and, taking the language of inspiration for my parable, to exhort you to "behold," in the expiring Jesus, "the Lamb of God that taketh away the sins of the world!"

The Saviour of the world is frequently represented in the sacred writings under the figure of a Lamb. For this there were divers reasons. Meek, innocent, and patient, this gentle animal presented a significant emblem of His character who would be "brought as a lamb to the slaughter, and as a sheep before her shearers is dumb, so he would not open his mouth." In that ritual, which, in the twilight of revelation, shadowed forth the distant substance of the Christian economy, the lamb, therefore, was appointed to be the sacrifice which should be offered daily for a sweet savour unto the Lord. But more especially in the Passover, when the victim was slain, by the mark of whose blood God's people were preserved, the lamb was chosen for the victim. In these types was Jesus Christ set forth anciently to the eye of faith, as the sacrifice with which the sins of the world were to be expiated, and, on account of the innocence of his nature and the efficacy of his blood, prophets, and apostles, and angels, conceive of him under the image of a lamb.

But he is also styled in the text, and in many other passages of the sacred writings, "the Lamb of God;" and for this I shall mention two reasons, which, while you are contemplating the sacrifice of the death of Christ, may impress you with a sense of the greatness of the victim, and of the wonderful loving kindness of our God.

Probably, on a part of the very mount on which Christ was crucified, Abraham said to Isaac, "My son, God will provide himself a lamb for a burnt offering." The words were prophetic. Jesus is styled emphatically "the Lamb of God," because he was provided for us by the Almighty. For the purposes for which Christ was slain, man had nothing to offer to his Maker. "All the beasts of the forest were" already "his, and the cattle upon the thousand hills." Could man have ranged through all worlds, and called the creatures which are in them his own, he could not have found a victim, whose blood would have been efficacious in the sight of God to wash away sin. Foreseeing the fall of man, and knowing that there could be found no voice to help, no arm to uphold, God, in infinite mercy, from the foundation of the world, provided the sacrifice by which the transgressions of his children might be expiated, and they ransomed from destruction. And in the ram caught providentially by his horns, and substituted by the Patriarch in the room of his son, who was first required, was typified the offering which the providence of the Almighty had prepared for our race, and should, in due time, be substituted in our stead. Well is he denominated "the Lamb of God" who was thus provided for and given to us by the Almighty.

But where was this precious sacrifice found? Whence came this victim, whose blood is of such unspeakable value and singular efficacy? It is further to be observed by us, that he is styled "the Lamb of God," because he was near and dear to the Most High. In the person of his Son, God beheld the image of his own glory. He who came down from heaven, to be offered in our behalf, was far above all principalities and powers in his state, and without equal in his nature. Near to the Father as his only begotten, and dear to him as his perfectly obedient Son, he was with the Father from all eternity, the object of his supreme regard, and heir of his glory and worship. Yet this exalted Being, whom angels adore, is sent to take upon him our flesh, and become obedient to death. This object of God's delight, this pure, and holy, and beloved heir of his perfections, is given to be our ransom and atonement. And it was, probably, with a particular view to him, as the Lamb provided to be the propitiation of our sins, and to teach us both the value and the efficacy of his blood, that the Father proclaimed at his entrance upon his office, "This is my beloved Son, in whom I am well pleased."

Our need of such an atonement it becomes us to-day to consider. This Son of the Almighty, this immaculate "Lamb of God," it is not without great expediency and use that he is sacrificed upon the cross. Not but for purposes of infinite moment hath it pleased the Father thus to bruise him. It is not without respect to the glory of his government that hath put him to this unparalleled grief. This "Lamb" was "slain" in the counsels of heaven "from the foundation of the world;" and it is in virtue of the mediation and atonement which he hath consummated on the cross, that the human race were saved from the doom of destruction, and have received from the Almighty the overtures of pardon and everlasting life. His blood is the purchase of our redemption.

Man is "by nature, born in sin," and, consequently, under the government of a holy God is "the child of wrath." This the pages of his history in every age prove. And of this every one has too sensible experience, too indubitable evidence in his own bosom. Of his inability to expiate his own offences he has everywhere manifested a common sentiment. Wherever we find him thoughtful of his condition and mindful of his God, we find him by an altar, offering a victim, with whose blood he is hoping to propitiate his Maker. Nowhere has he reposed with confidence in his own righteousness. Nowhere has he trusted wholly to his contrition and tears. The universal prevalence of this idea indicates that it is either very obvious to natural reason, or has been derived to all men from the same external source. That the soul, in some solemn moments, may have just apprehensions of her inability to make reparation for her offences, might perhaps be admitted. But there is no congruity in the nature of the things, between shedding of blood, and remission of sins; the connection between one and the other is by no means obvious to reason; and we are left to infer that God who only could be the one unchangeable source of instruction, informed man soon after his fall, of his inability to be justified without an atonement, and graciously taught him to stay his faith and soothe his anxieties with typical sacrifices, till the great sacrifice should be offered for him, in which he should find his peace.

In truth, by the first transgression man became a debtor to the divine justice in a sum which he could never have paid. The arm of vengeance was stretched out against him, and but for the intervention of Christ, he must have gone into irretrievable perdition. And we, his posterity, "wherewith should we have come before the Lord, and bowed ourselves before the Most High God?" With the sorrows of our first parents, we inherit also their sinfulness. And guilty in the sight of the Almighty, on what ground should we plead for pardon and favour? Should we trust to our good deeds? Alas! they are inconstant, and the best of them alloyed with many imperfections. Should we trust to our repentance? That, too, is imperfect, and utterly disproportionate to our offences, and followed often by repeated transgression. Should we betake ourselves to the mercy of God? One of his attributes is never exerted in opposition to another; and both the honour of his government and the happiness of his creatures would require the execution of his righteous laws. Should we, then, have recourse, with Jews and heathens, to victims and oblations? In themselves, the Lord hath no delight in burnt offerings. Though countless lambs should bleed upon a thousand altars, they could never take away sin. We need "an advocate with the Father," such as the Father only could appoint; we need a "propitiation for our sins," such as God only could provide. Were it not for this precious victim upon whom the Father looks from his throne, and remembers his covenant and mercies, we should have nothing to plead in mitigation of our sentence, but might justly expect to be driven from his presence and to lie down in sorrow. At best we should wander through life uncertain of his favour; and death would overtake us unconsoled with the knowledge that there is a fountain set open in which the stain of our iniquities may be washed away, and a price paid for our redemption from destruction.

The certainty and efficacy of this sacrifice of Christ, as that which God, in his great love towards mankind, had prepared to take away their sins, remains yet to be considered. Intimations of this his mercy, the Almighty gave in the hour of their conviction, to the first offenders. He afterwards gradually unfolded the scheme of it in prophecies, types, and figures, to his chosen servants in every age. And all the marks by which "the Lamb of God" was to be known; all the qualities and sufferings and circumstances of death, by which he was to be distinguished, are found united in Christ.

You behold him to-day offered precisely at the time appointed in the midst of the predicted week; when "the sceptre was departed from Judah," while the second temple was yet standing, whose "vail was" presently "rent from top to the bottom." You see all things that were written, that the Messiah should suffer; by such sufferings it was requisite we should be delivered. The remembrance of the cross should be an incitement in us to all goodness. How shall we, for whom our Lord has done and suffered such things, by living in sin, "crucify him afresh, and put him again to shame."

Finally. Let us justly estimate the obligations we are under to the Lord, our Redeemer. In heaven he is known as "the Lamb of God;" and "ten thousand times ten thousand, and thousands of thousands" of angels bow, we are told, before him, "saying, with a loud voice, Worthy is the Lamb that was slain, to receive power, and riches, and wisdom, and strength, and honour, and glory, and blessing." "The four and twenty elders" also "fall down before him, having, every one of them, harps, and golden vials full of odours, which are the prayers of saints." How great is our obligation to love and adore him, for whose sakes he was slain. To the praises, then, which we know to be chanted in the temple above, let our lips and lives say amen: "Blessing, and honour, and glory, and power, be unto Him that sitteth upon the throne, and unto the Lamb, for ever and ever."

SERMON XL.

ON GOOD FRIDAY.

LUKE, xxiii. 48.

"And all the people that came together to that sight, beholding the things which were done, smote their breasts and returned."

THE crucifixion of Jesus Christ is, to us, the most stupendous and interesting part of the economy of God. Creation is an astonishing display. The scenes of nature strongly interest, through the consciousness that we have in them a part. Every object about us fills the contemplative with amazement. But before them all, for grandeur of design, for solemnity of circumstance, for greatness of expression, and for connection with man's destiny and duty, is the mystery of the cross. This envelops all that is important to our race; all that will nourish astonishment forever, and ever deserve our most grateful consideration. To be, indeed, actual spectators of the crucifixion, and with "the people who came together at that sight, to behold the things which were done," was not our lot. Yet, to ponder it as a thing accomplished, with its mighty consequences, the sacred narrative, and our interest in it, require; nor will reflection ever fail to furnish such views of the subject as will compel the good man to smite his breast with even deeper amazement, and juster determinations than theirs, whom the text exhibits returning, awe-struck, from the solemn scene.

It is now the season in which the mighty event had its accomplishment. Having carried us through the sad occurrences which preceded it, the Church has brought us, to-day, to the foot of the cross, that we may contemplate its truth, magnitude, and import. But who shall set these in a full light. For me; I am lost in this "depth of the riches both of the wisdom and goodness of God;" yea, it is a theme too deep for human expression. Yet, to assist your conceptions of its greatness, and suitably to improve this holy time, I would raise your contemplations to the greatness of the Person who suffered, the greatness of the sufferings he endured, and the greatness of the end, or consequence of his suffering. These are points with which your breasts should be thoroughly penetrated, on this sacred day, and, if properly considered, may exceed, in impressiveness upon the believing mind, the actual sight of the transactions, which wrought such emotions in the Jewish spectators.

Of the greatness of the Person who suffered, how shall I give you an adequate idea! Consider his origin. An eternal emanation of God. "The only begotten," and "well beloved Son" of the Father. The equal sharer of the glories of the Godhead; the noblest inhabitant of heaven. Consider his state. It was "he, by whom all things were made, and without whom, was not any thing made, that was made;" he, into whose hands the everlasting Father had put all power; the Creator and Lord of heaven and of earth. Consider his character; he lived on earth a perfect being. The unsullied purity and sublimity which were in him, and shone through the veil of his flesh, realize, in fact, all that the mind can form of ideal beauty, or rather, furnish the only image of perfect excellence with which the mind is acquainted. He "did no sin, neither was guile found in his mouth." Before him the sages who approach nearest to perfection, are as nothing; yea, our conceptions of angelic excellence will not raise us to the majesty of his character; for, with conscious inferiority, they bow themselves in his presence, and are commanded by the Highest to worship him. His unconquerable meekness and patience; his unequalled love and dignity of soul; the signals of divinity which he displayed at death, and the agitations of all nature as he expired, wrung from his foes, even from his guards and crucifiers, the just acknowledgment of his greatness, "Truly, this was the Son of God." Like the sun, he rose amidst the mists of morn; brightened on his course, and set without contracting spot or blemish, or sustaining any diminution of his glory, in all that lustre which he unceasingly shed, while travelling in the greatness of his strength.

Here the transition is easy from the Person to the greatness of the sufferings he endured. Prophecy, the mysterious messenger of heaven, was early, and at various periods, sent to announce to mankind the appearance of this great Personage in their world. With different degrees of precision, at different times, she drew the character she described, the course of the coming Christ. But in every portrait, in every sketch, conflict and suffering were conspicuous. Her first whisper was, that "his heel" should be wounded by the serpent, whose "head" he would "bruise." As time advanced, she unfolded, gradually, all he should endure, from the persecutions of his infancy to the last insult of the piercing spear. Now, she breaks forth as if beholding one covered with anxiety and blood: and now, with pencil dipped in saddest hue, she gives the entire and affecting piece. "He shall grow up as a tender plant, and as a root out of a dry ground; he hath no form nor comeliness; and when we shall see him, there is no beauty that we should desire him. He is despised and rejected of men; a man of sorrows, and acquainted with grief. He was oppressed, and he was afflicted, yet he opened not his mouth. He is brought as a lamb to the slaughter; and as a sheep before her shearers is dumb, so he openeth not his mouth. He was taken from prison and from judgment; and who shall declare his generation; for he was cut off out of the land of the living."

Such was the description which prophecy gave of him, whose ancient herald she was. Her picture of his griefs was not too highly wrought. He realized them all. To pass over his early humiliation and poverty; to omit the persecutions, troubles, and difficulties which marked his life; the guest chamber and judgment hall, Gethsemane and Calvary, will furnish specimens of all the sorrows which human nature can taste and deprecate. Behold the commencement of his Passion, when, with deep anguish, he perceives that one, whom he had honoured, should betray him. Dread apprehension of the approaching weight of woe, brings on "an agony," in which nature scarcely sustains, sweating, "as it were, great drops of blood," through intense distress. In sorrowful retreat, he is arrested as a thief at night, and friendship's token is prostituted, to designate him. Now he is dragged before a heathen tribunal, and mockeries, buffeting and spitting, from a rabble populace, are silently endured. Though pronounced innocent, he is delivered to the scourge, and wanton cruelty contrives new pains. At length he is doomed to death, and hurried, with malefactors, to the shame and tortures of the cross.

Great as is the Person who is immolated on the cross, and uncommon as is the measure of his sorrows, the manner is equally wonderful in which he endures them. It is here that we may learn to endure. Observe his meekness and patience. This Son of God is led "as a lamb to the slaughter, and as a sheep before her shearers is dumb, so he openeth not his mouth." Ponder his humility. He is God; but he takes upon him "the form of a servant." He submits to be bound, to be scourged, to be mocked; he humbles himself "to death, even the death of the cross." Consider his conduct towards his crucifiers. They exhaust their ingenuity to torment him. They spend their strength in vexing him. No insult, no mockery, no cruelty which they can devise, is omitted. But not an emotion of resentment rises. There is something of the God in his deportment. They excite his commiseration: "Father, forgive them, for they know not what they do." Examine his resignation. His "soul is exceedingly sorrowful." "Being in an agony" under the woe he sustains, "his sweat was as it were great drops of blood falling down to the ground." Under the feelings of nature he wishes, if it were possible, this dreadful hour might pass from him;

"nevertheless, not my will, but thine be done." See him die. His anguish ruffles not his bosom. To show that nature is not exhausted, and his death voluntary, he cries "with a loud voice." And what are his words? "Father, into thy hands I commend my spirit." And when he had so said, "he yielded up the ghost." Search the pages of history. Go to all the scenes of death. Bring together all the great ones of the earth; where will you find such meekness, such patience, such piety, such benevolence, such fortitude, such generosity, such equanimity? Who hath suffered, who hath died like Jesus Christ? The lustre of his greatness illumines the body of death. We forget, for a moment, the cross, in admiration of the wonderful virtue which encompasses the victim upon it. Surely, thou virgin mother, though "thy soul be now pierced through with a sword," some admiration of his transcendent greatness in death, must occasionally brighten thy mind; thou wilt keep all these things, and ponder them in thy heart.

Amazing scene! Unparalleled sufferings! How exact a counterpart of prophecy's descriptions! We can scarcely contemplate them without adopting her words: "Was ever sorrow like unto his sorrow, which was done unto him, wherewith the Lord afflicted him in the day of his fierce anger." But, observe the testimonies which God, in this awful hour, gives to the character of his Son. The situation of the heavenly bodies admits of no eclipse. But, nevertheless, the sun is darkened! It is not the country nor the season of extraordinary throes of nature. But the earth quakes; the rocks are rent; the graves are opened! No voice of an archangel is heard; no trump of God sounds; yet, many of them that sleep in the dust, now hear the voice of the Son of Man, and awake, and are seen with him in the city, partakers of his resurrection! Long has the Holy of Holies been hidden from every eye but that of the high priest. Man saw not yet the mercy-seat. But, as Jesus dies, the veil of the temple is rent from before the cherubim, and shortly after the temple itself is demolished, and Jerusalem, the glorious holy city, passes away.

Do any question the extremity of the sufferings which Christ endured? They are recorded by heathen and Jewish, as well as sacred historians. Are the supernatural concomitants of the crucifixion doubted? The awful darkness is particularized by several profane writers, which, at that season, could not have been caused by eclipse, and there are not wanting considerate men, who conceive that the earth yet bears the marks of her convulsions. Are the effects of the scene upon the minds of the crucifiers thought improbable? Scarcely can the skeptic, who has not lost all feeling, ponder the account of it without similar emotions. The circumstances of Christ's suffering wrought deep conviction of his divinity in one of the most famous and ingenious of his adversaries, to whom prophecy had in vain opened her wonders, and miracles their strength.

But we hasten to what gives still more interest to the crucifixion; the purpose of it. Wherefore is the Son of God thus bruised? Why does this spotless, glorious Being thus die? These are sorrows "wherewith the Lord hath afflicted him in the day of his fierce anger." But is God displeased with his beloved Son? Is there anger for him who hath done "no sin?" No. He suffers, "the just for the unjust." "The Lord hath laid on him the iniquity of us all." Alienated from his Maker by transgression, and having voluntarily subjected himself to the penalty of sin, man must have perished had not the Eternal Son appeared in his behalf, to expiate his sins, and satisfy the requirements of offended justice. We see human nature desolate. Men are subject to sin, and to the consequences of it, pain, and misery, and death. Every person carries the evidence of this in himself. He sees it in all about him. Fallen and helpless, he has nothing to offer to propitiate his Maker. Repentance he cannot have without his Maker's help, and when he has it, it makes no atonement. Future obedience he would have owed if he had not sinned. This, therefore, makes not satisfaction. Besides, his obedience, when he has turned to his Maker, is all imperfect. His own righteousness, to the end of his days, is much alloyed. How, then, shall his

Maker be reconciled? How shall the wrath of heaven be turned away? He needs some friend to stand between him and his God and make his peace. Satisfied would be the justice of heaven, and sure his salvation, if there were some one to take his sins, and sustain the punishment of them. But where should such a prevailing intercessor; where should such a disinterested Saviour be found? His fellow-men—they can do nothing. Every one for himself needs a deliverer. No man may "redeem his brother, or give to God any ransom" for his own soul. The angels—they owe for themselves a perpetual obedience, and who among them would be of sufficient strength if, indeed, of sufficient benevolence, to sustain for a sinful world the wrath of its offended God? God looked, but there was none to help. Therefore his own arm brought salvation. In the person of the Son, he came down from heaven to purchase our redemption with his blood. He is our peace. "He hath borne our griefs, and carried our sorrows." God "hath made him to be sin for us, who knew no sin; that we might be made the righteousness of God in him."

By graciously giving himself a ransom for us, and consenting to pour out his soul unto death, Christ arrested the arm raised to execute the just sentence upon the sinner, and restored man to the favour of his God. To make this atonement for fallen man, and effect this reconciliation between him and his offended Creator, was the vast purpose of the Saviour's death. A world of beings is saved by it from impending destruction. Having interceded for them, he, in the fulness of time, made their satisfaction, by bearing "their sins in his own body" upon the cross, and through the everlasting righteousness which he brought in, became their peace. The Prophets and Apostles, though remotely distant, in sweet accord proclaim "he was wounded for our transgressions, he was bruised for our iniquities." "He was delivered for our offences." "We are saved through his blood." "By his stripes we are healed." But not only life, the hope also of eternal life is given us in this redemption. "For if," says St. Paul, "when we were enemies, we were reconciled to God by the death of his Son, much more, being reconciled, we shall be saved by his life." While we behold in the cross the seal of the remittance of the penalty to which man had subjected himself, we behold in it also the earnest of his future felicity. Having by "his oblation of himself, made the full, perfect, and sufficient sacrifice and satisfaction for the sins of the world," Christ entered into the Holy of Holies with his own blood, there "to appear in the presence of God for us." While thus we contemplate him, pleading his merits with the Father, and think, amazed, how, in this work, the Father hath commended to us his love, we are enabled to adopt the inspired sentiment: "He that spared not his own Son, but delivered him up for us all, how shall he not with him also freely give us all things?"

And yet we have, perhaps, but an imperfect knowledge of the consequences of this great event. That there are higher orders of moral beings, and that it has reference to them, the Scriptures plainly evidence and declare. But what their natures, numbers, or condition, and how they are interested in the mystery of redemption we are not informed. We know that, by it is made known "to principalities and powers," the "manifold wisdom of God;" that angels make it the subject of their consideration; that the hosts of heaven are not less occupied than the ransomed of the Lord, in celebrating the praises of the Lamb. Still, to perceive the Christian mystery in all its connections; to behold it in all its importance and results, is, doubtless, impossible, till the final consummation, when we shall cease to "see through a glass darkly," and be admitted to the presence and full fruition of God.

Christians: these are some of the most striking parts of the crucifixion. As we ponder, we should profit. The Church brings us to the cross, that we should think of them, and that we should think of them for our good. While we consider who it is that died upon the cross, we may learn how much love and gratitude we owe to God, who "spared not his own Son, but gave him up for us all," and to the Son, who consented to empty himself of all his glory; to be thus abased; thus to die; that he might make "satisfaction for the sins of the world," and redeem men from destruction to eternal life. While we contemplate the extraordinary sorrows which the Son of God sustained, and by which he made the expiation, we may learn how great an evil sin is, and find the strongest incitement to repent of our past offences, and to endeavour to cultivate the dispositions and duties which are pleasing in God's sight. From the manner in which we have seen our Lord sustaining his sorrows, we should learn to be meek and humble; to be patient; to be gentle towards all men; to forgive our enemies; to be obedient to the will of God. The testimonies which, at his death, confirmed the character of the Son of God, should establish our confidence in him; and from our knowledge of the end for which he suffered and died, we should draw hope, and faith, and peace.

Thus, I have endeavoured to assist your conceptions of the magnitude of the event we commemorate, by setting before you the greatness of the Person who suffered, the greatness of his sufferings, and the greatness of the ends which they effected. When collecting our views of the subject, with how much greater amazement and devotion should we "smite our breast," than the awe-struck multitude who saw only the solemnity, without the import of the scene. For us, the Son of God laid down his life. Impressed with the odiousness of sin, which required thus to be expiated, let his blood purge our consciences from evil works. With gratitude for his sufferings, "let us go forth to him without the camp, bearing his reproach." Let it be the holiest occupation of our hearts, to "show forth his death till he come." And, kindling our love at the exhaustless source of his, let it be the main object of our lives to attain, through his merit, to a union with the ten thousands that surround his throne, in singing, "Worthy is the Lamb that was slain, to receive power, and riches, and wisdom, and strength, and honour, and glory, and blessing."

SERMON XLI.

ON GOOD FRIDAY.

ISAIAH, liii. 5.

"But he was wounded for our transgressions, he was bruised for our iniquities; the chastisement of our peace was upon him; and with his stripes we are healed.

WE are called, this day, to witness a scene of such sufferings, as have been but once realized upon earth. The innocent Jesus, who descended from heaven to bless and instruct our race; "who did no sin, neither was guile found in his mouth;" whose life had been one uniform display of love to mankind, and divine perfections, is betrayed by his disciple, seized by a rabble band, dragged to judgment as a base criminal, and, amidst the most wanton barbarities, and aggravated humiliations, condemned to be crucified. By inconceivable agonies of body and mind, his condemnation is preceded. It is followed by every cruelty which unfeeling malice can inflict. To the torture and mockery of a crown of thorns, they bind his sacred head. "He hides not his face from shame and spitting." The cruelties of the scourge lacerate his body. And it is not till humanity is fainting under its burthen, that they lead him away to crucify him. At Golgotha, the cup of suffering overflows. Every ingredient which can embitter it, is infused. To the cross, the most ignominious and painful instrument of death, the patient victim is nailed. With taunts and insults, inhumanity, and outrage, are the agonies of crucifixion aggravated. An awful withdrawing of the divine smile, compels, from the overwhelmed sufferer, the cry, "My God, my God, why hast thou forsaken me!" A pause ensues. The wonderful man, in patience possesses his spirit. Exhausted, at length, with the weight he bears, and conscious of the accomplishment of some mighty purpose, the Author of our faith, cries, "It is finished," and with unsullied innocence, "gives up the ghost." Earth feels the death, and quakes. The heavens are wrapt in gloom. The guards appalled, confess a Divinity. The spectators amazed, "smite their breasts and return."

Great God! Is this the Son of thy love, whom thou didst send to visit and instruct our world? Under thy government, is he thus received by those whom he came to bless; and requited with a heavier fate than is allotted to the basest of the sons of men? Wherefore hath it pleased thee, thus to "bruise" him? Wherefore, while thou dost behold, is the innocent heir of thy perfections and love, put to this unparalleled grief, ignominy, and death?

The end and design of the sufferings of Christ are explained to us by the Prophet of the Most High, in the pathetic words of my text: "He was wounded for our transgressions; he was bruised for our iniquities; the chastisement of our peace was upon him; and by his stripes we are healed."

But what means the Prophet, when he speaks of beings without health or peace, and obnoxious to punishment? The offspring of the Eternal must necessarily be all pure; and, as man was made and fashioned by him, he must have come from his Maker's hands without sin, unhappiness, or imperfection. It is evidently of a ruined race the Prophet speaks; for to no beings, not corrupted from the state in which the Almighty formed them, can the character of trangressors laden with iniquity and misery, be ever applied.

The truth is, the wretched condition which the text supposes to belong to man, is the condition in which he is left by the fall. Revelation teaches us what it would be difficult not to believe, that when the Almighty formed man, he made him upright and just, furnished with the means and fitted for the enjoyment of unadulterated happiness. That moral nature, which was his glory, and capacitated him for the felicities for which he was designed, required that he should be free, and his Sovereign Creator thought it best, that a sense of his dependence should be impressed on him, and his obedience tried by an easy, benevolent, and explicit law, which, with his own lips, he gave him. Had we time, we might show in this economy, the wisdom and goodness of the Deity, and his royal regard to the welfare of his new moral creatures. But at present it concerns us only to observe, that in the use of that freedom with which he was ennobled, man violated the law of his Maker, in defiance of the awful penalty of death with which it was sanctioned. The divine displeasure was now incurred; misery and destruction became the sinner's doom, and thus the race were ruined. The solemn monuments of this fall are everywhere too numerous. Alas! we, too, certainly carry them about us, in this earthly tabernacle. All that we inherit from the first Adam, is a nature subject to a curse; its peace with its author and with itself broken; its spiritual and moral health impaired; and death its awful desert. If the justice of the Most High should be executed according to his law, the fruit of the transgression must inevitably be, an utter extinction from his creation, or a hopeless state of continually increasing sinfulness and misery.

But, loved for ever be our God; his feelings for the creatures of his hand, are the feelings of a parent; and he was tenderly solicitous, in some way consistently with his truth and holiness, to recover his prodigal offspring from the ruin which they had incurred. His holiness filled him with an abhorrence of sin. His immutable truth required that the law he had given should be executed. The honour of his government over all orders of intelligent beings, and for aught we know, the measure of their respect for it, were implicated in the punishment of the transgressors. Yet his infinite mercy pitied the victims of temptation; his benevolence wished to save this fair portion of his creation from the fatal fruit of their sin.

Here, it was, that the fulness of the Father's wisdom and holiness, and love, were displayed, in devising the scheme by which he would accomplish his gracious desire. If any one could be found to take man's guilt upon him, and bear its desert; if there were any being sufficiently holy to expiate sin, and sufficiently benevolent to devote himself to the work; who would place himself in the stead of man, and answer fully for his transgressions, the hapless creature might be rescued from death, and the justice of heaven, at the same time, satisfied. There is nothing in reason, or the nature of things, with which this would be incompatible; but if the act were voluntary in the substitute, everything to aggrandize his virtue; to manifest the immutability of the divine government; while it displayed its mercy, filled the redeemed with gratitude, and the strongest motives to future obedience. But how great, how disinterested, how infinite, must be the love which would undertake the work! How spotless and exalted in himself, must the being be, to expiate with the Almighty, the sins of man! And would not such a deliverance entitle the benefactor, who could consent to devote himself for its accomplishment, to as great returns of homage and love from men, as their creation claims? These considerations indicate the propriety, if not the necessity, that the person who should be the propitiation for our sins, should himself be divine. Such a person the Father beheld in his own adorable Son; the eternal emanation of his glory, and "image of his person." Him he resolved to give for our ransom. On him he determined to lay our iniquities, and, by making him an offering for sin every way adequate and acceptable, to redeem us from the awful demand of the law, and defeat the triumph of the adversary. To him who was to be our peace, how solemn the work. Yet he was a Son who inherited all the Father's compassion, and whose Father's will was his own. He saw and pitied man. He rejoiced to accomplish the gracious purpose of God. In his Father's pleasure and the travail of his soul, the sons and daughters whom his death would bring unto glory, he saw the reward of his sufferings, and was satisfied. When, therefore, neither sacrifice, nor offering, nor burnt-offering for sin, presented the means of fulfilling Jehovah's desire to save our race, then said this dutiful and benevolent Son, "Lo, I come to do thy will, O God!" Thy pleasure is my pleasure. The honour of thy government I am concerned to uphold, while I compassionate these helpless beings. Myself I offer, to bear their sins, and make reconciliation. "I am contented to do it; yea, thy law is within my heart."

By this stupendous arrangement in the council of heaven, the awful cloud was removed which hung over man, and the beamings of divine favour returned upon the dismayed offenders. They were taught to trust in the divine mercy, and though solemnly instructed in the unhappy consequences of their transgressions, received from the mouth of their Judge the promise of a Redeemer. Sacrifice was instituted to cherish in them the hope of pardon, by darkly revealing the method in which it should be obtained, and carrying the spirit of faith forward to the great atonement. And in the fulness of that time, which the Father, for reasons of inscrutable wisdom, had chosen, our gracious Deliverer, the Eternal Son of the Highest, appeared in our flesh, "to put away sin by the sacrifice of himself." This was the end of the amazing sufferings which, without sin or murmur, Christ endured. Not for himself was he cut off. For us men, and for our salvation, he came down from heaven, and on the cross paid the price of our deliverance. He perfected obedience in our nature; submitted to the curse of the law in our behalf; offered himself without spot or blemish to God, a full satisfaction for our sins, and through the efficacy of his precious blood we live; an everlasting righteousness is brought in, and God is reconciled to us; and we are made capable of obtaining eternal glory. Thus, "was he wounded for our transgressions, and bruised for our iniquities; the chastisement of our peace was upon him, and with his stripes we are healed."

There are ever men to whom all the ways of heaven are grievous; whom nothing pleases but the vain offspring of their own proud minds. To these, it is to be expected, "the cross of Christ" will yet be "foolishness." From the doctrine of their depravity, from the mysterious nature of Christ, and from their own views of the character of the Deity, they will attempt to raise a scorn upon the sufferings of the Redeemer for our salvation. But shall our faith, which rests upon the fullest evidences of the truth of the Gospel, be shaken by the cavils of speculative men? Shall we, who have found in the doctrines of Christ, that rest for our spirits which they need, quit it, because it presents to us wonders which surpass our comprehension? There is, indeed, something in our redemption through the blood of Christ, which fills us with amazement. The Apostle styles it the "mystery" of the cross. And what is not mysterious with which we are acquainted? Can we more clearly discern the wisdom of the arrangements for our present subsistence; or the mercy of the Deity in the miseries with which the earth is filled? Badly, then, must it become us to doubt the expediency of the means which the Most High hath chosen for our salvation. Whether any other way might have been devised for man's deliverance; why the expiatory sacrifice was deferred to so late a period; whether the sufferings of the Saviour might not have been dispensed with or diminished, it is not our business to inquire. It is enough for us to know that those things which God had before showed by the mouth of all his prophets, that Christ should suffer, he hath so fulfilled. Consider, then, ye doubtful, the evidences which encompass you; that "we are born in sin, and are the children of wrath." Reflect, how imperfect, with all your efforts and attainments, is the purity and virtue of your character. Contemplate yourselves as going into the presence of the infinitely holy and awfully just God, and ask yourselves, if you have not need of a Mediator with him; of something more than your merits to propitiate his favour? But, turn from the Son, whom he hath set forth as your Redeemer, and to whom else will you go? Will you make atonement for your own transgressions? Ah! wherewith will you make it? Look back, and see everywhere the indications which man has given of his sense of the need of an expiation of his guilt. See, in the thousand libations, and the ten thousand sacrifices with which he hath sought to propitiate his God, his want of something more than his own virtue to commend him to his Maker; his want of something more than his sorrow to turn away the wrath of the Most High. Rejoice, then, that God hath condescended to provide for the world a sacrifice which would be acceptable in his sight; whose blood would be of sufficient value and efficacy to take away sin. Under your consciousness of the wounds of the serpent, for the healing of which, Jesus, by divine appointment, is lifted up upon the cross; "Look unto him, and be ye saved, all the ends of the earth."

Such is the solution which the Scriptures furnish of this day's stupendous scene; the Son of God, in the form of man, expiring beneath the ignominy and agonies of the cross. This is that wonderful scheme, into which, St. Peter tells us, "the angels desire to look;" and the contemplation of which must compel the Christian to exclaim, "O, the depth of the riches both of the wisdom and goodness of God!"

By our meditations on this subject, we may be led to appreciate, with chastened joy, the deliverance purchased with Christ's blood. We find ourselves by nature the slaves of sin, the children of sorrow, and the prey of death. Tracing these evils to their source, by the light of revelation we discover that a transgression, of which they are the consequences, subjected man, who, till then, was the possessor of innocence and peace, to the most fearful expectation of destruction. He stood upon the brink of perdition; and, had he been left to himself, must, with his race, have perished forever. What words, then, can express the magnitude of the deliverance wrought by the mediation of the Son of God! Is there anything valuable in life? Is there anything pleasant in hope? Is there anything precious in the favour of God? Is it our happiness that the sceptres of sin and death are broken? Do we rejoice that the kingdom of heaven is opened to our anxious spirits, and that "we have an Advocate with the Father," whose intercessions cannot fail to prevail? We owe all to the merits of that atonement which the Redeemer made for us "in his own body on the tree." It was this which rendered "Jesus Christ, and him crucified," the only object which the transported Apostle desired to know. The remembrance that man was the occasion of these sufferings of the Saviour, will ever mix with our sense of salvation, emotions of sadness and regret. But we are unjust to the cross, if we do not glory in it, as the foundation of our redemption from ruin to our present hopes of eternal life, and consider its efficacy in procuring the remission of the first transgression, as our best assurance that He who expired upon it "is able to save them to the uttermost, who come unto God by him."

We should further be impressed by the mystery we commemorate, with the immeasurability of the love of God. Of this, indeed, we are conscious in our being and capacity for happiness. We learn it from his daily providence, and it is proclaimed by all his works. But, in the gift of his Son for our salvation, it is brought home to our hearts. In this we are made most sensibly to feel that "God is love." The attributes of the Deity are all displayed in the accomplishment of our redemption, exhibiting a Deity whom we are both to love, and fear, to reverence and adore. But mercy rules the work. The attribute which absorbs our attention is love. In the gift of the beloved of his bosom to ransom us from the penalties of sin, he has furnished a pledge of his compassionate regard for the welfare of his creatures, as great as it is affecting. And what return shall we make for infinite, unmerited benignity? "He hath showed thee, O man, what is good; and what doth the Lord thy God require of thee, but to do justly, to love mercy, and to walk humbly with thy God."

But I pass to the peculiar obligations we are under to the Being, whose sufferings we are commemorating. "Greater love," as he told his disciples, "hath no man than this, that a man should lay down his life for his friends." But, to rank among his friends, men had no title. They had no claim to his regards. Upon the authority of his Father they had trampled; yea, they would be his foes, and crucify him. Yet, for their sakes, he left a dignity and happiness greater than the highest seraph possessed; "humbled himself to be found in fashion as a man, and became obedient to death, even the death of the cross." Herein, indeed is love. Let me lead you to Calvary, and with other emotions than Pilate felt, bid you "Behold the man!" Surely, "he bears your griefs, and carries your sorrows, and the Lord hath laid on him the iniquity of you all." For you he suffers. For you he dies. And the emphatic, "It is finished," is but the requiem of his departing spirit, that he has completely accomplished your redemption. How transcendent this benevolence! At what a price hath he purchased our safety! Shall we be ashamed of his name, or indifferent to the prosperity of his gospel in the world? Shall we not devote to him our best affections, and "go forth to him, without the camp, bearing his reproach?" Shall we not, with the symbols which he hath hallowed, frequently place before ourselves and others, memorials of his death, and, by every mean in our power, increase his satisfaction in the work he hath wrought? Surely, it is our duty to acknowledge him in all our ways; and, to the utmost extent of our ability, to save the pain of beholding base ingrates in those whom he died to redeem. If there be anything like moral obligation, his love may challenge our most ardent attachment; and, "if ye love me," says he, "keep my commandments."

This leads us to remark, in the last place, how much it behooves us, by complying with the terms of the gospel, to see that this sacrifice of Christ be a "savour of life unto life, and not of death unto death" to us. You have seen with what paternal solicitude, at what an amazing expense, with what unmerited mercy, our Creator hath rescued us from the jaws of destruction. With the blood of his Son he hath sealed to us a gracious covenant, and given us a new opportunity to become heirs of immortality and glory. "How," then, "shall we escape, if we neglect so great salvation?" Is this redemption a ground for presuming on the divine mercy? Have we now nothing to fear or do? Because Christ gave himself an offering for the world, may we continue in sin, and hope for glory? Far otherwise. If there were any ingenuousness in us, the sufferings of our Redeemer should fill us with an abhorrence of vice; and his cross be the strongest motive which could influence us to strive, in future, for a perfect obedience. We are not our own; we are "bought with a price;" and God forbid, that he should ransom any of his creatures from death to a liberty of transgressing his laws, without a fear of punishment. To this end, saith the Apostle, Christ "died for all, that they who live, should not henceforth live unto themselves, but unto him who died for them, and rose again." It is an humble, though exalted; an holy, though free; a probationary, though immortal life, to which we are begotten, through the blood of the Redeemer. And if with such inducements and aids to a "patient continuance in well doing," we fall through our own perverseness, greater must be our condemnation. Wherefore, beloved, as the word of our God exhorts, "pass the time of your sojourning here, in fear; forasmuch as ye know, that ye were not redeemed with corruptible things, as silver and gold; but with the precious blood of Christ, as of a lamb without blemish, and without spot."

SERMON XLII.

ON EASTER-DAY.

LUKE, xxiv. 5, 6.

"Why seek ye the living among the dead? He is not here, but is risen."

THE Church, this morning, hastens, with the amiable women whose affection for Jesus was stronger than death, to the sepulchre of their departed Lord. At the mouth of the tomb, they were met by two men of wonderful appearance; their "countenances like lightning, and their raiment white as snow." As they stoop to look into the sepulchre, these messengers from the court of heaven, for such they are, address to them tidings which disperse their sorrows and fill their bosoms with rapturous joy: "Why seek ye the living among the dead? He is not here, but is risen." "Come see the place where the Lord lay." They descend into the sepulchre. Jesus is not there. They see "the linen clothes lie, and the napkin that was about his head, not lying with the linen clothes, but wrapped together in a place by itself." They remember that thus it was written, that when he had suffered, "he should rise from the dead the third day." Transported with admiration, they send forth their praises unto God.

This resurrection of him whom we have lately contemplated, offering himself upon the cross for our sins, is a subject for mutual congratulations to the whole human race. The memory of it is worthy to be kept a feast for ever, in all their generations.

"For ages mankind had been subject to the dreadful dominion of the king of terrors. The dismal grave waited for them in awful succession. It closed upon them, and they were heard of no more. Whether they had any continuance of being beyond this impenetrable confine of life, was a question of doubtful speculation. It is probable that some knowledge of their destiny had been revealed to the first men, of which, as of other important revelations, we find some tattered and defaced remnants in the heathen world. The most virtuous of the philosophers gathered from these, and their own reflections, a sentiment that another state of existence awaited them. But it amounted only to a hope; a hope, dubious and lingering, like the light of the expiring taper; and this so remote that it had no influence upon the mass of mankind. They saw their fellow beings descend irrecoverably into the tomb. They followed in their turns. And the grim monarch of the dreary domain seemed as sovereign as he was inexorable. It was reserved for the blessed Author of our faith to break his sceptre, and to bring "life and immortality to light, through his" most precious "gospel."

As an exemplification of the most interesting truth which the human mind can consider, the resurrection of Christ ranks before all other events in the annals of our world. Whatever conceptions the more considerate of the heathens acquired, respecting the continuance of their souls in being after the present life; of the resurrection of the body they had no idea. This they relinquished forever to corruption. Among the chosen people of God, with whom, as in a last receptacle, he deposited the truths which the world would not retain in their knowledge, some sentiments of this mystery were promulgated. That David and the Prophets were acquainted with it, is evident from their predictions of the Messiah's resurrection; and Job felt its consoling influences upon his heart, when he rejoiced that, "though after his skin worms would destroy his body, yet in his flesh he should see God." Still, however, the knowledge which the Jews had of this matter was obscure and contested.

It is to the sepulchre of the Arimathean that the children of men must come to behold, in a clear and convincing light, the interesting truth, that in these forms, in which we have known each other, and our nature has been known, we shall rise to renovated life, after sleeping an appointed time in the chambers of the dead. It is here we may behold a brother, made in all things like unto us, sin only excepted, and over whom death had exerted the utmost and most cruel extent of his power, bursting the adamantine fetters which the tyrant had imposed; coming forth from the grave in the form in which he had once dwelt among men; seen, heard, and handled by the companions of his former days. Nor is his resurrection unconnected with our own. He rises as "the Captain of our salvation," as "the first fruits of them that slept." In his resurrection, the Everlasting Father, who hath the keys of life and death, hath given us an earnest and pledge that he will also quicken our mortal bodies, and make us to sit together in heavenly places with Christ Jesus.

Need I now set before you the consolations and joys which spring from the assurance of our future resurrection! Need I demand of you, considerate men, whether there is any other light than that which flows from the knowledge of man's immortality, in which there is meaning or satisfaction, consistent with the wisdom or with the goodness of God, in this present promiscuous and perishable state! Need I, ye modest pilgrims in the paths of virtue, inquire of you, what encouragement you have to perseverance in your arduous course, but the animating assurance that a book of remembrance is kept, and that "your Father who seeth in secret, will," one day, "reward you openly!" Need I appeal to you, sons and daughters of sorrow, who are bowed down to the dust by the dissolution of the friends who were dear to you, and tender as the apple of your eyes, whether they have left anything behind them so soothing and precious as the knowledge that they are not struck out of the scale of being; and the hope that you may again enjoy them in a better world! Need I inquire of you, virtuous widow, from whom death hath torn the partner of your cares and your joys; of you, dutiful child, whose heart is yet wrung at the remembrance of a parent gone down to the dust; of you, disconsolate mother, who bewail the darling of your hopes, untimely taken from your fond embrace; of you, affectionate sister, who sighest for some beloved brother, whom you shall see here no more? Need I call upon you all, my brethren, who are journeying rapidly onward with me to that bourne whence no traveller returns, to say, soberly, if our hearts might not die within us as we approached the grave, if an utter extinction of our being were about to take place upon its brink? No; I need not. The consolations and joys which flow from the prospect of an immortal existence, you have felt and appreciated on every occasion which has required them since you received the Gospel. Among the sincerest offerings which you bring to the God of heaven, are your constant thanksgivings for "the hope of glory."

But it may be questioned, whether we do fully and habitually consider how much our joy in believing the resurrection of the dead is connected with the resurrection of Jesus Christ. Take this away, and all would be uncertainty. But for this instance and pledge of the fact, with what painful hesitation would our minds labour over the dubious inquiry, whether the vital spark, when once extinguished, could be rekindled in these perishable frames. But for our relation to the Redeemer, and our adoption by the Father, for his sake, how would the consciousness of our sins, and of the little value of our race among the immense productions of his hand, damp our expectations of being fostered into an eternal state by his power, who, if he needed, might only speak, and his universe would instantly be filled with far more excellent and purer creatures. In a word, how would our thoughts waver with all the fluctuation of heathen hope; what clouds and darkness would be raised over the grave by our fears, our fancies, and our foe, did not our faith remind us that we are purchased with the blood of the Son of God, and that because he lives we shall live also. It is the resurrection of the Saviour which gives a basis and stability to the expectation of another life. And this it does so completely and permanently that, among Christians, there is scarcely room for the question, "Why should it be thought a thing incredible with you, that God should raise the dead?"

Ungrateful it is in those who have received such an inestimable gift as the hope of immortality, to "kick" against the just and all-wise donor, because of the way in which he hath chosen to testify its reality. What mean the complaints of the partial appearance of the risen Saviour? Is it not enough that we have more evidence of the truth of this fact than of any of the articles of belief to which our minds are daily assenting? Is it not enough that his resurrection was attested by "above five hundred brethren at once;" to the greater part of whom, the historian of it appeals, as still living? Is it not enough that it rallied a disheartened, scattered, and feeble band of followers, and inspired them with a confidence, fortitude, and virtue which nothing could restrain or subdue? Is it not enough that the witnesses of the event were proverbial for integrity and simplicity, and exhibited all that consistence and correspondent behaviour which ever characterize the promulgators of truth? Is it not enough, that without wealth to support or power to befriend them, and without room for any of the motives to deceive, by which the mind is in such cases actuated, they asserted the fact before great and small, with uniform harmony and perseverance, and willingly evidenced the sincerity of their belief in it by sealing their declarations with their blood? Is it not enough that the power of his resurrection alone, established the Church against the opposition of policy and vice, and has been acknowledged and felt in every age, by the wisest and most virtuous of the human race? I know not upon what ground it is assumed that the Most High is obliged to give the utmost demonstration of any truth which he sees fit to require his moral subjects to believe. And with respect to the Jews, as they had disregarded "Moses and the Prophets," we have no reason to suppose they would have been persuaded by one risen "from the dead."

We stand, then, my hearers, contemplating a joyous and most important event; an event pregnant with consequences of unspeakable magnitude to the human race. "The Lord is risen," and our nature is risen in him, "and our life is hid with him in God." Shake off, then, O Zion, the mourning in which the crucifixion had enveloped thee. Put on thy beautiful garments, O Jerusalem, the holy city. Take to yourselves, Christians, a song of victory; and be ye all attired in robes of praise. What gratitude to God should be in your hearts; what hallelujahs to your Redeemer should be on your lips; what transports of joy should pervade your souls, while you contemplate the king of terrors stript of his sceptre, and the hour appointed in which himself shall be bound, and the captives of his dominion be all released! Behold, "the Lord himself shall descend with a shout, and with the voice of the archangel, and with the trump of God." Death shall be destroyed, and from the innumerable prisons in which he hath confined them, the human race shall be at once set free. But, ah! amongst the rising, what means this gloom, amazement, and horror, with which the countenances of so many are overspread! Alas! they have had no part in the regeneration; they are covered with the guilt of their evil deeds; they are rising to shame and contempt; they are coming forth to be consigned to everlasting perdition. Awful, afflicting view! O, let us turn from it to those upon whose faces peace has spread her smiles; into whose hands angels are putting palms of victory; unto whom seraphs are bearing white robes from the wardrobe of heaven; whom the Lamb is conducting into the presence of God. Behold, he presents them triumphantly to the Ancient of Days. "These are they," saith their leader to his Father, "who have embraced thy covenant and kept thy word. In the days of their flesh, it was their anxious care to do justly, to love mercy, and to walk humbly with thee their God. And now they plead no merit before thee, but ask acceptance in my name." The Son ceases. A pulse of joy shoots through the hosts of heaven, as the Everlasting Father smiles upon his offspring, brought back unto glory. "Children of the regeneration," saith he, "good and faithful servants, enter ye into the joy of your Lord." They range through regions of bliss. They quaff of the rivers of everlasting pleasure. They eat of the trees of immortality in the gardens of God. They remember their unworthiness, and look back upon their toils and their sorrows; but the hand of the Almighty hath wiped away all tears from their eyes. Gracious Redeemer, in this blessed company, grant, through thy mercy, we may all be found. If we are not already thine, O make us so, and leave us not to any vice or error which shall compel thee to reject us when thou comest in thy kingdom.

SERMON XLIII.

ON EASTER-DAY.

PSALM cxviii. 24.

"This is the day which the Lord hath made; we will rejoice and be glad in it."

WHEN light first shone through the darkness of chaos, awfully magnificent must have been the scene. Then was the first natural day. But how incomparably more grand was the display, when life first shone through the darkness of the tomb! Then dawned immortal day. The sun which rose in the lustre of the former dispelled an unfelt and material gloom; illumined and animated a world of bodies; is limited in its influences, and will, at some future period, set forever. The Sun which rose in the lustre of the latter, dispelled an afflicting and intellectual gloom; illumined and animated a world of spirits; is in its influences unbounded, and will, in meridian glory, be eternal. Well did the earliest Christians unite the commemoration of the two creations, and hallow the first day of the week as the Lord's Day. With still more striking propriety may the Church, at the annual recurrence of the Easter festival, adopt the exultation of the Psalmist, uttered as he prophetically contemplated the resurrection of the Messiah: "This is the day which the Lord hath made; we will rejoice and be glad in it."

Suitably to improve the season, and to illustrate the propriety of the exultation in the text, it will be my endeavour, in the following discourse, to show how great sources of joy and gladness were opened unto us, by the event which we this day commemorate. The extensiveness of the subject, renders me fearful of being tedious to your patience. But it is more important than any other upon which you can bestow your attention; and it shall be my aim, to render the discourse as concise and perspicuous as the scope of it will admit. In no way, perhaps, can this better be accomplished than by considering the resurrection of our Lord first, as the grand evidence of the truth of our religion, and secondly, as the genuine earnest of our immortality.

It will appear an august evidence of our religion, if we contemplate it, first, as the greatest and most decisive miracle of which we can form an idea. Miracles are credentials which we should naturally expect would accompany a mission from heaven. Hence, the Jews, who expected an extraordinary personage, sought after signs; and to pretences of these, Gentile impostors have always resorted. Of all miracles the restoration of life to the dead, is the most astonishing and satisfactory. To recall the spirit, when once it has fled; to rekindle the vital spark, when once it has expired; to resuscitate the corpse over which the desolating hand of death hath once passed, can be the act of Him alone, who holds, as an unalienable prerogative, the attribute of Omnipotence. Other wonders may be attributed to art, to sleight, or to infernal agency. But the keys of life and death are in the hands of the Almighty; and from him can in no way be obtained. So incontrolable is this miracle, that the pagan Pliny, imagined it impossible to any of his gods, and the skeptical Porphyry declared, if he could credit one instance of it, he would renounce his unbelief. If, then, to restore life to another be such unanswerable testimony of authority from heaven, what shall we say of the resurrection of Christ? To other cases of resuscitation of the dead obstinacy might object that there was connivance between the subject and the author of the miracle. But here, the fact, when ascertained, admitted of no evasion. The subject of the miracle was deprived of life by a public execution, and deposited in a tomb, which his foes studiously secured; "sealing the stone and setting a watch." The aid of no second person was employed in his resurrection. His disciples did not pretend that they had raised him; which they certainly would have done, had they accomplished a fraud. But the Saviour was the author of his own resurrection. The captive of the tomb burst his fetters by the energy of his divine omnipotence, and himself reanimated his sleeping dust. This, surely, was the greatest and most decisive miracle of which we can form an idea; and is the corner stone of the solid base upon which Christianity stands.

Its importance as an evidence of the truth of our religion will further appear, if we consider it as that to which the Saviour made his ultimate appeal; and on which he rested the truth of all that he delivered. "Destroy this temple, and I will raise it in three days." The candour of our blessed Lord was conspicuous, in declaring his intention previous to his death, and in pointing to a miracle which, while it should vouch for his authority, would actually exemplify the principal doctrines which he taught of his divinity, the acceptance of his sacrifice with the Father, and the abolition of death. He had so openly predicted his resurrection, and so firmly referred to it as his best voucher, that his foes took every measure to prevent an imposture. They ran to Pilate, and reminded him of the "deceiver's" assertion. Pilate recollected it; and bade them use every precaution. And yesterday we saw them strenuously engaged in making the sepulchre as sure as they could. And had they confuted his predictions; had the tomb retained its noble prisoner; had death held Christ in fetters, as other men, who could have felt the fulness of joy in believing? Great as are the other evidences of his religion, they were insufficient to sustain the faith, even of his twelve Apostles. Death scarcely took possession of their Master, before some, ashamed and intimidated, shrunk from sight; others, sad and sorrowing, were journeying to their former occupations; and but for the tenderness of woman, there had been none to visit his remains. Could his adversaries have produced his corpse, after the lapse of the third day, a fatal blow would, in all probability, have been given to the faith of the

Redeemer. And this we learn from the records of the times, they were equally anxious and determined to do. But "Why do the heathen so furiously rage, and the people imagine a vain thing? The kings of the earth stand up, and the rulers take counsel together against the Lord, and against his anointed. He that dwelleth in the heavens shall laugh them to scorn; the Lord shall have them in derision." He comes forth triumphantly from the tomb, at the time appointed, and his exact fulfilment of his promise leaves incredulity without a plea. It rallied the disheartened disciples, and inspired that unconquerable zeal with which the Church was established. It reduced the adversaries of Christ to their first and last resort, bribery and lies. It gave to the Christian fabric that finishing stroke, without which its foundation would have been unstable, and its consistence and majesty, very incomplete.

The worth of the resurrection, as an evidence of our religion, will appear still greater if we consider it as capable of removing the principal reluctances which the proud mind of man may feel at embracing the Christian faith. The doctrine of Christ crucified, is the doctrine which unbelievers find it most difficult to receive. No one can deny that human nature is prone to vice, and that vice is intrinsically odious. It is seen and felt everywhere. No one can doubt the need which mankind have of an instructor. It has been acknowledged in all ages. No one can question the possibility of another state, and immortal life. Of these, the soul has a strong presage and ardent desire. No one can disregard a proffer of pardon from his Creator, and overtures of his mercy and favour. It is what man has everywhere sought with trembling hope, and soothing devices. But there is something in the Almighty's laying such sufferings upon an innocent being; something in the Son of God's enduring all the abasements of humanity, and expiring in agonies upon a cross, at which infidel reason revolts. It "is a hard saying, they cannot hear it." This, however, is an uncandid way of judging of Christianity. It is to condemn a system upon a view only of one of its parts. To fix our thoughts upon the crucifixion, and disbelieve, without connecting it with the resurrection, is surely an unfair examination of the gospel. Would it be right, from a contemplation of the earth when the shades of night are spread over it, to pronounce the world dark and gloomy, without continuing our contemplation to the effulgent glory which is diffused by the rising of the sun? Every objection to the cross vanishes before the grandeur and felicity of the resurrection. The Son of God appears no longer abased; his humiliations no longer severe or useless; the exactions of the Almighty from him, no longer incompatible with the most affectionate goodness, when we consider Christ Jesus, for the sufferings of death, thus "crowned with glory and worship." The Jews, not regarding the satisfactory testimony which the Lord had promised, exclaimed while he hung upon the tree, "If thou be the Son of God, come down from the cross, and we will believe." Had their obstinacy permitted them to have gone with the wonder-struck watch to his tomb, they would have found even stronger demonstration than that which they demanded. But their eyes were blinded, that they should not see. God grant that the film may soon be removed from their sight; and they enabled to confess in the risen Saviour, a greater and more glorious Messiah than they have idly expected! But, more deplorable blindness has existed in the Christian world. The deluded Paine, from whom thousands have received a cup of poison, deadly as the most depraved nature could compose, has, with insolent infidelity, averred, that the story of the crucifixion is too cruel and ridiculous to be told by Christians to their children! Had he humbly contemplated it in its connection with the event, which millions of the best of his race are to-day commemorating, he might have thought it a story so full of compassion, wisdom and sublimity, that angels might ponder it with admiration. He is passed to the place of his account; and far be it from us, my friends, to load his followers with epithets of opprobrium and malevolence. Would heaven, they might be led from the cross to the sepulchre of our Lord; and, beholding the seeming contemptibleness of the former, lost in the majesty of the latter, there render homage to Him, "unto whom every knee shall" be compelled to "bow;" and whom "every tongue shall," one day "confess to be Lord, to the glory of God the Father." The triumph of Christ over the awful monarch whose sceptre had, for ages, dealt destruction through the world, is sufficient to satisfy the doubts, and remove the reluctance of every mind. When by means of death, he overcomes death, and "destroys him who had the power of death, that is the devil;" this fruit of the crucifixion commends it as the wisdom of God. The despised "Nazarene," the humiliated victim, is here "declared the Son of God with power." Amidst the glorious lustre of the resurrection, the cross no longer appears either "a stumbling block," or "foolishness."

Such are some of the considerations which show that the event we, to-day commemorate, is the grand and indispensable evidence of the truth of our holy religion, which leads me to observe, secondly, that it is to be considered as establishing for us the best joys of life, and especially as the earnest of our own immortality.

The most confirmed skeptic will, I believe, allow that Christianity, to those who feel satisfied of its truth, is the source of such happiness as cannot elsewhere be found. Its tidings of joy, and its inimitable instructions, the truths it delivers, and the prospects it opens, how happily are they adapted to the perplexities and sorrows, to the necessities and desires of our nature. I might speak of the provision it makes for our pardon and salvation. I might mention the revelation it gives concerning God and his worship. I might state its tendency to promote tranquillity in the bosom, satisfaction in the mind, and order, peace, and felicity in the world. I might adduce the ideas which swelled the notes of the heavenly choir, as they chanted at the birth of its Author, "Glory to God in the Highest, and on earth peace; good will towards men." I might take the light of prophecy in my hand, and carry you forward to the blissful scenes of the consummated influences of this religion, when "the wilderness and the solitary place shall be glad for them, and the desert shall rejoice, and blossom as the rose." Recalling your attention to these things, and reminding you that we have seen them deriving from the resurrection their confirmation, I might demand, whether, on this day, "which the Lord hath made," we may not well be filled with holy exultance and ardent praise? But, the time elapsing too rapidly to permit me to dwell on each of these topics, I hasten to one doctrine of our religion, which, on this occasion, is peculiarly pertinent, and on every occasion most interesting. It is in the gospel that "life and immortality are brought to light." What nature, obscurely desired; what reason, feebly hoped; what virtue, earnestly supplicated, is here clearly revealed. As an essential part of Christianity, this joyful doctrine shares in that general certainty which is given to all the truths of the gospel, by the resurrection of its Author from the dead. It were enough, to read upon the pages, which this event hath stamped with the seal of divine authority, that the time shall be, when "all who are in the grave shall hear the voice" of the Son of God, "and come forth;" "when this corruptible shall put on incorruption, and this mortal shall put on immortality." For who shall not be satisfied with the declaration of God?

But, on account of the anxiety of our nature, and the weak ness of our faith, God hath graciously condescended to grant, that this truth should be exemplified as well as taught. With all the hopes and expectations which nature can give him, man longs for evidence of the possibility of his future being. He stands gazing upon the remains of mortality in the chambers of the dead, and scarcely dares to ask, "Can these dry bones live?" His mind roves through the regions of invisible space, calling anxiously, Spirits of the departed, where are you! He sees that the plant perishes, and is renewed from its seed. He sees that the sun sets, and rises on the morrow. He sees that nature fades in winter, and in spring is renewed. But "man giveth up the ghost, and where is he?" Some evidence, in fact, that the dead may live, would be to his soul welcome and enlivening, as the light of the morning. This evidence, Christ, in his resurrection has furnished. One in our own nature and form, has lain in the grave the prey of death; and from the dominion of this king of terrors, has come forth triumphantly in new life, and is passed into heaven, leaving us assurance, that he who raised him up, will "also quicken our mortal bodies."

Let it not be objected, that his ashes were entire and composed, while those of other men are commixed and scattered. The omniscience of the Deity can accurately discriminate every atom, and know to what body it peculiarly belongs. Does not "he tell the number of the stars, and call them all by their names?" Does not he bring forth from the dust the various tribes of plants, reserving, to each, its proper form, and qualities, and season? Does he not, annually, restore to every flower, its infinitely fine and varied hues, and give "to every seed, its own body?" Can he, then, be at a loss to know what matter must give to any person his proper identity, "or with what body" every man should "come?" Nor is his power less than his wisdom. No single atom in the universe can secrete itself from his view; nor for a single moment resist his word. "Whither shall they go from his presence? Whither shall they flee from his spirit? If they ascend up into heaven, he is there. If they go down to hell, he is there. If they are borne on the wings of the morning, to the uttermost parts of the seas, even there" his power guides and will control them. Having resolved, that "as in Adam all die, even so in Christ all shall be made alive," he holds the infinity of particles, of which, at the resurrection, men must be composed, under the power of his might, each ready to take its proper station, when "the trumpet shall sound," and "the Captain of our salvation," shall give the great command. "Behold," saith he, "I am the LORD, the God of all flesh, is there anything too hard for me?"

Now the resurrection of Christ is not only an exemplification of the possibility of our own resurrection, but also "a pledge to assure us thereof." He rose as "the first born of many brethren." He is taken as "the first fruits of them that slept," into the temple of God, an earnest and consecration of the mighty harvest which shall be gathered in the end of the world, from all the beds of death. By raising him up from the dead, God hath testified his acceptance of the expiation he hath made for sin, and what but sin gave death a claim to our race? By raising him up from the dead, God hath given us assurance that he hath appointed him to "judge the world in righteousness." And shall they not, then, be gathered before him? By raising him up from the dead, God hath testified the redemption wherewith he undertook to redeem us from the miseries into which we were fallen. And among these, how afflicting were the loss of immortality and of the hopes of heaven. By raising him up from the dead, God hath exhibited the sceptre of death broken, before our eyes, that, "amidst the changes and chances of this mortal life," his faithful servants might flee for refuge, to the hope set before them. "If we believe," says the Apostle, "that Jesus died and rose again, even so them that sleep in Jesus shall God bring with him." "Because I live," said the Redeemer himself, to his sorrowing disciples, "ye shall live also."

And now, brethren, is not the doctrine of our resurrection to immortal life, that which dispels the deepest glooms of our present existence? Is it not this which gives to virtue her best encouragement and most fervent zeal? Does it not afford the only consolation under the loss of those whose lives and whose love were the zest of our felicity? Does it not illumine and cheer the valley, at the entrance of which our nature exerts its most powerful recoil; the valley of death? Hath it not erased from the tomb the inscription paralyzing to all the noble properties of our nature, "Death is an eternal sleep;" and inscribed in its stead, the invigorating truth, Man here takes the rest, from which he shall awake to eternal day? If, then, these choicest of our consolations, these most precious of our hopes, have their certainty from the event we are commemorating, with what fervent joy should we return from the sepulchre, with what holy gratitude should we keep this feast? Mourning widow, have you a husband, who, you hope, when he passed from this life, entered upon the joys of immortality? Weeping parent, have you a child whose little spirit, you trust, having been washed in the laver of regeneration, was taken at its death into Abraham's bosom? Dutiful son, have you a mother, whose absence from you you mourn, but, concerning whom, it is the solace of your grief to believe that she is among the spirits of the just, before the throne of the Eternal? Affectionate sister, have you a brother for whom your tears still flow, and would flow without intermission, were it not for the faith which checks them with the assurance, "thy brother shall rise again?" How great should be your gratitude to the Redeemer, who hath purchased by his death and resurrection, for these, your friends, the immortality and joys upon which they have entered, forever and ever!

SERMON XLIV.

THE GOSPEL TO BE GLORIED IN.

Romans, i. 16.

"I am not ashamed of the Gospel of Christ."

IT is the glory of man that he is constituted capable of an acquaintance with religion. There is no property of his nature which so clearly distinguishes him from the inferior animals of our system, and connects him with the spirits of the invisible world, as his power of knowing and worshipping his Creator, and of discovering and cultivating virtue. The materialists, who have denoted man by his erect form and bodily organization, have been controverted by those who have traced in other animals a similarity of lines bounding their shape and correspondent corpuscular organs. They who have considered speech as the peculiar property of man, have been opposed by some who have advocated the supposition that animals of many species possess a limited power of conversing with those of their own species, though by us their signs and modes of expression are utterly unintelligible. Even they who have esteemed reason as the distinguishing principle of our nature, have found adversaries, who have discerned something in other animals analogous to this rational faculty, and have derived arguments from their various sagacities in defence of the theory that reason, like sensation, ascends by immeasurable gradations from the being which seemingly vegetates to man who profoundly thinks. But no one ever yet conjectured that any other visible being than man is capable of conceiving spiritual ideas, and possesses a power of investigating and applying religious truth. To contemplate and admire the beauties of moral science, to look through nature up to nature's God, to receive instructions from the Eternal Mind, to hold high converse with the Sovereign of Eternity, to rise above the influence of visible things, and reason of righteousness, temperance, and a judgment to come—these glorious privileges are bestowed exclusively, as far as respects the creatures of this diurnal sphere, upon the being who was made little lower than the angels, and crowned with glory and worship. It is this spiritual nature, this religious capacity which makes man man, and gives him his superiority over the lower orders of existence. Now, of all religions which the world has known, Christianity is incomparably the most excellent. No other system has exhibited such purity of precept, such sublimity of doctrine, such adaptation to man's necessities, such strength of evidence, or such demonstration of the protection of heaven. The mind, therefore, when contemplating the nature of man in conjunction with the perfection of the Christian revelation, is filled with wonder that there should ever have been any occasion for the declaration of the Apostle in the text. Under the influence of these combined views, it is ready to demand, with a mixture of confidence and surprise, can any person be ashamed of the Gospel of Christ? Many, however, there were in St. Paul's day, and there are many, too many, at the present day, to whom the Gospel of Christ is either a "stumbling block" or "foolishness." Some are ashamed of a system which they have never, or at best but superficially examined. Others are ashamed to embrace a belief which, at the same time, they are afraid and unable to reject; and others are ashamed to avow openly the faith which secretly they are willing and anxious to embrace. Suffer me, my respected hearers, to solicit your attention, while I endeavour to show you the folly of being in any degree ashamed of the Gospel, by illustrating, in the first place, its transcendent excellence. And secondly, by disclosing the corruption of the principles from which a shame of it generally proceeds.

1. Christianity is *excellent in its origin.* It is not a system of ethics resulting from the speculations of philosophy, nor a religious scheme devised by the ingenuity of intrigue. It comes from God. It is an emanation from the source of light, and consequently, like all emanations, participates of the essential nature of the source from which it proceeds. The proper object of the mind is truth. Any communication, therefore, from the Author of truth, when once proved to be such, is so far from being an occasion of shame, that it is entitled to the most profound veneration. Whatever may be the matter which it contains, whether alone or within the comprehension of our reason, whether coincident with, or opposed to, our preconceived opinions, if it bear the sanction of divine authority, it merits devout observance and respect. Shall angels listen with attention when Jehovah speaks, and receive with eagerness and pleasure the counsels of the Most High? Shall the hosts of heaven wait humbly by his throne anxious to hearken unto the voice of his word, and shall man treat that Gospel with contempt which comes to him in the character of a revelation from God? Shall he even view with indifference a system for whose bare existence, under its peculiar circumstances, he can in no way satisfactorily account, but by confessing with the astonished centurian, that its author was truly the Son of God? The origin of his religion should be the Christian's boast. If in the heathen world, men were proud of sitting at the feet of this or that learned sage, and embraced opinions upon no other ground than the mere name of their author, surely he who sits at the feet of the spiritual Gamaliel, and receives his instructions from the only all-wise, must perceive new dignity conferred upon human nature, and need not be ashamed of the master of whom he is taught. As we esteem a gift in the compound proportion of its intrinsic value, and the love and respect we feel for the giver, so ought we to prize the best gift of heaven to men, as much for the greatness and goodness of the donor as for the in-

estimable treasure which it contains. It is impossible to realize that it is the power of God, and at the same time be ashamed of the Gospel of Christ.

2. Again. Christianity is *excellent in its nature.* We view the visible creation with astonishment, and are irresistibly led by it to acknowledge and adore its author. But the prospects which the Gospel presents to the spiritual eye are as far superior to the objects of corporeal vision as the pleasures of intellect to the pleasures of sense, or as the paradise of Adam to the habitations of his posterity. Every part of the Christian system is in itself perfectly good and beautiful; and the union of all the parts forms a fabric exhibiting such wisdom in the contrivance, such greatness in the execution, and such harmony in the effect, as have excited the wonder of the profligate and commanded the admiration even of the infidel, when employing its engines to accomplish its demolition.

Examine the morality of the Gospel. How much purer than the most refined conceptions to which the mind of man had ever attained. There is not a vice, not an evil propensity of which human nature is capable, that Christian morality does not prohibit. There is not a virtue, not an amiable inclination that human nature can possess, which Christian morality does not recommend. The finest feelings of the heart are strengthened and directed, the sublimest views of the mind are cleared and extended, and all the graces of life are shown and exemplified in the religion of Jesus Christ. For every imperfection of humanity it discovers a remedy; for every virtuous sentiment it affords a sanction; to every immortal hope it promises fruition.

Examine the doctrines of the Gospel. These are not less excellent than its morality. The very nature of many of them proves that they cannot be the offspring of the human mind; for unaided reason has not access to the high regions where they are found, and neither strength nor inducement for the conjecture cf them. What views do the Scriptures give of man; his origin and nature, his condition and destruction! How clear—

how satisfactory—how transporting! The mind, when it has embraced Christianity, ceases to consider man as an enigma, and is no longer perplexed by the condition and events of human life. It finds a clue in the Bible to that labyrinth of intricacies, in which every reflecting infidel must find himself bewildered. Does it teach you that human nature is corrupt? Who does not behold proof of it in the world? Who does not carry evidence of it in his own bosom? Does it teach you the necessity of an atonement for sin? Where has not man manifested his consciousness of it, by seeking with victims to appease, and with oblations to propitiate his gods? Does it teach you the need of the aid of divine grace in the renewal of your nature? Who feels it not when he aspires after virtue—who sighs not for it amidst the pressing temptations of this infectious world? Does it disclose to you a future retribution and eternal life? When has not enlightened conscience foreboded the one—when has not contemplative virtue longed after the other? From the views it gives of man, turn to the views it gives of his Creator. How sublime, how instructive, how consoling! It erases the dark inscription, "To the unknown God," from every altar, and dedicates it to "The Father and friend of man." It represents him, indeed, as just to punish iniquity; but, at the same time, as commending most affectingly his love to his creatures, in reconciling a guilty world unto himself by the sacrifice of his beloved Son. It turns the deluded idolator from his phantoms, and his vision from his stocks and stones to the living and true God, whom it exhibits as one, as spiritual, as omnipotent, as all-wise, as eternal, worthy of all homage, trust, and obedience, in that he perpetually displays in his government of the universe, the utmost perfection of justice and mercy, of goodness and truth. Consider the doctrine of the Gospel with regard to the worship of God.

During the night of heathenism men were left to grope in the dark for the object of worship, and were liable, through the infirmities of their nature, to adore the creature rather than the Creator. But by the light of the Gospel the darkness is dispersed; and the only proper object of religious adoration clearly revealed. To the services which the gospel prescribes, reason instantly accedes, as perfectly becoming the beings for whom they are designed. It takes the children of ignorance and superstition from immolating victims, pouring their fruitless libations, and counting their beads, and leads them forth in the garments of holiness and in the spirit of love, to the throne of their Father in heaven, teaching them to worship him "in spirit and in truth." No unmeaning ceremonies, no costly expiations, no fatiguing rounds of duty does it enjoin, but its yoke is easy and its burthen light. The sacraments of Christianity are neither so numerous as to be tedious, nor so showy as to be ridiculous. Few in number and simple in nature, they are calculated wholly to sublime the affections and inspire the purest devotion. In short, the excellent nature of our religion, separate from every other consideration, is abundantly sufficient to make it the pride rather than the shame of the rational mind. Did the disciples of Socrates employ every faculty to maintain his speculative principles? Did the disciples of Pythagoras submit to privations and self-denials for the sake of his visionary theories? Did the disciples of Confucius advocate his practical tenets in opposition to the corruption of a court and grandees? Were the disciples of Mahomet ready to propagate, at the expense of their lives, his gross opinions? And shall they whom the "Best Beloved of the Father" hath descended from heaven to instruct, neglect his communications? Shall the disciples of Christ shrink from their master and be ashamed of his excellent cause? Forbid it, common sense! forbid it, every principle of reason! independently of the regard due to revelation.

3. Once more, Christianity is *excellent in its purpose or design.* This is no other than to render men happy here and hereafter. It tends to make them happy here, by bringing them to the pardon and favour of God, and restoring to them their original assimilation to the divine nature. It aims to rekindle in the bosom that spirit of celestial love which, when possessed, diffuses itself into all the affections, and creates a delightful har-

mony between the soul and every external object. It is calculated to regulate the exultance of those whose lot is cast upon life's lofty summits, and at the same time to furnish peace and contentment to those who are doomed to dwell in its obscurest vales. It is designed to hush the murmurs of the disappointed, to relieve the cares of the anxious, to cheer the spirits of the desponding, to dry the tears of the afflicted, to support the hopes of the righteous, to encourage the repentance of the sinner, to bring man to an assurance and sense of safety under the shadow of his Maker's wings, to introduce peace, and righteousness and charity upon earth, to make of the human race one happy family, united in loving and honouring one common Parent and Protector, the great and benevolent God. Were the principles of this religion fully and universally operative in their purity, upon individuals and communities, what a scene of love, tranquillity, holiness and bliss would our world exhibit!

But this is not all. It was peculiarly the object of Christianity to rend the veil between the present and a future state; and to show that this world is but the outer court of an eternal temple, where man, if he will avail himself of his Maker's goodness, shall reach the perfection of his nature, and find the reality of happiness, for the enjoyment of which he was originally created. The gospel of Christ was not designed merely to make man happy during his short pilgrimage here,—but to illumine his tomb,—to divest death of his terrific aspect,—to take from him his sceptre and his sting, and convert him into a messenger sent by the Disposer of events, to conduct his children to a state of bliss beyond the confines of this sublunary state. For this purpose it points them to the cross, that they may behold the wonderful victim sustaining the burthen of sin which has been transferred to him from their shoulders, and may rejoice in the knowledge of forgiveness. For this purpose it brings to them the "earnest of the spirit," that with this pledge of the favour of God in their hearts they may look up to him with the confidence and affection of children, crying "Abba, Father." And for this purpose it leads them to the sepulchre of Christ, that they may behold the sceptre of death actually broken by his mighty resurrection, who submitted to death "that he might destroy him who had the power of death, that is the devil, and deliver those who, through fear of death, were all their lifetime subject to bondage." Such is the aim of the gospel of Christ,—to make men happy, to restore them to their alliance with the Most High, to recover them "from the death of sin to the life of righteousness," to raise them from corruption to incorruption; from mortality to immortality, from earth to heaven. "I am not ashamed of the gospel of Christ," says the apostle, "for it is the power of God unto salvation to every one who believeth."

Thus we have seen the transcendent excellence of Christianity, in its origin, its nature, and its end. Permit me now to ask, is there anything in it of which man can be ashamed? Is not its excellence sufficient to preserve it from neglect? yea, to make it the boast of the beings to whom it is addressed? Is it not calculated to elevate the faculties of the mind, to invigorate the amiable affections of the heart, to confirm the best hopes of the soul, to give character and felicity to life, and increase the quantity of happiness in every situation in which man can be placed. So benign indeed are its influences, that even if it were a delusion it would be a pleasing delusion, for it enhances every joy and mitigates every sorrow of human existence. It would be a desirable delusion, for it alone is capable of reconciling the contemplative mind to life and its events. Take his belief from the real Christian and you give a mortal stab to his comfort,—you deprive him of a treasure for which the world cannot compensate,—you obliterate from the face of nature every lovely feature, and obscure that light, by the reflection of which he had discovered something significant in life,—something desirable in existence.

Whence then is it that any are found, who are in any way ashamed of the gospel of Christ? Perhaps if we turn our attention to the human heart, and trace this shame to some of the causes from which it proceeds, we shall see how weak, foolish, and corrupt it is; how exceedingly unworthy of an intelligent being.

A powerful cause of this shame both in believers and unbelievers, is a fear of the remarks of the world. There are many who are afraid to profess openly their faith in the gospel, or even soberly to examine its evidences, lest they should excite the observation of their less serious acquaintances, and incur the imputation of hypocrisy or weakness. If they go to Jesus, it must be with Nicodemus, "by night, for fear of the Jews." Now a more unworthy principle cannot operate upon the mind of man. It augurs a want of manly independence which would be considered disgraceful in any other cause, and is dangerous as well as disgraceful, where such momentous interests are at stake. "Who art thou, that thou shouldest be afraid of a man that shall die, and of the sons of men who shall be as dust, and forgettest the Lord thy Maker?" What are the sneers of which thou art so apprehensive? They are the shafts, the feeble shafts with which the irreligious attempt to protect their own negligence or depravity. Their libertine hearts are unwilling to receive the truth in the love of it. Like evil spirits they are uneasy to see others aspiring after a purity which they do not possess. Restless and rash, they wish to disturb the foundation of the piety which reproaches them; but unable to find in it any imperfection, they have recourse to sarcasm; and hope to laugh down a religion to whose restraints they are resolved not to submit. Yet the fear of what such persons may say is often the cause of the backwardness of many to be found among the professing disciples of the Redeemer. Deplorable infirmity of human nature! that it can be brought to dissemble at the tribunal of vice,—to dissemble at that tribunal its fear of God and its attachment to virtue! Reason surely must recoil from the idea that truth, the fairest daughter of heaven, should exclude herself for fear of observation, much less should bow the knee to error. And religion makes an appeal, to which she expects not a reply, when in the energetic language of inspiration, she demands—

"Whether it be right in the sight of God to hearken unto man more than unto God, judge ye."

Another cause of the shame which the apostle renounced, is inconsideration. It is not want of conviction which renders all men inattentive to the claims or negligent of the duties of religion. In many there is an habitual thoughtlessness, which is carried along with the tide of the world, without considering how this tide moves or whither it will conduct them. Accordingly we find that an aversion to the profession and an inattention to the ordinances of Christianity, is the more general among those who are in the inconsiderate period of life. Innumerable are the instances of those who in their juvenile years have been chief among the thoughtless and boldest among the profane, but when they have advanced to the more sober seasons of maturer age, they have embraced the faith and duties which they once despised, and found their joy and peace in them. But to consider is in every age man's privilege and duty,—a privilege which raises him above the lower orders of being—a duty, for the discharge of which he is accountable. And inconsideration, when that which is nothing, or which is everything, demands his attention, is one of his follies, over which, if there be tears in heaven, angels weep.

The last source of a shame of the gospel which I shall mention is the unsubdued strength of vice. Any person who has the smallest acquaintance with human nature must have observed how easily the passions can bias reason, decoy the will from the path of duty, and veil the deformity of sin. Virtue and vice are so directly in opposition, that our contempt for one will be as exactly proportioned to our attachment to the other, as the elevation of one part of a balance to the depression of its counterpoise. The man who is in subjection to vice will have little relish for the pleasures of religion. The sense is diseased, which is adapted to the perception of them. Christianity is as grievous to his corrupt mind, as the light of the sun to the disordered eye. Even if he have some darling affection which he is unwilling to sacrifice, some beloved passion which he wishes to indulge, he will persuade himself to question the necessity or indubitableness of the principle which interferes with his wishes, and at length becomes tired, if not ashamed, of an authority which he neither respects nor discards. Such was the case of the young man in the gospel. He loved the principle of virtue, and had kept the commandments from his youth. But the ease and pleasures and distinction which attend on wealth had a dominion over him, and when the spirit of the gospel tried him,—when Jesus required him, trusting to the treasures he would have in heaven, to sell all his possessions and follow him, instead of rejoicing to become the disciple of a Being in connection with whom he would possess all things, he went away sorrowing, because discipleship would cost him the sacrifice of great riches. Such was the case of the unhappy Agrippa. He believed the prophets, and Paul's arguments and appeals forced conviction upon his soul. But he was not prepared to resign the luxuries of a court—he was not ready to forego the pleasures which his rank and the indulgences which his coffers put in his power; and he probably aimed as much to silence his own conscience as to compliment the apostle when evidencing at once the force of truth, and perverseness of depravity, he said, "Almost thou persuadest me to be a Christian." And such was the case of the wretched Felix. He was anxious to hear the apostle concerning the faith of Christ. And as he "reasoned of righteousness, temperance and a judgment to come, Felix trembled." He could not withstand the word of God,—the power of truth, and it shook him to his inmost soul. But the remembrance of past pleasures, and the hope of future indulgences, enslaved him. Drusilla sat by him, and he was surrounded by companions of his debaucheries, and sycophants of his power. Ashamed to yield to the convictions of his mind, he dismissed the apostle, deluding himself, while he promises the eloquent prisoner that at a more "convenient season" he will call for him. They who are truly brought out of darkness into light, in whom the Holy Spirit hath broken the power of sin, and who are thus turned from Satan unto God, can never be ashamed of the name, the gospel, the ordinances, the friends of the Redeemer. So far as you find yourselves reluctant to acknowledge Christ, to rejoice in his name and word, and to follow his steps, so far unquestionably are you from being perfectly turned to the living God. The reason assigned by him why "men love darkness rather than light" is "because their deeds are evil." And he hath left us an axiom which with its illustration is peculiarly memorable, as a declaration from him of the power of vice in its unsubdued strength, to bias the judgment and corrupt the will; "He that is of God heareth God's word; ye therefore hear him not because ye are not of God."

From what has been said, be induced, my brethren, to esteem the revelation of the gospel as the best blessing which the Most High has conferred on the human race. Guard against those corrupt principles which interfere with the acknowledgment of its truth or the discharge of any of its duties. Ye, who are lovers of moral improvement, will ye be ashamed of that faith which has been the delight of Abraham and Moses, of David and Samuel, of the "glorious company of the apostles, the goodly fellowship of the prophets, the noble army of martyrs," and the host of Christian worthies whose virtues have formed the purest lustre which yet has rested upon the human character? Ye who are admirers of reason, will ye be ashamed of the faith, in which these masters of reason, a Locke and a Newton, a Boyle and a Hale, a Washington and a Jones, have found their peace and satisfaction? Ye who are willing and glad to avail yourselves of "the redemption that is in Christ Jesus," will ye be ashamed to appear as his followers and defenders of his cause, when, to secure for you this redemption, he "endured the cross, despising the shame," though he was heir of the glory and bliss of heaven?

This shame may be manifested by an acquiescence in the words and deeds of those who are opposed to the gospel. It may be manifested by a backwardness to confess its authority, and assert its excellency, and an equivocation of its principles when they would be derided or contested. It may be manifested by a reluctance to come forward to its ordinances, baptism and the Lord's Supper, because of the eyes of a mixed world, or the vibration of the heart to and from the Redeemer. It may be manifested by a desertion of any of the duties he enjoins,—by a neglect of any of the services he requires,—by a contempt of any of the humiliations he recommends,—and by forbearing at proper times, and in suitable manner, to extol the deeds he has done and the instructions he has given. In these or any other ways, will ye, my brethren, who have seen the excellency of the gospel, and the corruption of the principles from which a shame of it proceeds, be found unfaithful to the God of your salvation? I call upon you to guard against this false shame, by your knowledge of the evils of which skepticism is productive. I call upon you to guard against it by your sense of the greatness of your privilege in walking amidst the light and comfort which the Christian revelation hath diffused. I call upon you to guard against it by the amazing debt of gratitude which you owe to Christ, and the unspeakable recompense which awaits the faithful. I call upon you to guard against it by the holy sign impressed upon you at your baptism, in token that you should not afterwards be "ashamed to confess the faith of Christ crucified—manfully to fight under his banners, and to continue his faithful soldier and servant unto your lives' end." I call upon you to guard against it by that transcendent tenderness, that ineffable goodness, which hath led him to offer his own body and blood to be your spiritual food and sustenance, and is ready, unworthy as we are, if we will go humbly to his table, to entertain us with heavenly food and spread over us the banner of love. And, finally, I call upon you to guard against it by that solemn declaration from his own lips with which I shall close this discourse, "Whosoever shall be ashamed of me and of my words in this adulterous and sinful generation, of him also shall the Son of Man be ashamed when he cometh in the glory of his Father, with the holy angels."

SERMON XLV.

THE DANGER OF NEGLECTING THE GOSPEL.

HEBREWS, ii. 3.

"How shall we escape, if we neglect so great salvation?"

THERE is not a more general cause of indifference to religion, than an habitual inconsideration of the magnitude of its importance. St. Paul, addressing the Hebrews, is chiefly anxious in the beginning of his epistle, to impress them with a sense of the pre-eminent greatness of the gospel of Christ, particularly of the redemption therein revealed to the human race. In this he aims a well-directed blow, not only at Jewish prejudices, but also at the principal obstruction to the efficiency of the Christian revelation. For, could the hearts of men be impressed with a deep and abiding sense of the greatness of the gift conveyed in it to this ruined world, and with a just estimate of the stupendous means by which its designs have been achieved, the sentiment in the text would rise spontaneously and forcibly in every mind, "How shall we escape, if we neglect so great salvation?"

It will well become us, my brethren, to make these words the theme of our sober meditations. My wish, therefore, will be to set before you, in the first place, the principal considerations which give such solemn magnitude to the redemption and promises of the gospel.

Secondly, to point out the way in which this great salvation may be neglected.

Thirdly, to illustrate the apostle's opinion of their dangerous condition who wilfully neglect it, to their own condemnation.

One important consideration which magnifies the redemption revealed to us in the gospel, is derived from its *origin*. It is the offspring of the divine mind—the work and care of God. An act done by a person of eminent power or wisdom, acquires consequence from the character of the agent. We affix a value to it correspondent to the excellence of the powers exerted in devising and promoting it. Anything, therefore, which comes from the Deity, about which his intelligence and goodness have concerned themselves, comes recommended with a high claim to the attention of his rational creatures. If it be promotive of our welfare, gratitude strengthens this claim. The mercy is magnified by the majesty of its author. Now, the scheme of redemption was formed in the councils of heaven. The everlasting Jehovah vouchsafed in mercy to be the author of this salvation. To give it being and efficacy, he deigned to employ his infinite wisdom and power, his tender compassion and care. It comes to you in the name and with the seal of God. Of that economy from the government of the universe, which the Almighty Creator evolved in his mind from everlasting, the mystery of redemption through the blood of Christ was a chosen part, by which he would save the race of mankind, and manifest the qualities of his nature and government to all his intelligent creatures. Although to the faithless this mystery be a "stumbling block," and to the carnal "foolishness," it is nevertheless so effectual and wonderful, so simple and sublime, that in the view of the humble mind which has experienced its power and studied its contrivance, it could have been devised only by those attributes of the Almighty, the beams of whose excellence are collected in it as in a mirror, and reflected for the comfort, instruction, and admiration both of angels and men. Now, consider the Being who is capable of infinite and eternal happiness in the contemplation of his own perfections, meditating what might be done for his creature man; consider divine wisdom, holiness, benevolence, and all the infinite attributes of the Most High, busy in preparing a plan for raising our fallen race to immortal life and glory. Consider the persons of the adorable Trinity becoming august parties in this work, jointly adopting it, establishing it, and bringing it into operation. Consider it thus, as coming from God, and engaging his care, and say if it be a small or indifferent thing which the gospel reveals—if it be not a great salvation.

But, further, it is magnified by the *dignity of the person* selected to accomplish it, and the wonderful apparatus provided for conveying and explaining it to man.

When the Deity was pleased to actuate chosen men with his spirit, for the benefit of their fellow beings, high was the claim which their instructions had to attention and respect. When angels were sent on errands of mercy to the humble inhabitants of this lower world, great was the honour conferred on our nature, and the messages they brought it would have been perilous to have disregarded. But lo, to accomplish the scheme which the attributes of the Almighty had been employed to devise, the Son of his bosom, the highest personage in the court of heaven, he who was of one substance and glory with the Father, is sent to earth. To him the work of salvation is entrusted. He is to unfold and finish it among men. To prepare his way, to explain his work, to attest his mission, to seal his doings, what a stupendous system of arrangements and events do I behold! See a combination of types and symbols, old as the reign of death,—wonderful, harmonious, significant,—bearing strong marks of a divine origin, and all meeting in the mysteries of the cross their marvellous fulfilment. Hark, what strains in every age from the harp of prophecy, various, sublime, affecting—describing with amazing harmony and precision the time, the deeds, the sorrows, and the death of the Redeemer. Behold, when the Saviour arrives, nature summoned to leave her appointed course and attest his character. Hosts from heaven gratulate the world on his arrival. To give assurance of his truth the dumb speak, the dead are raised, heaven is opened, the voice of God is heard: and when he finishes the work all nature feels and witnesses the mighty deed! What pains, if I may use the expression, has the Most High taken in all this to give clearness and majesty to the revelation of our redemption, and conviction to men of its truth and value! Who can avoid seeing his hand, labouring in the movements of this vast system of types, prophecies, and wonders, to impress upon us the importance of the salvation which they introduce and explain. Who, as he contemplates these amazing arrangements, pervading all time, is not filled with the sentiment that it is a very momentous work! The illustrious character of the bearer of divine mercy, and the ancient, august, supernatural apparatus which unfolds and illustrates it, are alone sufficient to excite reverence, to apprise us that it is a great salvation.

There is, however, a yet more interesting consideration. The redemption of the gospel is great in *the happiness it hath wrought* for our race. It is not a little favour that is done for us. It is no small benefit they forego who neglect this gift. Were it a lengthened lease of life, were it instruction how to spend the present short period of human existence properly and happily, were it but a restoration to us of the knowledge of the one only living and true God, it would be worthy of high estimation. But these fall infinitely short of the aggregate good implied in this salvation. To have a fair estimate of it, we must turn our attention to two points: the state from which it takes us, and the ultimate situation to which it would bring us.

The state from which it takes us is a state of sin, misery, and death. Having transgressed the law of his creation, man became obnoxious to the wrath of the Almighty. Miserably helpless was his condition. His nature was depraved. Ignorance and vice overspread his abode. He was dead in trespasses and sins while he lived, and the corruption of the grave was the end to which he was hastening. Contrast with this forlorn situation the condition in which the gospel places him. We there see the dread penalty of transgression remitted; his ignorance of God, duty, and happiness, dispersed; the strength of sin destroyed; death's awful sceptre broken; the gates of heaven set open before him; pardon and eternal life assured to his faith; a happiness placed within his reach pure as the glory of God, great as the most extended desires of his soul, and durable as eternity. To have brought us to this blessedness from any state would have been doing our race, yea, any race, the utmost kindness. But to have brought us to it from a condition miserable and forlorn, to have thus taken us out of the mire and the clay, and set our feet upon a rock, and ordered our going, is a service which finite conception can never weigh, nor human language express. Fain would I impress upon you its extent and efficacy. But words incumber the subject. Your own minds must perceive your condition by nature, and it must be left to the Spirit of the Most High to enable you to estimate the greatness of your deliverance.

I pass therefore to a remaining consideration which raises to an affecting magnitude the salvation offered to us in the gospel. It is *the price at which it was procured:* the sufferings and sacrifice of the Son of God. Why are the heavens overspread with gloom and the angels hovering over Calvary in astonishment? Who is this that cometh from Jerusalem, with dyed garments, to the trembling mount, this that is marred in his visage, travelling to the agonies of the cross? What are these sufferings at which the sun turns pale and nature quivers through all her massy frame? The dignified personage from the court of heaven, Jesus Immanuel, dies. Behold, he "is led as a lamb to the slaughter, and as a sheep before her shearers is dumb, so he openeth not his mouth." Listen to the few significant words which fall from his lips as he bows his head and yields up the ghost. He pronounces it is finished. What means the interesting sufferer? What is finished by the sacrifice of this innocent and heavenly victim? Amazing economy of heaven! It is your salvation. He is "wounded for our transgressions," he is "bruised for our iniquities, the chastisement of our peace is upon him and by his stripes we are healed." Yes, our ransom from destruction, and restoration to the favour of the Most High were effected by the blood of Christ. To accomplish that redemption, and establish that blessed hope which are proclaimed to us in the gospel, no less than "the only begotten of the Father" is made "the propitiation for our sins." No less than the second of the adorable Trinity is "found in fashion as a man," and becomes "obedient unto death, even the death of the cross." We are "not redeemed with corruptible things, as silver and gold, but with the precious blood of Christ, as of a lamb, without blemish and without spot." Look at the cross! Behold there at what an expense our salvation is procured. See in the wounded side of the wonderful victim the source of the stream which cleanseth us from sin. Observe the costly sacrifice, and unparalleled sufferings, which expiate our offences and purchase our peace. There hangs, expiring for the redemption of this world, "he who knew no sin," the everlasting Son of God. Amazing dispensation of divine mercy! Overwhelming instance of the Almighty's love! This price, at which we are redeemed, enhances the value of our salvation beyond the utmost measure of our astonishment and praise. Oh, the height, the depth, the length, the breadth of the love of God revealed to us in Christ Jesus!

Such are the leading considerations which give a most solemn magnitude to the redemption of the human race. It is great as a work upon which the Most High has employed his wisdom and care. It is great, because the eternal and beloved Son was sent to accomplish it. It is great, because it is the end and fulfilment of a stupendous display of types, prophecies, and wonders, which have been employed to prepare its way from the beginning of the world. It is great, because it snatches us from awful perdition and eternal death, to pardon, renovation and immortality. And it is great, transcendently great, great beyond the power of language to express, because the Lamb of God, whose value not the worlds of the universe could equal, whose place not millions of races of created beings could fill, was slain to purchase it, and to establish the promises.

If now the gospel of this redemption be by any neglected, how can they hope for forgiveness and safety. If this amazing mercy of the Almighty be despised, on what ground can the helpless children of men look for the pardon of those sins of which they are consciously guilty; or for that deliverance from death, after which enlightened nature earnestly aspires? There are two ways in which we may neglect this great salvation—by wilfully rejecting it; and by presumptuously omitting to comply with its conditions. I tremble at the thought, that in either of these ways any one of my hearers, yea, or any one of our race, to whom the tidings of it are proclaimed, should suffer himself to neglect it: for awful are the declarations, and unchangeably just and true, that none such can hope to escape the anger and vengeance of the Almighty.

How indeed shall they escape? The violation of the covenant in Eden drew after it very awful consequences, and but for the intervention and atonement of the blessed Mediator, would have involved man in hopeless perdition. The sanctions of the law given from Sinai, are of an unaccommodating nature, and were executed with solemn precision. "If, then," says the apostle, "the word spoken by angels was steadfast, and every transgression and disobedience received a just recompense and reward, how shall we escape, if we neglect so great salvation?" He that despised Moses' law died without mercy under two or three witnesses; of how much sorer punishment, suppose ye, shall he be thought worthy, who hath trodden under foot the Son of God, and counted the blood of the covenant, wherewith he was sanctified, an unholy thing, and done despite unto the spirit of grace!

Again, how shall they escape? For if, as the wisest even of the heathens surmised, as the experience of the world has proved, and as the conscience of every one will attest in the hour of sober reflection, it be necessary to man's hopes and happiness that the Deity should interpose to purify his nature and provide a pardon for his sins, can we conceive of any dispensation greater, more suitable, or more effectual than this? Is there a better victim to be offered for our sins? Can a purer gospel be preached? May the mercy and justice, the righteousness and truth of the Deity be more happily combined, or more endearingly displayed? What can be done more unto this vineyard, than its gracious and merciful owner hath not done in it? We should find ourselves unable to frame a scheme of redemption more worthy of God, and more consistent with the honour of his government, and the best interests of his universal kingdom. And what says his own unerring voice? "There is none other name given among men whereby they may be saved." "There remaineth no more sacrifice for sin."

Once more, how shall they escape? Proportioned to the greatness of this salvation, is the enormity of their ingratitude and atrocity of their guilt, who reject or abuse it. Consider the language which their conduct implies. They practically say, God may be concerned for our salvation; his dispensations to the world in all ages may have reference to its accomplishment; his Son may become incarnate and bleed; the treasures of his wisdom and love may be opened and lavished upon us, but we regard not his mercies and desire not the knowledge of his ways. They in effect pass by the cross. They behold the Son of God extended upon it. The venerable sufferer calls to them in accents of melting tenderness, "Is it nothing unto you, all ye that pass by? behold and see if there be any sorrow like unto my sorrow, which is done unto me wherewith the Lord has afflicted me," for your sakes. But with cold indifference they turn their heads; with disobedient heedlessness, they go their way. When the Saviour of this most costly sacrifice which the Father hath provided for the expiation of their sins, has reached unto him in the heavens, they refuse to comply with the easy and necessary conditions upon which they may avail themselves of its unspeakable benefits. Surely such must flatter themselves, notwithstanding the declaration of the Almighty, that there is some other way to escape, or else they have never considered how great is this salvation.

Come, then, my hearers, and place yourselves at the foot of

the cross. Behold the Almighty making his Son an offering for your sins. Impress your bosoms with a sense of the amazing greatness of the redemption which God hath wrought. Amidst the stupendous testimonies which the law and the prophets, types and miracles, heaven and earth, and the unexampled behaviour of the sufferer, are giving to his character and offices, are there any unmoved and wilfully blind? Yes. Unhappy unbeliever who makest God a liar, and rejectest his counsel against thyself, "thou art the man." Amidst the unparalleled humiliation and sorrows of the innocent Jesus, are there any who would add a pang to his anguish, and prolong his grief? Yes, hypocritical professor, who, by the inconsistency and unholiness of thy life, dost crucify the Son of God afresh and put him to open shame, "thou art the man." Amidst the all-sufficiency of this sacrifice for the sins of the world, and the wonderful proclamations of its acceptance by the Father, are there any to whom it shall be a savour of death unto death? Yes, hardened sinner, who goest on still in thy wickedness, refusing God's counsels and despising his reproofs, "thou art the man!" And, alas, when these are removed how few of the rest are found cleaving unto their crucified Lord, ready to be crucified with him! Of those who are called by his name, how many are there, who, like his first friends, stand looking upon him far off from the cross! Christians, arise! Go forth to your Master "without the camp, bearing his reproach." Resolve from henceforth to know nothing as the basis of your hopes and banner of your confidence, but "Jesus Christ, and him crucified."

SERMON XLVI.

GLORYING NOT IN THE THINGS OF THIS LIFE, BUT IN THE LORD.

2 TIMOTHY, iii. 4.

"Lovers of pleasures more than lovers of God."

PLEASURE, in the worldly idea of it, is perhaps the strongest foe to virtue and the most subtle enemy of man. She presents herself to him, arrayed in a variety of charms, displaying the most enticing allurements, and making her court to the blindest and most ungovernable feelings of his nature. She too often succeeds,—leads her captive in chosen chains, and in the end proves a vixen to his soul, tormenting and distracting him. That man must have occasional relaxation from the main pursuits of life, and renovate exhausted nature by unbending to amusement, is perfectly the sentiment of reason and religion. Neither the one nor the other requires that he should forego all innocent gratifications for the furtherance of his salvation, nor endeavour to appease and honour his Maker by masking himself in the austerity of a monk. But both unite in assigning limits to indulgence; in divesting pleasure of unreal charms, and prohibiting expressly the fatal folly of making it the business of life. The apostle Paul, writing to his beloved Timothy, warns him of a sad degeneracy which would come in the latter days. Having mentioned many of the gross iniquities which would distinguish these perilous times, iniquities, alas, too strikingly descriptive of the corruption of the world in the present age, he adds, in the words of my text, that men should be "lovers of pleasures more than lovers of God," and that they should be so infatuated with this syren who entices only to destroy, as wholly to despise the restraints of religion and virtue—nay, to prefer pleasure to their God.

Whatever may be the period alluded to by the prophetic apostle, we may certainly see in the picture he has drawn the features of the modern dissolution of piety and principles. Moved by the alarming resemblance, I would solicit your attention while I endeavour, in the first place, to show when men may be said to be lovers of pleasure more than lovers of God.

Secondly, to point out the folly and danger of the conduct which affixes upon men this hideous character.

And thirdly, to give you some rules for so regulating your pleasures that in this respect you may be blameless and without offence, unto the coming of your Lord and Saviour Jesus Christ.

In the first place, men are "lovers of pleasures more than lovers of God" when they indulge in any gratifications which in their nature or by precept are improper and sinful. All pleasures, whether sensual, social, or mental, which are condemned by cool reason, or the injunctions of the Most High, are of this description. Every temptation, when it would seduce a man, addresses him in the beguiling language of the serpent to Eve, "You shall not surely die." Passion, that able artificer of deceit, suggests to the heated fancy some delusory thoughts, which would lead us to believe that the pleasures before us are not so vicious as they are represented, that they cannot be unpardonable, and that we may indulge now upon condition that we will refrain in future. But whoever listens to these suggestions, and unresistingly throws himself into the arms of forbidden pleasure, acts with the boldest effrontery towards his Maker. Are your pleasures impure? Are they such as conscience condemns? Are they prohibited by the commandments of the Almighty? They are then incompatible with a love of God. It is impossible to have a sincere and genuine affection for Deity, and at the same time to delight in gratifications which he, by the reason he has implanted in us, or by the revelation he has given us, has denounced as criminal.

Presuming that this point is clear to every sober mind, I will dwell no longer upon it; but proceed to observe, that the charge in the text may be alleged against many who indulge in pleasures which are not unlawful, but in themselves innocent. Almost any gratification, although in itself harmless, may be rendered criminal by abuse. If men are so engaged in making "provision for the flesh to fulfil the lusts thereof," that their thoughts are never fixed upon the Supreme Being, nor upon the obligations he has imposed on them; if they are so involved in the schemes and delighted with the enjoyments of this life, that the objects of the invisible world have no place in their hearts; if they are so infatuated with the pomps, the luxuries, or the recreations of the world, that they prefer them to the more rational and sublime delights of religion and virtue: then are they "lovers of pleasures more than lovers of God." There are many persons so immoderately attached to amusements and gratifications that they readily resign for them the pleasures of religious worship, both public and private, the advantages of virtuous company and conversation, and the happiness of discharging those amiable offices of benevolence and relative duty, which ennoble the character and life of man. When this is the case, the love of God is evidently abandoned for secondary joys; because none can love him who do not delight in his service and keep his commandments.

Again, they who by constantly or intemperately pursuing worldly pleasures, impair their faculties, relax their energy, injure their health, waste their substance, neglect their families, and dissipate their time, may be said to love pleasure rather than God, even though their gratifications should seem in themselves to be innocent. For all these certain consequences of an immoderate attachment to pleasure are utterly incompatible with the will and wishes of the Most High. Can he love God who squanders the time which should be spent to his glory in the ruinous occupation of the gamester; or he who wastes the substance which he has given him for the support of his family in riotous living? Can he love God, who, for a momentary gratification, parts with his resemblance to his Maker, or he who prefers the prostitution of the faculties which should adorn his rational creation, to the application of them to the advancement of the good of the community and his own spiritual improvement? No. Whoever truly loves God will be anxious to honour him with his body and his spirit, with his faculties, his time, and all that he has given him. In short, when a man's soul is so bound up in any temporal pleasures, that they are preferred to the discharge of his duty; when he cannot relinquish any enjoyments which may come in competition with his usefulness to society, with the welfare of his fellow beings, with the feelings of virtuous friends, or with the dignity of the divine image with which his nature is impressed; the foe of God and religion may be said to have gained the affection of his heart. Do you find that you are ready for a sensual ecstasy to part with the joys of a good conscience? Is the theatre a source of more lively gratification to you than the sanctuary? Are you more pleased with the splendour of a ball and the gayeties of dress than with the beauty of holiness or the cultivation of virtue? Then have you reason to suspect that the divine and holy principle of love to your Creator has not the place which it ought to have in your bosoms, nor its proper influence upon your lives.

Thus you have seen that men are lovers of pleasures more than lovers of God, when they indulge in any sinful gratifications, and when, confining themselves to those which are not forbidden, they make them the chief sources of happiness, and are enslaved by them with chains which neither reason nor religion can break. I now proceed, secondly, to show the folly and danger of the conduct which affixes upon man this hideous character.

The very idea of loving pleasure rather than God, has in it something peculiarly shocking. If we reflect a moment, we shall perceive that it is debasing to the nature of man. That which elevates us above the brute is our capacity for spiritual and moral joys. To make, therefore, those pleasures, some of which are groveling, many of which are frivolous, and which are all transient as the moments of fruition, objects of exclusive regard and perpetual pursuit, is to put off the greatness with which our Maker hath invested us, and to level ourselves with the lower orders of creation. How must it excite the astonishment of superior intelligences, to behold beings who are capable of participating with them the pure, the exalted, the imperishable joys which flow from the knowledge and love of God, and from the employment of religion and virtue, devoting a probationary life and immortal souls to pleasures, sensual as those of brutes, to pursuits unprofitable as those of children, to pleasures and pursuits, which may occasion remorse but can yield no happiness in the sober hours of reflection, and will furnish them with nothing that will be valuable or necessary in their future eternal existence! This total devotion to pleasure diminishes the dignity of man. It is his highest privilege, that which ennobles his nature, that he is capable of walking with God. When he forgets his intellectual faculties, and spiritual relations, when he turns from the fields of sublime speculation and virtuous pursuit to which reason and religion invite him, and on never-resting wings spends his short day in pleasure's ground, enamoured of flowers which fade in his embrace, and revelling upon air with unsatisfied avidity, he exhibits more of the butterfly than the angel, and causes astonishment in heaven at such vacancy and debasement in heirs of immortality, in children of God.

Again, this conduct is irrational. It is the part of reason to estimate things according to their real worth. Now what are the pleasures which engross the affections of those whom the text describes, compared with the duties and pursuits to which our vocation in Christ Jesus directs us? Are they capable of making men wiser or better? Are they noble in themselves, useful in their effects, and lasting as our desires? Like the pleasures of virtue, do they elevate while they delight, become finer with age, and prove sweetest upon reflection? No; they are gratifications, which sometimes disgust before they die, and generally die as soon as they are enjoyed. To say the best of them, they are delights which gratify for a moment, and when they vanish, leave neither improvement nor satisfaction. Sorrow is not prevented by them, nor death dismantled of his terrors. On the other hand, the pursuits of pleasures which spring from the love of God are sublime in themselves. They are adapted to the necessities and infirmities—to the powers and destiny of our nature. They will be useful to us in every situation; in adversity as well as prosperity, in the approach of death as well as in the progress of life. Their sole tendency is to advance us towards perfection, and in them we shall attain to the true end which our Maker proposed in giving us existence. What, then, can be more irrational than for beings, endowed and informed as men are, to follow the former and neglect the latter? What do I say! Can enlightened children of the Most High prefer riot and mirth to the services of his sanctuary and the blessings of his favour? Can reasonable creatures prefer the ignoble haunts where chance presides, and whither idleness and intemperance, profanity and strife resort, to the expecting home where dwell the offspring of once fond affection and all the sweet charities of relative life? Can beings who have been ransomed from destruction by the blood of the Son of God, and with whom it remains to make their election sure, give a more willing ear to the harp and the tabret than to the oracles of truth, and prefer debauches which corrupt and amusements which fill with ennui, to the deeds of virtue which elevate the heart and the promises of religion which tranquillize the soul? In a word, can men, beings endowed with reason, accountable beings, yea, enlightened also by revelation, and taught that they shall be happy or miserable forever according to their use of this probationary life, can they be seduced by vain and fleeting gratifications from the paths of truth and duty? can they turn their ears from the voice of inspiration, and for devotion to pleasure depart from God? It should seem incredible. Yet thus irrational are many of mankind; and it would be less painful if the number were confined to those from whom we might expect no better. But, alas, many act thus under the remonstrance of conscience and their better judgment, under the advantages of a pious education and frequent instruction; sacrificing with a willingness and perseverance, which nothing but the most unhappy infatuation can occasion, the favour of heaven and the true happiness of men, for the enjoyments of brutes and the laughter of fools. How wide is their choice from the dictates of sound wisdom! "My son, enter not into the path of the wicked and go not in the way of evil men. Avoid it, pass not by it, turn from it and pass away." "The fear of the Lord is the beginning of wisdom, and to depart from evil is understanding."

Once more, the conduct we are considering cannot but fail of the end it proposes, and may lead to misery and perdition. Every man who is a lover of pleasure promises himself happiness. And is happiness the fruit of his pursuit? Alas! I know not a more prolific source of restlessness and discontent, of sorrow and sadness, than this criminal love of pleasure. What evil has it not introduced into our world! Observe the wretch whose fallen eyes and languid limbs may well attract your notice. He has loved pleasure more than God. It pleased the Most High to give him a family, in which virtue and discretion, had he made them his friends, would have rendered him useful, and crowned him with bliss. But sinful indulgence decoyed him from the straight path of duty. He became intemperate, and on the altar of his pleasures sacrificed, with his innocence, his substance, his talents, and his time. Poverty and remorse, contempt and disease, are now his portion; and he who might have been like the olive tree, encompassed with the branches of its strength, must now behold the wife of his bosom pining with sorrow, and his little ones crying unanswered for bread. Mark yon widow, between whose brows care has a furrowed seat. She had a son, to whom, when heaven bereaved her of her husband, she, with a mother's blindness, looked for support. Alas! her son was a lover of pleasure more than a lover of God. He was not destitute of filial affections; but the gaming-table stupefied all his sensibilities. They who there stripped him of his wealth, led him to the impure abodes where he might spoil others of their innocence. One vice familiarized him with another, and a vagrant now, he wanders without food, without peace, without a name—a living monument of the truth of the wise man's remark, that "A foolish son is the heaviness of his mother." Enter the burial-yard, and stop by the stone which is rendered pathetic by its date. There is an air of mystery in its inscription. Inquire of some one what brought the victim to his untimely grave. He, too, loved pleasure more than God. Religion he considered as an injurious restraint upon the appetites of nature and the pursuits of life. He therefore despised her bonds, and withheld not his heart from any joy. Satiated, at length, with his immoderate indulgence, he became disgusted with pleasure, and pleasure in revenge sent melancholy into his bosom. He grew dissatisfied with himself, dissatisfied with society, dissatisfied with nature, and dissatisfied with God. In an awful moment he extinguished in himself the spark which the Almighty had kindled; and pleasure must forever be rebuked by the tear which piety will shed near the grave of the suicide.

Sufficiently unhappy are the effects of a sinful attachment to pleasure, even in this world. If man could always live thoughtless, if reflective age should not overtake him, and if his existence ceased at his death, still it may be questioned whether he could with safety adopt the suggestion of pleasure, "Let us eat and drink, for to-morrow we die." But this is not the case. Reflection in no man will always slumber, and every man is destined to live hereafter. And what are the joys with which the ministers of pleasure furnish a man for the hours of reflection? They have enervated his fortitude, enfeebled his piety, and turned him from the principles and duties which, if attended to, are productive of peace. Perhaps they have impaired his health, wasted his time and property, diminished his respectability, and rendered him a broken vessel, empty himself and useless to the world. At any rate, they have counteracted the will of the Almighty by fastening the affections, which he would have attracted to heavenly and enduring objects, upon earthly and fading joys. What satisfaction, then, can they afford when reviewed! To every man there are moments when he must turn his thoughts inward, and would there look for comfort and support. But what support, or comfort, can be found, or expected, in the remembrance of pleasures which defiled when they delighted, and are vanished like the visions of night? In the hour of his ecstasy he may have smiled exultingly, and fancied himself happy. But Solomon has strikingly compared his joys to "the crackling of thorns under a pot," and taught us that the "end of his mirth is heaviness."

There is, however, a yet more dreadful censor of pleasure, in death. It is appointed unto all men once to die, and this seductive syren can never commute, though she may accelerate the fate of her victims. Awful is their state when brought by some minister of the "king of terrors" to the borders of eternity. They have loved pleasure, but she has given them none of the qualifications of faith and holiness, which enlighten the soul in its passage through the tomb and soothe the hours of expiring life. On the contrary, having for the sake of pleasure renounced God, they have turned from themselves the favour of heaven, and by wasting their probation in a round of follies and indulgences, have exposed themselves to the sentence—"in your lifetime ye received your good things," "depart from me, ye workers of iniquity." Imagine, then, one of this unhappy class of men brought suddenly to the brink of the grave. The remembrance of his life comes like a cloud over his mind. The sun is darkened light. It chills his spirit. Compelled at length by the gloominess of his condition to think, his mind flutters dismayed over some such reflections as these: "Oh, foolish man that I have been! I have spent my life in vanity and folly. The pleasures I pursued have never yielded me the satisfaction they promised; and I have frequently pursued them in defiance of remonstrances within me, which perhaps were the whispers of God. Life is gone, and I am hasting into eternity. What have I to carry into the presence of the Almighty but a defiled body and a soul 'dead in trespasses and sins!' Can I expect that God will love me, when I have loved pleasure more than I have loved him? O, that some one could assure me that *that* blood of the Redeemer which I have thoughtlessly despised, will cleanse me now from my pollutions, and expiate my sins! Would God be pleased to prolong my days I would choose him for my portion, and spend my life in his service. But I fear I shall die." This is not an imaginary picture. It is taken from life. How far that repentance is effectual, which commences when we have no longer inducement or power to sin, it is not easy for us to determine. Of one thing we may be sure, that safety is always on that side where no risk is run. God is merciful; but he is not mutable. He is "long-suffering and of great kindness;" but he will not "clear the guilty." The wise man, to whom he communicated much of his ways, and who has gathered more from experience than perhaps any other mortal, taking to his use a strong and solemn irony, has given us a caution upon this subject, pertinent and impressive. "Rejoice, O young man, in thy youth, and let thy heart cheer thee in the days of thy youth, and walk in the ways of thy heart and in the sight of thine eyes; but know thou that for all these things God will bring thee into judgment."

Such is the folly and danger of the conduct which affixes upon men the hideous character of "lovers of pleasures more than lovers of God." It derogates from the dignity of our nature; it is wholly unbecoming rational beings, especially professors of Christianity; it must fail of the end it proposes, and may involve us in misery and perdition. Had I time, it might be shown to be a fever, destructive of public as well as private greatness and happiness; bringing upon nations as well as individuals, oftentimes a delirium, sometimes dissolution. But I must haste to give you, as was proposed, some rules for so regulating your pleasures that in this respect ye may be blameless and without offence unto the coming of your Lord and Saviour Jesus Christ.

In the first place, when any pleasure solicits your embrace or pursuit, ask yourselves always whether it is lawful; if it is not, nothing should induce you to yield yourselves to it. Turn from it resolutely, and haste away. Regard not its allurements. Mind not its charms. Whatever its appearance, a sinful qualification must do you harm. Though it should be sweet in the mouth, it will assuredly convey poison through the system. Though it present itself to you in all the loveliness of beauty and deck itself in all the desirableness of delight, it conceals a sting which it will leave in your bosom. The extraction of that sting, should it ever be removed, must give you unspeakable anguish. It may never be extracted; but festering and gangrening may render you wretched till death. You may carry it into the eternal world; and there, when place for repentance shall no longer be found, it may become in you a worm which shall never die. From indulgences, then, which you know to be criminal, make it a rule to turn resolutely away. It will not answer in these cases to hesitate. He who stops to deliberate with forbidden pleasure will generally be undone. She has powers of fascination: and whoever, instead of winging his way to the regions of safety, hovers with irresolute delay over the snare she has spread, will be drawn nearer and nearer by the strange action of her spells, till he is suddenly entangled in its meshes; and may in the same moment discover that his freedom and his virtue are gone. There is danger in listening a moment to unlawful appetite. It is instant and persevering resistance which will put the prince of darkness to flight. Take for your example the renowned Joseph. Consider always the high claim which the laws of the author of your being have to your observance. When tempted by any pleasure which conscience, reason, or religion tells you is sinful, turn to the reflection which will ever be the best safeguard of virtue, "How can I do this great wickedness and sin against God?"

Again, if you are satisfied that the pleasure which invites you is lawful, ask yourselves before indulgence, whether it will interfere with any duty. If it will, a less good is never to be preferred to a greater; we must not sacrifice duty to any joy. It may interfere with our duty, either by occupying that time which should be otherwise employed, or by unfitting us in our talents, substance, health, or spirits, for those actions which it is incumbent on us to perform. I will illustrate this by a few examples. We are advised by our holy religion to owe no man anything but our love; and the common principles of justice and honour require the payment of debts. This high duty, economy and industry will enable every man to discharge. If men, then, in the pursuit of pleasure, involve themselves in expenses which they never expect to defray, or if, being by imprudence or misfortune, or by any other means, already embarrassed, they indulge themselves in the joys of extravagance, or even in the ease of indolence, while their creditors are deprived of their due; they sacrifice to pleasure the brightest gem in the breast-plate of integrity, and, though it may seem venial to themselves, become offensive to the eyes of the God of righteousness. Allow me another instance: it is the duty of every man to provide for the subsistence and to promote the comfort of the family which the Most High has given him. With this tender duty, whose influence upon the happiness of the world is incalculably great, pleasure may often interfere. If a man suffer her to withhold his presence from his home when he should be there, for the protection, the guidance, or the comfort of his household; or if she lead him to neglect the business, or enfeeble the faculties, by means of which he is to provide for their sustenance and improvement, though he may quiet himself with the thought that the gratifications to which she leads him are not unlawful ones, we have the highest authority to say, that he "denieth the faith, and is worse than an infidel." Take a third example. I know not that religion has anywhere prohibited our excursions in pursuit of rural pleasures, or the innocent hilarity of our social meals;—but all considerate persons will confess that to reverence the Sabbath and join in the public services of the Lord our God, are the reasonable duties of every sincere Christian and good citizen. Whatever pleasures therefore interfere with these duties, though they may be innocent in themselves, become criminal by the unseasonable use of them. If the festivity of the table, or the allurements of a ride, or even the ease of repose, detain us from the sanctuary, where the Most High expects on his holy day to receive the acknowledgments and adoration of his children, he, our Creator and Redeemer, is made to give place to pleasure, and we prefer her blandishments to his commands. Your own consciences will enable you to apply this rule of never sacrificing duty to pleasure, to innumerable other cases, in which indulgences, innocent in themselves, may be incompatible with the proper improvement of ourselves, with the requirements of piety or benevolence, with the feelings of virtuous friends, or with that general sobriety which is so meet in this state of probation and mortality, and so favourable to the growth of the best qualities of the soul. Our blessed Lord carries the self-denial, with which truth and duty are to be preferred before all other gratifications, to a sublime degree—"He that loveth father and mother more than me is not worthy of me." And an inspired apostle gives to the sacrifices of innocent indulgences which a good man should make, a wide extent and powerful motive,—"It is good neither to eat flesh, nor to drink wine nor anything whereby thy brother stumbleth, or is offended, or is made weak."

Further, in the pursuit of pleasure it will be found a useful rule, never to go to the utmost extent of innocent gratification. Our minds, to be trained and preserved in the ways of virtue, must be kept under control. If we would not love pleasure more than we ought, our inclinations for it should always feel the reins of discipline. The passion for pleasure is encouraged by freedom and strengthened by indulgence. Though the desires should be limited to lawful gratifications, yet if within these limits they have an uncontrolled sway, they will at length grow imperious; and, often weakening the influence of sedate principles, and the attraction of sober pursuits, become most unhappily the ruling springs of life. Besides, it is often but a line which separates virtue from vice. He who allows himself to go to the last boundary of innocent indulgence, will, in all probability, be seduced into the regions of transgression. We may give ourselves an impetus even in a pleasant course, which we may not be able to arrest, when it has brought us to the brink of a precipice. Look at the unhappy wretch whom pleasure has made her victim with the cup of intemperance. Think ye, he plunged at once into his iniquity? No. When he first tasted the intoxicating draught, his virtue remained unchanged. Appetite presently led him beyond the necessities of nature. He looked with more and more delight upon the sparkling of the cup; and, fancying himself still within the bounds of moderation, recurred with increasing avidity to its exhilarating influence. But, alas! when he came to the point which separates moderation from excess, he was unable to discern it. He passed it, and became the slave of the most tyrannic of vices; and it is not among the least of the compunctions which now torture his bosom, that he must attribute his ruin to his neglect of early restraint. Safety is greatest far within the boundaries of virtue. Go not to the utmost extent of innocent indulgence. "Hast thou found honey? eat so much as is sufficient for thee; lest thou be filled therewith and it cause thee disease."

Once more, if you would escape the snares of pleasure, avoid idleness. Prescribe it to yourselves as one of the best defences against her allurements, to have something to do. It is in the hours of indolence that she plants her dominion over the hearts of men. It is among the listless tribe, whose faculties have no employment, whose time is heavy upon their hands, and whose minds for want of engagement, are exposed to the intrusion of whatever promises present joy, that she finds the greatest number of her votaries. When men are engaged in honest pursuits and virtuous employments, she seldom approaches them, or she does it unsuccessfully. It was not while David was penning with piety his transcendent Psalms, nor while he was fighting with holy zeal the battles of his country, but it was in an hour of indolent relaxation, when he was walking vacantly upon the top of his house, that he was beguiled by pleasure to conceive the crime, in which he seems for once to have lost sight of his God. Let a man be busily devoted to the employments and duties of "that state of life unto which it hath pleased God to call him," and pleasure will hardly be able to gain such influence in his bosom as will turn him from the paths of sobriety and virtue. It is want of more important employment, that favours her solicitations. Show me the person who has no avocation, to whom there belongs neither profession nor pursuit, and I will point you to one, whom pleasure, if she attempt it, will be sure to overcome, and in all probability will then exalt as a supporter of her unhallowed dominion.

Again, let me not forbear to remark that in order to escape whatever is injurious in the pleasures of life, and the true interests of the soul, it is necessary that you should dwell near to God. Conscious of the harm to which we are exposed in this world of temptation and frailty, we should betake ourselves to the shadow of those wings under which we may be sure of safety. The more we know of God, the more we shall love him, and the more we love God, the less we shall regard the vain and sinful pleasures of this fleeting life. An eye to his presence will check our volatility. To contemplate his perfections and the joys which his mercy has provided for us in Christ Jesus, will raise our affections to better objects: our communion with him and supplication to him, will procure us the protection of his grace; and the riches of his good word, and the powers of the world to come, will enable us to say of carnal pursuits and criminal joys, that we have no pleasure in them. Abide in God. Choose him for your counsellor and friend. If you cleave to him, he "will not suffer you to be tempted above that ye are able, but will with the temptation also make a way to escape, that ye may be able to bear it."

Lastly, there is another rule of infinite worth and of easy application. When tempted by any pleasure, ask yourselves how your heavenly Master would have conducted himself in similar circumstances. The example of Christ is a perfect model of conduct for all his disciples. His injunction is, "Learn of me." Would his followers make him the pattern for regulating their lives, would they desire no gratifications which he would have disdained, and indulge themselves in no pursuit which he would have avoided, they might always regulate their joys without perplexity or error. Be it your care, with regard to the pleasures of life, to walk as Christ walked, and you will not fail to be blameless in this respect, and without offence unto the day of his coming.

I have now finished what was proposed, when I introduced this subject to your attention. So long as you are continued in the flesh, you will be surrounded, my brethren, by the allurements of pleasure. The conflict with them is an arduous and perilous part of the Christian warfare. "Ponder your paths and let all your ways be established." "Supplicate often, your heavenly Father, to prevent you in all your doings with his most gracious favour and to preserve you with his continual help. Apply the rules which have been suggested, to the regulation of your own conduct, and train, by them, the desires of the young, whom Providence may have committed to your care. Keep ever in remembrance, that to "seek the kingdom of God and his righteousness" is your principal concern; and should you be brought, in the course of your probation into the gardens of pleasure, let not wisdom and understanding forsake you. So shall you be "blameless and harmless, the sons of God without rebuke, in the midst of a crooked and perverse generation;" and they who are of the contrary part, having no evil thing to say of you, may haply be led, by your steady uniform goodness, to admire the ways of virtue and glorify their Father who is in heaven.

SERMON XLVII.

GLORYING NOT IN THE THINGS OF THIS LIFE, BUT IN THE LORD.

JEREMIAH, ix. 23 and 24.

"Thus saith the Lord, Let not the wise man glory in his wisdom, neither let the mighty man glory in his might; let not the rich man glory in his riches;—but let him that glorieth glory in this, that he understandeth and knoweth me, that I am the Lord, who exercise loving-kindness, judgment, and righteousness in the earth."

THERE is nothing in which men more unfortunately err than in the estimate which they make of the acquisitions and distinctions of this transitory life. Ruled by imperious passions, confining their views to the present scene, and their desires to the gratifications which it offers, they are wholly absorbed in the pursuit of riches, honours and fame, whilst the principles are neglected which should elevate them above the world and its illusions, and are the basis of everything which is truly great and godlike in the human character. Against this madness or folly, with which almost all men are more or less infatuated, the prophet Jeremiah inveighs with the voice and words of divine authority. "Thus saith the Lord, Let not the wise man glory in his wisdom, neither let the mighty man glory in his might; let not the rich man glory in his riches, but let him that glorieth glory in this, that he understandeth and knoweth me, that I am the Lord who exercise loving kindness, judgment, and righteousness in the earth."

The word "glory," here signifies that exultance which indicates a belief that the cause of it is a source of safety and happiness. It is distinct from the presumption of vanity, and the arrogance of pride; neither of which may be innocently indulged, even upon those grounds on which the text exhorts men to glory. The import of the passage I take to be this: Thus saith the all-wise Counsellor, the Sovereign God, trust ye not in the wisdom, power, and wealth of this world, nor build with them the fabric of your happiness, but let a reasonable assurance and religious reverence of my gracious, wise, and equitable government of the affairs of men be the source of all your joy and ground of all your confidence.

The words thus explained present two propositions, which I shall endeavour to illustrate in the sequel of this discourse.

First, that the temporary acquisitions and distinctions of this life are unworthy of our reliance as sources of happiness and safety.

And secondly, that a religious knowledge of the government of God, properly improved, is the genuine source of confidence and peace.

The absurdity of glorying in the distinctions and acquisitions of the world will be evident if we consider that they are promiscuously shared by the virtuous and the vicious. The paths of knowledge are not open exclusively to the upright. They are not always the worthy who are vested with power, and bear rule among men. Wealth does not always flow in an undeviating course to the doors of the honest and good. On the contrary, riches are often accumulated by the hard and defiled hands of the oppressor—power is acquired and used by those who are the spots and scourges of society, and the knave is often armed with cunning and well versed in human science. Pitiful occasions then are these things for glory. If they were the means of security and gladness, would they be bestowed upon those in whom the Most High can have no pleasure? Under his providence it is reasonable to suppose, that to the sacred ground of peaceful confidence and pure joy, the obdurate transgressor of his laws can have no access. Accordingly we are taught in his word that the distinctions of this life are not the tokens of his favour. He is of purer eyes than to behold iniquity, and cannot look upon sin. And since they only in whom he delights can be happy, the wisdom and honours and wealth of this world, which are frequently acquired by those whom his soul hateth, can never be the sources of safety and satisfactory joy. While it should diminish every man's pride, it should also weaken his confidence in them to reflect that they are participated by those to whom the Almighty hath declared "there is no peace"—to whom, though vengeance may a long time linger, there is a fearful looking for of judgment.

But their unworthiness to be the objects of our trust and expectation will be further evident, if we consider that they are mutable and uncertain. We need a rock for our reliance, amidst the waves of this troublesome world. That which may be worthy of our confidence and glory must be stable and permanent. But to which of man's temporal endowments do those properties belong? Wisdom is undoubtedly the best of all earthly acquisitions. But who can trust to his own wisdom? Its utmost glance can traverse but a narrow circle. Precarious, awfully precarious is its tenure. Look only for a moment at those from whom wisdom is fled, whom accident, disease, or the inexplicable providence of God has deprived of that reason which once beamed in them, with superior lustre. How are the treasures of the well-stored mind changed to confusion, and all dignity and elevation of thought converted to abasement! Look but on one such subject of delirium, and nothing more can be necessary to deter the wise man from glorying in his wisdom.

There are some, however, who rely more upon their might than upon their wisdom. Their personal qualities of body or of mind, or the public predilection, has raised them above their fellows, and given them great sway and extensive influence in society. This is apt to make men forgetful of a superior power, and to fill them with complacency in themselves. But if their might be founded in personal properties, these are perishable.—

The most mighty strength, the most heroic courage, the most superior skill, time will impair as a moth fretting a garment. If it depend upon the public voice, this is extremely uncertain. The light of popular favour which has brought them into conspicuous notice, waxes and wanes like the phases of the moon. Nothing is more inconstant. To-day it shines upon Cæsar, to-morrow upon his subject; and he is in obscurity. A prince on his throne now, and anon carrying the chains of his vassal, is a reverse of fate which men have often witnessed. What more absurd then than to glory in our might! Whatever be the properties which give men pre-eminence in the world, or however extensive their power, he who has no other source of peace and security, gathers for himself vexations and disappointment. He rests upon a reed which the winds will shake, and his own weight may destroy.

But more than in their wisdom or might men glory in their riches. These are the idol to which the many bow, and sacrifice and offer their confidence—and in the busy pursuit and anxious care of them all other sources of safety and complacence are easily forgotten. Yet their mutability is notorious. They are in perpetual fluctuation. From the hands of one they are gone he knows not how. Misfortune overtakes another, and while he is felicitating himself in his abundance, strips him of all he possesses. From a third they descend to his offspring, and what the father accumulated with the labours of his life, the son in a little while dissipates. Wealth is of too transitory a nature to afford men security, or be chosen by them as the source of satisfaction and glory. And in his observation of this truth, Solomon founded those pertinent proverbs, "Labour not to be rich," "Cease from thine own wisdom. Wilt thou set thine eyes upon that which is not? For riches certainly make themselves wings, they fly away as an eagle towards heaven."

In short, instability is so inseparable a property of everything human—the acquisitions and distinctions of this life are so mutable and uncertain, that it should seem the Almighty has disqualified them for our reliance. He who trusts in them for his safety and peace, and has no other resource, depends like Jonah upon the shelter of a gourd, which while it rapidly grows and promises to abide, some fatal worm is destroying at the roots.

But the unworthiness of these things to be the cause of our glory, is brought into the strongest light by the consideration that they are prostrated by death. If they were constant and sufficient, and allotted only to the worthy, it would, nevertheless, much disparage them that they are unable to offer resistance to the arms of "the king of terrors." This unrelenting chastiser of human folly bids defiance to the wisdom and the might of men, and most impressively teaches the rich man the absurdity of glorying in his riches. Let us pause, and observe the course of all human grandeur—how it passes away. Look back though the long series of years since the creation. What multitudes renowned for wisdom, and might, and wealth, have exulted on life's stage, while these passed to corruption! And what is the fruit of their attainments! Where now are the philosophers and sages of heathen days, and the luminaries of the centuries since the promulgation of the gospel, in whose souls the rays of human wisdom were gloriously diffused? Where now are those who ruled the world, the Alexanders and Cæsars, whose personal powers or the popular voice raised to the utmost pre-eminence of might? Where now are the rich ones of former years, who amassed wealth till they were unable to estimate it, and rolled in all the pomp and indulgences which it could procure? They moulder in the dust! And where are the traces of the splendour in which they gloried? It is humiliating, yet instructive, from our own point of time to review in the ages which are past, the end of all human distinctions and attainments. We see beforehand in what our complacence and confidence in the temporal acquisitions must terminate. Though wisdom, and might, and riches were combined in our portion, they could not elevate above the reach of death. We must go down into the same abyss into which the wise, and great, and wealthy of former times have lost their grandeur and distinction. And they, to use the bold figure of the sublime Isaiah, will say, "Art thou become weak as we? Art thou become like unto us? Thy pomp is brought down to the grave; thy skill, and the noise of thy viols; the worm is spread under thee and the worms cover thee."

If we could suppose that temporal acquisitions would be of any utility in the future existence, there would be some plea for the ardour with which they are sought, some reason for glorying in them, notwithstanding their inability to save their possessor from the grave. But the rich man leaveth his treasures to he knows not whom when he dieth. He can carry nothing with him. All his abundance for which he hath laboured, rising early and late taking rest, is useful only in this short life, and can avail him no more after death than the dust in which he reposes. "Be not then afraid," says the Psalmist, "when one is made rich, when the glory of his house is increased; for when he dieth he shall carry nothing away, his glory shall not descend after him."

The distinctions which are here necessary for the order and comfort of society, will also be disregarded in the future state. The ruler and the subject, the man of might and the humble tenant of the vale will stand on a level at the bar of God. "He that doeth wrong shall receive for the wrong he hath done, and there is no respect of persons."

What parts of human knowledge may be confirmed, and have operation in the future state, we are unable to say. The systems in which reason betrays her weakness, while intending to display her strength, in attempting to explain the ways and works of God, and to improve the condition of men, are mutable even in this world. One generation confounds, rejects, and ridicules the opinions of another. Most of them, though here they amuse us, may perhaps in our improved existence, be acknowledged to be futile. Of this we may be assured, that the art of virtue and science of theology will be chiefly studied and esteemed in the kingdom of heaven.

Now, to exult in earthly wisdom, power, and wealth, as sources of security and happiness, when they may be useless in the greatest and most important part of our being; yea, when at best they can serve us only in this short life which is passing away, and at death will be effaced by the waves of oblivion, must be the grossest of absurdities, if we are moral and intelligent creatures, and candidates for immortality. "Let not the wise man glory in his wisdom, neither let the mighty man glory in his might; let not the rich man glory in his riches."

Having thus fully shown how unworthy of reliance the acquisitions and distinctions of this life are, it remains that we consider and appreciate the substitute proposed in the text. But this will open a field too extensive to be now investigated. It must, therefore, be reserved for the employment of a future opportunity. Meantime, I shall have accomplished much, if in any degree your affection be withdrawn from the impressive charms of earthly wisdom, power, and wealth, which must be done before they can be placed upon things above. The allurements and illusions of the world are the snares in which men are so easily taken. Entangled in these, they forget the transitoriness of life and importance of holiness, their dependence on God, and their eternal concerns. On this account, the Author of our religion levelled against them his most earnest exhortations; and hence, when we put on his name, we are required to renounce them. Not that Christianity is of an austere spirit. By any measure of their importance to our happiness or usefulness in the world, they may be innocently desired and pursued. So far as wisdom will increase our admiration of the Eternal Mind, and enable us to promote the welfare of men, let us study to be wise. So far as power and influence in society are acquired by honest means, in order to be used in the accomplishment of pure and beneficent purposes, let them be considered as blessings from above. So far as wealth is necessary for the comfort of our families, and will be used by us to alleviate the suffering and increase the joys of our fellows, it would be wrong to view it with indifference. But we must forget that we are strangers and sojourners here as our fathers were, and become insensible of the genius and design of our religion before we can indulge a complacent confidence in any human acquisitions as affording our proper security and joy. They can never repay this unqualified devotion to them. Whoever trusts in them without blending with them the hopes of religion and the pleasures of virtue, will find by experience that Solomon was not declaiming when he declared them vanity and vexation of spirit.

But the prophet does not take from men the objects on which they lean and indulge a fallacious complacency, to leave them destitute of any grounds of confidence and glory. In the conclusion of the text he provides a great and inestimable substitute. "Let him that glorieth glory in this, that he understandeth and knoweth me, that I am the Lord who exercise loving-kindness, judgment and righteousness in the earth."

The government of God is the grand foundation of the hopes, and safeguard of the happiness, of every intelligent creature. In that knowledge of the Deity, that understanding of his ways, and assurance of his providence over the affairs of men, that intimate acquaintance with the nature and principles of his administration, which the prophet recommends man, may find a sure basis of composure, confidence and joy. Besides this there is no rock of reliance, no source of safety and peace.

We find ourselves here with a complex nature in a precarious state. Life's courses are various, its evils are numerous, its anxieties great, and its wants problematical. Every person of reflection must desire something on which his spirit may rest and feel itself safe; some ground of dependence, some object of trust for happiness amidst the troubles, and safety amidst the dangers of his condition. If we should think ourselves masters of our own fate, we should have little cause to glory. A consciousness of the narrow limits of our view, a sense of the feebleness of our virtue, daily experience of the infirmity of our nature, are so many barriers to our deriving rational confidence from any reliance upon our own faculties and exertions. Deplorable is our condition if we are dependent only on ourselves. No beings can be more destitute of the hopes of safety and assurances of happiness than those of our race who know no sources of protection and joy but their own confined powers.

The skeptical principles of chance or fate furnish a miserable resource. Who that has feeling can be happy, if no knowledge of an intelligent design in the tribulations of life divest them in part of their gloom? Who that reflects can think himself secure, if life and its events are fortuitous and he is perpetually exposed to all the evils which may be found in the infinitude of possibilities? These systems are very fallacious, which, to solve man's dependence and enlighten his mind, turn him over to blind destiny or chance. While they promise him a noble enlargement, freedom from fear, and much cause for excellence, they reduce him to a condition in which he is exposed to the utmost and every evil which can be possible: and nothing but mere chance will preserve him.

It is a knowledge of the Almighty that he exists, a God infinite in every perfection, and governs supreme by the universe which is the work of his hands,—that furnishes assurance of safety and the means of peace and joy to all rational beings. To us men, how important is this knowledge! We are the sport of uncertainties. Our world is forlorn. Misfortune is uncontrolled. Vice fears no retribution, and death is triumphant until we understand and know the Deity, that he is the Lord, and are informed of his ways and the unchangeable principles of his mind. An acquaintance with his being and his government over the affairs of men, dispels the darkness and disarms the miseries of life, and is a foundation on which every humble expectation of safety and every reasonable hope of felicity may be established in the upright heart.

For I hasten to observe that the government of the Deity is immutably gracious, wise and equitable, and a knowledge of this is essential to that acquaintance with him in which we are exhorted to glory. Indeed these characters of his administration cannot be hidden from any who faithfully study and understand the manifestations he has made of his nature and purposes.

That the Lord is a God of kindness, gracious in an immeasurable degree, we need not be long learning. That he hath made us when he needed us not, and administers his government for the benefit of his creatures rather than for his own aggrandizement, is unanswerable proof of his benevolence. The bounty with which he provides for our sustenance and delight, and his patience, and forbearance, and kindness towards the most obdurate offenders, magnify the praises of his benignity. The care and expense, with which he recovered a race, who are rebellious against him, evidence most affectingly that he is a sovereign in whom the beamings of mercy do always adorn the dignity of justice. His word and his works, and the daily operations of his providence, teach us that he exerciseth loving-kindness in the earth.

Of the wisdom and judgment with which he conducts the affairs of the universe we have indubitable assurance. All excellences emanate from him; in him, therefore, all wisdom is concentrated. That he uses it is necessarily implied in his possessing it. Nor are we ignorant of its effects. In the economy of nature we see the most stupendous contrivance, and the most perfect adaptation of means to their end. The system of moral government which he administers, so far as we are acquainted with it, appears admirably calculated to promote the improvement of his moral creatures and the honour of his supremacy. Of some dispensations of his providence we may not see the reason. His judgments in the earth may be sometimes inexplicable. But our powers should be measured before we undertake to scan the proceedings of God. From the reflections of reason and the revelations of his word we may obtain a general and sufficient assurance that his understanding is infinite, and all his ways unalterably just. He always sees what is best to be done. Nothing can conceal from him the result of any operation nor the connections of any events. Of man's necessities, and how he may be conducted to happiness, he alone is fully informed. He, therefore, cannot err in any of his dispensations to the children of men.

The equity of the divine government is not less certain than any other attribute of it. By our finite sight this is not always immediately discernible. But it is among the wisest principles of religious knowledge. Rectitude is essentially inherent in the nature of the Deity. His will is the standard of right. Free from the passions and prejudices of men, he is without partiality. In his survey of his creatures he beholds them with an equal eye, and with everlasting righteousness regulates their concerns. Though to some a fairer position seems given than to others, though we see not always that merit is the measure of prosperity, though the wicked sometimes triumph, and the worthy are in depression, yet we cannot doubt that justice is forever in the council of heaven. Under every form which his providence may assume, in every event which he ordains, we know from his nature and his word that he is watchful of the interests of the upright, and will cause all things to work together for good, to those who love him. "The Lord is holy in all his ways, and righteous in all his works. His commandments stand fast forever and ever, and are done in truth and equity."

That the government of the Deity is thus gracious, wise, and equitable, we must believe, before we can rightly know and understand him. "In those things I delight, saith the Lord." Of a faithful contemplation of his works and providence and word the declaration of Moses happily expresses the result. "He is the rock; his work is perfect; all his ways are judgment; a God of truth and without iniquity, just and right is he."

Now what greater cause for glory can there be than to know that all things are under the inspection and government of such a being!—that this God is our God, and will be the guide of his servants unto death. To be under his government, to have our lives and all the concerns of them in his hands; to serve him who is thus gracious, wise, and equitable, and have him for the only object of our trust, is the safest and happiest condition in which we can live. Of the numerous definitions of happiness this perhaps would be most unexceptionable, that it is a persuasion of our dependence upon an infinite Being, whose power is able to give efficacy to his will, and whose will is wholly guided by benevolence. Such a Being must be a safeguard in danger, a refuge in trouble, and a source of supplies for all our wants. If we may glory in any knowledge, it must be in knowing his existence and character, his promises and will. If we may glory in any might, it must be in the might of him who is our governor and sole dependence. If we may glory in any riches, it must be in the riches of the wisdom and goodness of our God. His being, and control of the affairs of men, and gracious purposes towards them, are to the upright, when properly understood, the only genuine source of confidence and peace.

SERMON XLVIII.

HOPE.

JEREMIAH, xviii. 12.

"And they said there is no hope, but we will walk after our own devices, and we will every one do the imagination of his evil heart."

TO soothe life's sorrows, animate man in every virtuous pursuit, and bear him onward with diligence and cheerfulness to his high destination, hope is implanted in the human bosom by its benevolent Creator. Its object is future good, and its range the present life and eternity. Nourished upon these grounds of expectation which nature, reason, and revelation furnish, it is the strong defender of virtue, and sure guide to greatness and peace. It is to this principle, as we may learn from the context, that the promises of the Most High are addressed. We are said to be saved by it, and it is named by an apostle as the inseparable companion of faith and charity. So important is it to the comfort and right management of life, that an abandonment of it is inevitably followed by the most unhappy and ruinous consequences. Yet we find that there were many in the prophet's time, and indeed there are in every age, who adopt the opinion that there is no reason to look for satisfaction here, or a better being hereafter, and therefore yield themselves to the impulses of present inclination, and do that which is right in their own eyes. They say, "There is no hope, but we will walk after our own devices, and will every one do the imagination of his evil heart."

In discoursing from these words, it will be my endeavour to set before you, in the first place, the unreasonableness of the opinion that there is no hope.

Secondly, to point out to you the temptations to imbibe this opinion, to which we are exposed.

And thirdly, to show the inseparable connection between the adoption of it and the abuse of life.

1st. Nature, reason, the charms of creation, every magnanimous emotion, the experience of every good man, all rise in opposition to the hostile sentiment that "there is no hope." So numerous are evidences of its unreasonableness, which crowd into the indignant mind, that it is difficult to determine how to arrange them or with which to begin. Those which are the most powerful, may, I think, be drawn from the situation in which we are placed, from the most natural and satisfactory sentiments which we have of a Supreme Being, and from the enlivening instructions and soothing consolations of revealed religion.

I begin with the *situation* in which we are placed. Surely, this world, with all the beauties which adorn it, its riches, and the scenes of stupendous grandeur which its inhabitants behold, is not the allotted residence of beings doomed to despair. Some unvaried desert, on which no star should glimmer, no flower should appear, no meandering stream should flow; some murky dungeon into which no beam of light should enter, no voice of joy be ever heard, would better suit the destiny of beings who were to know no comfort and indulge no hope, than this magnificent world, where all is beautiful, lively, and animating, and leads to lofty conceptions and manly designs. Cheerfulness predominates in all the works that surround us. The scenes in every part of our abode invite to pleasure and improvement. The rising sun rebukes despondence, and when it sets it reproaches distrust. Indeed, the external circumstances of our situation inspire hope by the delights which they yield.

Who that abides beneath the canopy of the skies, and walks amidst the beauties of the varied year, has not innumerable sources of elevating delight constantly set open before him? What virtuous mind, unstrung by accident or exertion, may not recur to the charms and wonders of nature, and in the contemplation of them acquire new tone, new energies, new motives to grateful satisfaction in his being, and invigorating expectation from its issue? Who that surveys this earth and all the grandeur about it, and reflects with the calm judgment of virtue upon his station in it, but will infer that there is something of high extract and happy destiny in man from his having dominion in so delightful a domain.

But let us consider the occupations of our existence. Is there no blessing of health, of satisfaction, and of reward, upon the manifold employments of industrious life? Is there no hope of competence and respectability in the upright efforts of the artist and the husbandman? Is there no certainty of noble and increasing pleasure in the active pursuit of knowledge? The happiness which shall crown assiduity, is so sure that men are able to anticipate it, and the anticipation is the life and joy of their exertions. To the satisfaction and rewards of laborious life, we need not, however, confine our views. Look to the pleasures of social virtue. In the endearing charities of father, son, and brother, what thousands are made happy! Is there no prospect of a pleasing recompense in gladdening a parent's heart, nor any expectation of consequent felicity in the exchange of those endearments, and cultivation of those virtues, to which consanguinity and friendship give birth? From the domestic circle, let us expand our views to enlarged society. In his connection with the world, every good character may improve his being, and experience a satisfaction exquisite and adapted to his nature in the paths of integrity. In the sphere of public usefulness, are there not avenues to noble pleasures in advancement, in the consciousness of worth, and in the esteem of the truly great and discerning? Are there not, in associating our efforts for the general welfare, and promoting in our stations the improvement and happiness of our community, our country, and mankind, such delights as would be worthy of the most exalted natures, and in a way suited to beings situated as we are, reward amply the labours of virtue? Is there not bliss, finer, in truth, than the quickest nerves of human sensibility, in having the blessing of him who was ready to perish come upon us, and causing the widow's heart to sing for joy? In the industrious application of his mental and corporeal powers to their proper subjects, in cherishing the pleasures and discharging the duties which spring from domestic relations, and in useful and benevolent offices among mankind, every considerate person may unceasingly improve his being, constantly look forward to good, lead a life correspondent to the properties of his abode, and experience in it a foretaste of virtue's reward. The connection between fidelity and satisfaction, between assiduity and success, will indicate to him a moral government, and habituated to avail himself of this connection, and to draw the pleasures which exalt his nature from the scenes and duties and charities of life, his mind will not easily be unbent by the opinion that there is no hope.

But it will be said things are not always as they have been represented. There are clouds and terrors as well as light and beauties in our situation. The sweet charities of life are sometimes embittered, and the best efforts at improvement and usefulness frustrated. True: and very great are the advantages of this economy. Both the natural and the moral atmosphere are purged by the thunder and the storm. That state of uniform, uninterrupted pleasure, for which the effeminate imagination sighs, would be miserably adapted to the hopes of beings who must presently leave it. Such a state would not yield us the delight of which we vainly dream, but would exhibit in a little time, the sickening sameness of a dead calm. Above all, we should forget in it our dependence; our attention would seldom be raised to the wonderful power which controls the complex and directs the changeful scene; and thus we should be deprived of one of the sources of the loftiest and most joyous hope.

For as we have already hinted, and shall proceed to show, an everlasting support of hope may be derived by the virtuous from the most natural and satisfactory sentiments of a Supreme Being. No man in the unperverted use of his senses can doubt that there presides over the universe an intelligent God. Into the sentiment which reason forms of this Being, goodness invariably enters. Whatever reflections we make upon his nature will terminate in the assurance that he is infinitely and immutably benevolent. In ten thousand ways he has displayed his character before us. Wherever we turn our eyes, we see the tokens of a gracious God. The effects of his power, which evidence his being, proclaim him wise and good. Sooner than we can believe him otherwise, we can believe that there is no God.

Now, if we consider ourselves as his creatures, we must know that we are under his observance. If we retire into ourselves, and reflect upon the faculties with which he has endowed us, and the station we occupy among his works, we shall be satisfied that we are not unmeaning expletives, but have a portion of his spirit and are formed with some high design. If we notice the relation of the riches, and beauties, and wonders which we behold, to our sustenance or delight, mark the unwearied providence by which our beings are continued and our capacities for pleasure supplied, we shall be convinced that we are objects of his bountiful love. If we observe in the course of our conduct the perpetual connection of vice with remorse and misery, we shall have reason to conclude that we are subjects of his moral government. In short, in the calm rational view of things, we are evidently related as creatures and subjects to a benevolent God, who for the communication of happiness caused the world to be made, and governs his creatures with a benignant hand.

And is it possible that in a life enlivened with a knowledge of this Being, there is no hope? Can we consider ourselves as under the wakeful eye and protecting hand of a heavenly Father and not think our condition happy? Is there no safety in his approbation? Is there no certainty of securing his smiles by an obedience to his will? Is there no hope of obtaining his aid by lifting up our hearts with our hands to him in the heavens? Is there no probability that in every adversity he will support the humble who trust in him, and cause all things to work together for their good? Can we believe that under his government there is no hope of satisfaction in the paths of virtue, either here or hereafter? Has this gracious Being constituted us as we are, consciously capable, and instinctively desirous of perpetual progress in life and happiness, and placed us here for nothing, or to be miserable? Has he turned off his offspring to a despondent fate, and will never bring them to the enjoyment of himself? The very sentiment of our connection with him inspires hope. The idea of his being and government sheds a light and joy and value upon life. The perfections of his character, taught us in all his works, are pledges to us of good, if we are not unfaithful to ourselves. If men will shut their eyes against the beamings of the sun, and then complain that there is no light, who shall convince or relieve them? But let them think of the adorable perfection of the Being who is the source and centre of all things; let them consider the happiness of living under his protection and smiles; let them appreciate the certainty of obtaining his approbation in the paths of integrity; and then while the slaves of vice and victims of despondence cry "Who will show us any good?" their hearts will be satisfied with the sacred wish—"Lord, lift thou up the light of thy countenance upon me."

But it will be urged, we are sinners and have not strength to reach the attainments you have mentioned; we are mortal, and must leave, in a few years at most, the scenes and pleasures you describe. Come, then, to the enlivening instructions and soothing consolations of revealed religion. Recur to that word which a gracious God has given to be a guide to our feet and a lamp to our paths. Is there no satisfaction in having duty explicitly stated, virtue clearly defined, and knowing that the paths in which we are to pursue them, are paths of peace? Is there no joy in the tidings of a Saviour, to correct the evils and expiate the imperfections of which we are concious?—no comfort in the declaration that "God so loved the world that he gave his only begotten son, to the end that all who believe in him should not perish but have everlasting life?" Is there no solace in the promise of the spirit to help our infirmities, nothing worthy of attention in the divine voice, "Come unto me, all ye that travail and are heavy laden, and I will give you rest?" Is there no hope in the assurance sought by nature, evidenced by reason, enforced by conscience, that our Father seeth in secret, and will bring the righteous through the vale of death to abundant and eternal rewards?

Perhaps you will reply, "This revelation is all a parable. We cannot receive it." But why can you not receive it? It has satisfied the greatest masters of reason, and noblest persons of the human race. There must be something of corruption in the heart, or perverseness in the will. The greatest and the best characters who have dwelt on the earth have laid hold on these hopes and found them precious. Do they not shed a cheerful and invigorating light upon the state of thousands who embrace them? And are not these the only characters who seem to be acting toward an end, and manifest dignity and happiness in every condition of life? Nature wishes for a guide, wants a Saviour, asks for assurance of immortality. There must be something wrong in the disposition which struggles against the proffer of these in the gospel. Surrender your hearts to religion. Live in the pursuit of those graces and the discharge of those duties which it commends. Learn of it to subdue every licentious, sullen, and depraved passion. Do good in your station. Cultivate an acquaintance with "the God of the spirits of all flesh." Strive to assimilate yourself to his perfection. Weigh well the reasonableness and authority of his word, and under its guidance seek, by a "patient continuance in well doing, for glory, honour, and immortality." Then shall thy light rise in obscurity, and thy darkness be as the noon day. Sweet shall be thy pleasure and increasing thy satisfaction, beneath the benign influences of the gospel of peace. "When thou goest it shall lead thee, when thou sleepest it shall keep thee, and when thou awakest it shall talk with thee." In the day of dismay, when the clouds of adversity lower upon thy life, and terrors take hold of thy mind, thou shalt no more say, "There is no hope;" but the animated language of thy heart shall be, "Why art thou cast down, O my soul, and why art thou disquieted within me? Hope thou in God, yea, I shall yet give him thanks, who is the health of my countenance and my God."

We have now seen the unreasonableness of the opinion that there is no hope. Yet there are temptations to imbibe it to which we are exposed, and which we shall now proceed to consider.

And, in the first place, we are liable to indulge this erroneous opinion from the limited nature of the views which we have of the divine administration. Situated as we are, we must be ignorant of the connection of events. Of the vast chain in which all things are combined in mysterious order and terminate in God, we see but a single link. Yet from what is before us we receive our impressions, and by the present are often drawn into mistaken opinions and unhappy conclusions. Our nature instinctively wishes for constant happiness. Like children, without knowing what is good for us, we would have instant gratification, and hence expect a course of things conformable with our views, and free from every interruption of our satisfaction and joy. But it may be necessary that our desires should sometimes be crossed. We know but in part, and what to us would seem right and delightful, would often be attended with the most injurious consequences. Pleasant is the sight of the sun. We are cheered and enlivened with the brightness which his beams dispense, and think all nature loveliest when he shines. Still it is the cloud that darkens the day which carries the shower by which the earth is fertilized, and the thunder which purifies the air.

The misfortune is, we measure the expediency of the divine economy by our finite and biased judgments. In the hour when the cloud comes near us, the spirits are dampea, and everything seems cheerless. Whatever does not comport with our immediate satisfaction is construed into an evidence of man's dismal state. If a wise and virtuous and useful character, against whose removal everything appears to plead, be suddenly taken from the earth in the midst of life, the most desponding sentiments will often lower in the bosoms of survivors. When the good and great are seen struggling under life's heaviest burdens, while the worthless roll on in the high course of prosperity, the mind is tempted to conclude that the world is abandoned to a blind chance, which scatters a little good with an undiscerning hand. If men are overpowered by poverty, and, after every upright and persevering effort, think themselves doomed to remain in the dreary back-ground of life, they are too liable to sink into the gloomy revery, "there is no hope." Instead of reflecting that the world is governed by a wisdom greater and better and surer than ours; instead of remembering how often we have known blessings to be wrapt in adversities, and have seen the day-spring break in upon the thickest darkness; instead of considering how elevated should be our position and correct our sight, to judge of the vast work which the Almighty is executing upon the earth, we are dissatisfied with some shades in the piece, whose effect we are not in a station to perceive, and conclude that the whole is dismal, without design or relief. The temptation is here in the disposition of man to make his own judgment the standard of what is good or expedient. Bounded as he is in his views, he must often meet with events which will seem dark and inexplicable, and if he have no other standard by which to correct his erroneous one, the shades of life may fill him with that despondence which the patriarch's strange case wrought in the bosom of his wife, when in the true spirit of the text, she urged the patient sufferer to "curse God and die."

Again, there are passions and affections in the human constitution, by which we may be drawn into the unreasonable sentiment that "there is no hope." It is the misfortune of pride, a passion too generally predominant, that certain points of a dependent nature are essential to its satisfaction. In any one of these, its whole happiness may be unhinged. Let its ambitious projects be frustrated; let the neglect and contumely of the world offend it; let some secret vexation perplex its thoughts, it catches disgust quickly, and is dissatisfied with the appointed course of things. It cannot bend to the evils of life. It cannot accommodate itself to the wrongs and disappointments which are to be expected in the world. If it has built its sanguine expectations upon some object and been disappointed, it blinds the unfortunate person in whose bosom it reigns to all the happiness within the good man's reach, and renders him dissatisfied with himself and the world. What an instance have we in Haman, the favourite of Ahasuerus, king of Persia. His pride had made his happiness so dependent on the obeisance of a certain Jew, that it could persuade him there was no work in life, no pleasure in the riches and honours he possessed, no satisfaction in any course he could pursue, while this obeisance was disdainfully withheld. Never was a stranger nor a weaker despondence than when he uttered the disgraceful confession, "All this availeth me nothing, so long as I see Mordecai the Jew sitting at the king's gate."

Nearly related to pride, is the sullen, morose disposition, which, like the jaundiced eye, puts its own hue upon every object which it beholds. It is sometimes constitutional. Oftener, however, it proceeds from erroneous views of men and things; and in some natures it arises from a dissatisfaction with themselves. But from whatever cause it springs, it shuts the bosom against many of the virtues which gladden life, leads on to discontent, and renders the perplexities of existence more perplexed. Persons of this description forego many of the delights which were designed to solace us in the present state. What to them are the sweet influences of nature's fairest scenes? What to them are the tender and endearing charities of life? What to them is the prosperity of others, or the approbation of the good and great? There is generally a mixture of obstinacy in their character. You cannot allure them into the steady course of virtue, nor the fair consideration of things that may be hereafter; for if it be only from disgust with the opinions of others, they say, "there is no hope."

But let us turn from them to another kind of advocates for this groundless opinion. I mean the melancholy. Approach them tenderly, only to learn the infirmity of nature. Of all the victims of mistaken notions, they most claim your tears. Melancholy is one of the strangest affections of the human mind. It can shut out the light of the sun. It can deaden the sensibilities of nature. Its deluded children see nothing but profound darkness hanging over all the paths of life, save where an awful flash of lightning gleams in the gloom. In the religionist this affection of the mind is most powerful. It raises fancy and fear above reason, or rather, reason catches its infatuating madness, and turns traitor to itself. Now it is overwhelmed by the awful majesty of God and of his requirements. And now it sinks under the weight of its own unworthiness. It leaves the mind with a triple force against the admission of hope, and never rouses but to look to it to see if it be secure.

I may add, that remorse is among the passions of nature which seduce men into the miseries of despondence. This emotion is wisely implanted in our constitution. It is a wholesome —and with offenders who are not hardened—an effectual corrective of vice. But such is the misery to which they expose themselves who incur its severity, it sometimes goes, like our passions, to an unhappy experience. The conscious offender is dismayed by the appearance of its scourge. The recollection of his crimes or follies harrows his soul. He fancies the arrows of the Almighty stick fast within him, and their poison drinketh up his spirits. Without adverting to the character of the Deity, or hearkening to the counsels of religion, or asking of repentance what may be expected from its aid, he often concludes that "there is no hope," and goes on to greater and yet greater iniquity. In all these cases you will observe that the passions are the cause of despondence. Unhappy he who is under their control They should never be consulted in the formation and adoption of any opinion, but kept constantly subjected to the principles of reason and religion.

But I hasten to observe, in the third place, that if we are exposed to imbibe the opinion under consideration, by the limited extent of our views of the divine economy, and by the passions and affections of our nature, we are much more so by the scheme of things which, in these modern days, is brought forward to ensnare the thoughtless and amaze the considerate. Christianity is the great basis of human hope. This the new philosophy would at once demolish, and exterminate its ruins from the earth. Yes, that precious faith, on which our assurance of immortality. rests, from which the encouragement of virtue is drawn, to which we can resort in the weary hour and be refreshed, this novel friend would tear from our bosoms. And what would it give us in its stead? A freedom from moral duty—a liberation from religious, watchful, and benignant care—a chilling declaration that beyond the grave man has no hope. To destroy the expectation of satisfaction in the paths of virtue here, and of a better existence hereafter is its avowed aim. It speaks no hope. Whoever receives it, cuts himself off from hope. What hope, indeed, can have any foundation, when the gospel and religious obligations are set loose? This scheme of things may, therefore, be considered as the most dangerous temptation to the unhappy abandonment of life's dearest friend. The young are most liable to be its victims. It flatters the strong propensities of nature under the plausible character of a liberal friend. With a syren voice, fascinating the unwary, it lures them to resistless destruction. Wretched philosophy! How dost thou spoil the young of the instructions, which would guide their steps, and of the hopes which would illumine the clouds of their life! How dost thou wound the venerable parent's heart by the profligacy and irregularity unto which thou leadest his child! How dost thou deprive society of the true usefulness of its members by making them instruments of corruption or occasions of shame! I see thee like some comet, whose horrid train is not yet disclosed, offering light, but bringing destruction, irretrievable destruction, if the Eternal did not watch thy course. It obtrudes itself, my brethren, into most of the subjects, which we have lately contemplated. Indeed, what subject that is dear to us does it not affect! My duty is unceasingly to warn you of its dangerous errors. "Son of man," says my God, "I have set thee as a watchman upon the wall of Jerusalem." And if there be an evil against which the ministers of the Gospel have reason to lift up their voices, it is this demoralizing philosophy. It is not the least among its evil tendencies that it leads to the unhappy belief that there is no hope: with the adoption of this error is inseparably connected the abuse of life.

When once the hope of finding a rational satisfactory happiness, either in the paths of wisdom here, or in a state of existence to which they will conduct us hereafter, is eradicated from the human bosom, there remains no nature sufficiently strong to keep men in the discharge of the duties of life. What shall influence them to persevere in the course in which these duties lie, in defiance of the temptations and obstacles which the world opposes, when they have fallen into the hopeless conclusion that "there is one event to the righteous and the wicked!" What shall reconcile them to the toils, vexations and self-denials, to which they must submit in discharging their domestic obligations! What shall animate them in the arduous and disinterested labours of patriotism, benevolence and philanthropy, if it avail nothing whether they be good or bad, and death shall obliterate forever the remembrance of them and their actions? What shall keep them in the path of excellence when they have persuaded themselves that all paths are alike, and that there is no satisfaction to be found in any path? Will the young man be industrious, will the public man be diligent, will the benevolent man go to the chambers of sickness, and to the dungeons of misery, will the assassin drop his dagger, will the suicide put away the fatal bowl, if they say there is no hope? Will men be good and useful, when they have yielded themselves up to the opinion that it matters nothing whether they are so or not? What is to impel them? what is to restrain them? While the path of useful life is smooth and pleasant, they may, perhaps, adhere to it. But when obstacles appear in it, which require labour and anguish to surmount them, or paths of a more alluring aspect present themselves on either side, motives are wanting, sufficiently powerful to produce in them fortitude and resolution. That a regular and constant application of life to the purposes for which it was bestowed is to be expected from those who have imbibed the gloomy sentiments we are combating, will appear unreasonable and incredible to every person who knows anything of the nature of man.

But this is not all. When the enlivening hope of future good is cut off, what will men consider as their best interest and wisdom? Evidently, present gratification; and, in seeking this, what will be their guide? There remains no other than their own inclinations. These must direct the choice, and govern the conduct, when the connection between virtue and happiness is disregarded, and there is no "respect" to a "recompence of reward."

Now, let us consider what would be the result of an unqualified submission of men to the guidance of their inclinations. It is the least of the imperfections of these that they are blind. They know not, and I can never indicate, what is good for man in this life. Intent always upon immediate gratification—taking their bent generally from the circumstances of the moment—and always unable or unwilling to forecast the consequences of things, they would lead men often into the most perplexed and dangerous paths. Resigned to their influence, the honeyed poison we should eagerly grasp, and the wholesome bitter would never be our choice.

But they are not only blind, they are for the most part evil. The guides, to which he must submit, who abandons the hope of satisfaction in a life of faith and usefulness, are prone to iniquity. The will, since the fall of man, is perverse; the passions are corrupt, and the thoughts and desires of the natural heart, are, as the Scriptures assure us, "evil continually." With all the guards and restrictions which religion puts upon us, scarcely are all our propensities to wrong at all times restrained in the most upright. Where the rude and tumultuous passions of our nature govern without any limitation or control, what discord and misery must they produce in society? What neglect, perversion and abuse, of all the powers of life! What vice can you conceive, what conduct can you imagine, what determination can the wildest and most barbarous imagination form, into which men, under the allurement of powerful temptation, or the pressure of imperious exigencies, may not be led, when they have relinquished all expectation of happiness in any of the walks of life, when they have ceased to value the pleasures of duty here, or to expect retribution hereafter? No matter how deep, how ominous, how awful the abyss into which they are plunging. They fancy they have nothing to hope, and consequently nothing to fear. Their inclination is their only guide, and for the gratification of their present desires, they will plunge into iniquities over which reflection shudders and virtue weeps.

It is hope which most animates us, in every right application of the powers of life. It is she who must keep us in the paths to which faith conducts us, and where charity, surrounded by all her lovely offspring, the duties of life, dwells. On this account she was given to man, to be the companion of his innocence in the garden of Eden, and the food, which was to sustain her, was on the tree of life. When man, for his fall, was driven from the garden, his compassionate Maker permitted her to accompany him, and she was sustained by the promise given to the wanderers, that "the seed of the woman" should "bruise the serpent's head." When a flood of vengeance had destroyed the world, and a few only of the human race remained, lest the retrospect of memory, and vestiges of desolation should paralyze the survivors with fear, she was sent to invigorate them, and her eye was fixed upon the bow in the clouds, upon which, while she looked, she lived. Under the Mosaic dispensation, when he who was circumcised became "a debtor to the law, to keep the whole law," that the faithful might be preserved from leaving the paths of duty, amidst the errors and sorrows to which their frailty subjected them, she dwelt among them by the tabernacle and the temple, and her food was the types and promises by which she was surrounded, and the blood of the sacrifices, which were the "shadows of good things to come." And now, under the Gospel economy she abideth, amidst the sins and sorrows, and mortality of life, supported on the one hand by faith, and on the other by charity, looking at the cross for her sustenance, and to heaven for unspeakable joy. The goods she promises are many of them distant, and "hope deferred maketh the heart sick," and therefore the Almighty hath provided for the enjoyment of them, as it were by anticipation, through that faith, which is to us, even in this world, "the substance of things hoped for." Thus careful has our Heavenly Father been to provide, at all times, an abode and adornment on earth for this heavenly virtue. He introduced her to man in the garden himself. He sent her to the fathers by the prophets. He hath restored her to us by his Son; and wherefore all this care? Doubtless, because of the importance of her influence on the conduct of his human creatures. He hath commanded us to cherish her, as a grace whereby we are saved, and hath illustrated for us in impressive examples, the happiness of keeping, the misery of abandoning her. I bring to you two, each striking, and rendered more so by the contrast which the other exhibits. They are found in him who betrayed, and him who denied his Lord. Both were unhappy. Both were dismayed. Both were stung with remorse. The latter had grace to keep his hope. He turned, and abode by his Lord, and became his first apostle. The former was left a prey to the thought, "there is no hope," and he departed and hanged himself.

In short, deprive men of the belief that in the course of a good, useful life, they may spend their days cheerfully here, and by the mercy of God will be received and rewarded through the merits of a Mediator hereafter, and you take from them every spring of generous and satisfactory exertion, you paralyze the whole system of nature, you leave them a prey to every bad propensity and passion, and from the clouds of perplexity and sorrow, which arise often over this probationary state, and sometimes lower thick and long upon it, you turn away the heavenly beams which would attenuate their darkness, and gild their edges. If once men can say "there is no hope," the consequent resolution is almost inevitable, but "we will walk after our own devices and will every one do the imagination of his evil heart."

You have now seen, my brethren, the unreasonableness of the opinion that "there is no hope." You have seen the temptations to imbibe this opinion, to which we are exposed. You have seen the connection between the adoption of it and the abuse of life. How important is it that we have right views of our condition, and destination! How important that the opinion we have been examining have no place in our breasts! Ye who are parents will naturally infer, from what has been said, the great consequence of imbuing your offspring with cheerful and elevating views of the state in which their Creator hath placed them. Not that they should be taught to consider it as a state of pleasure in which, like Leviathan in the sea, they have only to "take their pastime;" but as a state of significant existence, as a state of goodly hopes, a state that is under the guidance and protection of a benignant God, a state designed for their advancement in virtue and happiness, and which shall terminate in the complete and eternal felicity of the righteous. Upon their entering the world with these views of life, and preserving them while they continue in it, their comfort, their safety and their usefulness, in a greater degree depend, than upon any endowments of wealth or wisdom, of elegance or power, which your most assiduous endeavours can procure for them. Teach them to consider hope as the friend, which God, with parental consideration, stationed in man's bosom, and the son of God descended to replace and establish there. Inscribe early upon their hearts the obligation of cherishing this friend. Accustom them to consider as a part of the duty of their probationary life, amidst its waves to cling to hope, with holy fervor and sacred pertinacity.

Our view of this subject should also induce the aged to manifest, by a uniform cheerfulness, a constant reliance on the enlivening prospect of a better world, that there is satisfaction in the paths they have chosen, even to the end. Instructive to the young is the peaceful eye and happy voice of the aged Christian. Let them not abate nor conceal their satisfaction. That hope, which in the beginning of their life was to them as the morning star, animating them with the expectation of a clear and pleasant day, let it, towards the close of life, be to them as the evening star, cheering and beautifying the approach of night, when the glare of day is departed. Happy the children who see in their parents, happy the young who see in their aged friends, this sweetest influence of Christian hope. They cannot but wish that in the evening of their own lives they may be under the same sky in which this star appears.

SERMON XLIX.

STABILITY IN RELIGION.

HEBREWS, xiii. 9.

"Be not carried about with divers and strange doctrines; for it is a good thing that the heart be established with grace."

THE design of the apostle in the context is to excite in the Christians whom he addresses, a stability in their religious opinions, by leading them to contemplate the steady faith and perseverance of their pastors and rulers, and the unchangeableness of the doctrines which they were appointed to administer. This stability is of great importance at all times, but especially so in an age when the religion of the Redeemer must be recommended to the world by the conduct of its professors; and when, as the same apostle foretold, schemes of faith are multiplied, heresies exist, false spirits are abroad in the Church, and the love of many is waxed cold. At such a time, instability in the professors of Christianity, cannot be guarded against with too much circumspection. It shall, therefore, be my endeavour, with the divine assistance, to point out to you some of the principal causes which produce this instability, and to bring under your consideration some of the most obvious consequences of it.

In the first place, a want of a proper knowledge of the nature and truths of religion, will expose Christians to much unsteadiness in their opinions. That they might "continue in the faith," St. Paul thought it important to the Colossians, that they should be well "grounded and settled;" that is, should be thoroughly acquainted with the evidences and doctrines, with the whole design, and all the parts of revelation. But there are many individuals who take up religion by halves. The doctrines which are congenial with their feelings, the truths which their own situation has rendered particularly interesting, the principles which incidental circumstances have most strongly impressed, are mistaken by them for "the whole counsel of God." Hence it arises, that when their feelings alter, or new circumstances occur, their opinions change and their conduct is varied. If Christians are thus imperfectly instructed in the nature and design of their religion, if they neglect to inform themselves for what end God has given them the gospel, and what it is which in his word he requireth of them, it cannot fail that, like the vessel which has neither anchor nor helm, they will be "driven of every wind, and tossed." On the contrary, let them acquaint themselves perfectly with the principles of the doctrine of Christ, as they are found in the only pure receptacle of them, the word of God; and then "leaving these," and not "laying again" and again "the foundation" of their faith, make it their single aim to "go on" steadily "unto perfection," and it is probable they will progress, under the blessing of the Divine Spirit, towards the true measure of Christian excellence, unmoved by any of the currents of human opinion, which flow in every direction, and change their courses as times and seasons change.

Another cause of instability in religious opinions, is the love of novelty. With whatever is new, human nature is prone to be captivated. It is this which gives to curiosity its powerful action in the human heart. It is upon this that imperious fashion founds her wonderful empire. And the influence of this, even in the religious world, has not always been resisted. Although it is an incontrovertible truth, that in matters of revelation the oldest opinion is the best, new systems of divinity come recommended to the weakness and the vanity of human nature, under greater advantages than the old one, which is better. That sameness which tires in the natural scene, is apt unfortunately to tire also in these things, of which, but for the capriciousness of our fancies, it would be esteemed a principal excellence. Hence, new interpretations of Scripture, various modes of worship, "divers and strange doctrines," have a powerful attraction upon the minds of men. This has always been the case. In all ages, curiosity has caused some to waver in their faith and to wander from the truth. Over such the apostle Paul sometimes laments, as "ever learning, and never able to come to the knowledge of the truth;" and sometimes he applies to them his severest sarcasm, that they will "heap to themselves teachers having itching ears." But neither our curiosity nor the novelty of opinions, can alter the truths or economy of the gospel. That which was the true faith, that which constituted the true Church, and that which was true holiness in the days of the apostles, will continue to be so till the end of the world. There is "one Lord, one faith, one baptism," and, like Jesus Christ, they are "the same yesterday, to-day, and forever."

Another cause of instability will be found in the secret influence of our passions and worldly interest. In religious investigations, it is of the utmost importance that we be affected by no motives whatever which do not spring from a pure love of truth and duty. Yet, we do not know our own hearts. Little prejudices, partialities which arise out of their feelings, a view to temporal convenience or emolument, do sway men's minds even in religious opinions with a powerful bias, whose strength, perhaps, lies in its imperceptibility. The influence of important friends, personal or political resentment, nay, an attachment to an individual instructor, has often—I blush to own it—converted him into a Unitarian, who once adored the divinity of his Redeemer, and these into advocates for the strange doctrine of the unconditional reprobation of a part of mankind to everlasting destruction, who were once fully persuaded that "Christ died for all men," and "that whosoever will," may "taste of the waters of life freely." Inconstancy proceeding from this source is deeply to be deplored. It is prostituting the dignity of religion. It is trifling with the immutability of truth. We should always, as the apostle exhorts the bishop of Ephesus, "continue in the things which we have learned and have been assured of," until a conviction of their error makes it our duty to relinguish them.

The last cause of instability in religion, which I shall mention, is a mistaken zeal; and as a cause this is peculiarly interesting, because the pious and well-meaning are sometimes inadvertently the subjects of its operation. There is no Christian, I believe, who finds in himself, while performing his warfare, that pure and uninterrupted perfection, after which he earnestly aspires. We carry about us a body of sin, of which we probably are not wholly divested till this body of flesh returns to the dust. But there are some, who, having formed high ideas of Christian holiness, love, and assurance, and still finding in themselves a portion of that frailty which belongs to every human being, are led to suppose, that good as the paths are in which they have been traveling, there must be others which are better. Comparing the honest internal state of their hearts with the external appearance of others, they fear that of all men they are least in favour with Christ, and far behind in the race which is set before them. Hence, they are led to seek in new opinions and untried modes for that perfection which they cannot find in their own. They desire to be brought nearer to Christ, to come even into his seat. So far, their humility and affections are good; but their reasonings are erroneous, and their affections may consequently misguide them. For, if they hear that Christ is "in the desert," thither they credulously go forth; if it is told them, behold, he is "in the secret chambers," there they expect to find him; not considering that in every stage of their earthly pilgrimage, they must be incumbered with the infirmities of their nature, and that they are advised by their Lord himself that "false Christs and false prophets will arise, to deceive, if it were possible, even the elect." It is not from change of opinions, nor from a fondness for all opinions, that the peace of God will spring; but from a holy and steady observance of his commandments. "If any man will do his will, he shall know of the doctrine" that it is from heaven, and Christ "will come unto him and make his abode with him."

Surrounded by such and so many causes which may render us unsteady in our religious opinions, with what propriety does our Church lead us in one of her collects, to pray that God would himself enable us both to "know and perceive what things we ought to do, and also give us grace and power faithfully to fulfil the same!" How important this prayer is will more strikingly appear, if we now proceed to consider some of the most obvious consequences of that instability, against which it is my anxious desire to caution you in this discourse.

And, in the first place, it much retards the Christian's progress towards perfection and peace. Nothing is accomplished in any arduous work without steadiness and perseverance. This is particularly true with respect to religion. Its object must be fixed. The means of attaining that object must be definite. And in the use of these means we must be uniform and constant. If men, to use the language of Scripture, will be "like children, tossed to and fro and carried about with every wind of doctrine;" if to-day they are with the world, and to-morrow with Christ; if they are now under the influence of one system of religion, and anon advocates of another, it is hardly possible they should find the true peace, or reach the genuine maturity of the Christian. Reuben, the first-born of Israel, was of this description. At one time his sentiments are according to truth. At another, according to his feelings and the company he is in. Now, we behold him led by his passions; and presently absorbed in holy and virtuous emotions. His venerable father observed his character with regret, and pronounced the prophecy concerning him, "Unstable as water thou shalt not excel." And St. James, a servant of God, teaching in his epistle to the scattered Christians of the twelve tribes, upon this very subject, has the pertinent and just observation, that "a double-minded man is unstable in all his ways." Indeed, whoever would try all the improvements, and enter into all the opinions in religion, which the fertility of modern times has produced, must traverse a labyrinth far more intricate than that of Crete; nor is it certain, when he is once involved, that he will easily obtain a clue which will conduct him back to the light of safety that he imprudently left. It often happens, that those who have tried all faiths, and wandered through all modes of religion, are finally a prey to a fatal indifference, or to an enthusiasm as dangerous, or else in unavailing sighs regret their departure from the ancient way, in which their companions have with steady steps followed the exalted worthies, who, through faith and patience, inherit the promises.

Another consequence of the instability of Christians is, that occasion is given to "the enemies of the Lord to blaspheme." It is with a scrutinizing eye that the world observes the conduct of those who call themselves the followers of the Redeemer. If they are unsteady in their virtue; if they are unsettled in their principles; if by any of the causes which have been mentioned, they are made examples of inconstancy and caprice, those who will not allow themselves the opportunity and means of judging more correctly, will not fail to infer that the peace and satisfaction which Christianity professes to bestow on its votaries, is more a fancy than a reality. Nor will the evil be confined to those who "are of the contrary part." When the young and inconsiderate among ourselves observe their parents and elders endeavouring to "serve both God and mammon," varying their conduct with their situation, or with a mistaken liberality leveling the distinction of things, and patronizing the most opposite tenets, there is danger of their acquiring very loose ideas concerning religion, if they do not imbibe skeptical ones. It is hardly possible that they will preserve much veneration for a thing so mutable, or conceive strong attachments to an object so indefinite. Hence it is that we are commanded to "walk circumspectly," "not to please ourselves," nor to seek our own benefit, but to have our eyes upon our brother, "for his good to edification."

Lastly, by the instability of Christians, the great and essential truths of the gospel may be endangered. There is no setting any bounds to the wanderings of the human mind, when it has passed the limits prescribed to it by the Almighty. What contrariety of opinions, what crude and monstrous systems of belief, what discord and confusion has it not produced in the world, when it has trusted to its own skill, and departed from the landmarks which the fathers had set! They who will permit themselves to deviate, must expose themselves to err. The truths of the gospel, so far as they may be affected by human conduct, can be preserved pure and entire only by the stability of its professors in resisting innovations, and in contenting themselves with the written word for a light to their feet and a lamp to their paths. It was with a view to this difficulty that St. Paul advised Timothy to "hold fast the form of sound. words," and that Jude deemed it needful to exhort all Christians that they should "earnestly contend for the faith once delivered to the saints." Indeed, the idea is absurd, that human reason should be capable of improving that which the Almighty has made perfect. Whoever will study the history of the human mind, may find occasion to sigh, that the frailnesses of our nature are so great as to render the unrestrained indulgence of freethinking upon religion a dangerous, if not a sinful experiment.

It is your happiness, my brethren, to have been called to a knowledge of the gospel in a church which is established "upon the foundation of the apostles and prophets, Jesus Christ himself being the chief corner stone;" a church venerable alike for the beauty of its economy, and the reasonableness of its worship, and destined, we hope, to be the ark in which the true terms of the covenant shall be preserved in their purity, notwithstanding the errors in doctrine, in discipline, and in practice, which in seasons of innovation and human vanity may spring from the ingenuity or perverseness of men. Gather, therefore, from her excellent services and from the Scriptures, which she has appointed to be read every Sabbath-day, a right knowledge of God and your religion. Bring this knowledge to the government of your lives. Endeavour by its light to remove from your nature whatever is evil, and strive through its blessed influences to honour your Maker by discharging with fidelity the various duties which belong to the stations and relations in which he has placed you. When you have done all, own with humility that you are "unprofitable servants," and trust, with a lively faith, for your final acceptance, to the merits of mediation of his Son, your Redeemer. Then if any man shall say unto you, "Lo, here is Christ, or lo he is there, go not after him." In the vocation wherein ye were called, therein abide. Make it your principal care to imitate the constancy and order of the primitive Church, by "continuing steadfastly in the apostle's doctrine and fellowship, and in breaking of bread and in prayers." Amen.

SERMON L.

THE TRUTH MAKING THE FAITHFUL FREE.

JOHN, viii. 31 and 32.

"If ye continue in my word then are ye my disciples indeed; and ye shall know the truth, and the truth shall make you free."

IN this chapter, the author of our religion proclaims himself "the light of the world." The Pharisees objected to his doctrine, and with all the pride and weakness of human reason, endeavoured to embarrass the heavenly Teacher. They told him that he bare witness of himself, and therefore was not to be credited; they insultingly asked who he was, that they might believe on him, and wished to see and know his Father to whom he so constantly appealed: and they boasted of their privileges as the descendants of Abraham, which raised them above the reach of his benefits, and rendered the freedom he proffered them contemptible in their sight. To these things the Saviour replied, with all that precision and dignity which characterized his preaching. He observed to them, that he knew his origin and himself, (of which they certainly were ignorant,) and was therefore credible, till they could convict him of falsehood or guile. Still, however, he was not alone in the record which he gave of himself. Their own law, which accepted the testimony of two witnesses, was complied with; for his Father was with him and confirmed all his declarations. He reminded them of their earthly nature and views, assured them that an humble, unprejudiced mind was all that was necessary to the reception of his doctrine; called upon them either to believe or disprove his authority, and told them that, though they supposed themselves the children of Abraham, they were slaves, and slaves of the vilest description. Declaring himself to be the same that he had said unto them from the beginning, he inculcated the necessity of faith in him to liberate them from their spiritual bondage and make them free indeed. He added, with peculiar emphasis, that after they had crucified him, the events which would follow would prove to them that he was the Son of God, and that the Father was in him and with him, attesting whatever he advanced, and sanctioning whatever he premised.

His plain, yet grand and powerful discourse, (enforced by the manner in which it was spoken,) produced a great effect. As he spoke these words, many believed on him. Addressing himself to these to animate and instruct them, and at the same time awaken an emulation in the rest of his audience, he then delivered the words of my text: "If ye continue in my word, then are ye my disciples indeed; and ye shall know the truth, and the truth shall make you free."

This passage, taken by itself, is as adapted to us as to those to whom it was originally spoken, and under the divine blessing may lead us to some useful and important contemplations.

The first thing it presents to our attention is *the character of the real disciples of Christ*—they continue in his word. By his word, is meant his gospel, the doctrines and precepts which he taught, the religion which he brought to man. By continuing in it we are to understand an acquaintance with its nature and end, a preference of it to all other opinions, a decided adherence to it, and an obedience to all its acquirements. They may be said to continue in his word who study the Scriptures, to acquire a knowledge of the spirit and design of Christianity, and, regardless of every other allurement, make it their chief care to cherish and personate them in their hearts and lives. These are Christ's disciples indeed. To be born of Christian parents, and observe the externals of religion, merely to refrain from joining with his adversaries, or with unmeaning formality to call him Lord, Lord, can entitle no one to this dignified character. Nor does it belong to those, whose minds assent to the truth of his mission, and all that is recorded of him, while their hearts are unpurified by his principles, and their lives debased with "the pollution that is in the world." His disciples, indeed, those to whom the character properly belongs, feel an attachment to his religion. They are anxious to know his will, and in every situation strive to conduct themselves upon the pure and upright principles of his gospel. They neglect nothing which he has commanded, and desire nothing which he has prohibited. They want no other Saviour, go after no other instructor, and seek no greater good than the happiness which he has revealed. They labour with him in the work, which he wishes accomplished, and to adorn his doctrine by virtuous lives is their first ambition and constant employment. This is to continue in his word; and when we continue in his word, then are we his disciples indeed.

Another thing which the text contains worthy of our consideration is *the promise made concerning the disciples of Christ*, that they shall know the truth. Truth is the object of our noblest faculties. It is our capacity for an acquaintance with it that raises us to our high station in the scale of beings. We have, too, a natural desire for it—a thirst inciting us to pursue it. The greatest of our race have devoted their labour and lives to the attainment of it, and in all ages it has employed the most anxious activity of the human mind. But, "what is truth?" Scarcely any two of the many that have attempted to solve the question have agreed in opinion. Sage has opposed sage. Philosophy has taught the most incongruous tenets. The human mind has vibrated from point to point, without remaining anywhere fixed and at rest. What difference of sentiment has divided mankind! What variety of doctrines distract our attention when we seek information among the productions of the thoughtful! How many systems, all inconsistent with each other, might be formed from the diverse reasonings and reveries of men! One point they all establish, the inability of our reason to discover the knowledge for which our nature thirsts. In the irreconcilable diversity of opinions, which has been the fruit fair experiment is more satisfactory than whole years of speculation. While the disciple of the Redeemer abides at his feet, he will find himself relieved of the burthens under which he travelled, and brought to a state of rest and hope. While he practices the virtues which the gospel inculcates, he will know from his own bosom, that they are conformable with right reason, and never lose their reward. While, in his intercourse with the world, he brings the Christian principles into use, he will find their tendency as happy, and their effects as beneficial as they are declared to be in the sacred records. While he seeks the divine assistance and grace, in and through the means which his religion ordains, he will feel his moral debility aided. The countenance of his Maker lifted up upon him, will shed abroad joy in his heart, and he will perceive that the promises of Scripture are authorized by him with whom is "the residue of the spirit," even God. In short, while he lives uniformly the Christian life, abiding in Christ, and walking as he walked, he will realize, to the honour of his religion and his own ineffable comfort, a fulfilment of the fair promise of the Saviour: "If any man will do his will he shall know of the doctrine whether it be of God, or whether I speak of myself."

Experience is a strong advocate for Christianity. The further the good man advances on his way, the more intimate and satisfactory is his acquaintance with truth. Nothing, I believe, will more contribute to fix those in the faith, who have not time or power to examine its tendencies, than to live uniformly by its instructions. The fruit of a conscientious obedience to its requirements is peace, and its result, "quietness and assurance forever." Few persons, if any, who have faithfully continued in Christ's word, have found cause to be dissatisfied with it. Apostates there doubtless have been. But it is to be feared that in the days of their profession their hearts went after their idols, and they neglected to observe that spiritual regimen, which the great Physician of souls has prescribed. In general, the Christian's experience confirms his faith. To the great praise of the gospel, they who have resorted to it for instruction, embraced its doctrines sincerely, have almost invariably found it a gospel of salvation. In their knowledge of the truth they have been happy and satisfied. It has been to them like "a light from heaven above the brightness of the sun," discovering to them, amidst the darkness of this benighted world, ways, which "are ways of pleasantness," and paths, which "are paths of peace."

Let others, then, talk of the guidance of nature, and the illumination of reason. These are flattering and fascinating terms. But, in the estimation of considerate minds, they are traps of eloquence to catch the unwary. How can nature guide, when her propensities are often evil—when the courses to which she points are frequently opposite? How can reason illumine when the experience of the world has proved, when her own voice has lamented, that she herself is in darkness? In examining the credentials of religion, in endeavouring rightly to understand her instructions, and in applying them circumspectly to life, reason has her proper employment. But as a source of truth, as a guide to the frail inhabitants of this sinful world, the perplexities and inconsistencies, the errors and vices of all ages, proclaim her imbecility. The disciples of Christ will not be deterred from continuing in his word, by any such fictions of the sufficiency of nature, which spring from the perverseness of the heart, and are cherished by the vanity of the mind. Their Master is "the way, the truth, and the life." In him, are hidden "all the treasures of wisdom and knowledge." "To whom," Lord, if we leave thee, "shall we go? thou hast the words of eternal life."

The last thing which the text offers to our consideration is *the freedom which the truth shall give* to those who continue in Christ's word, and are his disciples indeed. "The truth shall make you free."

Here we are not to consider the Saviour as promising civil liberty to his followers. This was the erroneous construction which the Jews put upon his words. They replied to him, "We be Abraham's seed, and were never in bondage to any man;

and how sayest thou ye shall be made free?" But of civil concerns he affected no control. No. He declared from the beginning that his kingdom was "not of this world." He endeavoured to correct the expectation of a *temporal* prince in the Messiah. He did not in any instance interfere with the political establishment of the earth. Though his religion, undoubtedly, tends to fill the bosom with those feelings and principles which originate, and to promote those habits and manners which secure, true civil liberty, yet, this is not the ultimate object of Christianity, nor the freedom promised in the text.

It is also to be remembered, that there is a liberty inherent in man, essential to him, and, therefore, not promised as something peculiar to the disciples of Christ. I mean that natural freedom, which constitutes him a free agent, and fits him to be made an accountable being. After all the idle disputations about this liberty, every man must feel that in this sense he is free. The rebukes of conscience, when he has done wrong, must spring from the supposition that he might have done otherwise; and reason, if she do not make herself dizzy, in pursuing a labyrinth of metaphysical subtlety, will clearly perceive that, could man be destitute of this liberty, he would be incapable of virtue or vice. Let no one think to secure himself in his sins under the covert of necessity. It is a shelter raised by the ingenuity of man, and will sooner crush than protect transgressors. The text, far from supposing men destitute of this freedom, goes upon the supposition that it belongs to them. Otherwise how could they be considered capable of complying with a condition, and invited to continue in Christ's word?

What, then, is the freedom, which the truth shall give to those who embrace it and are disciples indeed? It is a moral freedom, a liberation from spiritual bondage, a freedom from the servitude and misery of sin. We are "by nature children of wrath," subject to the dominion of passions and vices, strongly affected by the temptations and events of the world, and heirs of death. It is from this wretched state of debasement and death that Christ would make us free. That this is the liberty prepared as the fruit of an obedience to the gospel, is evident from the answer which the Saviour gave to the Jews, when they contemned his promises, as unnecessary to the free descendants of Abraham: "Verily, verily, I say unto you, whosoever committeth sin is the servant of sin."

Let us adjust our ideas of this servitude. When we reflect upon the operations of our minds, we find that there are some things which they will approve and choose. Reason always gives her testimony to the excellence of virtue and the sacredness of duty, to the authority of God and the purity of his laws. Now, the perfection of our freedom as moral beings, consists in our ability to act according to the choice and direction of our judgment. Our passions are inferior parts of our nature. They evidently should be in subordination to our reason. Our minds are intrinsically superior. What they determine without restraint is our real choice. Our moral liberty consists in the power of regulating our conduct by resolutions which they have rightly formed, or by laws to which they have assented as good, or as coming from an acknowledged authority. "As in a civil state," says a good writer upon this subject, "as in a civil state, and political capacity, men are free, when they are under no government or direction, but that of laws which they themselves have made, or which they have approved and voluntarily consented to; so in regard of their inward condition, and considering them as rational and moral agents, they are free, when the deliberate judgment and election of their minds, are the only rule of their conduct and they can always act according to this rule, easily and without interruption." But, alas! when we come to reflect on man's conduct, how little do we see of this freedom! Where shall we find him steadily pursuing what he perceives to be his interest and duty, unrestrained by the influence of any inferior principle, or uninterrupted by the occurrences of this evil world? The heart is so corrupt, passion is so strong, habit is so imperious, the concerns of this life have such influence over the soul, that he is unable of himself to live as conscience dictates, to serve his God, and become fit for heaven. He sees a path to be good and pleasant; he resolves to pursue it; but he is held from it by some evil propensity, or stopped in it by some adverse event of this mutable state. The good which he would, he does not; and the evil which he would not, that he does. But where, then, is the independence of the soul? Where is man's moral freedom? Not to be able to do what his mind determines to be fit and excellent to be done, and to be restrained from doing it by principles which the mind condemns—surely, this is slavery, vile, debasing slavery! Yet, thus are sinners slaves! "Know ye not, that to whomsoever ye yield yourselves servants to obey, his servants ye are whom ye obey; whether of sin unto death, or of righteousness unto life and peace?"

The debasement and misery of this servitude is the greatest that can be conceived. It prostrates all the greatness, and all the hopes of man. It reduces beings capable of fellowship with the Father of spirits, and with the angels that surround his throne, to a humbling affinity with the basest creatures. It withholds them from the exalted pleasures of pure intelligent natures, and feeds them on vile and beggarly joys. Its wages are dreadful. Wretchedness is its recompense. In the necessary, established order of things, and by the everlasting law of the Almighty, the wages of sin is death. So that men are held by sin in an ignoble, unhappy servitude, and when it has alienated them from God, when it has marred the peace, and blasted the hopes of their bosoms, it binds them over to its dreadful offspring, death, through fear of whom "they are all their lifetime subject to bondage."

It is this deplorable state, it is this miserable servitude, from which Christ promises his disciples freedom. The leading end and grand tendency of his gospel, is to liberate men from the ignoble chains of ignorance, passion, evil inclinations, and vicious habits, by which sin holds them under its dominion, and to restore them to the glorious liberty and joyful inheritance of the children of God. If they will continue in his word, and obey from the heart that "form of doctrine" which he hath delivered unto them, they shall be made free from sin, and become the servants of God, and, consequently, have their fruit unto holiness, and the end everlasting life."

But, how is it that the truth shall make us free? It powerfully operates to this purpose by revealing to us an everlasting righteousness, brought in for us in the merits, and by the sacrifice of Christ, who, under the interesting character of Saviour of men, is of God "made unto us wisdom, righteousness, sanctification and redemption." He hath received the wages of sin in our behalf. Our iniquities he hath "borne in his own body on the tree." By his own death he hath "destroyed death, and begotten us again, through faith in him, to the blessed hope of everlasting life." Here, in the knowledge of remission of sins, is encouragement to repentance. These precious truths release us from the bonds and fears, with which the consciousness of sin enslaved us. They are the tidings, at which "the lame man will leap as an hart, and the tongue of the dumb shall sing." They are the tidings, which "proclaim liberty to the captives, and the opening of the prison to them that are bound."

Again, the promise of the aid of divine grace, which the gospel makes to all them who love the Lord Jesus in sincerity, as it is peculiar to Christianity, so it greatly elucidates its efficacy to rescue men from the bondage of corruption. It is by this aid alone, that man's efforts to throw off the fetters of vice, and regain and preserve his moral freedom, can be successful. The strength of nature is inadequate to the arduous achievement. Her powers are corrupt. Her propensities are evil. The dominion of sin is so strong, that reason and conscience, wearied sometimes with fruitlessly remonstrating against it, sink silently into the servitude, and are unable to rouse themselves to a new struggle. But by the spirit of God, acting in and with the word and sacraments, we are begotten to a new life—a life of strength and holiness. This grace is a source of great power and exertion. By it the obstacles to our moral liberty are removed. Through its assistance, we are enabled to conform our lives to the dictates of conscience, and the requirements of God. It "worketh in us to will and to do," advancing us "from strength to strength," and "from glory to glory," "until we all come, in the unity of the faith, and of the knowledge of the Son of God, unto a perfect man, unto the measure of the stature of the fulness of Christ." This spirit is what Plato conceived must have actuated him whenever he was virtuous. This grace is the assistance which Socrates confessed must be given from heaven to man, before they could correct the errors of their minds, and the vices of their lives. And every Christian is assured that, as the merit and sacrifice of Christ release him, upon repentance, from the punishment of sin, so his grace and holy spirit, accompanying the gospel in the hearts of all them who believe, are sufficient to liberate them from the dominion of it.

The moral freedom of men may be, and doubtlessly often has been, accomplished by the immediate operation of the divine power upon the heart. But we observe further, that the ordinary operation of the spirit of Christ, under the gospel dispensation, is through the instrumentality of the word and sacraments. We are born again of the word of God. The truth, a knowledge of which is acquired by continuing in Christ's word, shall make us free. The written Scriptures remove the veil of ignorance which was spread over the sons of men. They sweep away the "refuges of lies." They disperse the darkness which covered the earth, and the thick darkness which overwhelmed the nations. The doctrines and precepts of Christianity are such as strike at the very foundation of the dominion of vice in our bosoms. Nothing is more necessary in promoting our freedom from sin, than to have our passions and affections in due subjection. To this the gospel greatly contributes, by declaring their true place and use; by inspiring that temperance and moderation, which is the best discipline for them, and by encouraging the cultivation of such virtue as will increase the strength of the soul in maintaining its dignity. It unveils the spirituality of the divine law. It applies its precepts to the heart, out of which are the issues of life." "The law of the Lord is perfect, converting the soul."

The sacraments of the gospel are also important instruments in releasing men from sin, and begetting in them the hopes and joys of liberated, redeemed beings. They are the appointed seals of that pardon through the blood of Christ, by which our bondage is broken, and the consecrated channels of that grace, through which we are enabled to preserve and enjoy our spiritual freedom.

And it may be added, that the motives to virtue and obedience which Christianity presents, are so new and weighty, that they must powerfully animate and strengthen men in their conflict with vice. The representation which it gives of the being, attributes, and government of God; the information which it furnishes of the dignity and destination of man; the prospect it opens, of pardon of sins, of freedom from death, from sorrow, and pain, the hold which the exertions of the Godhead for our redemption are calculated to take, and the bright exemplars of goodness which are presented for our imitation, form together such a phalanx of motives as cannot fail to encourage us to resist, and enable us to vanquish, whatever opposes our progress in holiness.

In short, the Christian system, the doctrines, precepts, and sacraments of the gospel, are as well adapted as anything we can conceive to break the power of our vicious propensities, and free us from the bondage of sin. From these, through the blessing of that spirit, which attends all those who resort to them in simplicity and sincerity, we derive that holy and complete "armour of God," in which we may "be able to stand in the evil day;" and who, let me ask, can plead in extenuation of persisting in wickedness, the ignorance or debility of nature, when such an armour is provided, and offered to him by the Most High?

In the first place we may learn from what has been said, how unjustly the gospel is considered as a curtailer of man's privileges and will. It is the true source of freedom, and justly styled "the perfect law of liberty." There are, indeed, those who assert that man is most free when he is left to act according to his inclinations, and that religious principles are shackles which enslave him. But as well might that state be thought a state of civil freedom, in which there is neither head nor subordination, laws nor regularity, but every man may do what he pleases, and he hold the reins who chances to get uppermost. *There is no genuine liberty, but the liberty to do what is right.* This is the freedom which is heaven-born. It is the freedom of the angels. It is the freedom of God. They who deceive themselves, or delude their fellow-beings, with the promise of any other liberty, will generally be found in their lives to be servants of corruption.

We may, secondly, learn from our subject, how to ascertain whether we have continued faithfully in Christ's word. Are we made free? Is the depravity of our nature corrected? Are we turned from the power of sin unto God? In the warfare between the flesh and the spirit, is the spirit victorious and the flesh subdued? If the answer be negative, there remains something more to be done; some principle of the gospel which we have not yet applied to our lives; some want of fidelity and perseverance in the discharge of our religious obligations. It is wise and safe to try yourselves by these tests. Instead of relying upon internal sensations, which, as a pious father of our Church has well observed, may puff us up with spiritual pride upon a fancied possession of what we have not, or give us great trouble and disquiet upon an imaginary want of what we really have, prove yourselves by that standard which cannot fail nor deceive you. "He that doeth righteousness, is born of God." "He that committeth sin is of the devil." "Hereby we do know that we know him, if we keep his commandments."

Lastly, we learn from the text, a most cogent motive for embracing the gospel, and continuing in Christ's word. What is this freedom which it proffers us? Is it not a release from all the incumbrances which bow down our nature, and humble it in the dust? To be freed from the guilt of sin by a sufficient atonement; to be freed from the dominion of sin by the spirit of the Almighty; to be freed from the fears and sorrows, and dreadful apprehensions of judgment to come, with which frail man is encompassed and incumbered; and instead of these, to be exalted to the glorious liberty and joyful expectations of sons of God, what is there on earth, or in heaven, more adapted to our necessities, more worthy of our desires! But this blissful emancipation can be wrought in us only by the truth, that truth which is mercifully promulgated for the benefit of all men in the word of Christ; but known in its clearness and efficacy to those only who "continue in his word, and are his disciples indeed." Hold yourselves, then, my brethren, to the instructions and discipline of the gospel. By faith, and meditation in God's word, and uniform practical obedience, endeavour to know and understand perfectly the truth as it is in Jesus, that so you may be liberated from the bonds of your nature, and experience in yourselves the blessedness of those of whom the voice of inspiration hath pronounced, "If the Son shall make you free, ye shall be free indeed."

END OF VOL. I.

www.ingramcontent.com/pod-product-compliance
Lightning Source LLC
LaVergne TN
LVHW021309110826
845150LV00003B/534

* 9 7 8 1 4 2 5 5 5 8 7 0 3 *